# The Knowledgeable Knitter

# The Knowledgeable Knitter

Understand the Inner Workings of Knitting
and Make Every Project a Success

MARGARET RADCLIFFE

Storey Publishing

The mission of Storey Publishing is to serve our customers by
publishing practical information that encourages
personal independence in harmony with the environment.

Edited by Gwen Steege
Art direction and book design by Mary Winkelman Velgos
Text production by Jennifer Jepson Smith
Indexed by Nancy D. Wood

Photography by John Polak
Pattern schematics by Missy Shepler
Appendix illustrations by Alison Kolesar
Charts by Ilona Sherratt

© 2014 by Margaret Radcliffe

**Storey Publishing**
210 MASS MoCA Way
North Adams, MA 01247
*www.storey.com*

Printed in China by Toppan Leefung Printing Ltd.
10  9  8  7  6  5  4  3  2  1

Library of Congress Cataloging-in-Publication Data on file

*For Anna,*
*without whom many things would not have been possible,*
*including this book*

# CONTENTS

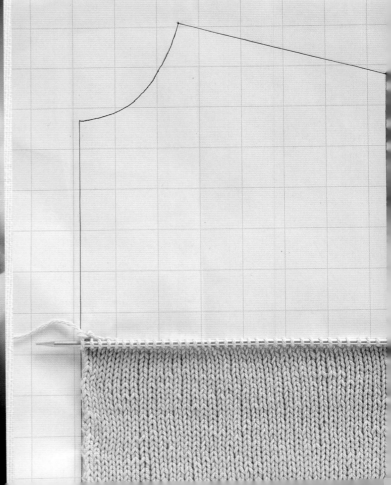

# Knowledge Is Power

**FOR MORE THAN TWO DECADES** I've been focusing my teaching and writing on helping knitters develop their skills and their judgment, on enhancing their creativity and independence. *The Knowledgeable Knitter* is intended to add to that effort, reaching far more knitters than I can possibly teach in my workshops.

So what good are enhanced judgment, a broader knowledge of knitting techniques, and well-developed knitting skills when all you really want to do is follow the directions and knit a sweater? They enable you, even while constructing wonderful sweaters using standard knitting patterns, to tweak each sweater, making it exactly the way *you* want it. You get to take charge of the entire process, both creatively and technically, using the pattern as a starting point.

*The Knowledgeable Knitter* follows the life cycle of a sweater, from selecting the yarn, pattern, and needles, through knitting and finishing. It focuses primarily on conventional, bottom-up sweaters and vests knit in pieces, because that offers the best opportunities for discussion of issues like how to handle edge stitches, shaping, and seaming. I've been careful, however, to include detailed discussions of other construction methods, including circular sweaters and those worked from the top down, as well as some tips for cuff-to-cuff garments.

In my other books, a good deal of the content is what I'd call "how-to" — step-by-step detailed instructions on how to perform specific knitting techniques. In this book, I've tried to step back from the techniques to get a wider perspective on the project as a whole. I think of *The Knowledgeable Knitter* as a "why-to" book rather than a "how-to" book. But don't worry, techniques that require in-depth discussion are included in the text, and you'll find detailed explanations of the rest in the appendix.

Successful sweaters, projects you're proud to show off or give as gifts, are all about the choices you make. Initially you'll need to choose the pattern or the yarn.

Sometimes you'll decide on both at the same time. Many knitting failures are the result of a bad matchup of pattern and yarn — they simply don't work well together. The next major choice is size. Determining the correct size to make is crucial, because it doesn't matter how well made a garment is, it's not going to look good if it doesn't fit. Before you start knitting, another significant choice is the needles — if you don't have the right size needles to get the correct gauge, the garment won't come out the size you expect. And then there's the cast on. This sounds insignificant, but if the cast on is too tight, too loose, or just doesn't look good, it will be there forever to haunt you (unless you decide to cover it up with some embellishment or take the bottom of the sweater off and replace it — but more about *that* later). And these decisions are just the beginning!

As you work your way through the garment, following the instructions, there will be numerous times when you ask yourself, "What do those directions actually mean? How do I do *that*? Where do I put whatever it is? Is it time to . . . ? But . . . ? What if . . . ?" We all like to get the knitting going, and then, whether we love the process itself or we just want to have the satisfaction of a finished object, we prefer the knitting to flow along as effortlessly as possible. Unfortunately, while we're on automatic pilot, bad things can happen without our ever noticing. Sometimes we get to the end, look at the results, and can only ask the ultimate question: "What was I thinking?"

An old friend of mine, who did consulting for businesses large and small, used to say that there are two keys to success: show up and pay attention. The fact is that these apply to knitting just as much as to anything else in life. You need to show up and knit, but you also really do need to pay attention. This book is designed to help you identify what to pay attention to, and how to judge for yourself the best course of action to take.

# First Choices:
# Pattern, Yarn, and Needles

THE VERY FIRST DECISIONS you make before you even start knitting will determine whether your project has every possibility of success, or is doomed to failure. Choosing the pattern, the yarn to go with it, the size you'll make, and the size needle you'll use are the most important issues you'll confront, so let's start by discussing those.

In this chapter, we'll cover how to recognize a well-written pattern, how to determine the size and desired fit for each project, what difference fiber content makes, how to take control of your gauge, and dozens of other small but important choices.

# What Makes a Well-Written Pattern?

We all know the frustration of picking out the pattern for a fabulous garment, finding just the right yarn, and then discovering that the instructions don't make sense. Sometimes it's a matter of misinterpretation on our part, but sometimes the pattern really *doesn't* make sense. Possibly it's been edited and some crucial piece of basic information is missing; sometimes it's a matter of terminology, where the designer calls a technique by a name we've never heard of; sometimes there are inconsistencies or errors. On your end as the knitter, you don't really care *why* there's a problem — you just want to know what to do to fix it.

When I worked in computer programming, we relied on "redundancy checks." In my programs, I'd make sure that any data fit the limitations we expected at the time it was entered, and then again just before doing anything with that information, to make sure it hadn't inadvertently been changed. "Redundancy check" really just means double-checking to make sure things appear to be internally consistent, to prevent future problems from cropping up. A good knitting pattern will present the information you need in more than one way so that it's possible for you to check to make sure that things are indeed going right or so that you can detect it when they've gone awry.

Some examples of redundancy checks possible in knitting patterns are listed below. Note that many of these are very rarely incorporated into published patterns. If you see them, you should bless the author, editor, and publisher for helping you out by providing more detail than usual!

▷ **Photos or drawings of the finished garment** are shown with enough clarity and detail so you can see how it's shaped, assembled, and finished. Beware of garments photographed on models where their arms or a large accessory obscure key details or distort the fit!

▷ **Gauge is given in rows as well as stitches.** This helps you to evaluate whether the fabric you're knitting really matches the designer's specifications.

▷ **Fabric quality.** The instructions include a gauge specification, but they also describe the quality of the fabric desired: for example, "a gauge of 5 stitches and 7 rows per inch, to produce a firm, resilient fabric" or "a gauge of 16 stitches and 22 rows per 4 inches, to produce a soft, stretchy fabric."

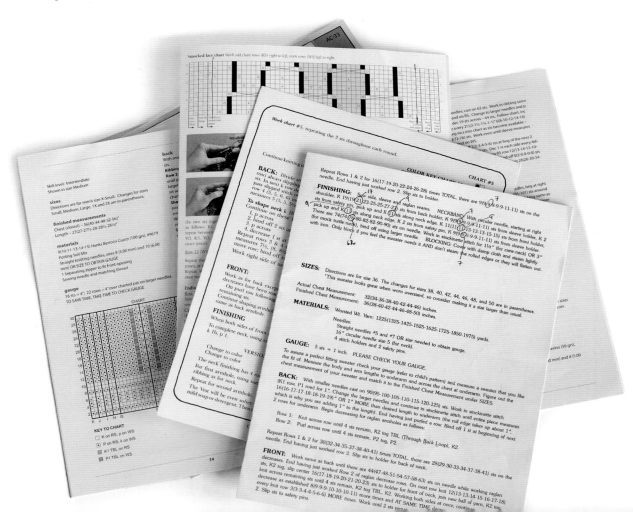

▷ **The yarn specifications** include the name of the yarn originally used by the designer, the yarn weight (sport, worsted, etc.), the fiber content of the yarn, how many yards are in each ball or skein, how much each ball or skein weighs, and how much yarn is required to make the garment (giving length and weight — not just the number of skeins of the original yarn).

▷ **Pattern format.** Pattern stitches are expressed in two ways: they are written out row by row, and they are charted. Some charts for pattern stitches, notably those with major changes in the number of stitches from row to row, are so confusing when charted that they are omitted because they add nothing to the understanding of the pattern.

▷ **Schematics.** The instructions tell you how many inches long to make a section, but they also include a schematic diagram (a simple drawing of the main garment sections with finished measurements). The measurements should include things like shoulder width and neck depth, not just overall length and circumference. I'll discuss schematics in more detail later on.

▷ **Diagrams.** If the construction techniques are unconventional (for example, cuff to cuff, or some sections are knit up while others are knit down), there are diagrams showing the order and direction of construction.

▷ **Stitch counts.** The instructions tell you not only how many times to increase or decrease but also how many total stitches you should end up with.

▷ **Row orientation.** When the instruction says to work in pattern for a certain length or a certain number of repeats, it also states what row of the pattern you should (ideally) end with. This is really only essential if the next step in the project relies on your working a particular row of the pattern stitch.

▷ **Technique illustrations.** The instructions not only describe how to perform an unfamiliar technique, such as a multistep decrease or increase, but they also include an illustration showing how it should look when it's completed.

Giving you both pieces of information, for example what to do, plus an idea of what the outcome should look or feel like, makes it possible for you to use your own judgment to determine whether you're following the directions correctly. It has another advantage: because errors do creep into knitting patterns (in spite of the best efforts of designers and editors), the additional information can help you determine when there is an error and exactly what the error consists of, so that you can correct it in your knitting and keep on working.

Not all knitting patterns will include all of these features, because there may not be space, or because they may not be appropriate to the project. For example, it's not really necessary to provide a schematic of a scarf that's a basic rectangle; providing just the length and width measurements is sufficient. It's not practical to provide a schematic for a garment knit in a spiral — it's three-dimensional, so a two-dimensional diagram showing the shape of the knitted strip that makes up the spiral isn't really going to be helpful. A schematic for the completed spiral garment would, however, be helpful in ensuring it's the correct size when assembled and during blocking.

So, when you look at a knitting pattern, look for the helpful information I've listed above, because it's a sign that the thoughtful designer had *your* needs in mind while writing the instructions. Many of these aids will be missing — use your common sense to determine whether they're really necessary or practical for the project you're contemplating.

15

# Understanding and Evaluating Schematics

Remember that schematics aren't necessarily to scale. This is because they represent all the different sizes of the garment, and the proportions of things like length to width and sleeves to bodies are different for each size. Schematics just provide a visual representation of the basic shape of each piece, with measurements for all the sizes.

For sweaters knit flat with separate pieces that must be seamed, the basic schematics should include each of the major garment pieces, for example the front(s), back, and sleeves (usually it will just show one sleeve assuming that they are identical). Sometimes the back and the front will be superimposed with

two necklines drawn, one for the back and one for the front. Measurements for lengths and widths of sections of each piece should be included. The more measurements the schematic provides (like the schematics shown here), the easier it is for you to check for proper fit. Shoulder width, neck width and depth, and armhole depth are all just as important as the overall circumference and length. Unfortunately, most schematics omit some of these measurements. Many stylistic features, like collars or hoods, are rarely included in the schematics. Here are some examples of schematics that go well beyond the minimum information.

**Garment Worked Conventionally in Pieces**

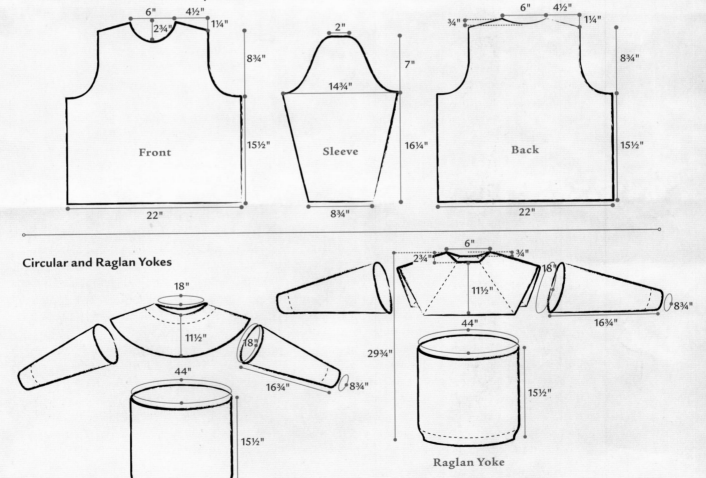

**Circular and Raglan Yokes**

**Schematics for sweaters knit in the round** won't always show separate garment pieces, although an exploded view like this one may be used. Lengths are given just as for a garment knit flat, but circumferences will be provided rather than widths.

First Choices: Pattern, Yarn, and Needles

## Swing Coat

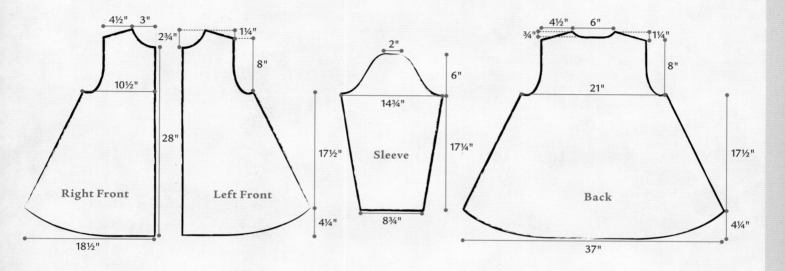

**Right Front** 4½" 3" 10½" 28" 18½"

**Left Front** 2¾" 1¼" 8"

**Sleeve** 2" 6" 14¾" 17½" 17¼" 4¼" 8¾"

**Back** ¾" 4½" 6" 1¼" 8" 21" 17½" 4¼" 37"

## Asymmetrical Fronts, with Bands

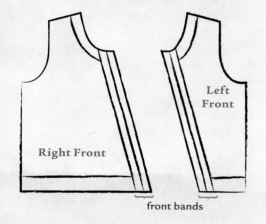

**Right Front**

**Left Front**

front bands

When a garment is asymmetrical, instead of showing just one half and letting you assume that the other is a mirror image of it, the schematic should show both pieces. This one shows not just the two fronts, but the bands that will be added to them. Each front band has a line down the center indicating the point where buttonholes and buttons should be aligned to overlap the two fronts.

## Sleeve Lengths, Superimposed

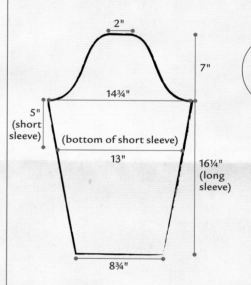

2" 7" 14¾" 5" (short sleeve) (bottom of short sleeve) 13" 16¼" (long sleeve) 8¾"

Short and long sleeve options for the same sweater may also be shown on a single sleeve diagram. The sleeve cap shaping is the same for both. Only the lengths and the widths at the bottom edges differ.

## V-Neck Front and Back Neck, Superimposed

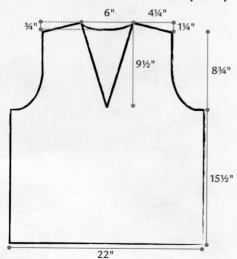

¾" 6" 4¼" 1¼" 9½" 8¾" 15½" 22"

Sometimes to save space when almost all of the measurements are the same, two garment pieces will be shown superimposed in the schematic. This schematic is for a V-necked vest with back neck shaping. The width of the back and front neck openings are identical. Measurements for the depth of the front and back neck opening are shown on the single diagram.

First Choices: Pattern, Yarn, and Needles

# Choosing the Right Size

The easiest way to determine which size will fit you the best is to compare the measurements of a similar garment that you already own and like the fit of with the measurements of the one you're contemplating. Obviously, you'll need to compare the chest measurements, but to ensure a really good fit through the shoulders, you need to compare the width between the armholes, the armhole depth, and the width and depth of the neck opening (both back and front). It's easy to adjust the width of the body; it's a lot harder to adjust the shoulder area of a fitted sweater, because with neck, shoulder, and armhole shaping all happening in close proximity to each other, things get complicated!

## What Ease Does for Your Garments

It's important to understand the concept of *ease*. Simply stated, ease is that little bit of extra space in a garment that makes it comfortable to wear. Without ease, all garments would be skintight. In some cases, this is desirable.

Consider, for example, a leotard. Leotards are designed so that they are actually smaller than the body and stretch to fit it very closely, so that a dancer's every stance and movement can be seen clearly. This is an example of *negative* ease, where the garment is smaller than the body measurements. Sometimes, you may want to construct a handknit garment with negative ease — imagine a body-hugging tank top made in K3, P3 ribbing. On the right body, it would be stunning. With sweaters, in most cases you'll want some ease added to your body-circumference measurements and to the armhole depth to allow for comfort in motion, space for whatever you'll wear under the sweater, and for the thickness of the knitted fabric.

If you have a similar knitted garment that you already like the fit of, compare its measurements with your measurements to discover how much ease is comfortable for you. If you don't have a similar garment, or you have one but you don't like the fit, you'll need to adjust for ease. Some of this is common sense — if the garment you have is too big in some areas, pinch a fold of the fabric until it's the size you'd like it to be, and then deduct the width or the length of what you pinched from the garment's measurement to get the desired measurement including ease. If you don't have a garment for comparison, dress in whatever you plan to wear under the sweater and get a friend to measure you (see How to Take Body Measurements, page 20).

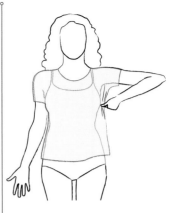

Pinching side of sweater to determine ease

The measurements will be more accurate if someone else takes them than if you do it yourself. Don't pull the tape measure tight around the circumference of your body; instead, hold it loosely around the clothing you're wearing. Compare these measurements with your actual body measurement without clothing and you'll get an idea of how much ease is required for you to be comfortable.

One variation you'll have to address is personal preference. Some people like their garments loose, while others prefer them more fitted. You may not have even considered your own personal preference. If not, this is the time to do so. Put on a sweater or other garment you like, pinch a fold of it at the side to see just how much ease there is, as shown in illustration above. If you're knitting for someone else, you may want to observe how they like their clothing to fit, or ask them to provide a well-fitting garment to help establish the correct size.

Allowing additional ease for the thickness of the knitted fabric can be a puzzle when you haven't yet knit the fabric, but you can also use a common-sense estimate. A thin sweater (made from sport-weight yarn) will need less ease than a thick sweater (made from bulky yarn). A stretchy sweater will need less ease than one knit firmly.

Deborah Newton's book *Designing Knitwear* has excellent discussions of measurements, fit, and ease, and the Craft Yarn Council has published sizing standards for handknit garment designs (see the appendix, page 284, for the website address). These are their ease recommendations, given for the circumference of the sweater.

▷ Very close-fitting: Actual chest/bust measurement or less

▷ Close-fitting: 1 to 2 inches

▷ Standard-fitting: 2 to 4 inches

▷ Loose-fitting: 4 to 6 inches

▷ Oversized: 6 inches or more

If the fabric will be thin and stretchy or you prefer a closer fit, head for the lower end of these ranges. If you prefer a looser fit or the fabric will be thick, lean toward the higher end.

# Recognizing Fit

You need to recognize the difference between fitted, relaxed-fit, and totally unfitted drop-shoulder sweaters. Three different styles result in very different sets of measurements to fit the same person. These are sized to fit a woman with a 36" chest, a 28" waist, and 38½" hips. The silhouette of the body is shown in green. The outlines of the garments are shown in black. Depending on how the garment is tailored, the body varies from 40" to 47" in circumference, and the sleeve width at the underarm ranges from 14¾" to 20".

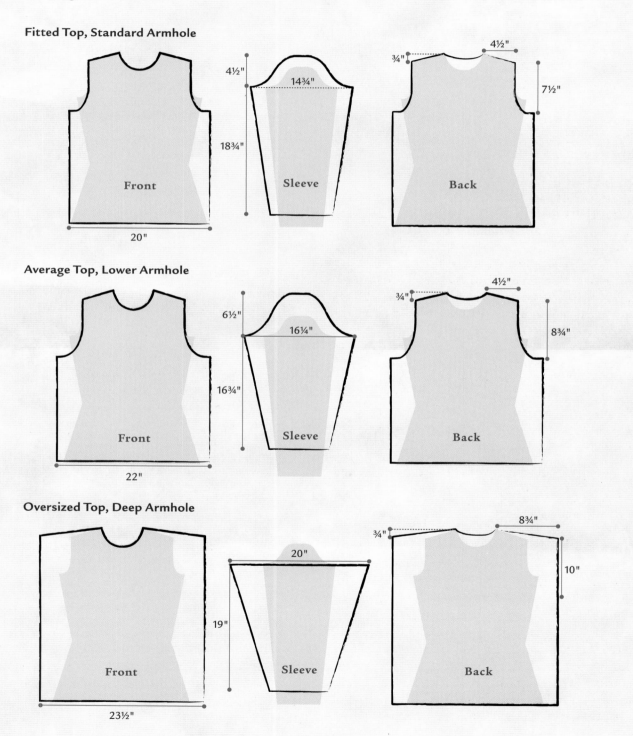

**Fitted Top, Standard Armhole**

Front — 20"
Sleeve — 4½", 14¾", 18¾"
Back — ¾", 4½", 7½"

**Average Top, Lower Armhole**

Front — 22"
Sleeve — 6½", 16¼", 16¾"
Back — ¾", 4½", 8¾"

**Oversized Top, Deep Armhole**

Front — 23½"
Sleeve — 20", 19"
Back — ¾", 8¾", 10"

# How to Take Body Measurements

Body measurements should be taken over under-garments. When making a coat or bulky sweater to be worn over additional layers of clothing, you may also want to measure over representative clothing and compare these larger measurements to the finished measurements of the size you plan to make, to ensure that the garment will fit comfortably when layered.

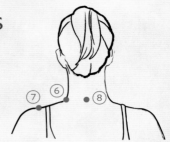

## Points from Which Other Measurements Are Taken

⑥ High shoulder point (where the shoulder meets the neck)

⑦ Low shoulder point (where the shoulder meets the top of your arm. This is the point farthest away from your neck that doesn't move when you raise and lower your arm.)

⑧ Back neck bone

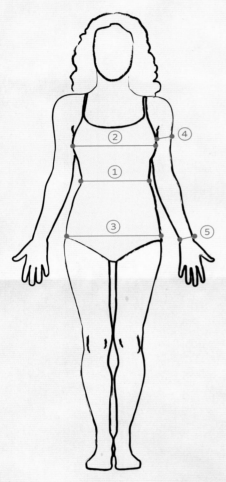

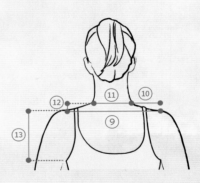

## Shoulder and Neck Area

⑨ Full shoulder width (between the two low shoulder points)

⑩ Individual shoulder width (parallel to the floor from the high shoulder point to a point directly above the low shoulder point)

⑪ Neck width (parallel to the floor, between the two high shoulder points). This is more easily calculated by subtracting the two individual shoulder widths from the full shoulder width, rather than actually attempting to measure neck width.

⑫ Shoulder depth (perpendicular to the floor, from the low shoulder point to a point even with the high shoulder point). This may be easier to calculate than to measure, by measuring waist to low shoulder and waist to high shoulder, and then subtracting to find the difference between the two.

⑬ Armhole depth (from the low shoulder point to the underarm)

## Circumference Measurements

① Waist circumference (narrowest point)

② Chest/bust circumference (widest point)

③ Hip circumference (widest point)

④ Upper arm circumference (widest point)

⑤ Wrist circumference

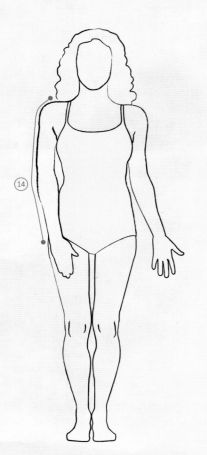
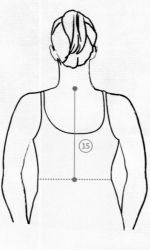
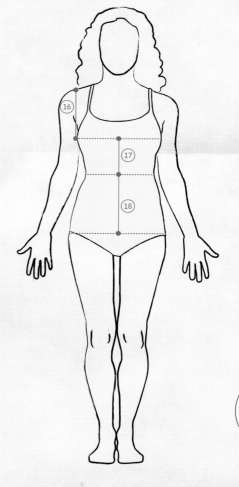

## Lengths

⑭ Arm length (low shoulder point to wrist, with arm slightly bent)

⑮ Back-waist length (perpendicular to the floor from waist to back neck bone). This is only necessary if there will be waist shaping.

⑯ Low shoulder-to-bust length (perpendicular to the floor, from widest bust/chest measurement to low shoulder point).

⑰ Bust-to-waist length (perpendicular to the floor from waist to widest bust/chest measurement). This is only necessary if there will be waist shaping.

⑱ Waist-to-hip length (perpendicular to the floor, from widest hip measurement to waist). This is only necessary if there will be waist shaping.

There are also a few specialized measurements you may want to make if you intend to add bust darts. These are discussed in Measuring for Bust Darts (page 120).

## What If the Pattern Doesn't Match Your Measurements?

When we purchase clothes off the rack, to get a good fit we have to buy the size that fits our largest measurement, and then take in or shorten the other areas to make them smaller. When knitting a sweater, we have the option of making sections larger or smaller. If instructions for a given size will make a garment that fits in some areas but not in others, the best bet is to choose the one that fits best through the shoulder, armhole, and neck area. This is the most complicated area to adjust because any changes to shoulders and armholes affect the shaping of the sleeves, and vice versa. It's easier to make the body, which is usually straight, larger or smaller to fit your bust, waist, and hips properly. See chapter 4 for detailed discussions of how to adjust almost any part of your sweater.

## Verifying Measurements versus Pattern Instructions

Once you've completed the comparison between your desired size and the pattern size, and selected the size you think you should make, do a quick check to see that the measurements given in the pattern are consistent with the instructions.

**Checking the width or circumference.** Read through the pattern to find the number of stitches for the body of a pullover just below the underarms, and then divide that by the number of stitches per inch and see if it matches the schematic. The best way to determine the circumference of a cardigan (assuming the back and fronts are shaped the same) is to find the width of the back just below the underarms and multiply it by two. Test the width at the shoulders, the neck opening, and the sleeve at the cuff and the underarm the same way. Remember that the individual shoulder width (from the armhole to the neck) on the schematic probably does not include the width of any neck or armhole borders, so check the width of the borders and allow for them. If the garment is shaped from waist to bust, check the waist measurement as well.

**Checking the length** isn't necessary unless there is shaping to taper the sleeves or the body, or there are diagonal sections like a crossover front or the yoke on a raglan-sleeved or circular sweater.

If you do need to verify the length, read the instructions to find out how many decreases or increases there are and how often they are done. Multiply to find out the total rows over which the shaping takes place, then divide by the number of rows per inch in the gauge to get the actual length. This may be off by a few rows if there are plain rows before and after the first and last shaping row, but it will still be close.

For example, if the sleeve instructions say to increase at both edges every 4th row 22 times and the row gauge is 7 rows per inch, multiply 4 rows by 22 increases to get 88, then divide by 7 rows per inch, and you'll find that the sleeve shaping will be about 12.6 inches. Add the length of any ribbing and the length that is worked straight between the top of the shaping and the underarm to get the total length from cuff to underarm.

When checking the fit of a raglan or circular yoked sweater, a key measurement is the distance from the neckline diagonally to the underarm; it must be long enough to fit you comfortably or it will be too tight under the arms. Yoked sweaters like these are commonly 1 to 2 inches longer to the underarm than sweaters with armholes and separate sleeves, to make their simpler shaping comfortable to wear. Take this measurement over a shirt that would be worn with the sweater to allow enough room for comfort.

Measuring diagonal from neck to underarm

If you find discrepancies, double-check them to be sure you haven't made a mathematical error, then mark the corrected measurement on the schematic. If you see variations between what you calculated and the measurements on the schematic, you'll need to rethink whether this really is the right size for you, perhaps by verifying several sizes to find the one that fits best.

Is all this checking necessary? It depends. If it's a fitted garment, with shaped armholes and sleeve caps, then it really needs to fit in order to look good. A fitted garment that doesn't actually fit will not only look bad, it may be very uncomfortable to wear. The only way you can be sure it will fit is to check the actual measurements. If it's a drop-shoulder garment, as long as it's comfortably big in the chest and upper sleeves and the sleeves aren't too short or too long, it will be fine, so the critical measurement on a drop-shoulder sweater is the finished length of the sleeve, measured from the center back neck to the cuff. To calculate this measurement for a sweater, take the width of the body at the shoulders, add the length of *both* sleeves, then divide by two.

# Finding a Yarn to Suit Your Pattern/Finding a Pattern to Suit Your Yarn

You have the best chance of a successful garment the more closely you match the yarn used in the original design; however, you shouldn't feel compelled to use the identical yarn. There are almost always appropriate yarns you can substitute. You just need to match the yarn's three key attributes as closely as possible: these are the thickness of the yarn, the fiber content, and the yarn's structure and texture. You should also consider the color of the yarn, but that's more a matter of aesthetics and personal preference.

## Understanding Yarn Weight

There are several systems for yarn weights in use. In the United States, the different thicknesses of yarn have traditionally been called by name, such as sport weight, worsted weight, and bulky weight. In the United Kingdom, the terms include 4-ply and DK ("double knitting"). The Craft Yarn Council has tried to standardize references to yarn weight for knitting and crochet using a numbered system that begins with size 0 for the thinnest yarns and ends with size 6 for the thickest (see the appendix, page 284, for the website address). In all of these cases, the label refers to a range of yarns with similar thicknesses that may or may not be close enough to the thickness you want.

To check for a comparable thickness, you need to compare the yards per ounce (or gram or pound). If you are lucky, the pattern will provide yarn specifications that include how many yards or meters are in each ball or skein and how much each ball or skein weighs. Divide the weight by the length for the yarn you're considering and compare the result to the original yarn. If one provides weight in grams and the other in ounces, you'll need to convert them to the same units. After decades of doing these conversions, I have memorized that 1.75 ounces equals 50 grams. This is really all you need to remember. Or, if it seems simpler to you, 3.5 ounces equals 100 grams.

For example, the pattern calls for a worsted-weight wool yarn with 110 yards per 50-gram ball. You want to substitute a wool yarn with 198 yards per 100-gram ball. The easiest thing to do is to multiply the yards in the original ball by two to see how many yards would be in a 100-gram ball: 110 yards × 2 = 220 yards. The substitute yarn has only 198 yards in the same weight, so it's a little thicker or denser than the original. A second

yarn you're considering is packaged with 225 yards in 4 ounces. To compare it to the original, you'll need to figure out how many yards are in 50 grams. Remember that 1.75 ounces = 50 grams. Divide 4 ounces by 1.75 ounces to discover how many 50-gram balls are in 4 ounces, and you get 2.29. Divide 225 yards by 2.29 to get 98.25 yards in 50 grams, which is also a little thicker or denser than the original (which you'll remember had 110 yards in a 50-gram ball). Are either of these yarns close enough to substitute? The answer is a solid maybe! You'll need to test them out by knitting a swatch to see if you like the fabric when you are knitting at the correct gauge, but you also need to consider fiber content and structure, so read on.

## When You Don't Know the Yarn Specs

If your yarn is missing a label or the label doesn't contain enough information, you can figure out what needle size would be appropriate by this simple test. Fold a strand of the yarn in half and hold it across the holes in a needle gauge. The hole that the double strand covers will indicate the needle size that will serve as a starting point. Knit a swatch with this size to see if you can match the gauge specifications and produce a suitable fabric. Adjust the needle size depending on your results: If you need to get more stitches per inch, use a smaller needle, which will make the fabric tighter and less stretchy; for fewer stitches per inch use a larger needle, which will result in a looser, stretchier fabric.

This also works if you substitute multiple strands of thinner yarn for a single thicker yarn. Twist the strands loosely together, then fold in half and lay them across the needle gauge. Stretch them a bit to prevent them from kinking up.

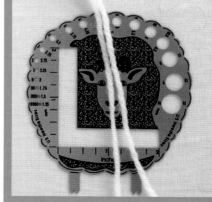

## Fiber Content and the Finished Fabric

The fiber content of the yarn plays two roles. The density of the underlying fiber affects how much length there is for the weight at any given thickness, and the inherent properties of the fiber affect how it behaves. As an example, let's compare cotton to wool. Sheep's wool is less dense, with air trapped inside the cell structures of each hair. Most sheep's wool used for handknitting is naturally crimped or waved. Cotton fibers are much denser, much shorter than the wool used for spinning yarn, and have no crimp.

The different characteristics of the fibers result in different yarn characteristics. Cotton yarns tend to be inelastic. They are usually more tightly spun than wool yarns, because more twist is required to hold the short fibers together so the yarn won't fall apart. Wool yarns are more elastic because the crimp in the individual hairs stretches out straight when pulled and returns to its original length when relaxed. If you take two pieces of yarn, one cotton and the other wool, that are the same thickness and the same length, with the same number of plies and the same amount of twist, the cotton yarn will be heavier than the wool.

Because of these dissimilarities, garments knitted from the two fibers will also behave differently. Cotton garments, because they are heavier, tend to gradually stretch in length while worn. If they shrink in the wash, they will usually end up shorter and wider. Wool garments, because the yarn is elastic and less dense, hold their shape better. If they do stretch out of shape, washing restores the fiber's natural crimp, and they can usually be blocked back to their original shape.

So, choose a fiber content that closely matches that of the original yarn. A wool and acrylic blend may substitute just fine for 100% wool. Nonstretchy plant fibers like cotton, linen, hemp, and bamboo can usually be substituted for each other. Silk, rayon, and other slippery inelastic yarns can also be substituted for each other. Less elastic animal fibers, like mohair, cashmere, and alpaca, can usually be substituted for each other, but depending on how tightly spun they are and whether they have been brushed to produce a fuzzy halo, their appearance and behavior can vary widely. And you can usually use all the nonstretchy yarns interchangeably. If the pattern calls for a 100% wool yarn, many times you can successfully substitute a wool-blend yarn that is at least one-third wool.

### Same Stitch Patterns, Different Yarns

Lamb's Pride (wool and mohair singles)

2-ply handspun (wool)

Generally speaking, any fiber you expect to stretch (anything heavy and inelastic, which includes anything that's not wool) will perform better in a garment structured with seams to help support it. These fibers will also perform better the thinner the yarn and the less dense the pattern stitch. Fine yarn worked up into a delicate lace fabric will cause far less trouble than bulky yarn worked into a thick fabric. Borders in all fibers besides wool present challenges, which I discuss in Fiber Makes a Difference in Borders (chapter 8, page 223).

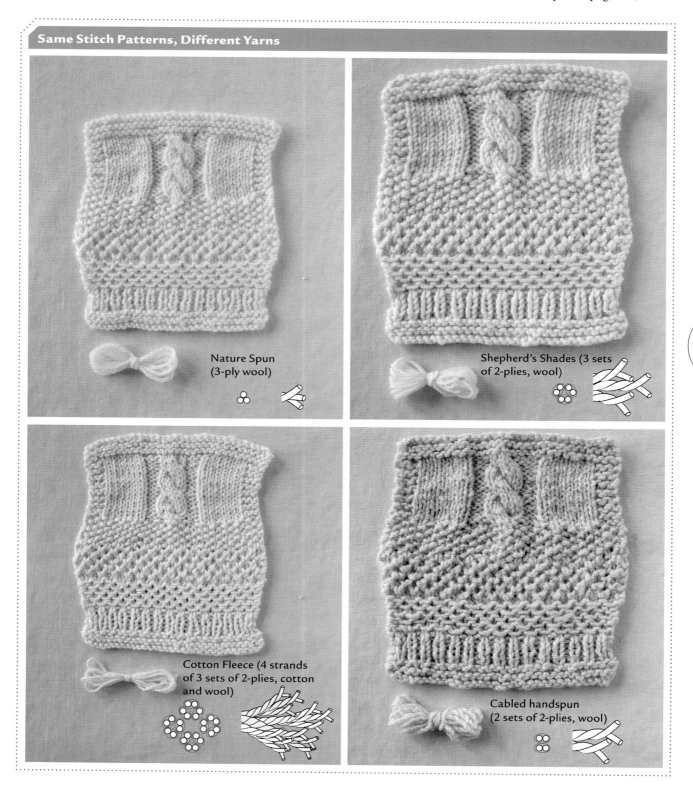

**Same Stitch Patterns, Different Yarns**

Nature Spun (3-ply wool)

Shepherd's Shades (3 sets of 2-plies, wool)

Cotton Fleece (4 strands of 3 sets of 2-plies, cotton and wool)

Cabled handspun (2 sets of 2-plies, wool)

## How Yarn Structure and Texture Affect the Fabric

One of the surprising things about yarn is how yarns that have the same fiber content, the same thickness, and are the same color can look completely different in the knitted fabric depending on their structure. It's obvious that fabric made from a fuzzy brushed mohair will look very different from fabric made from a smooth yarn. For this reason, it's best not to take a complicated textured pattern stitch and knit it in a highly textured yarn, because the texture of the yarn will partially or completely obscure the pattern stitch. What's not so intuitive is the difference in appearance that the ply structure and the amount of twist make.

The major difference is stitch definition. You can really see the stitch patterns in some yarns, and in others they can look like a disorganized jumble. In single-ply yarn, the twist of the yarn itself is very noticeable, making the individual stitches appear crooked because the fibers within the yarn are almost parallel to one side of the stitch and almost perpendicular to the other. The rounder the cross-section of the yarn, the better the stitch definition. The amount of twist also plays a role — loosely twisted yarns tend to have poorer stitch definition (see photos pages 24–25 and below).

So, if there will be textured pattern stitches and you want to clearly see every stitch, avoid loosely spun 2-ply and highly textured yarns. If you will be working color patterns, keep in mind that using a fuzzy yarn will make the color changes less crisp and may obscure subtle stranded work, slipped-stitch colorwork, or intarsia altogether.

**Similar Patterns, Different Textures and Colors**

**Effect of yarn structure and texture on fabric:**
(A) 3-ply with good twist shows off the textured pattern stitches in spite of the color variations; (B) dark yarn hides the textured stitches completely; (C) brushed mohair obscures the textured patterns; (D) variegated handspun yarn with different colored plies provides an interesting variation of effects in the different pattern stitches, although you can't tell what the patterns are.

## Choosing Your Colors

You can use any color you like. I should probably say this again: you really can use any color you like. You don't need to match the color of the garment illustrated with the pattern. But you do need to employ common sense. It doesn't make sense to take a subtle textured pattern stitch and knit it in a dark yarn where it can't be seen, or to use a multicolor yarn so busy that it obscures the pattern stitch. Sometimes you may want to work a pattern stitch simply to amuse yourself or to break the tedium of endless acreage of stockinette stitch, knowing that it won't be obvious to the casual observer. But if you want the pattern stitch to be the highlight of the garment, pick a yarn that will enable everyone to see it.

Selecting multiple colors for a garment, whether to be used in stripes, in stranded knitting, or in other pattern stitches, can be challenging. You may visualize what you want, but be unable to find the colors you need. You may have no idea what colors to choose. There are a couple of approaches you can use to dealing with both problems, but the main advice I have is to experiment. Collect yarns and hold them together to see how you like them in various combinations. To check for contrast to see whether colorwork will show up, twist strands of all the yarns together and look at them in dim light — if you can still see each color clearly, then there's enough contrast so that they'll all show up in the knitted fabric. Wrap cards, varying the proportions and placement of each color, to determine how much of each to use and which will be the best neighbors.

The most important thing to remember when working with color is that there are no right or wrong color combinations. There are no bad colors. What suits you might not appeal to others, but you're the knitter and it's *your* judgment that matters when deciding what colors to use in your own projects. (For an in-depth discussion of color in knitting, see my *The Essential Guide to Color Knitting Techniques.*)

Another issue to consider when choosing multiple colors for a project is whether they are colorfast. If the garment is multicolor, one color may run during washing and stain the other colors, ruining it. Protect yourself from problems like this by testing all the yarns before you combine them. Cut off a sample of each color. Run hot water into a white basin, bowl, or cup, and soak each color separately to see whether the water changes color. Rub the wet yarn on a white paper towel to see whether any dye comes off. If any of the colors run, wash them until the rinse water runs clear to remove all the excess dye before knitting with them. Using a surfactant like Dharma Professional Textile Detergent or Synthrapol (see Online References, page 284 for information) will help to speed this process, because they prevent excess dye from settling back onto the surface of the yarn. Before washing, balls of yarn must be wound into skeins and tied in several places to prevent tangling. Roll them in a towel to remove excess water, then hang to dry completely before winding into balls. Washing in hot water may shrink the yarn, but that's good! It means the fabric knit from it won't shrink after it's completed. If this sounds like too much work, try to find a yarn you can substitute that doesn't run.

### Evaluating Multiple Colors

Wrapping sample cards and twisting yarns together can help you see how the colors interact.

## Keep Quality Assurance in Mind

Check to make sure that all the balls or skeins are from the same dye lot, because the color may vary noticeably from batch to batch. Handpainted or hand-dyed yarns may vary in color even if they are from the same batch. If you do end up with yarns from more than one dye lot, or you suspect there's a color variation, test the yarns by twisting them together. Hold the twisted strands under a bright light or take them outside and see if the difference in colors is noticeable. If you can't tell that two different yarns are twisted together, then you probably won't see a difference in the finished garment.

When purchasing handspun yarn, check to see that all the skeins appear to be the same thickness. If one skein appears to be thicker or thinner throughout than the others, you should put it back. If you love the yarn and need to use a skein that doesn't match, then see When Your Yarn Causes Problems (chapter 5, page 151) and Other Yarn Inconsistencies (chapter 5, page 152) for techniques that will help to disguise the variations.

## Choosing Needles

The brand of needles you use is a matter of personal preference. If you knit loosely, you will probably find wood or bamboo needles comfortable to use because the knitting is less likely to slip off the needles. If you knit tightly, slippery coated metal needles may appeal because it's easier to move the stitches along as you work. If you enjoy knitting lace, cables, or other patterns with lots of stitch manipulations, you'll probably prefer

**Effect of different needles.** The fingers of this glove were worked on a different set of double-pointed needles than the hand. The fingers are tight, with even stitches, while the hand is looser and less even.

needles with sharper points. But, if you are like most knitters, you'll just use the needles you have unless you find them annoying for a particular project, at which point you should go out and find needles that work better for you. Changing between brands of needles or between needles made of different materials during the course of a project may result in variations in the size of your stitches. If you change from bamboo or wood to metal needles to work different sections of a garment, look critically at the fabric you're creating to make sure there's no noticeable change in the stitch size or quality of the knitting.

## Types of Needles: Straights, Circulars, and Double Points

The choice of circular versus straight versus double-pointed needles will be obvious in many cases. Like the brand of needle you use, the first choice will be whatever needles you already own, unless they simply won't work. Since you can knit a flat piece on straight needles or back and forth on circular needles (assuming the needles are long enough to accommodate all your stitches), suit yourself as to which you use. I personally like to use double points for narrow pieces of flat knitting, just ignoring the point at the other end. Because they are shorter than regular straight needles, I find the length more convenient for carrying around and knitting in armchairs or tight spaces like airplanes.

The choice of whether to work narrow tubes using Magic Loop (page 268), two circulars, or double points is also entirely a matter of personal preference, but if you experiment, you may discover that you like one of these for a particular type of project and another for a different type of project. I prefer short double-pointed needles for very small tubes like fingers and thumbs, but will happily work slightly larger tubes (like the hands of mittens, socks, and the bottom of sleeves) circularly on whatever type of needle is available. I don't really like using two circular needles because I find the dangling ends of the needle not in use annoying, but when I am working a sweater circularly from cuff to cuff, I like to put the front on one needle and the back on a second needle because it makes it easier to keep track of where I am in the project and I can lay it out flat to measure it. It also means that, assuming I separate the front and back to work the neck and bottom opening, the stitches on the half that is not in use don't need to be moved to another needle or holder — they are already on one. I don't waste time counting and rearranging stitches in the course of the project — it can all be worked on the same two needles. It's worth it to become comfortable with several ways of working tubes, because one may be far more convenient than another in a particular project.

## Needle Length Matters

The length of knitting needles ranges from 5-inch double-pointed needles to circular needles that are 60 inches or even longer. Whether you choose single points, double points, or circular needles, choose a length that will not impair the knitting. If stitches are jammed tightly on the needle, it's difficult to work consistently and to catch mistakes. If stitches are severely stretched to go around a too-long circular needle, it's difficult to slide them up onto the points, difficult to pass them from point to point as you work, and it may force you to knit more loosely in order to be able to knit at all. With circular needles used the conventional way (not Magic Loop or two circular needles), it's important that the needle be shorter than the circumference of the knitting.

**Inappropriate Needle Lengths**

Top, too few stitches on a circular needle. Bottom, too many stitches on a straight needle

## Needle Size Determines Gauge

The critical choice is the *size* of the needle. It's simply common sense that thicker needles make bigger stitches resulting in a looser, lighter knitted fabric and thinner needles make smaller stitches resulting in tighter, denser fabric.

When you're working from pattern instructions, it's very, very important to match the number of stitches and rows per inch specified by the pattern, either in stockinette stitch or in the pattern stitch specified. Every knitter is different — some knit tightly, some knit loosely, and some vary from day to day. If you already know you knit tightly, then start out with a needle one or two sizes larger than the instructions suggest. If, on the contrary, you knit loosely, start with a needle one or two sizes smaller than the instructions suggest. If you know that you are inconsistent, once you find the needle size that seems to work, keep an eye on your knitting to make sure it looks consistent. You may even want to measure the gauge (in both rows and stitches) periodically while garment making is in progress.

## Why You May Need More Than One Type of Needle for the Same Project

All of the pieces of garments that are knit flat can sometimes be made on a single pair of straight needles, with perhaps the addition of a smaller pair for the ribbing. You may need or want additional needles, however, in order to make work on specific sections of the garment more pleasant and efficient. For example, a medium-length circular needle (24 inches or longer) is nice for working the flat front or back of an adult-size garment because it can be laid out flat for easy measurement. The stitches for a large garment will fit more easily on the circular needle than on a straight needle. The neck or armhole borders could be worked flat and then seamed at the shoulder or underarm, but if you use a 16-inch circular needle for your neck border, you can make a very neat, seamless neck border instead.

When working a garment in the round, you may want different length circular needles or sets of double-pointed needles to most comfortably work sections with various circumferences. You may also want additional needles so that sections can be held on them until wanted, instead of transferring the stitches to another needle, a stitch holder, or a piece of yarn.

29

# Matching Gauge

Be patient while testing out the needles and yarn trying to match the correct gauge. You need to knit swatches at least 6 inches square to get a reasonable measurement of stitches and rows. I like to cast on, work for a few inches, and then do a preliminary measurement across the stitches. If it seems to be coming out okay, I'll continue until I have a square, take it off the needle, and measure both stitches and rows to make sure the gauges of both dimensions match the pattern gauge. If they don't, I'll put the swatch back on the needle, work a row or round in reverse stockinette, then adjust my needle size up or down and repeat the process. I'll keep doing this, making a long test strip or tube with ridges marking each needle change, until I get the required gauge. Sometimes, one of the earlier sections ends up being the closest match. If I had unraveled it, I wouldn't know that. Of course, you need to keep a record of what size needle you used for each section, so make a list in the same order that you knit the test strip.

You could also work a reminder into each section of your swatch, to keep track of the needle size you used:

▷ Work a series of K2tog, yo, where the number of yarnovers matches the needle size.

▷ If working in stockinette, work part of a row in reverse stockinette with the number of stitches to match the needle size.

▷ Weave in a piece of waste yarn across the same number of stitches as the needle size.

▷ Attach a piece of waste yarn with knots tied in it to indicate the needle size.

We all have a tendency to play with our swatches when we measure them, patting them flat, stretching them out a bit in width or length in hopes they will match the correct gauge. Of course, this can be a recipe for disaster. When you do this, you're kidding yourself. It's like adjusting the bathroom scale to read five pounds lower so you feel like you've lost weight. So avoid the temptation — lay your swatch out on a smooth flat surface, like a tabletop, lay your ruler on top of it, and count the stitches in 4 inches. Without moving your swatch, move the ruler and count the rows in 4 inches. Do they both match the specified gauge? Excellent — you're ready to wash your swatch!

## For a More Accurate Gauge Count

Put your swatch on a surface you can pin to. Insert T-pins at the zero and 4-inch measure, then count the stitches or rows between pins. Be sure to include partial stitches!

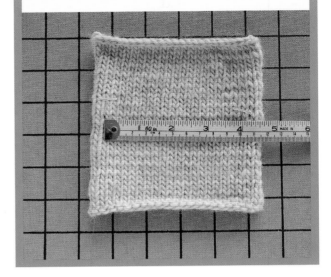

## Why Row Gauge Matters

Row gauge matters because knitting stretches. In plain stockinette stitch that's knit fairly firmly, the fabric will hold its shape so you can be pretty sure of getting realistic counts of both rows and stitches. If the fabric is ribbed, lace, or very loosely knit, you can easily and accidentally lay it out with the fabric stretched so that the stitches match the desired gauge, but the rows are way off. In cases like these, it's important to stretch the fabric gently to the correct number of stitches in 4 inches. If it will stay in place on its own, count the rows in 4 inches to see whether the row gauge is also correct. If it won't stay in place, you may need to pin it out on a bulletin board, blocking board, or towel while you measure. Don't stretch it horizontally to measure the stitches, then re-stretch it vertically to measure the rows! If it stretches easily to the correct measurements in both dimensions *at the same time,* you're ready to wash it to check for shrinkage or expansion.

## It's Not Done Until You Wash It

Some yarn shrinks. It's a fact of life. And when it shrinks, your garment will change shape. Other yarns expand or relax when washed. To know how much your swatch will shrink (or expand) in both dimensions, you'll need to wash it just as you will wash the planned garment and dry it just as you will dry the planned garment. If you will lay the wet garment flat and block it, then you need to do the same to your swatch (see Blocking Knitted Pieces, chapter 7, page 194). Measure your swatch as described on the facing page and note the stitch and row count in 4 inches before you wash. After the swatch is dry, measure all over again. If the rows and stitches in 4 inches haven't changed, you should jump for joy because it makes the process of creating a garment exactly the size and shape you want much, much easier. If the rows or stitches per inch have changed, you must allow for this while knitting.

If there are more stitches per 4 inches than you want after washing and blocking, you'll need to use a larger needle so that the number of stitches in 4 inches matches the gauge after it shrinks. Yes, this means you'll have to swatch, wash, and dry all over again. But if you knitted a test strip with various needle sizes and kept a record of what size you used for each section, you can just use the needle size for the section that matches the correct gauge.

If the row gauge in this section also matches the specifications in the instructions, you're all set, assuming the directions are given in rows throughout the garment. Usually you'll find they are not. If your row gauge doesn't match that specified in the pattern, or if the instructions are given in measurements rather than rows, you'll need to adjust proportionally. You'll knit more rows if your fabric shrank, so that it will shrink to the correct length, and knit fewer rows if your fabric grew, so that it will grow to the correct length when washed.

---

## CASE STUDY #1-1

# Planning for Shrinkage in Length

① **Calculate the proportion of shrinkage.** If the swatch started out with 28 rows in 4 inches, but those same 28 rows measure 3.75 inches after washing, this is a reduction of 0.0625 in proportion to the original length. To calculate the proportion of shrinkage, subtract the shrunk length from the original length, then divide the difference by the original length. If you prefer to work in percent, you can multiply by 100 to make the answer a percentage.

$$(4" - 3.75") \div 4" = 0.0625 \text{ or } 6.25\%$$

② **Calculate the required length before shrinkage.** Multiply the desired length by 1 plus the amount of shrinkage. This example assumes the desired length is 14".

$$14" \times (1 + 0.0625) = 14.875"$$

The result is the length that you will actually knit. When the garment is washed, it should shrink to the correct length.

A second approach to planning for shrinkage or growth, which you might find simpler because there are fewer calculations, is to figure out the number of rows you'll need to reach the required length after washing. Take the length measurement, multiply it by the rows per inch in the gauge after washing, and you'll have the number or rows you need to work. In the example above, that would be 14" × 7.47 rows per inch = 105 rows. Of course, you'll have to count those 105 rows as you knit to be sure you've reached the correct length.

# Swatching for Gauge in Circular Knitting

MANY PEOPLE KNIT MORE TIGHTLY than they purl, or purl more tightly than they knit. This means that their gauge in stockinette and many other patterns when working flat will be different from the gauge when working in the round. How do you know if you have this problem?

① Work a flat swatch at least 5 inches square in stockinette and look at the purl side of it. Stretch it a little from top to bottom. If the ridges are evenly spaced, then there's no problem. If the ridges alternate being closer together and then farther apart, as in the photo above, you definitely have a difference of tension between your knits and your purls.

② Work a circular swatch in stockinette at least 10 inches around.

③ Count the number of stitches in 4 inches on both swatches. If the circular swatch is smaller (with *more* stitches per inch), then your knits are tighter than your purls. If the circular swatch is larger (with *fewer* stitches per inch), then your purls are tighter than your knits.

Even if you don't have a problem with flat versus circular tension differences in stockinette, you might when working other pattern stitches. For this reason, you should always make a circular gauge swatch if you plan to make a garment in the round. If the garment has both flat and circular sections, work the circular swatch, then bind off about half the stitches and continue the swatch working flat. Check the gauge in both sections to make sure it's the same. Also take a critical look at the two sections to make sure they look the same, on both the right side and the wrong side, because you want all the sections of your garment to match.

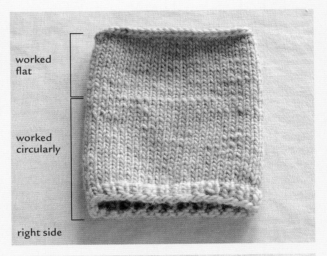

worked flat

worked circularly

right side

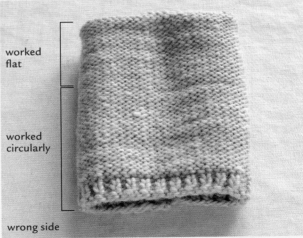

worked flat

worked circularly

wrong side

**The bottom of this swatch** was worked circularly while the top was worked flat. On the right side (above), the stitches in the flat section look just a little tighter. On the wrong side (below), the variation in the ridges in the top half is barely noticeable.

If you work at it, you may be able to adjust your tension to solve the problem. This is the ideal solution, because then your knits and purls will be consistent with each other and so will your flat and circular knitting in the future. Once you figure out which is looser, your knits or your purls, try to make those stitches just a little tighter. You may be able to accomplish this by trying one of the following adjustments.

▶ Wrap the yarn an extra time around one finger to prevent it from sliding as easily.

▶ Change the angle at which you hold your yarn, which can pull the stitch open when forming it. Hold it lower or higher to see if it makes any difference.

▶ Work the stitches on the tips of your needles, which have a smaller circumference and will produce a smaller stitch.

▶ Form the stitches in the opposite direction (by wrapping the yarn the other way around the needle). This can make them smaller or larger. You'd need to experiment with working the knit stitches this way, and then the purl stitches, to see if it affects either of them in your knitting. Remember that you need to work into the back of these stitches on the following row or round so that they don't end up twisted.

▶ Knit backward across the whole row, instead of turning and purling. (See Knit To and Fro in the appendix, page 276.)

If you are unable to adjust your knits or purls so they match each other, another solution when working stockinette is to use a different size needle for the purl rows. Use a smaller needle if your purls are too loose and a larger needle if they are too tight. You'll need to experiment to find the best size.

# There's More to Swatching Than Matching the Gauge

We all want to get past the swatching stage as quickly as possible, assuming we don't (go ahead and confess) skip it completely. But there's more to swatching than matching the gauge. This is your chance to make sure you really like working with the combination of pattern stitch, yarn, and needles. It gives you a chance to learn the pattern stitch so that you'll have an easier time doing it correctly and consistently when you start the garment. You may discover that you hate, Hate, HATE working the pattern stitch, or working with the yarn, or that you have the correct needle size, but the needles are too blunt or too slippery to work with easily. Before making the ultimate commitment, decide whether you really want to be wed to the pattern, tools, and materials until the final finishing doth you part.

## Evaluating the Fabric in Your Swatch

Even if you're confident you've selected just the right yarn to go with your pattern and you've got exactly the right gauge, evaluate whether you're happy with the fabric in the swatch. Does it look as good as you expected? Does it look good both up close and from across the room? Does it feel good, or is it scratchy? Does is stretch just the right amount (some for a baggy sweater, a lot for a loose lacy garment, not much for a coat or long vest)? If it still seems perfect to you, forge ahead, but if not, you might want to reconsider the project.

## How Will You Manage Your Yarn?

The swatch is also your opportunity to test out how to handle your yarn. If it is difficult to work with the yarn and needles you've selected, see whether things improve when you change to a different type of needle. Many stitch manipulations are easier to work on needles with long tapered points. Some yarns behave better on wooden needles; others are easier to work with on slick metal needles or on plastic needles.

### Working with Multiple Balls

Whether it's for stripes, Fair Isle, intarsia, or slipped-stitch patterns, whenever you use multiple balls of yarn, they'll twist around each other. While swatching, you'll get a feel for how annoying this will be. If you want to avoid wasting time with tangles, here are a few tips:

▷ Set all the balls on a table in front of you, instead of letting them roll around in a basket or bag. You'll notice when the strands cross and can just reposition the balls as this occurs. Arranging the yarns in small jars or in a box where they fit fairly tightly keeps them from moving around. Winding them into center-pull balls also helps.

▷ If using just two balls in stranded knitting, put one to your left and one to your right. If the strands twist, you'll realize you've twisted them while working and can resolve the problem immediately.

▷ When using multiple colors in intarsia, wind each yarn supply on a bobbin or into a butterfly; secure these close to the back of the knitting so they don't twist around each other, or abandon the bobbins entirely and use a loose arm's length of each color.

Another issue with all kinds of colorwork is ends: What to do with them? Will you weave them in as you knit or leave them for later? Will you carry the yarn up a few rows when it's used again, or cut it? Experiment with this in the swatch to determine what will work best. (See Weaving in Ends as You Go, appendix, page 281); and Dealing with Ends, chapter 7, page 200).

## Working with Difficult Yarns

Slippery yarns require special handling. Balls wound from them tend to dissolve into a tangled mess. If a slippery yarn is in a skein, wind it by hand into a firm ball and place the ball inside a ziplock bag or a knee-high stocking to prevent the ball from falling apart. Or wind the ball around a core (like a dowel or a toilet-paper roll) to help support it. Pull the yarn out a little at a time as you use it. Avoid winding a slippery yarn into a center-pull ball with a ball winder. If you pull from the center, the ball will collapse into a puddle that could require hours to untangle.

Similarly, do not use a ball winder for a flat yarn, either woven or knit in a tiny tube, because it will get twisted. Instead, wind the yarn by hand onto a toilet-paper tube, being careful not to twist the yarn. Put the tube on an extra knitting needle and suspend it between two holes in the sides of a cardboard box, so the yarn can unroll neatly. If you have a swift (equipment that holds a skein of yarn as it's wound into a ball) that you can dedicate to this yarn while you knit, set it up nearby, put the skein on it, and knit directly from that.

## Swatching to Refine the Details

With the needle size decided, you can fine-tune the details in one perfect swatch. Make sure the borders, cast on, bind off, and edge stitches are all fully integrated — that they look as good as they possibly can.

### How to Handle Flat Yarns

To prevent twisting, wind flat yarns onto a tube, suspend the tube on a knitting needle, and let the yarn unroll as you work.

Cast on enough stitches to make a swatch about 8 inches wide, then incorporate the following details included in your garment, plus any others you can think of. Working out these details in the swatch is time well spent, because it's quicker to rip out and rework a swatch than to rip out and revise a full-size garment.

## Test the Cast On, Border, and Bind Off

Start and end your perfect swatch just as you will the actual garment — with the same size needle (usually two sizes smaller for the borders than for the body). Use the same cast on, bind off, pattern stitches, and border you plan to use. Increase at the top of the border (or decrease if you are working top down) as called for in the directions (usually it's an increase or decrease of about 10 percent of the stitches to make sure that the ribbing doesn't stretch out of shape).

▷ To increase by 10 percent, work K10, M1 (or K9, Kfb) repeatedly across, or substitute your preferred increase.

▷ To decrease by 10 percent, work K8, K2tog repeated across.

## Audition the Edge Stitches

If you're going to sew seams or pick up stitches along the sides, it will be much easier if the edges are smooth and neat. Usually you'll want to keep at least one stitch at the edge in either stockinette or in garter stitch. If it will be an exposed finished edge all on its own, a possible way to neaten it is to slip the first stitch of each row. See Managing Edge Stitches, in chapter 2 (page 54).

## Shaping and Curved Borders

To test out shaped edges, work a curve in your swatch that can masquerade as either an armhole or part of a neck opening. When working from the bottom up, bind off about a quarter of the stitches at the beginning of a right-side row. Continue to work in your pattern and decrease 1 stitch at the beginning of each right-side row until another quarter of the stitches are gone. Work straight in pattern for a few inches, then bind off the remaining stitches.

When working from the top down, cast on about 2 inches of stitches, work straight for a few inches, then increase at the beginning of each right-side row for a couple of inches. Finally cast on about the same number of stitches that you increased. Work even for a few more inches, transition to and complete the bottom border, and then bind off the swatch.

If you are concerned about making the right and left shaping look consistent, then make a wider swatch and work the shaping at both edges to test it out (see Shaping a Garment at the Edge, chapter 4, page 101).

## How to Evaluate Your Swatch

Look at your swatch critically.

▷ Do the cast on and bind off look good? Do you like the other side of either one better? Do they pull in too much or look too loose?

▷ Is the bottom border nice and neat? Does it flow beautifully out of the cast on or into the bind off? Study the border in relation to the rest of the swatch — does it pull in or flare out? Can you stretch it easily to the same width as the rest of the swatch? Does it return to its original width when you let go? Are the increases or decreases at the top of the border either unobtrusive or decorative? Does the body fabric flow nicely from the border, or does it look messy and disorganized? Does the border's pattern stitch integrate well with the bind off/ cast on?

▷ Take a close look at the shaped section of the swatch. Does the bind off/cast on integrate well with the pattern stitch, or should it have been done on a different pattern row? How do the increases or decreases look? Were they difficult to integrate into the pattern stitch? Can you improve them by substituting a different increase (M1, Kfb, or lifted) or using ssk instead of K2tog? Would they look better worked further from the edge or closer to the edge? Is the edge neat so it will be easy to pick up stitches for the neck or armhole border? Pick up

**A Shaped Swatch**

Make a shaped swatch to test edges and borders.

stitches along the curved edge and try out the neck or armhole border (using smaller needles, if called for). Pick up stitches along the straight side of the swatch to replicate picking up for button bands on the front of a cardigan. This is an opportunity to try out your buttonholes!

If any of the details bother you, this is the time to work them out. Make notes on what you did to make the swatch look as perfect as possible and refer to them, and to the swatch, as you work your garment.

▷ Try a different cast on or bind off, use the back side of either as the "public" side, or use a larger or smaller needle for either of them. For cast ons, see chapter 2 (page 43); for bind offs, see chapter 5 (page 163).

▷ If you don't like the way the increases or decreases look at the transition to or from the border, try using a different technique or hiding them in a purl rib. If it looks messy at the point where the border meets the pattern stitch, work 1 or 2 rows of stockinette or reverse stockinette to ease the transition.

▷ If you are unhappy with your shaped edge and borders, see more about shaping at the edge on page 101, integrating shaping with pattern stitches starting on page 102, and making perfect borders on page 50.

*Second Thoughts:*

# Planning the Project

NOW THAT YOU'VE MADE the major decisions — yarn, needles, pattern — you're ready to jump right in and get started, right? Probably not.

This is the moment to consider whether there are any other decisions you need to make before you begin. Is there anything you want to change about the sweater? Even if you plan to follow the pattern instructions without any modifications, is there something that worries you about any of the techniques, shaping, or finishing?

Taking charge now, thinking ahead to plan the best approach for your project and the best way to handle the finishing will make the whole process of knitting and completing the garment go more smoothly. You'll be able to work more efficiently, there'll be less chance of major problems that could force you to rip out, and finishing will be much easier if you plan ahead based on the suggestions in this chapter. You'll be glad you did!

## Order of Construction

Most patterns instruct you to begin with the back of the garment, then proceed with the front, the sleeves, seaming, and borders. There are, however, reasons why you might not want to do things in this order. Let's say that you ignored all of the excellent advice in chapter 1 about working gauge swatches and want to jump right in. In this case, it's much better to begin with a sleeve than with the back of the sweater. The sleeve will be narrower in width, so it will grow more quickly. When you've worked a few inches, stop and measure to ensure that you really are working at the desired gauge. If not, unravel and switch needle sizes — you'll have a lot less invested in the project after a few inches of a sleeve than after a few inches of the back. If you're working your sweater circularly, there's even more of a difference, because working a few inches of the back plus the front is double the work of starting just the back. In the next few pages you'll find several different approaches to garment construction.

## The Conventional Approach to Flat Construction

The back is usually worked before the front because the shaping of the back is usually simpler: the back neck begins closer to the shoulders, so the underarm shaping has usually been finished before you are required to embark on the neck shaping. This gives you a chance to warm up. Having successfully completed the back, it's assumed you're ready for the additional challenge of shaping the front neck, which may occur at the same time as the armhole shaping. Another assumption is that you're more likely to make mistakes on the first piece of the sweater, or to have second thoughts, and you can then use your experience to improve the front. The logic is that the front, which is more noticeable, will look better than the back. But, if you know yourself to be the kind of knitter who is interested and excited at the beginning of a project, and becomes bored with the repetition of maintaining a pattern row after row, garment piece after garment piece, this may not work to your advantage. If you do your best work early in a project and then rush carelessly to the end, you might want to make the front first. Except for considerations like these, with any garment knit in pieces and then sewn together, it really doesn't matter in what order you construct the pieces.

Except (isn't there always an "except"?) . . . if you want to ensure that the sleeves are the perfect length, it's really best to save them for last. How, you ask, can you make the sleeve both first (in place of a gauge swatch) *and* last? Easy, start the sleeve and don't work any farther than the underarm, then leave it on a spare needle or a piece of yarn until you're ready to check the length.

The order of construction that I prefer, to ensure that the sleeves really are the right length, is to make the back and front (it doesn't matter which comes first), block these pieces, then join the shoulders, and add the neck border *before* completing the sleeves. Blocking is necessary with fabrics that will be stretched to size during the process (made from fabrics that are ribbed, cabled, lace, or in any other pattern stitch that should be flattened for best effect). Blocking is also the best practice in plain stockinette stitch and other pattern stitches, because it will help to uncurl and neaten the edges, which makes seaming easier, and will allow you to verify the finished dimensions. Try the garment on. Make sure the neck fits the way you like it. If not, fix it before moving on. (See Getting Neck Borders Right in chapter 3, page 71.)

If it's a drop-shoulder sweater, the edge of the armhole will fall some distance down the arm from the shoulder, so the sleeve must be shorter than you might expect to fit properly. Take a look at the schematics showing different armhole and sleeve styles for the same size sweater (Recognizing Fit, page 19) to see just how much the sleeve length can vary between a capped sleeve and a drop-shoulder sleeve. Try on the partially finished sweater. Measure from the edge of the armhole at the top of the shoulder down the arm with the elbow slightly bent, to the point where the sleeve should end. That's the length that the sleeve must be in order to fit well.

Sometimes the weight of the sleeve once attached will stretch the shoulder seam out, so plan for this by testing the shoulder to see how much it stretches and deduct a little bit from the sleeve measurements if necessary. Binding off the shoulders and sewing them together or using three-needle bind off (see appendix, page 261) to join them will usually provide enough

support to minimize stretching. (For more on stabilizing shoulders that may stretch, see chapter 8, Seams, page 257.)

If it's a fitted sweater, with a shaped armhole and sleeve cap, the critical length is from the underarm to the cuff. To be able to measure this accurately, it's best to baste the side seams of the sweater, put it on, and then measure from the top of the side seam at the underarm along the inside of the arm to the cuff. Make sure that your sleeve is this length to the underarm. Because the height of the sleeve cap will vary depending on the width of the sleeve and the shape of the armhole, it is not a good indicator.

Finish the first sleeve, baste or pin it in place (with safety pins) and try on the one-armed sweater. Basting is the only way to get a good feel for the fit of a shaped armhole and sleeve cap, but you can get away with pinning on a drop-shoulder design. A smooth, contrasting basting yarn will be easy to remove; avoid a fuzzy yarn that may leave noticeable residue. If the sleeve fits, make a second just like the first. If it doesn't fit, figure out what needs to change, unravel and revise the top of the sleeve, and try it on again. See the section on designing a sleeve cap under Adjustments for a Round Armhole in chapter 4 (page 125) for making adjustments to sleeve caps. Make a note of what you did so that you can make the second sleeve identical to the first once you get it exactly right.

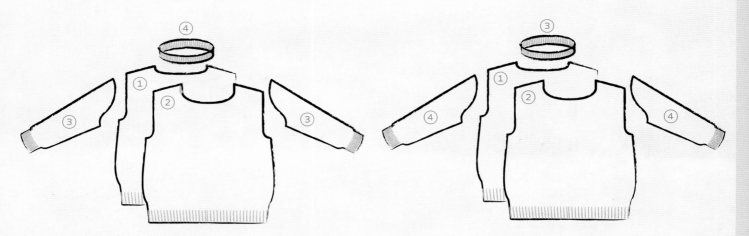

Conventional order of construction: 1 back, 2 front, 3 sleeves, 4 neck border

My preferred order of construction: 1 back, 2 front, 3 neck border, 4 sleeves

# Going Beyond Conventional Construction

## Bottom-Up Construction of Seamless Garments

So far I've focused on bottom-up construction of sweaters made from separate pieces and then seamed, but there are plenty of other ways to make a sweater. First let's look at seamless sweaters worked from the bottom up.

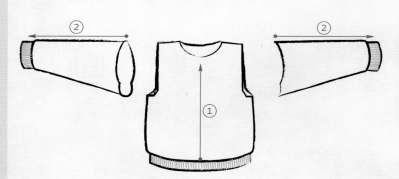

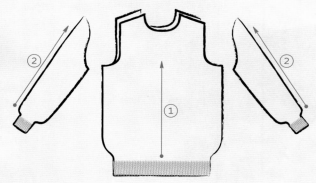

**Pullover vest.** Knit the body circularly up to the underarms, the front and back separately from that point to the shoulder, and then join the shoulders using three-needle bind off.

**Drop-shoulder pullover.** Make the body the same as the pullover vest, but without underarm shaping. Sleeves can be knit circularly from the bottom up and then sewn into the armhole, or knit down from stitches picked up around the armhole, thus avoiding seams. Working the sleeves from the top down makes it easy to ensure they're the correct length.

**Tailored pullover.** A fitted sweater with set-in sleeves and shoulder shaping can also be knit circularly. Make the body as described for the drop-shoulder pullover. Work the sleeves circularly from the bottom up until you reach the underarm, then flat through the cap, and sew them into the armholes. Alternatively, using short-row shaping for the cap, set-in sleeves can be picked up and worked down from the armholes. (See Case Study #3-3, page 80.)

**Cardigan vests and sweaters.** Work the body flat in one piece to the underarms, then complete the armholes, shoulders, neck, and sleeves as described for the pullover versions above.

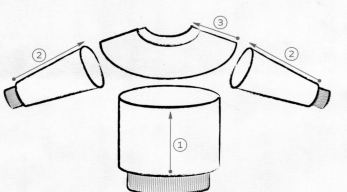

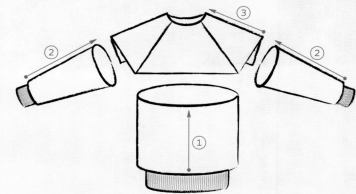

**Circular-yoked pullover.** Work the front, back, and both sleeves circularly to the underarm, then assemble them all on one needle to work a circular yoke, decreasing as you approach the neck opening.

**Raglan-sleeved pullover.** Work just as for a circular yoke above, but line the decreases up at four corner points to define the sleeves within the yoke area.

**Raglan or circular-yoked cardigans.** Work flat in one piece up to the underarms, then add sleeves and shape the yoke as described for the circular and raglan-sleeved pullovers, but work the yoke area flat, leaving the center front open.

## Top-Down Construction in Separate Pieces

Identical to bottom-up construction, except that you begin each piece at the top and work down to the bottom, this is advantageous if you are working a pattern stitch that you like better when seen upside down. It also allows you to fit the neckline, armholes, and sleeve length as you work. In this case, I give the same advice as I offer above for working bottom to top in separate pieces: complete the back and the front, join them at the shoulders, and complete the neck border before working the sleeves. When working the sleeves from the top town, stop at the underarm (assuming you've got shaped armholes and a sleeve cap) and evaluate whether the sleeve cap will fit properly, then continue working down the sleeve until it's just the right length.

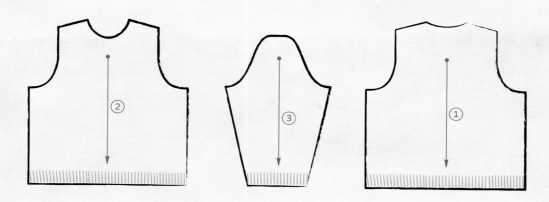

Top-down flat knitting. Order of construction,
1 back; 2 front; 3 sleeves

# Going Beyond Conventional Construction (continued)

## Top-Down Seamless Garments

Follow the same process as bottom up, except in reverse. What's important is that the distance from the neckline or shoulder to the underarm join be long enough that it's comfortable to wear. After you divorce the sleeves from the body, continue to work each of the sections until they are the right length. Because it's easy to try on the garment and check the length, many knitters advocate this as the best method for making sweaters that fit well. Versions of all of the following garments can easily be made with open fronts. Instead of joining into a round to work circularly, leave the knitting open at the center front and work back and forth, making the fronts and back all in one piece.

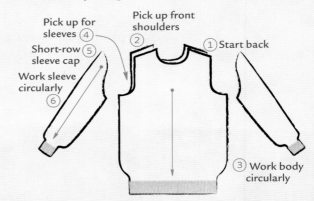

**Pullover vest.** Work the front and back separately down to the underarms. One of them can be made first, then stitches for the other can be picked up along the shoulder instead of casting on, to avoid having to sew a seam. Use a very firm cast on at the shoulders to prevent the shoulder seam from stretching and spoiling the fit. After you reach the underarm, begin working the whole body (back and front) circularly.

**Drop-shoulder pullover.** Work the body as described for a vest above. Pick up stitches for the sleeves around the armholes and work them down as well.

**Tailored pullover.** To make the sloped shoulders, cast on small groups of stitches until the shoulder is wide enough. You'll have to sew the shoulder seams later on. For true seamless construction, cast on all the stitches for the shoulder (using a firm cast on so that the shoulder won't stretch and spoil the fit, then work short-row shaping as described in Adding Shoulder Shaping (chapter 4, page 136). When starting the opposite piece, pick up along the shoulder cast on and work another set of short rows, reversing the shaping. Pick up stitches for the sleeves around the armhole, then work short rows to create a sleeve cap as described in Case Study #3-3 (page 80).

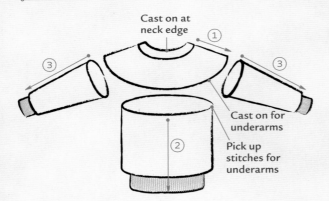

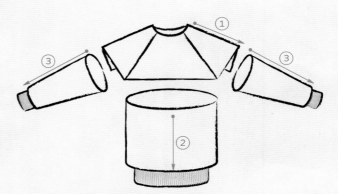

**Circular-yoked pullover.** Cast on at the neck edge, work the border, then increase to make a circular yoke. Divide the stitches, setting aside the sleeve stitches, cast on for the underarms at both sides of the body, and work the body (front and back) circularly down to the bottom. Work the sleeves down, picking up stitches across the underarms of the body.

**Raglan-sleeved pullover.** For an unshaped neckline, make this identical to a circular yoke, but place the increases at four points to define the sleeves. To make a shaped raglan neckline, begin by working flat on just the stitches for the back neck and shoulders. You'll increase at four points to define the sleeves and also will increase and/or cast on to shape the front neck opening. When the neck opening is complete, begin working circularly.

# Cast Ons

Occasionally pattern writers specify which cast on to use, but it's far more likely that your pattern will simply instruct you to "cast on." If you're like most knitters, there's one cast on you use all the time, never considering whether it's the best one for the job. I'll put my professional standing on the line and say that, if you're only going to learn and use one cast on, the best is the long-tail cast on. It is neat, stretchy but not loose, and, once learned, you can work it faster than any other cast on. But even this versatile cast on won't be a practical option in some situations.

## Choosing the Best Cast On for the Job

It's really best to be familiar with several cast ons and to choose among them depending on how the cast on needs to behave, as well as how it looks. You'll find instructions for each of the cast ons mentioned below in the appendix (pages 264–67).

## Stretchy Cast Ons versus Supportive Ones

The most important consideration for a cast on is whether it's elastic or firm. For example, at the neckline of a pullover, it will need to stretch enough to go over the head but be supportive enough to prevent the neckline from stretching out of shape. At the cuff of a sweater, it will need to stretch enough to pass easily over the hand but have enough memory to return neatly to its original length. If the cast on is at a rolled edge or the edge of a ruffle, it needs to be very stretchy or the rolled edge won't roll and the ruffle won't ruffle to its full potential.

Very stretchy cast ons include knitted, half-hitch, lace, and tubular. Moderately stretchy cast ons include long-tail, Channel Islands, and ribbed cable. Supportive casts ons stretch just a little, and then no farther. The cable cast on is a good supportive cast on. (See photographs below and on the following page for examples of each of these.)

### Very Stretchy Cast Ons

**Knitted cast on**, if not worked very firmly, tends to look loose and loopy, but this is an advantage if you want a stretchy edge.

**Lace cast on** is formed by working a yarnover between each stitch in a cabled cast on. It stretches magnificently, with decorative loops that can stand alone, be used to join to another piece of knitting, or support other ornaments like beads or fringes.

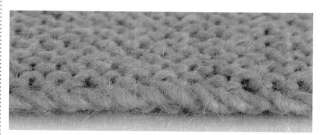

**Half-hitch cast on.** The tension of the half-hitch cast on is easy to adjust by simply spacing the stitches out more or placing them closer together on the needle. It can be difficult to work into on the first row, however, so is best reserved for short cast ons where you want a minimum of bulk, like the underarms of sweaters when working top down.

**Tubular cast on** makes a very stretchy edge that integrates perfectly with K1, P1 ribbing. Tubular knitting can be worked following the cast on to make a casing for elastic or a drawstring.

Long-tail cast on is the best all-around cast on. It looks neat when relaxed but stretches well under tension. You can control how tight it is by how tightly you tension the tail and how closely you space the stitches on the needle when working it.

Channel Islands cast on is a little more complicated to learn and execute than the others shown here. It can take a little practice to be able to work it with consistent tension, but it's worth the effort. The double strand across the bottom means this cast on will wear well, while the tiny bumps every other stitch make a lovely embellishment. It integrates extremely well with K1, P1 ribbing, but looks good with almost any pattern stitch.

Ribbed cable cast on also makes a doubled strand across the edge of the fabric that will wear well over time, transitions perfectly to K1, P1 ribbing, looks almost identical on both the front and back, and stretches well.

## Supportive Cast On

Cable cast on is a variation of the knitted cast on that produces a noticeable ropelike edge. Its ability to stretch is limited, making it perfect for an edge that you don't want to stretch very much. You can work the stitches farther apart to make it stretch more.

## Durable Cast On

Long-tail cast on made with thumb strand doubled

## Cast Ons under Tension

Cast ons under tension, from top to bottom: tubular on K1, P1, Channel Islands on K1, P1, half hitch on garter, lace on faggoting rib

## Does Your Cast On Need to Be Durable?

Will the cast-on edge be subject to wear? The bottom back edge and the cuffs of sweaters are subjected to significant abrasion and abuse, especially in children's garments, so you'll need a cast on that will stand up to wear and tear. On the other hand, the delicate edge of a lace shawl to be worn only on formal occasions can be gossamer thin, in keeping with its intended use. In a situation where high durability is desirable, choose the cable cast on or work the long-tail cast on with the thumb strand doubled.

## Will Your Cast On Be Visible or Hidden?

Will you be able to see the cast on once the garment is finished? If the edge will be hidden in a seam, behind the picked-up edge of a border, or rolled up in stockinette stitch, it doesn't matter how it looks. If, on the other hand, the cast on will be visible every time the garment is worn, think about how it will look. Will it integrate agreeably with the adjacent ribbing or pattern stitch? Some cast ons produce a very definite ridge across the bottom of the fabric, some produce a twisted, ropelike edge, while others look ribbed or purled.

If the edge will normally be relaxed, then the relaxed tension of the cast on should match the tension of the fabric it's attached to. A fabric where the stitches are wide in proportion to their height, like garter stitch or open lace, may require a different or looser cast on than a fabric like ribbing or cables where the stitches are proportionately narrower. If the edge will normally be stretched when the garment is in use, make sure the cast on is still pleasing when stretched.

▷ **For ribbing.** These have a ribbed appearance, and stretch and rebound like the ribbing: ribbed cable, Channel Islands, and tubular cast ons.

▷ **For lace.** These are open and very stretchy: knitted and lace cast ons.

▷ **For stockinette.** Stockinette edges will naturally curl. Starting with a hem prevents the edge from curling, but the whole hem will have a tendency to flip up to the knit side. To prevent this, make the hem slightly narrower than the fabric above it by working it on fewer stitches or on smaller needles.

▷ **For cables.** Use a moderately stretchy cast on, but cast on 1 or 2 fewer stitches where each cable will fall. On the first row, work increases at these points so you have the correct number of stitches.

**Working with Hems**

Hems, from top to bottom: folded, picot, rolled

**Handling Cables**

Long-tail cast on *without* increases at base of cables

Long-tail cast on *with* increases at base of cables

**Decorative Cast Ons**

Channel Islands with garter stitch (right side)

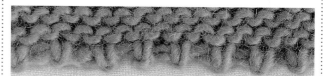

Channel Islands with garter stitch (wrong side)

## Embellishments at the Cast On

To add an embellishment or special effect at the beginning of your knitting, choose a decorative cast on, or work an edging as long as the width of the desired cast on and then pick up the required number of stitches along the side of the edging. Decorative treatments include Channel Islands cast on (for a picot edge),

casting on additional stitches to make a ruffle, lace cast on, multicolor cast ons like the two-color versions of the long-tail and cable cast ons, and hems. Edgings can be as simple as a strip of garter stitch or an I-cord, or they can be a complex lace pattern. For a ruffled edging, make a strip of edging longer than required, pick up stitches along it, then decrease to the correct number of stitches.

### Decorative Cast Ons (continued)

**Ruffle at cast on**

**Long-tail cast on using multiple strands in different colors**

**Long-tail cast on with one color on thumb and another color on finger**

**Long-tail cast on alternating colors**

**Cable cast on alternating colors**

### Decorative Edgings

**Stockinette picked up along garter stitch edging**

**Stockinette picked up along I-cord edging**

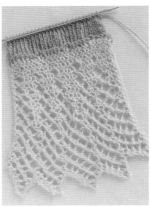

**Picked up along lace edging** to make a ruffle (left) and without a ruffle (right).

## Adding On to Work in Progress

Casting on at the edge of your work to shape a neckline or armhole when working from the top down, over an opening like a buttonhole, or when starting a steek requires a single-strand cast on. See Casting On to Work in Progress, page 162 for more information on choosing the best cast ons for these situations.

## Easy-to-Remove Provisional Cast Ons

There are situations where you'll want to begin your work in the middle, for example, if you plan to add the borders later. In these cases you'll need to use a provisional cast on, which is simply a cast on worked in contrasting waste yarn that is easy to remove. Once removed, the bottoms of the original stitches are placed on a needle, and you can work seamlessly in the opposite direction.

Using a strong, smooth, slippery waste yarn (such as mercerized crochet cotton) will make removal easier and ensures that no contrast-color residue is left on your project. Several provisional cast ons are explained in the appendix (pages 266–67). Choose whichever one you feel most comfortable with.

As an alternative to using a removable cast on, you can simply cast on and knit a few rows in contrasting yarn, cut it, and begin working with the yarn for your project. When you are ready to remove the waste yarn, take a pair of sharp scissors and cut across the top row of the waste yarn. Slip a needle into the first row of stitches in the project yarn and pick out any remaining snips of the waste yarn.

## Using Waste Yarn Instead of a Provisional Cast On

① **Carefully cut off waste yarn** to expose first row of stitches in project yarn.

② **Slip needle in** to pick up first row of stitches. Remove remaining bits of waste yarn.

## Thinking Ahead

If there will be a seam starting from the corner at the cast on, be sure to leave a long tail for sewing it up later. You'll have fewer ends to weave in that way. Make the tail into a butterfly to keep it out of the way. Secure the butterfly to the fabric with a safety pin to keep it from pulling loose.

If cutting your knitting (even if it is waste yarn) makes you nervous, you can steal a trick from machine knitters and use ravel cord. This is a very strong, very smooth cord that can be removed just by pulling on the end of it. If you don't have access to machine knitting supplies, you can substitute a soft nylon macramé cord or dental floss. Cast on and work just one row in waste yarn. Change to your ravel cord and work one row. Change to your project yarn and begin working the garment. Because the ravel cord is very slippery, you may want to tie the ends to the waste yarn and project yarn. (Be sure to make knots you can easily untie.) When it comes time to remove the cast on, check that both ends of the ravel cord are untied and aren't twisted back on themselves through the stitches at the ends of the row. Pull on the ravel cord until all the slack is taken out of it and the row becomes very tight. Continue pulling and it will slide out of the row, separating the stitches in waste yarn from those in the project yarn. Slip a needle into the first row of stitches in the project yarn. You can also slip the needle in before removing the ravel cord, but this can make it more difficult to remove the cord; placing the stitches on a very thin needle or the cable of a circular needle will make removing the cord easier.

## Joining Beginning and End of Round in Circular Knitting

How you join the beginning and end of round when working circularly depends on your personal preferences. The appendix provides instructions for three different methods of joining (pages 269–70). It's good to be familiar with all three, because any one may be preferable depending on the project you're working on. If the beginning/end of round at the edge won't show (for example, when it's hidden in a seam, behind a border, or in a rolled edge), then choose whichever is most comfortable for you to work. If the cast on will be visible, experiment to see which one looks the best and is the most practical when beginning your project.

## Why Not Jettison the Cast On?

If you are never happy with your cast on, consider adding the borders later. Start with a provisional cast on, casting on the number of stitches needed after the border, and work the rest of the piece. Remove the cast on, place the stitches on the size needle needed for the border, work one row or round, increasing or decreasing to the correct number of stitches, and finally work the border and bind off. The result is no cast-on edge at all — only matching bound-off edges at top and bottom.

# Centering Pattern Stitches

Most knitting designers have taken care of placing any pattern stitches so that they look good on the garment. But, if you're making fitting adjustments, changing the pattern stitch, or you want to add your own large motif, consider where to place it on the garment before you begin. The larger the motif, the more care you'll have to take. Avoid putting prominent sections of the motif at the points of the bust, or centered on a prominent stomach or bum! Also avoid having the edges of the motif cut off by armhole or neck shaping. If it doesn't fit in the space available, it's best to downsize the motif to make it fit. Center large motifs horizontally on the front, back, and sleeves. Consider where the pattern will fall at the shoulders and arrange it so that the shoulder seams cut across the motifs at a pleasing point. The easiest way to plan the placement is to create a chart for the actual shape of each garment piece, in rows and stitches, then chart the pattern on it. Remember that the outer edges of motifs that extend all the way to the side seams will be obscured when the sweater wraps around the body.

## Planning Placement of Stranded Motifs

If the major motif has an odd number of stitches (as is usually the case with stranded knitting), you'll need an odd number of stitches in each section of the garment in order to center it. Plan the front and back so that the shoulder seams fall either above a major section of the pattern or at the center of a motif; then the pattern will

**Planning Stranded Motifs**

top of motif missing at shoulder seam

top of motif ends at seamline

center of motif falls at shoulder seam

motif cut off

top of motif missing

Compare the differences between shoulder details and top-of-sleeve details in these two illustrations.

look continuous across the shoulder from front to back. Plan the sleeves so that the top of the sleeve and the bottom where it meets the cuff fall between major sections of the stranded pattern.

For example, in the top chart for the stranded pattern opposite, notice that the shoulder seam falls at the top of two major horizontal patterns, but, because the darker narrow pattern that divides them is missing, the overall pattern is noticeably interrupted at this point. The sleeve layout is more pleasing, with the dark chain pattern falling at both top and bottom.

In the version of the same chart shown below it, slight changes in the way the pattern is laid out on the garment result in major differences. The shoulder seam of this version is much more pleasing because it falls at the center of a motif, but the sleeve is less satisfying because the dark chain motif that defined its top and bottom edges in the other version is missing.

## Planning Placement of Large Cabled Motifs

If the major motif has an even number of stitches (as is frequently the case for cabled patterns), you'll need an even number of stitches for each section of the garment in order to center it. Centering the major pattern elements horizontally is simplified if a small pattern, such as Seed Stitch or repeated 2-stitch cables, is used at the sides of the front, back, and sleeves.

With large cabled motifs, it's important to plan the placement vertically as well, so that the cabled pattern integrates nicely with the neck opening and any other shaping. Cables should also end symmetrically at the shoulder seam, with the final cable crossing the same distance below the seam on both front and back. Ideally, the seam should fall at the halfway point between crossings so that the cabled pattern appears almost continuous from front to back.

**Planning Cabled Motifs**

**Planning cables.** Care was taken to place the bottom of the neck opening at a point in the complex cable design where it does not cut across any major cable crossing and where the outer ribs of the cables frame the opening (*left*). Notice how the neck shaping integrates with the Gull-Wing Cables on either side. Half of each cable disappears, making it easy to continue the pattern on the other half all the way to the shoulder seam.

At right, you can see that the shoulder seams were planned so that the Gull-Wing Cables mirror each other perfectly.

# Planning Ahead for Perfect Finishing

Once you've selected your pattern and yarn, taken the time to test-drive your needles by working a swatch, checked for shrinkage (or growth) and planned for it, you're going to want to jump right in and start your garment. Don't. Exercise your patience once again and do just a little more planning. Before you start, think about what will happen when you finish. Unless you're making a seamless circular garment, you're going to need to sew the thing together. Decisions you make before you work the garment pieces will have major impacts on how easy it is to join the pieces and pick up borders, and how good the finishing details look when you're done.

## Beginning with the Very Best Borders

First let's talk a little bit about bottom borders, since most sweaters start at the bottom edge with some sort of noncurling border. It can be difficult to make the borders in the correct proportion to the body of a garment. The basic rule of thumb for ribbed borders attached to stockinette stitch is to make the borders with needles two sizes smaller and with 10 percent fewer stitches than the body. This works just fine if you happen to get the same gauge as the designer on the borders, if you're working with a wool or wool-blend yarn that has good memory so the ribbing pulls in the proper amount, and if the rest of your garment is worked in stockinette stitch.

This border was worked circularly, while the garment is seamed above the border.

It also requires forethought and excellent finishing skills to make the borders of garments look good where seams are sewn. With a little care in centering ribbing, however, you can noticeably improve the appearance of seamed borders. Many knitters (myself included) have messy-looking ribbing because of inconsistencies in tension between knit stitches and purl stitches. Both of these problems can be mitigated by making the borders circularly, even if the rest of the garment is worked in flat pieces as in the photo bottom left.

## Making Borders Just the Right Size

Before you start your garment, test and evaluate the borders on a swatch as described in Swatching to Refine the Details (chapter 1, page 34).

The convention for well-behaved borders (10 percent fewer stitches and needles two sizes smaller) doesn't always work. All knitters are not alike: some knitters work ribbing that is much looser or much tighter than the original designer expected, and they must adjust their needle size accordingly to get good results. You'll find out whether this applies to you when you swatch; you can adjust for it automatically on future garments. All yarns and fibers are not alike: the 10 percent and two-sizes-smaller rule usually applies for stretchy wool yarns, but not for yarns with no elasticity or fibers that are not wool. You may need to go as much as four needle sizes smaller and 15 percent fewer stitches when working with inelastic yarns that don't return to the original width after stretching the border. (See Fiber Content and the Finished Fabric, chapter 1, page 24.)

Why are borders worked on fewer stitches than the body of the garment? Borders are at the edges of the garment and are frequently under tension either from the weight of the garment (neck and armhole borders), when we move or sit down (bottom borders), and when we push our sleeves up (sleeve borders). All of these borders are stretched whenever we put the garment on or take it off. They tend, therefore, to get stretched in width. Making them narrower to begin with means that when they do stretch out of shape, they are still the same width or narrower than the body of the garment, which keeps them looking neat. Stockinette stitch naturally curls to the outside at the top and the bottom, so making the bottom borders slightly narrower than the body or sleeve they are attached to also prevents them from flipping to the outside of a garment whose main fabric is stockinette stitch.

The traditional ribbed border that's narrower than the body of the garment may not be what you want aesthetically, or it may simply not be practical with the

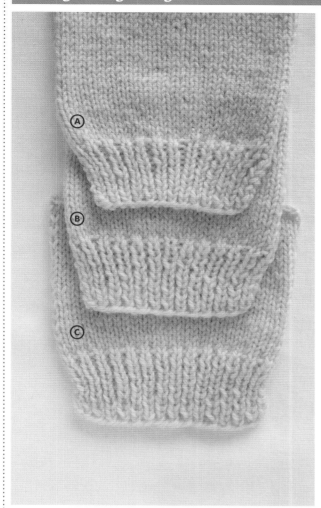

**Getting ribbing right.** Border worked on 10 percent fewer stitches and needles two sizes smaller Ⓐ; border worked on 10 percent fewer stitches and same size needles Ⓑ; border worked on same number of stitches and same size needles Ⓒ. Ⓐ is what you want.

**Dealing with inelastic yarns.** Linen yarn in a K1, P1 border with 10 percent fewer stitches and needles four sizes smaller Ⓐ; same yarn in a K1, P1 border with 10 percent fewer stitches worked on needles two sizes smaller Ⓑ.

**K3, P3 ribbing** in linen yarn is very elastic.

**K1b, P1 ribbing** in linen yarn makes very neat ribs.

yarn and fiber you've selected. In this case, you might want to make a bottom border that doesn't curl, but one that also doesn't pull in like a standard ribbing. You can substitute a garter stitch or Seed Stitch border, or a decorative edging. Be sure to check the gauge of these and make them exactly the same width or a tiny bit narrower than the section of the garment they are attached to, so they don't flare or flip up annoyingly.

For more about designing the best borders and about shaped borders for necklines and armholes, as well as the bottom borders I've discussed here, see Changing the Borders in chapter 3 (page 70) and The Special Challenge of Shaped Borders in chapter 8 (page 224).

**Seed Stitch,** for a nonribbed, noncurling border

## Making Borders Look Continuous across Seams

One of my pet peeves in knitting patterns is being told to begin by casting on an even number of stitches and then work in K1, P1 ribbing for the bottom border. When you go back to sew the seams, whether it's a sleeve seam or a side seam joining the front to the back, there's no way to make the ribbing look good at the seam. The same thing happens when you cast on a multiple of 4 stitches and work in K2, P2 ribbing.

This is because one side of the ribbing ends in a knit rib and the other ends in a purl rib. To make a neat seam, the ribbing needs to be sewn so it looks continuous across the seams, as shown in the following photos.

In K1, P1 ribbing (top); in K2, P2 ribbing (bottom)

**Two Ways to Seam K1, P1 Ribbing**

**Seaming K2, P2 Ribbing**

Work K2, P2 ribbing on a multiple of 4 plus 2 stitches, placing 2 knit stitches at each end on the right-side rows, then seam a full stitch from the edge.

(*Left*) Work K1, P1 ribbing on an odd number of stitches, placing a knit stitch at the beginning and the end of the right-side rows, then work mattress stitch a half a stitch from the edge. This is a good choice when the seam of the garment above the ribbing will be worked only a half stitch from the edge.

(*Right*) This illustrates Nancie Wiseman's method for managing ribbing. Work K1, P1 ribbing on an even number of stitches, placing 2 knit stitches at one end and 1 at the other on the right-side rows, then seam a full stitch from the edge. This makes a neater seam than the previous example and is the best choice when the seam of the garment above the ribbing will be worked a full stitch from the edge.

## Making Seamless Borders

If you are unhappy with seams in ribbing or unhappy with your ribbing, you might consider making the borders circularly. My own purl stitches always look neater than my knit stitches. It's not that they're larger or smaller, it's that when I purl a stitch, then turn the fabric over and look at it on the back, the two sides of the now-apparent knit stitch look closer together than the two sides of a stitch I actually knitted. The result is that my ribbing, when worked back and forth, looks inconsistent, with larger- and smaller-looking stitches alternating up each knit rib. If I work K1, P1 ribbing in the round, the wrong side (that is, the side away from me while I was making it) always looks neater because the knit stitches are narrower. For this reason, I sometimes plan ahead and work my K1, P1 borders circularly

**Working Borders Circularly**

**K1, P1 ribbing** worked circularly with knit stitches looking loose (wide)

**"Wrong" side of K1, P1 ribbing** shown above worked circularly. Notice that the knit stitches (originally worked as purls from the other side) look tighter and neater.

**K1, P1 ribbing** worked flat. Ribs are inconsistent.

from the wrong side. When the garment is easier to work flat (for example, something with intarsia colorwork), I begin the flat pieces with a provisional cast on, complete the whole garment except for the bottom border, then remove the cast on, put the resulting live stitches onto a circular needle, and work the border down with the wrong side facing me.

Analyze your own ribbing. Does it look the same when worked flat as when worked circularly? If so, lucky you! If not, decide which one you like the look of, and which side of it looks the best. Make that the public side of your ribbing.

## Starting with the Ideal Neck Border

When you work a sweater from the top down starting with the border, you need to take into account the function of the neck border. The neck opening of a pullover needs to be big enough to go over the head, but the border mustn't stretch too much or the garment won't fit correctly. Choose a cast on that stretches but looks neat when relaxed. I like to begin with either the long-tail cast on or the tubular cast on. Work the border on needles two sizes smaller than the body to help it keep its shape. The pattern instructions will tell you how many stitches to cast on. If you have reversed the direction of construction and the instructions were originally to be worked from the bottom up, cast on the number of stitches specified for the neck border. After you've completed this border, check to see that it will pull over the head (if a pullover) and will fit comfortably around the neck before continuing with the rest of the sweater.

## Planning for the Best Edges and Seams

A point I touched on in chapter 1 is that the way you handle the stitches at the beginning and end of the row should depend on what you plan to do with those stitches later on. If it will be a finished edge (say the front of a cardigan where a section of garter stitch at the edge serves as the button band), you'll want the edge to look as nice as possible without any further finishing. If the edge will be joined to another piece with a seam or if stitches will be picked up along it to add a border (for example, along a neckline) or another piece of the garment (as when sleeves are picked up along the shoulder and knit down), how you handle the edge stitches affects both how easy it is to complete the finishing and how good the finishing will look. Some of these choices require a few extra stitches, so you'll need to plan ahead in order to cast on the right number of stitches or to increase to the correct number at the top of the bottom border.

## Managing Edge Stitches

Many people are taught to slip the first stitch of every row, regardless of what will be done with that edge later. This is fine if it will be an exposed edge, because it smooths the edge, preventing the alternation of long and short stitches by creating only 1 long stitch for every 2 rows. The problem with making this a habit comes when you must seam or pick up stitches along a slipped-stitch edge: there are only half as many slipped stitches as there are rows, and they are tall, loose stitches. When I plan to pick up stitches or to seam, my preference is to maintain at least 1 edge stitch in either stockinette stitch or garter stitch.

### When to Use a Stockinette Stitch Edge

If the base fabric is stockinette, reverse stockinette, or a pattern stitch based on stockinette, I prefer to use a stockinette edge stitch. What do I mean by a "pattern stitch based on stockinette"? This is one where half the rows are mostly knitted and the other half are mostly purled. A good example would be a lace pattern where the right-side rows incorporate yarnovers and decreases to make the pattern and the wrong-side rows are just purled, or a textured pattern where a design of reverse stockinette stitches appears on a stockinette background.

It is rare for stockinette stitch edges to be left exposed. The only exception is when the edge is intended to curl. Top and bottom edges in stockinette naturally curl to the knit side of the fabric. Side edges curl to the purl side. In both cases, the edges are hidden by the curling, so it doesn't matter what the stitches look like.

In the more frequent cases where you'll either pick up a border or sew a seam, for a stockinette fabric, I always knit the first and last stitches (or perhaps the first and last 2 stitches) on the right-side rows and purl these same stitches on the wrong-side rows. Working 2 edge stitches (or even more), rather than 1, is particularly useful when the pattern stitch has yarnovers close to the edge, incorporates increases and decreases that distort the stitches at the edge, or is reverse stockinette that causes the edge to curl to the front of the fabric. In all of these cases, the additional stitches will make the seam easier to sew and neater in appearance.

Sometimes it's necessary to cast on a couple of additional stitches to accommodate the edge stitches if the pattern stitch requires increases, decreases, or other stitch manipulations at the very beginning or end of the row. It's important to realize that these additional stitches may change the fit of the garment. One more

**Stockinette-based pattern stitch** with one stockinette edge stitch. Border added at right.

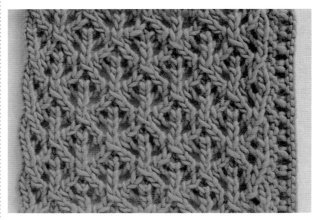

**Same pattern stitch** with two edge stitches. Border added at right. With the additional stitch, the edge of the pattern is more clearly defined.

stitch at each end of the row on the front and back of a sweater means there will be 4 additional stitches. At a gauge of 20 stitches to 4 inches (5 stitches per inch — a normal gauge for worsted-weight yarn), this will make the circumference of the sweater almost an inch larger. In a finer yarn it would have less effect overall, but in a bulky yarn, with a gauge of 10 stitches to 4 inches (2½ stitches per inch), an additional 4 stitches will result in a circumference that is more than 1½ inches larger. If you cast on for additional stitches, be sure to consider whether the garment will be too big. Calculate the expected finished circumference of the garment, allowing for the fact that either a half or a whole stitch at each edge will disappear into the seams, depending on what seaming technique you choose.

### When to Use a Garter Stitch Edge

If, on the other hand, the base fabric is garter stitch, a pattern based on garter stitch (where all the rows are mostly knit stitches), or Seed Stitch (where the edge is already garter stitch), I usually use garter stitch at the edge.

For exposed edges in a garter-stitch-type fabric, you can make the aesthetic choice to take the pattern stitch to the very edge or to substitute plain garter stitch at the edges. If the edge looks messy or you don't like the characteristic alternating long stitch and short bump at the edge of the fabric, you have the option of making a slipped-stitch edge.

### When to Use a Slipped-Stitch Edge

Slipped-stitch edges are appropriate in any fabric, either to make an exposed edge look neat or when half as many stitches will be picked up along the edge as there are rows, which usually occurs only when working in garter stitch or making a ruffle.

Some knitters prefer working with slipped-stitch edges all the time, but I don't recommend it when there will be neck or armhole borders to pick up, or when seams will be sewn. Having fewer edge stitches to work into makes it difficult to pick up enough stitches. Working with looser stitches can also result in loose, messy-looking seams.

But sometimes slipped edge stitches can be an advantage. When worked very firmly, they reduce the bulk in the seams. In thin yarn worked on very small needles, you can sometimes get away with the looseness caused by slipped-stitch edges, because even the slipped stitches are very small. Some knitters prefer crocheting their seams together. The longer, more regular stitches along a slipped stitch edge make a crocheted seam easier to execute.

---

**More Edge Stitch Treatments**

Garter stitch all the way to the edges

Seed Stitch with garter stitch edge at right, stockinette at left

Seed Stitch all the way to the edge

---

**Exposed Slipped-Stitch Edge**

The chained edge on this swatch was created by slipping the first stitch of each row knitwise, then purling the last stitch of the row. You can achieve exactly the same effect by slipping the first stitch of the row purlwise (being careful to keep the yarn in back while doing so) and knitting the last stitch of each row.

Slipped-stitch edge. Both garter stitch borders were picked up, allowing 1 stitch for every 2 rows of the base swatch. The stitches at right were picked up and knit under both strands of the slipped edge stitch. Those at left were picked up and knit under just the back strand of the slipped edge stitch, creating a ropelike effect at the inner edge of the border.

Non-slipped-stitch edge. Both borders on this stockinette stitch swatch were picked up, allowing 3 stitches for every 4 rows of the swatch. The border at left is worked in K1, P1 ribbing; the one at right is K2, P2 ribbing.

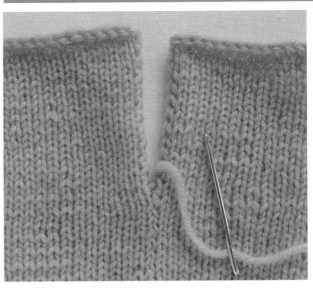

Seam in stockinette stitch with firm slipped-stitch edge. Notice how the stitches along the seam vary in tension, with loose stitches at one side crowding into tight stitches on the other.

Seam in stockinette stitch with loose slipped-stitch edge. The stitches on both sides of the seam are more even, and the seam looks almost perfect when relaxed as shown in this photo. When placed under tension, however, the gaps are very obvious.

Mattress-stitch seam in garter stitch with firm slipped-stitch edge. In garter stitch, mattress-stitch seams result in a noticeable dip or ditch along the seam line.

Mattress-stitch seam in garter stitch with loose slipped-stitch edge. When relaxed, the seam looks identical to one worked along a firm slipped-stitch edge, but when the seam is placed under tension, the gaps are obvious.

## A Decorative Option: Corded Edges

Another option that can be used on the finished edge of a garter stitch–based fabric is to work a slipped cord on 2 or 3 edge stitches. This makes a more substantial edge that is smooth and neat. To ensure that the fabric is as wide as it should be, cast on 1 or 2 additional stitches to accommodate the cord. When you reach the end of the row, bring the yarn to the front and slip the last 2 or 3 stitches. Turn to begin the following row. Pull the yarn firmly across behind the slipped stitches, and then knit them firmly before continuing across the row.

You can work this at both edges of the fabric or at just one. If the edge is shaped, all shaping should be worked in the main fabric of the knitting, not in the cord. In other words, if working decreases or increases at the end of a row, work them in the stitches immediately before bringing the yarn forward and slipping the stitches. If working the shaping at the beginning of a row, knit the slipped cord stitches first, then work the required shaping.

### Working a Corded Edge

At the end of the row, bring the yarn forward and slip the last 2 or 3 stitches purlwise.

At the beginning of the row, pull the yarn across the back and knit firmly.

Corded edge on garter stitch

Shaping along a diagonal corded edge

The corded edge doesn't work well with stockinette stitch fabrics (purl side shown for clarity). It is too short and pulls the edge in, but you still might choose to use it if this is the effect you want.

## Add a Yarnover Edge

Working a yarnover at the beginning of every row provides neat loops that can be used for joining later on. These are particularly useful when attempting to join pieces of lace together neatly.

To make loops at the edge, work the yarnover, followed by a decrease, at the beginning of every row. If this looks messy or is too tight, try working the yarnover, knit or purl a stitch, then decrease 1 stitch.

Use a crochet hook to join the pieces. You can pull the loops themselves through each other if they are loose enough, or use an additional strand of yarn to crochet them together (see Joining Yarnover Edges in chapter 7, page 216).

Yarnover edges on lace prepare the pieces for decorative crocheted seams.

## Planning for Increases and Decreases

When shaping is involved, it's important to plan the placement of your increases and decreases so that they don't mess up your nice neat edges. I prefer to work all increases and decreases a stitch or two away from the edge of the fabric, maintaining the edge stitches in garter stitch, stockinette, a slipped stitch, or a cord, just as described below. Working the shaping at the very edge makes it uneven, bumpy, and difficult to deal with later on. Shifting the shaping just 1 stitch farther into the fabric leaves an even, consistent edge that's a joy to behold and a pleasure to work along.

If you're also working a pattern stitch, you'll need to maintain it in spite of any shaping that's going on. How you do this depends on the characteristics of the pattern stitch itself. See chapter 4 for case studies that investigate increasing and decreasing in a variety of pattern stitches.

Take a little time before starting your project (or at least before you progress to the point where any shaping is required), to decide what type of increase or decrease will work best for you. It will save time in the long run if you experiment with shaping in your swatch rather than in the full-size garment (see Swatching to Refine the Details, chapter 1, page 34). Your range of options will depend on whether you need a single or double increase or decrease (see the appendix, pages 270–71 and 274–75, for options and instructions for each type). Choose based on what looks best in your yarn and pattern stitch, what is most easily worked with your yarn and needles, and which way they slant. See the material that follows on placement and on symmetry, as well as the case studies in chapter 4 for examples.

## Where to Place Increases and Decreases

To make the shaping disappear into a seam or when a border is picked up, work it at the very edge. Keep in mind that the edge will be irregular wherever the shaping occurs, so it may be difficult to pick up or seam neatly.

If you want a nice neat edge that's easy to work with when picking up or seaming, place the shaping at least 1 stitch away from the edge; depending on your pattern stitch, it may look better to work the shaping 2 or more stitches from the edge. Decide exactly how many stitches away based entirely on your personal preference (see following page).

### DECREASES AT THE VERY EDGE

Garter stitch

Stockinette stitch

K2, P2 ribbing

Slipped honeycomb stitch

## DECREASES ONE STITCH FROM EDGE

Garter stitch

Stockinette stitch

K2, P2 ribbing

Slipped honeycomb stitch

## DECREASES TWO STITCHES FROM EDGE

Garter stitch

Stockinette stitch

K2, P2 ribbing

Slipped honeycomb stitch

## Symmetrical Increases and Decreases

Knit 2 together (K2tog) and slip, slip, knit (ssk) decreases are mirror images of each other, with one leaning right (K2tog) and the other leaning left (ssk). I like to place ssk at the beginning of the row and K2tog at the end of the row so they appear to parallel the edge. Worked in combination with a single edge stitch, the decreases make two neat columns of stockinette stitches along each edge that are easy to follow visually when seaming or picking up.

If you prefer, you can do the opposite, placing the K2tog at the beginning of the row and the ssk at the end. In fact, this is particularly nice when working stranded knitting, because it ensures that the color pattern remains undistorted up to the edge stitch, since the decreases will appear the proper color and vertical rather than slanted.

What's important is to use one of these decreases at one edge and the other at the other edge of armholes, necklines, and tapered seams so that the two edges appear symmetrical.

Increases should also be worked symmetrically in similar situations. For example, when working a sleeve from the bottom up, work increases that slant in the opposite direction so that the edges appear to be mirror images of each other.

The knit-front-and-back (Kfb) increase doesn't appear to lean in either direction, but it is asymmetrical, with a knit stitch on the right and what appears to be a purled stitch to the left. To make opposite edges appear to match when using this increase, you need to shift the Kfb at the end of a row 1 stitch farther from the edge. In the photo bottom right, a Kfb was worked next to the last stitch before the neck opening, so that the purled segment appears 1 stitch away from the edge. On the opposite side of the neck, the Kfb was worked in the first stitch, so that its purled segment also appears 1 stitch from the edge. The Kfb increase tightens the stitch it is worked into, and it can make the edge too tight and distort the edge stitches if worked into the first stitch of a row. To avoid this problem, shift the increases 1 stitch farther from the edge by working K1, Kfb. To make the end of a row look symmetrical, stop when 3 stitches remain, and work Kfb, K2.

### Increase/Decrease Options for Symmetry

**Placing the K2tog before the neck opening** and the ssk after it makes it look like two columns of knitted stitches parallel the neck edge.

**Symmetrical increases paralleling a neck edge**, with M1R at one edge, M1L at the other

**Placing the decreases in the opposite positions**, with ssk before the neck opening and K2tog after it, leaves just one column of knit stitches running parallel to the neck edge.

**Symmetrical increases paralleling a neck edge**, with Kfb increases

## Options for Seaming and Joining

Before you begin a major project, consider how you plan to put the pieces together. Will all the pieces be knit separately and then joined together? Is there anything about the project that will make seaming difficult? If so, what are your options to make joining the pieces easier? Or will it all be knit in one piece, with no seams or only a few seams? Will new sections be picked up from existing sections of the garment, rather than worked separately and sewn together?

Keep in mind that at this point you're only *thinking* about the best way to put your garment together — this isn't a commitment, and you can always change your mind later. In fact, you should consider this issue periodically while you are knitting the garment, because your answers to the questions above may change as you get to know your materials and see how they behave in the fabric you're creating.

### To Sew or Not to Sew?

Let's consider what seams you'll need to deal with and what the options are for working them. In a traditionally constructed garment, worked flat from the bottom up, with separate front, back, and sleeves, there will be:

▷ Shoulder seams and side seams joining the front to the back

▷ Sleeve seams forming the flat sleeves into tubes

▷ Armhole seams joining the sleeves to the body

### *Seams: Joining after the Knitting Is Complete*

You have multiple choices for joining each of these seams. You may want to use different techniques on different seams, but if you do, keep in mind that the seams may look noticeably different from each other. I've provided an overview with pros and cons for each of these below. You'll find a more detailed discussion of seaming and other ways of joining in chapter 7 (page 192), and instructions on how to seam in the appendix (pages 278–79).

**Sewn seams** have the advantage of supporting the garment, preventing it from stretching in length or twisting if the yarn has a tendency to cause biasing in the knitted fabric. They look the neatest and are the least bulky option for seams that support the garment. They can be used to join side edges, top and bottom edges, or a combination of the two. You can adjust the amount of stretch in the seam depending on how tightly you sew it. They can be difficult to work if the edges of the garment pieces are not worked neatly and consistently; if the yarn is dark or textured, making it hard to see what you're doing; or if the yarn is textured or the plies stretch at different rates, making it difficult or impossible to sew with.

**Joining sweater edges**

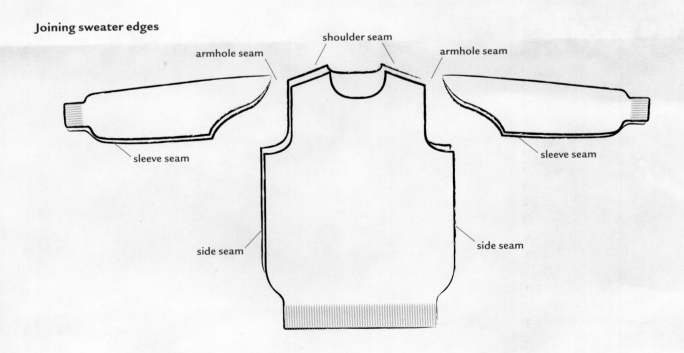

Crocheted seams have the advantage of being easily worked even in yarns that are textured or otherwise difficult to sew with. They are somewhat stretchy, but more supportive than a join made using Kitchener stitch (see appendix, page 276). They can, unfortunately, result in bulkier seams.

Three-needle bind off can be used to join two pieces of knitting while binding off (for illustration, see the appendix, page 261). It is especially useful to make neat, supportive, but slightly stretchy joins at the shoulders of sweaters. It's less bulky than crocheted seams and most sewn seams. It makes it easy to perfectly match the stitches of two pieces of knitting, but it only joins live stitches. This means you can join the tops of any two pieces if they have not yet been bound off. To join the top of a piece to the bottom of a piece, you must begin with a provisional cast on; when you remove it, you'll have live stitches that can be used in a three-needle bind off. It can also be used to join the side edges of two pieces of knitting by picking up the same number of stitches along each edge and then binding them off together, which is very useful for joining edges that don't match exactly, like the curved edge of a sleeve cap and the differently shaped edge of its matching armhole. The same technique is useful for joining panels or strips of knitting together. When worked from the wrong side, however, it does result in a very noticeable seam. This can be turned to advantage if it is worked on the right side with an embellishment like an I-cord bind off or a decorative bind off that looks like rickrack (see the photo for three-needle bind off, chapter 7, page 214).

Kitchener stitch, like three-needle bind off, must be worked on live stitches. It's the obvious choice if you need a join that appears to be seamless and is perfect for the underarms of sweaters worked with circular or raglan yokes. This is also a good way to join a sweater knit from side to side at the center back: make the two halves identically from sleeve cuff to center, then join them seamlessly at the center back to make a cardigan, or join both the front and back to make a pullover. It's impractical to use it to join the side seams of conventional sweaters. Sewing a side seam is a one-step process — you just sew the seam. Joining side seams using Kitchener stitch is a three-step process: pick up stitches along one edge, pick up stitches along the other edge, and finally sew the seam using Kitchener stitch. In addition to being triple the work, it will also look strange to have three rows of knitting at the side seam perpendicular to the rest of the body. Kitchener stitch provides no support to the garment at all, so should never be used for the shoulders of conventionally knit garments because they will stretch out of shape.

### Seamless: Converting to Circular

Another option, of course, is to combine the pieces of your sweater and knit it circularly so that it's seamless. How to do this is discussed in detail in chapter 3 (page 74). The advantage of working circularly is that you can very easily eliminate many, if not all, of the seams. This is great boon when working with a yarn that is difficult to sew with. On the other hand, it offers no support or protection against biasing when working with thick heavy yarns or fibers prone to losing their shape, such as cotton, linen, hemp, bamboo, silk, mohair, and so on. Garments that are completely seamless are more likely to be successful when worked in nice, elastic wool, and in thinner yarns (worsted weight or finer).

### Joining as You Knit

You can join the side edges of two pieces of knitting as you work. Complete the first section (say the back of a sweater). While you work the second section (the front of the same sweater), attach the end of each row to the back at the side seam by picking up a stitch and working a decrease to get rid of that extra stitch. The advantage of this method is that, by the time you've completed the knitting, you've also completed the seam. One disadvantage is that it can become annoying to work with as the project gets larger, heavier, and more unwieldy. Another is that the pieces are joined only every other row and the "seam" can be quite noticeable. You'll find complete instructions on joining using this method in Knitting On, chapter 6, page 182.

### When You Need to Think Ahead

With all of these options to choose from, it can be difficult to make decisions when you start your sweater. Luckily, you don't need to decide everything now.

▷ **Circular or flat?** The first decision, obviously, is whether you'll convert the pattern to circular knitting and make it seamless. You really do need to decide this before you cast on.

▷ **Kitchener stitch option.** If you will be using Kitchener stitch to join the cast-on edge seamlessly to any other edge (perhaps if working a side-to-side sweater starting from the center and working out), you need to begin with a provisional cast on. If, in the end, you decide not to use Kitchener stitch, you can still join these stitches using three-needle bind off, crochet them together, or put them on a needle, bind them off, and then sew a seam.

▷ **Perfecting edges.** If you plan to make the garment in pieces (front, back, and sleeves — all separate), it doesn't matter now whether you'll use sewn seams, crocheted seams, or some other method once they are done. All you need to do is to follow the advice in Planning for the Best Edges and Seams (page 53) to make neat edges, so that whatever technique you use to join will be easier and look its best when you're done.

▷ **Managing shoulders.** If you think you might want to join the shoulders using three-needle bind off, then you need to decide that before you bind off the first shoulder you come to. If there is no shoulder shaping, just put the shoulder stitches on an extra circular needle, a stitch holder, or a piece of yarn to wait patiently until the matching shoulder is completed and ready to be joined. If there is sloped shoulder shaping, you can't work this as a stepped bind off because you need live stitches for the three-needle bind off. Instead, you'll need to work the shoulder shaping using short rows (see Adding Shoulder Shaping, chapter 4, page 136). It's quite reasonable to put this decision off until you need to make it, which is just before you work the shoulder shaping. If you're coping with a pattern stitch that's difficult to work, you may decide that it's easiest just to bind off when the time comes. On the other hand, if you're working with a challenging yarn (for example, one that is highly textured or splits easily) that will make sewing up difficult, you may decide it's easiest to use three-needle bind off and avoid sewing altogether. If you determine that short rows are the best approach, you'll need to make the decision and start working the shoulder shaping 1 or 2 rows earlier than called for in the pattern to prevent the neckline from being too low.

▷ **Scheduling the side seams.** If you want to join the side seams as you go, then you must decide this after you make the back (or front if you work it first) and before you start the front (or back, if you worked the front first). When making a full-size sweater, keep in mind that it can become very bulky to work with all the pieces attached together.

▷ **Planning underarm seams.** The underarm seams of bottom-up raglan-sleeved and circular-yoked sweaters should, ideally, be worked seamlessly using Kitchener stitch. To prepare for this, you must put the underarm stitches of both the body and the sleeves on stitch holders or pieces of yarn rather than binding them off. Do this as you complete the body and sleeves, then you can join them after everything else is finished.

▷ **Planning for sleeves.** If you want to pick up the sleeves and work them down from the armhole, then you need to decide this before you begin the sleeves, and you need to first complete the front and back and join them at the shoulders. If you started a sleeve instead of working a gauge swatch, then you're already committed to working the sleeves separately, unless you unravel it and start over. Even sleeves with shaped sleeve caps can be picked up along the armhole edge and knit down, eliminating the need to set in and sew the sleeve to the armhole. If the sleeve is worked in a pattern stitch that is noticeably different when turned upside down, so that it won't match the body when knit from the top down, you may need to reverse the pattern stitch to make this look good; to figure this out, you may need to work a swatch of the pattern stitch upside down. Many lace patterns, patterns where the yarn is carried on the right side of the fabric while slipping stitches, and colorwork in stockinette will look noticeably different from the original when inverted, so your swatch may prove that it's just not possible to reverse the pattern stitch. Shaped sleeve caps, rather than drop-shoulder, T-shaped sweaters will require the additional effort of working short rows after picking up the stitches, matching the shape of the original cap. (See Case Study #3-3, page 80, for details.) Whether you choose to work the sleeves from the top down will depend on whether it seems easier to pick up stitches and make all the adaptations necessary or whether it's easier to just knit them separately and sew them on.

## Joining Difficult Fabrics

Sewing together a plain stretchy stockinette stitch fabric made from smooth, responsive yarn is a pleasant and gratifying experience once you are comfortable with the rudiments of seaming. Not all knitting is as easy to work with, however. Sewing together pieces of very loose or openwork knitting requires different techniques than sewing solid pieces. Joining very tight knitting can be just as challenging, because it's difficult to force the yarn and needle between the stitches and it's very hard on the yarn being pulled repeatedly through the fabric. Seams in bulky fabrics add to the bulk at points you'd prefer to be flat and supple. Fragile yarns, highly textured or fuzzy yarns, and yarns where the plies stretch at different rates can be impossible to sew with. You'll find suggestions for coping with all of these difficulties in Joining the Pieces, chapter 7 (page 203). It's good to consider such problems in advance, however, because they are all reasons why you might want to employ alternatives to conventional sewn seams, such as crocheted seams, picking up sections instead of attaching them later, knitting on parallel sections as you go (Knitting On, pages 182–83), or making yarnover edges to accommodate a decorative join.

## Planning for Ends

The biggest problem knitters face when dealing with ends is trying to work with an end that's too short. Whenever you cut the yarn or start a new ball, be sure to leave an end long enough to work with later — at least 4 inches.

When you start a new ball of yarn or run into a knot, you can splice the ends together, weave them in while you're knitting, or leave them to weave in later. There should be only a few of these, so there's no need to plan ahead for them.

When you're working in stripes, with multiple colors, or with small sections of several different yarns, you'll have far more ends to cope with, and in those cases, it is best to plan ahead. Before you start, decide whether you can carry the yarns up to future rows or rounds, or whether they should really be cut between uses. If you're not sure, try both out in your swatch. Carrying the yarns up the edge of the fabric can distort the edge stitches, but weaving in the ends takes time and makes the edge of the fabric thicker. If you're working circularly, you may want to carry the yarns from round to round to avoid excess ends, or you may choose to always cut the yarn and use the ends to hide the jog at the beginning/end of round (see Disguising the Jog, chapter 5, page 155). You'll find details on dealing with ends in the middle of your knitting in chapter 5 as well (page 152). Methods for taking care of ends after the knitting is completed are covered in Dealing with Ends, chapter 7 (page 200).

## When There Are Lots of Color Changes

When you are changing colors very frequently at the beginning of a row, it's possible to turn the ends into a decorative element, incorporating them in fringe or braids (see page 203), but you need to consistently leave ends long enough for the fringes or braids. Leave ends longer than you think you'll need and test out braids ahead of time on your swatch — you'll be surprised at how much extra length they require.

If you prefer to hide the ends on the inside of the garment, you can braid them along the seam line, using a method similar to working a French braid in hair, rather than weaving in each individual end (see Working Ends in Along Seams, chapter 7, page 202). This is much faster than weaving in individual ends, but it can prevent the garment from stretching, so should be used only along a supportive seam. If you want to do this, leave ends that are at least 6 inches long; it's difficult to work with shorter ends.

When the ends fall along the edge of the garment, rather than along a seam line, you can hide them inside a binding. This is just a two-layer border, with the ends encased inside. There are several ways to make bindings (see chapter 8, pages 235–37).

## Planning Ahead for Cutting

If you are working your garment circularly, especially in stranded knitting, you may want to continue circularly throughout the armhole, neck, and shoulder area. Circular sweaters with raglan or circular yokes incorporate the neck and armhole openings seamlessly, but if you're working a conventional sweater architecture, with separate sleeves, you'll need to plan how to handle the openings for the armholes and neck. You have three options:

▷ Continue in a straight tube up to the shoulders and add shaping later by simply cutting open the armholes and neck.

▷ Add steeks at each of the openings and work any shaping around the steeks.

▷ Use a combination of these, adding steeks and shaping at some openings, but not others.

Steeks are extra stitches added at armholes, neck openings, and cardigan fronts that serve as seam allowances when the openings are cut open later. They allow you to make the entire garment circularly, so that you can work colored and textured patterns from the right side throughout the construction process. They work best in garments made from natural (not superwash) wool or other animal fibers, because the cut ends will felt, preventing unraveling. While they offer the convenience of working circularly throughout the garment, cutting creates a multitude of ends that you must deal with in order to complete it. See The Whys and Hows of Steeks in chapter 3 (page 88) for details on how to incorporate various types of steeks into your garments. You'll find finishing information for cut edges in chapter 6 (page 187).

## Planning Ahead for Embellishments and Additions

Adding pockets, ruffles, cords, and other embellishments is much easier if you plan for them. Purl stitches can act as markers and provide an easy place to pick up stitches. Adding a row of increases or a partial row of waste yarn while you work the garment takes the trauma out of opening up the knitting to add pockets later on.

### Adding Ridges for Ruffles, I-Cord, and Other Applied Finishes

If you want to add surface decorations like ruffles or I-cords, work purl stitches on the public side wherever they will be attached. A row or round of purled stitches makes a neat, regular base for picking up or attaching embellishments later on. To pick up along it, fold the fabric along the purled stitches, then knit up 1 stitch in each "smile" or "frown" along the purled ridge. Patch pockets can be started this way, too. Pick up stitches along the ridge for the bottom of the pocket. You can either pick up along the sides of the pocket as well, or sew the sides down once it's completed.

Complex shapes, with twists and zigzags, are not easily picked up and knit on. Instead, outline the shape you want with the purled stitches, then use them as a guide to sew the embellishment on later. (For more information on adding pockets and other embellishments, see chapter 8, page 246.)

## Creating Live Stitches to Attach Pockets and Welts

Rather than picking up stitches later, it's also possible to create live stitches while you're knitting and set them aside on a holder or an extra circular needle until they are needed. This is most easily done when the addition will be horizontal, along a row of knitting.

For a practically seamless, stretchy effect, place all your stitches on a circular needle; the ones where the live stitches will be attached should be on the thin cable of the needle. Using a second circular needle and a second ball of yarn, pick up and knit 1 stitch under the strand between each of the existing stitches where the second layer of knitting will be added. Leave these on the second circular needle until you're ready to work with them.

### Picking Up for Ruffles

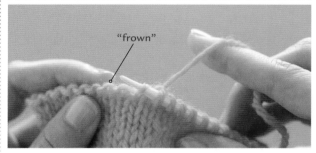

"frown"

Picking up in each "frown" along a row of purled stitches

Finished ruffle

### Picking Up Between Existing Stitches

Picking up and knitting new stitches between existing stitches

You can also work an increase after every stitch across the section where you need to add stitches. An M1 with the working yarn works best, because it doesn't tighten up the fabric. On the following row, knit the original stitches and slip all the increases to a second circular needle.

**M1s between every stitch**

**M1s slipped onto a second needle**

**If you are very clever with your hands,** you can work this all in one step by holding the two needles together as you work across, alternately knitting the original stitches while making the increases on the new needle.

**Waste yarn at center for pocket**

## Waste Yarn for Openings

Wherever you will need an opening later, you can just knit in a piece of waste yarn for as many stitches as you need for the width of your opening. Cut the project yarn, leaving a 6-inch tail for security and to weave in later. Using contrasting yarn in the same weight as the original, knit across the width of your opening. Leave 6-inch tails at both ends of the waste yarn. Start working with your project yarn again, leaving yet another tail. When you're ready to add the pocket or finish the opening, pick out the waste yarn, slip the stitches onto needles, and add whatever you like. The tails of the project yarn will come in handy for closing up any looseness at the ends of the opening. Note that you can only take advantage of this technique if you are absolutely sure of where the opening should be when you come to that point in your knitting. If not, then an "afterthought" addition will be a better choice. In this case, just keep on knitting. Later, when you can determine exactly where the opening should be, cut a single stitch at the center and unravel out to the sides to make the opening. See chapter 8 (page 249) for more information on making afterthought pockets.

67

*Third Time Lucky:*

# Modifying Your Pattern

YOU'VE CHOSEN YOUR materials, pattern, and tools; you've planned ahead and know how you're going to handle your edge stitches; and you've got an idea of what you'll do with your cut ends and how you'll put the pieces together. You're finally ready to cast on and get started, right? Not so fast! There are a few more adjustments you might want to consider to customize your sweater. These changes will be much easier to make if you decide about them *before* you cast on.

In chapters 1 and 2, I gave some practical reasons why you might want to change the pattern stitch, fit, or construction, so you may have already skipped ahead to this chapter to check out how to make these changes. But ultimately the reason (and the decision) is up to you. Do you like to work top down rather than bottom up? Do you prefer a pattern stitch to plain stockinette? If so, now is the time to think through the ramifications of making such changes and plan them out — before you cast on.

## Changing Color or Stitch Pattern

If you're thinking of playing with the pattern stitch, substituting stripes, incorporating intarsia, or fabricating some Fair Isle, and you haven't already been making swatches with this in mind, you need to swatch for gauge again. If you are changing a textured pattern stitch (knit/purl, ribbing, cables, and so on) or adding stranded colorwork, it's absolutely necessary to swatch the actual stitch and color changes, because they *will* influence the gauge. If you are planning to add stripes or intarsia with the same kind of yarn, you *may* be able to assume that the gauge will be the same in all colors, but that's not always the case — the thickness and density of the yarn may vary between colors even within a single line of yarn. And, you can test out what you plan to do with all the ends as you swatch.

If you get the correct gauge in your new pattern stitch, you *may* be able to work according to the original instructions for stitch count, length, and shaping, assuming that the new fabric you designed behaves like the original, but you'll also need to consider whether any pattern repeat will fit evenly into the original number of pattern stitches and how to center the pattern on the major garment pieces. You may need to add filler stitches (in something simple, like stockinette, garter, Seed Stitch, or a tiny stranded color pattern) at both edges to achieve the correct width. The more changes you make, the less likely it is that you'll be able to match the original gauge and follow the original instructions. For a better understanding of the issues involved, reread Matching Gauge (page 30) and There's More to Swatching Than Matching the Gauge (page 33) in chapter 1.

## Adding Embellishments

You can add ruffles, beads, lace, cords, or anything else you can think of that makes your sweater unique. Some embellishments use quite a lot of yarn, so ensure that you'll have enough. If the embellishment is added after the garment is finished, you can abandon the idea if you run out of yarn. If the garment starts with it (for example, a ruffle at the cast on), it will cause major problems if you run out before the end of the project.

How you approach these additions depends on the embellishment you choose. A fancy cast on or bind off will obviously be worked when casting on or binding off. A decorative panel in an otherwise plain fabric can be worked in the middle of the fabric, or you can work the panel first, then add plain panels on either side using the technique of Knitting On (page 182). Adding the panels later allows you to adjust for any change in width caused by the panel. Surface and edge ornamentation will be worked after the garment is completed. (See pages 246–52, for adding pockets, ruffles, and cording.)

## Changing the Borders

It's difficult to explain simply how to change a border, because there are so many different kinds of borders and ways to change them. You can make them fancier or plainer, narrower or wider; you may adjust the fit by making an opening larger or smaller without modifying the rest of the garment; you may be substituting a different fiber or pattern stitch and expect the borders to behave differently from the original. You may discover your gauge in ribbing doesn't match the designer's gauge, so your borders don't behave like the original. When you consider changes like these, keep in mind that borders serve an important structural role. If you change them, the garment may misbehave, becoming too tight, too loose, too elastic, or too inelastic to function properly in that particular garment.

Given the vast range of possibilities, I think the best thing to do is to explain how to design the best borders. Then, if you design the best possible border whenever you make any changes, the garment should come out okay. (For how to pick up and work the borders, see chapter 8.)

There are two key qualities that always need to be considered, plus a third aesthetic issue.

1. **Stretch.** Should the border stretch? Does it need to stretch to fit over a head, or at one edge, but not the other, to fill in a rounded opening like a neckline or armhole? Or does it need to *not* stretch to support the garment, or to keep a heavy fabric from stretching a neckline out of shape? Is it under tension all the time? Does it need to be resilient and regain its shape after stretching, like bottom and cuff borders?

2. **Length.** Does it fit the edge it's attached to? Not too long, because it will ruffle, but not too short because the garment will pucker.

3. **Transition.** How does the base fabric of the garment transition to the border? Will the stitches be picked up? Will the border be knitted first and then the garment continued from that point? Will increases or decreases be required to adjust the stitch count? How does the point where the border meets the rest of the garment look?

## Getting Neck Borders Right

First let's talk about whether and how much the border should stretch in various situations. Neck borders are extremely important, because they need to support the entire garment. If the neck border doesn't do this, it will stretch when subjected to the weight of the sleeves, the shoulder line will fall too far out, and the sleeves will be too long. Armhole and sleeve cap shaping will end up out over the upper arm, and the fit of a well-constructed shoulder area will be destroyed. In a sleeveless garment, the weight will be to the front and back, so a neck border that doesn't stand up to the weight of the garment will tend to stretch to the front and back. Any body shaping (such as bust or waist darts) will fall too low, and the overall fit of the garment will be affected. On the other hand, neck borders must stretch and curve to adapt to the edge of the knitted fabric they support. The base of a ribbed border, where it meets the garment, can stretch to fit the edge of the garment, while the bind off or cast on at the upper edge of the neck ribbing must be tight enough to support the entire sweater. Nonstretchy neck borders must be shaped so that they are long enough to fit the edge of the garment, but do not flare or pull in too much at their outer edge. Most importantly, all neck borders must be big enough to go over the wearer's head.

To design the border, knit a separate gauge swatch with the needles and in the pattern stitch you plan to use. Measure the number of stitches per inch. If you plan to block the border on the finished garment and stretch it to the max, block it before measuring. If you plan on a traditional stretchy border, stretch it slightly while measuring to simulate how it will behave under tension. Assuming that you are adding the border after the garment is completed, join the front and back at the shoulder, measure along the edge of the neck opening, and multiply by the gauge to determine how many stitches to pick up. On the other hand, if you are beginning a top-down garment with the neck border, you'll need to determine the size of your neck opening before you start and cast on the required number of stitches.

Another difficulty in discussing how to design a neck border is that there are so many possible ways to shape a neck — round, scoop, boat, turtle, and V are just a few.

**Round and scoop necks.** For rounded necks, you need to plan for the shorter circumference at the upper edge of the border, a bigger problem as the border gets wider. A border only 1 inch wide usually requires no shaping, while a border 4 inches wide always requires shaping. A wool ribbing, if left unblocked,

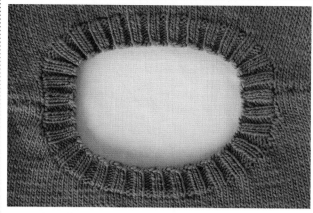

Round neck with unshaped ribbed border

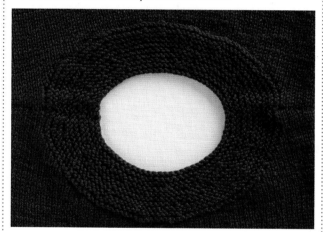

Circular neck with shaped garter stitch border

frequently closes up enough when relaxed to prevent flaring. A nonstretchy border (either because it's not ribbed or not wool) will need to be shaped to lie flat. If you start top down with the border, use a firm cast on to help stabilize the upper edge of the neck (assuming that it will stretch enough to go over the head) and consider increasing a bit at the bottom of the ribbing to enlarge the outer circumference of your border as you make the transition to the body of the garment. For details on designing a shaped border, see Case Study #8-1, page 226.

**Turtlenecks** must be worked in a stretchy fabric that will slip easily over the head and then relax back to the original dimensions. It must be thin enough to be comfortable when doubled. A soft fabric is the only practical option, but it could be ribbing, stockinette (with a stretchable border at the very edge that doesn't curl), or any other pattern stitch that is comfortable to wear and stretches easily to go over the head. Turtlenecks are usually worked with the same number of

V-neck with mitered corner in ribbing

V-neck with overlapped corner in ribbing

stitches throughout, but sometimes the outer layer is worked on larger needles, so that it has a slightly larger circumference and will lie neatly when folded over.

**V- or square-neck** openings require corners, which can be mitered or overlapped and sewn down at the corners. For mitering guidelines, see Case Studies #4-6 and #4-7 (pages 111–12) and Working a Border with Corners (page 224).

## Armhole Border Essentials

Like neck borders, armhole borders on sleeveless garments stabilize the garment, keeping the top of the garment from stretching in length, especially if it has a deep V-neck. Similarly, they must curve to fit the underarm shaping, but not flare or pull in too much

at their outer edge. Ribbing will stretch to do this, but nonstretchy borders require shaping to fit the edge. Armhole borders are designed just the same as neck borders.

## Front Border Requirements

The front borders or button bands on sweaters must lie flat, helping to support the fronts without either stretching out of shape or pulling in. Determine the required number of stitches just as for a neckline, but measure the border's gauge under very slight or no tension. Because they are usually straight, they don't need shaping, but care must be taken to bind off at just the right tension so the edge doesn't flare or pull in. Doubled front borders keep their shape better and look neater than single-layer front borders, but they can be a little bulky.

## Working Ideal Bottom Borders

Bottom borders and sleeve cuffs keep the bottom edges looking neat. Unlike neck and armhole borders, they don't support any weight, but they must be stretchy enough (or loose enough) so the garment is easy to put on. The important issue is that they mustn't stretch out and become limp and lifeless.

When worked in wool or wool-blend yarn, stretchy ribbed bottom borders on a stockinette stitch body should be knit on about 10 percent fewer stitches than the body, generally on needles two sizes smaller. In other pattern stitches, ribbed borders should be made about 10 percent narrower than the body. If your ribbing stitches tend to be loose, you may want to use an even smaller needle. Working the ribbing on a smaller number of stitches and smaller needles helps to ensure it doesn't lose its shape entirely under tension, but holds the lower edge of the body and sleeves in rather than flaring. In fibers other than wool, you may need to work ribbings on up to 15 percent fewer stitches and needles up to four sizes smaller. Test on a swatch before you commit yourself to the garment, and to be sure you don't overcompensate and make the borders too tight to be comfortable.

In nonwool fibers, it may be better to plan a bottom border in a pattern stitch other than ribbing that doesn't curl. In this case, rather than pulling in, you want the border to be the same circumference as the fabric it's attached to. The best way to figure out how many stitches will be required is to knit a swatch in the border pattern, measure it while it's relaxed (that is, not under tension), and calculate how many stitches will exactly match the width or circumference of the garment section for which it will serve as a border. (See Making Borders Just the Right Size in chapter 2, page 50, for examples of border variations.)

You can also substitute hems for ribbed borders. Like any other nonstretchy edge, they won't pull in but they will prevent curling. Because hems are double thickness, make them slightly narrower than the bottom edge so they don't bulge out. You can do this by working the inner layer of the hem on a smaller needle, with thinner yarn, or on fewer stitches. The shorter circumference of the hem also keeps it from flipping up when attached to stockinette stitch. (See appendix, page 273.)

## Transitioning to the Border

You will almost always need to work borders on a different number of stitches than the body or sleeves, and on necklines and armholes you will usually need to pick up stitches for borders. Depending on the yarn, the transition from the base fabric to the border may be extremely noticeable, especially if your yarn is smooth, light colored, and has good stitch definition. Smooth cotton, linen, or silk yarns, in particular, will show off any variation in tension or consistency, so the point where the border meets the garment may look wonky.

Stitches picked up along an edge, especially a curved edge, frequently look inconsistent, because you need to pick up unevenly to end up with the correct number of stitches and pick up along the vertical, diagonal, and horizontal areas using different methods. Any variation or unevenness automatically attracts attention. For advice, see the suggestions in Perfecting Transitions from Garment to Border, page 234).

# Changing Direction: Top Down versus Bottom Up

Is there any reason why it would be better to work in the opposite direction from that dictated by the instructions? Perhaps you think you have barely enough yarn: starting at the top lets you make the sweater as long as possible with what you have. Or, you may find it easier to work the shaping in the armholes and neck using decreases rather than increases, requiring you to begin at the bottom.

## Converting to Top Down

The two best reasons to convert a sweater to top down are that you like this construction technique and you're concerned about making your sweater long enough. Working from the top down lets you complete the shoulder area and the sleeves so that they fit properly, then work the body in one piece until you run out of yarn. Many knitters advocate top-down seamless construction because it's so easy to try on the sweater and fit the neck, shoulders, and sleeves as you go, but you can work from the top down in separate flat pieces as well. You may also prefer the way the pattern stitch looks worked in this direction.

When shaping a sweater from the bottom up, you are normally dealing with bind offs and decreases at

**Old Shale: Up and Down**

**Right side up.** The traditional Old Shale pattern features groups of eyelets that fan out upward when looked at right side up. The cast-on edge makes a scallop with slight points at the base of the eyelets.

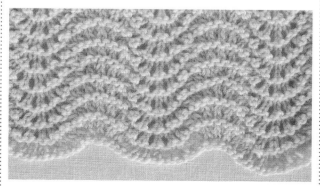

**Upside down.** In contrast, when deployed upside down, the eyelets make sprays that are wider at the bottom, and the bound-off edge creates a more even scallop.

the armholes, sleeve caps, and neck opening. These are easily worked to look symmetrical by using K2tog decreases opposite ssk decreases. Working from the top down requires that you work the shaping using increases and cast ons. Some increases are more difficult to work symmetrically. Top-down construction also requires you to jump right in and shape while working pattern stitches and color changes. With bottom-up construction, you make the usually straight body of the sweater first, and then deal with the added complication of shaping after you've mastered the pattern stitch.

To adapt a pattern to work from neckline to bottom border, you must invert all the instructions, casting on the number of stitches that the instructions say to bind off, increasing rather than decreasing, and binding off at the bottom rather than casting on. You can work your way backward through the pattern instructions, reversing all of these elements, but I find that approach confusing. It's more straightforward to create a schematic of the original garment, marked with stitch counts, length and width measurements, and notes on shaping. I then knit directly from the schematic or rewrite the instructions based on the schematic.

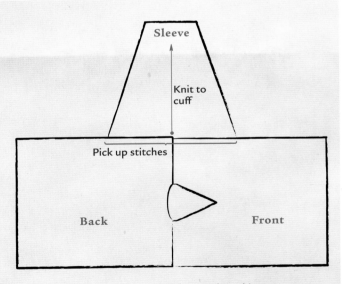

**Picking up the sleeve stitches** and working top to bottom is very easily accomplished on a drop-shoulder sweater where the top of the sleeve cap isn't shaped. Just pick up the stitches and begin tapering the sleeve down to the cuff, as shown in the schematic.

## Picking Up the Sleeves and Knitting Down

Regardless of how the body of the garment was worked, once the front and back are completed and joined at the shoulders, you can work the sleeves either from the bottom or from the top. If you work them from the top, you have the option of picking up stitches along the armhole edges of the front and back and working the sleeve from there, eliminating the need to set in the sleeve and sew the seam later.

## Converting from Top Down to Bottom Up

Many newer designs are worked from the top down, and you may want to convert those top-down instructions to work in the opposite direction, because you prefer working from the bottom up, the pattern stitch looks better worked in this direction, or you like the way decreases (rather than increases) look around the armholes and neck.

To rewrite the directions, reverse the process described in Case Studies #3-1 and #3-2 (pages 76–79). The original instructions will read like the Top-Down Front and Top-Down Sleeves in these case studies. Your instructions will read like the Bottom-Up Front and Sleeve. Remember that a schematic with detailed measurements, stitch counts, and shaping notes will make this process easier and help to prevent errors from creeping into your revised instructions.

# Converting Flat to Circular

Circular sweaters have fewer or no seams, so finishing takes less time. When either the yarn or the pattern stitch makes neatly finished seams difficult, circular construction can reduce or eliminate this problem. Some color and stitch patterns are more easily worked in the round than flat, because there are no wrong-side rows. Circular knitting also allows you to construct sweaters with architectures that aren't possible in flat knitting. A good example is sweaters with circular yokes: Working the front and back circularly in one piece means that you can be sure they are the same length without any need to measure or count rows. Horizontal patterns and stripes will match on the front and back because they are worked at the same time.

Circular construction, however, is not always the best choice. If the sweater is heavy, loosely knit, or made from fibers other than wool, it may be prone to stretching in length. Seams help to support garments and prevent stretching. Some pattern stitches and techniques are more difficult or impossible to work in the round. It's easier to work tailored fitted sweaters flat, and their seams provide support to ensure that stretching doesn't impair a good fit. Horizontal patterns will exhibit a one-row jog at the beginning and end of the round (but this can be disguised somewhat using slipped stitches, a seam stitch, or when weaving in the ends of colored stripes; see Disguising the Jog, chapter 5, page 155).

Sweaters can be worked circularly from the top down or from the bottom up. It will be easiest to work in the same direction as the original instructions, but you can follow the guidelines in Case Studies #3-1 and #3-2 for reversing the direction of work (pages 76–79) and then convert to circular knitting as described here.

① **Review the instructions.** First read through the original pattern and make sure you understand it completely, including all shaping and finishing.

② **Convert the pattern stitches.** Convert any pattern stitches to circular knitting. See Case Study #3-4 (page 82) for how to do this. Make a circular swatch to test out the new instructions as well as to check the gauge. If the effect looks bad at the beginning and end of round, experiment to see if you can improve it. See Disguising the Jog in chapter 5 for ways to do this. If some sections of the garment will be worked flat (see item 5 below), you'll also need to make a flat swatch based on the original instructions and make sure the gauge and the pattern stitch are identical on both swatches.

③ **Make flat schematics.** If the pattern doesn't provide complete labeled schematics, create your own, including stitch counts, lengths, and notes on shaping for all the separate garment pieces, as shown in Case Studies #3-1 (page 76) and #3-2 (page 78).

④ **Locate the beginning of the round.** Decide where the beginning of the round will be. Put the beginning/end of round where it will be least apparent (for a pullover, usually the side seam). Will the first half of the round be the back or the front? If the back and front are the same up to the underarms or neck opening, then you don't need to decide which is which until you start those openings.

⑤ **Determine the order of construction.** Decide whether to work some sections flat, or to use steeks and cut the garment open later. (For steeks, see page 88.) Decide whether the sleeves will be worked separately or picked up and knit on. See Case Study #3-5 (page 84) for more details.

⑥ **Plan the finishing details.** Consider how you will shape and join the shoulders (see Planning Ahead for Perfect Finishing in chapter 2, page 50). Will the neck border be worked as part of the body, or do you prefer to pick up stitches and add it later? Keep in mind that neck and shoulder shaping are most easily worked flat, which requires you to complete the front and back, join the shoulders, and add the border later. If there will be steeks, you'll need to plan for cutting and finishing them (see Cutting Your Knitting, chapter 6, page 186).

⑦ **Make circular schematics.** Sketch a simple schematic for your garment, including measurements, stitch counts, and shaping notes. See Case Study #3-5 (page 84) for details.

⑧ **Rewrite the garment instructions.** Convert the instructions from rows to rounds. See Case Study #3-5 (page 84) for an example.

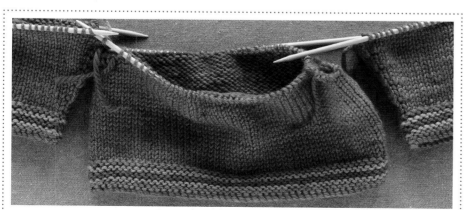

**For this circular-yoke sweater,** the sleeves and body were knit circularly to the underarm from the bottom up. They are now ready to be joined to work the yoke in the round to the neck.

# Converting the Body from Bottom Up to Top Down

Here's a set of basic instructions for the front of a sweater worked from the bottom up, assuming a gauge of 20 stitches and 28 rows = 4 inches, followed by an explanation of converting it to top down. To convert the back from bottom up to top down, you will follow exactly the same procedure, except that the neck shaping will be different from the front. Wherever you would have bound off in the bottom-up version, you'll cast on, and wherever you would have decreased, you'll increase.

## Bottom-Up Front

Cast on 99 stitches. Work K1, P1 ribbing for 2 inches, ending with a right-side row. Increase 11 stitches evenly spaced across next row (110 stitches). Work even in pattern until the piece measures 15½ inches. Continue to work in pattern as established while working the armhole, neck, and shoulder shaping.

**Left front armhole and V-neck.** At the beginning of the next 2 rows, bind off 9 stitches for the underarm (92 stitches remain). On the following right-side row, K1, ssk, work 40 stitches in pattern, K2tog, K1. Leave the stitches for the right front on the needle unworked, or transfer them to a circular needle or piece of yarn to get them out of your way. Turn and continue working in pattern on just the left front, decreasing as above every right-side row at the armhole edge until a total of 9 decreases have been completed. *At the same time*, decrease every 4th row at the neck edge until a total of 15 decreases have been completed and 22 stitches remain for the shoulder. Work even (if necessary) on 22 stitches until armhole measures 8¾ inches from underarm bind off. Shape shoulders: *At the beginning of the next right-side row, bind off 5 stitches. At the beginning of the following right-side row, bind off 6 stitches. Repeat from * once more. All stitches have been bound off. Cut yarn.

**Right armhole and V-neck.** Place stitches for right front back on needle, if necessary. With the right side facing, attach a ball of yarn at the center of the neck opening and work the right front, reversing the shaping for the left front as follows: K1, ssk, work 40 stitches in pattern, K2tog, K1. Turn and continue decreasing, as above, every right-side row at the armhole edge until a total of 9 decreases have been completed. *At the same time*, decrease every 4th row at the neck edge until a total of 15 decreases have been completed and 22 stitches remain for the shoulder. Work even (if necessary) on 22 stitches until right armhole measures 8¾ inches from underarm bind off. Shape shoulders: *At the beginning of the next wrong-side row, bind off 5 stitches. At the beginning of the following wrong-side row, bind off 6 stitches. Repeat from * once more. All stitches have been bound off.

## The Same Front Top-Down

To work the front top down, you will need to start each shoulder separately, join them at the bottom of the neck, then continue down, adding stitches to shape the underarms, and casting off at the bottom. Here are the reverse-direction instructions:

**Left shoulder.** You'll need a firm cast on to prevent the shoulders from stretching out of shape, and you'll need a single-strand cast on because you'll be casting on groups of stitches at the beginning of several rows to shape the shoulder, so use the cable cast on (see appendix, page 264). *Cast on 6 stitches and work 1 right-side row in pattern. Turn and work 1 wrong-side row in pattern. Cast on 5 more stitches at the beginning of the next right-side row (11 stitches). Work 1 right-side row and 1 wrong-side row. Repeat from * once (22 stitches). Continue working in pattern throughout. Beginning with the following right-side row, increase 1 stitch at the end of the row for the neck edge every 4th row until 10 increases have been completed and there are 32 stitches. While continuing to increase every 4th row at the neck edge, increase

1 stitch for the armhole at the beginning of every right-side row until 15 total increases have been completed at the neck and 9 have been completed at the armhole edge (46 stitches). Stop immediately after completing the final right-side increase row. Cut the yarn and leave these stitches on a spare needle or a holder.

**Right shoulder.** To make the second shoulder, reverse the shaping for the first as follows: *Cast on 6 stitches and work 1 wrong-side row in pattern. Turn and work 1 right-side row in pattern. Cast on 5 more stitches at the beginning of the next wrong-side row (11 stitches). Work 1 wrong-side row and 1 right-side row. Repeat from * once (22 stitches). Work 1 wrong-side row in pattern. Beginning with the following right-side row, increase 1 stitch at the beginning of the row for the neck edge every 4th row until 10 increases have been completed and there are 32 stitches. While continuing to increase every 4th row at the neck edge, increase 1 stitch for the armhole at the end of the row on every right-side row until 15 total increases have been completed at the neck, and 9 have been completed at the armhole edge (46 stitches). Stop immediately after completing the final right-side increase row. The yarn should be attached at the armhole edge of the knitting. Do not cut the yarn.

Place all the stitches on one needle, with the neck edges together to form the V-neck opening (92 stitches). Beginning with a wrong-side row, work across all 92 stitches for body.

**Underarms.** At the beginning of the next 2 rows, cast on 9 stitches (110 stitches).

**Body.** Work even in pattern until body measures 13½ inches from the underarm.

**Bottom border.** Decrease 11 stitches evenly spaced across the row (99 stitches). Work K1, P1 ribbing for 2 inches. Body should measure 15½ inches to underarm. Bind off in ribbing.

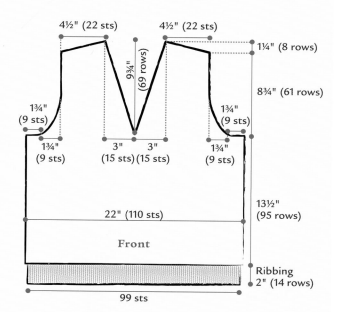

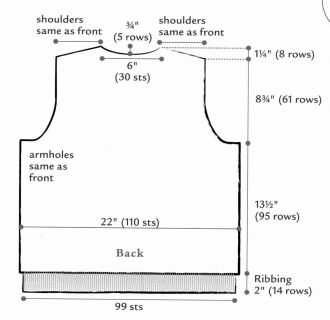

# Converting the Sleeves from Bottom Up to Top Down

When working from the bottom up, sleeves are usually made beginning with a bottom border or ribbing, increasing about 10 percent of the stitches at the top of the ribbing, and then increasing along both edges to slowly widen the sleeve up to the underarm. The underarm bind off begins the sleeve cap shaping, which is rounded using a series of decreases and further bind offs. Like the example in Case Study #3-1, it's helpful to make a schematic of the sleeve and to refer to it often to keep yourself oriented while rewriting the instructions. Here is an example of a common sleeve:

### Bottom-Up Sleeve

**Ribbing.** Cast on 41 stitches. Work in K1, P1 ribbing for 2 inches, ending with a wrong-side row. Increase 3 stitches evenly spaced across on next right-side row (44 stitches).

**Taper sleeve.** Work 5 rows even in pattern. On the next right-side row, increase 1 stitch at each end of the row. Continue to increase 1 stitch at each edge every 6th row until 15 increases have been completed and there are 74 stitches. Sleeve should be about 15 inches long. Work even until it measures 16¼ inches.

**Shape sleeve cap.** At the beginning of the next 2 rows, bind off 9 stitches (56 stitches remain). Decrease 1 stitch at each edge every right-side row four times (48 stitches remain). Decrease 1 stitch at each edge every 4th row six times (36 stitches remain). Decrease 1 stitch at each edge every right-side row six times (24 stitches remain). At the beginning of the next 2 rows, bind off 2 stitches (20 stitches remain). At the beginning of the next 2 rows, bind off 3 stitches (14 stitches remain). Bind off all remaining stitches.

### Top-Down Sleeve

To work the sleeve top down, you will need to start at the top of the sleeve cap, cast on and increase to make it wider, cast on at the underarm, and then decrease along the edges to taper the sleeve down to the wrist. Finish it off by decreasing just before the ribbing, working the ribbing, and binding off.

You can knit right from the detailed shaping information on the schematic, or you can use it to write out instructions like these:

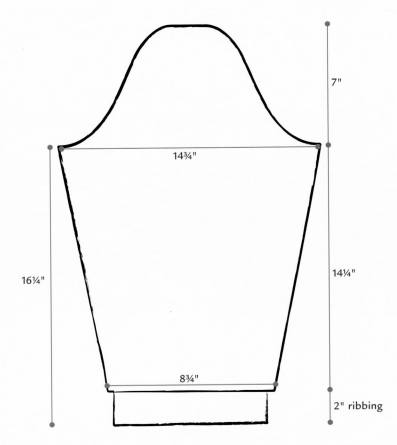

14¾"

7"

14¼"

16¼"

8¾"

2" ribbing

78

**Shape sleeve cap.** Cast on 14 stitches. Work in pattern throughout the sleeve. Cast on 3 stitches at the beginning of the next 2 rows (20 stitches). Cast on 2 stitches at the beginning of the next 2 rows (24 stitches). On the next 6 right-side rows, increase 1 stitch at each edge (36 stitches). Increase 1 stitch at each edge every 4th row six times (48 stitches). On the next 4 right-side rows, increase 1 stitch at each edge (56 stitches). At the beginning of the next 2 rows, cast on 9 stitches (74 stitches).

**Taper Sleeve.** Work about 1 inch even on these 74 stitches, then work your first decreases on the following right-side row. Decrease 1 stitch at each edge every 6th row until 15 decreases have been completed and 44 stitches remain. Work even on these 44 stitches until sleeve measures 14¼ inches from underarm.

**Ribbing.** Decrease 3 stitches evenly spaced across the next right-side row (41 stitches remain). Work in K1, P1 ribbing for 2 inches. Sleeve should measure 16¼ inches from underarm. Bind off in ribbing.

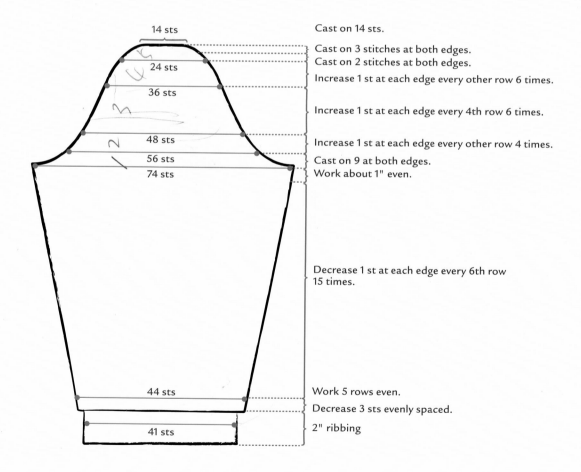

14 sts

Cast on 14 sts.

24 sts

Cast on 3 stitches at both edges.
Cast on 2 stitches at both edges.
Increase 1 st at each edge every other row 6 times.

36 sts

Increase 1 st at each edge every 4th row 6 times.

48 sts

Increase 1 st at each edge every other row 4 times.

56 sts

Cast on 9 at both edges.

74 sts

Work about 1" even.

Decrease 1 st at each edge every 6th row 15 times.

44 sts

Work 5 rows even.
Decrease 3 sts evenly spaced.

41 sts

2" ribbing

# Short-Row Sleeve Caps

With a little extra effort, you can also work a set-in sleeve from the top down, shaping the sleeve cap using short rows. Let's use the same sleeve and body instructions as in Case Study #3-2.

Along the whole armhole edge, pick up the total number of stitches you'll need at the underarm (74 stitches in this example). Make sure half are on each side of the shoulder seam (37 stitches in each half).

Follow the top-down instructions, but instead of casting on or increasing, work back and forth in short rows (see appendix, page 279). On each of these short rows, work past the last turning point for the number of stitches you would have cast on or increased. Be sure to wrap and turn at the end of each short row. Here's a comparison of the instructions for working the sleeve independently, and working it using short rows.

## Comparing Instructions

| Original Top Down | Short Row |
| --- | --- |
| Cast on 14 stitches. | After picking up along the armhole edge, you will be at the underarm. Turn and work back to the shoulder seam, and then 7 more stitches (half of the 14 that would have been cast on). Wrap and turn, then work 14 stitches (7 stitches on each side of the shoulder seam), wrap and turn. |

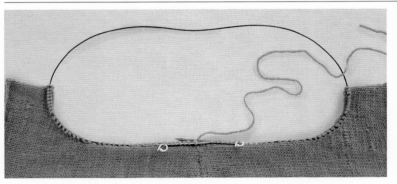

The first 2 short rows have been completed. The wrapped stitches are indicated by the markers.

| | |
| --- | --- |
| Cast on 3 stitches at the beginning of the next 2 rows (20 stitches). | Work until you are 7 stitches past the shoulder seam, pick up the wrap and work it together with its base stitch, work 2 more stitches, wrap and turn. Work back to the wrapped stitch on the other side of the shoulder seam, pick up the wrap and work it together with its base stitch, then work 2 more stitches, wrap and turn. There will be 20 stitches between the last 2 wrapped stitches. |
| Cast on 2 stitches at the beginning of the next 2 rows (24 stitches). | *Work back to the wrapped stitch on the other side of the shoulder seam, pick up the wrap and work it together with its base stitch, then work 1 more stitch, wrap and turn. Repeat from the * once more (in the opposite direction). There will be 24 stitches between the last 2 wrapped stitches. |

| Original Top Down | Short Row |
|---|---|
| On the next 6 right-side rows, increase 1 stitch at each edge (36 stitches). | *Work back to the wrapped stitch on the other side of the shoulder seam, pick up the wrap and work it together with its base stitch, then wrap and turn the next stitch. Repeat from * 11 more times. There will be 36 stitches between the last 2 wrapped stitches. |
| Increase 1 stitch at each edge every 4th row six times (48 stitches). | (1) Work back to the wrapped stitch on the other side of the shoulder seam, pick up the wrap and work it together with its base stitch, then wrap and turn the next stitch. Repeat this in the other direction. (2) Work back to the wrapped stitch from step 1, wrap and turn the same stitch again. Repeat this in the other direction. (3) Work back to the wrapped stitch from steps 1 and 2, pick up both of the wraps and work them together with their base stitch, wrap and turn the next stitch. Repeat this in the other direction. Repeat steps 2 and 3 five more times. There will be 48 stitches between the last 2 wrapped stitches. |
| On the next 4 right-side rows, increase 1 stitch at each armhole edge (56 stitches). | *Work back to the wrapped stitch on the other side of the shoulder seam, pick up the wrap and work it together with its base stitch, wrap and turn the next stitch. Repeat in the opposite direction. Repeat from *, working these 2 short rows three more times. There will be 56 stitches between the last 2 wrapped stitches. |

# Original Top Down

At the beginning of the next 2 rows, cast on 9 stitches (74 stitches).

Work all the way to the end of the row at the underarm, picking up the wrap at the previous turning point and working it together with its base stitch, turn. Repeat in the other direction. Short-row sleeve cap is complete. Work the rest of the sleeve to the cuff without short rows.

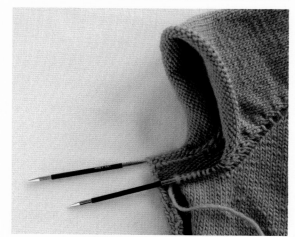

Completed short-row **sleeve cap**

## Shaping Sleeve Cap When Working in the Round

Exactly the same technique can be used to shape sleeve caps when you're working in the round. Work the whole sleeve cap in short rows. When all the sleeve stitches have been worked down to the underarm, and you are ready to work a right-side row, just start working circularly to complete the sleeve.

## More about Short Rows

For complete instructions on working short rows, including the wrap and turn and picking up the wrap

on subsequent rows, see Short Rows in the appendix (page 279). Note that if you are working in garter stitch, you should wrap the turning stitch, but there's no need to pick up the wrap when you come to it; the wraps will integrate nicely with the garter stitch ridges and will be unnoticeable. If you are working a pattern with yarnovers, you may not need to wrap at all; the hole that is left at the turning will contribute to the openwork effect.

# Converting Pattern Stitches from Flat to Circular

When you are working circularly, there are no wrong-side rows, so you must convert the instructions for wrong-side rows to right-side rows. When you knit on the wrong side, it looks like purl on the right side, and vice versa, so the first step is to change all the references in wrong-side instructions, substituting knit for purl and purl for knit. The wrong-side rows in flat knitting are worked in the opposite direction from the right-side rows, so you will also need to reverse the instructions, starting from the end of the row and working back to the beginning. If there are any edge stitches to center the pattern when working it flat, these are usually not needed when working circularly. Selvedge stitches, which disappear into the seams, should also be eliminated if they will affect the fit of the sweater significantly: at a gauge of 12 stitches per 4 inches, eliminating the seams but not the selvedge stitches means that the circular sweater is 1⅓ inches larger in circumference than the original. You may find it helpful to create a chart of the pattern stitch, which can easily be used for both flat and circular knitting, and then either work directly from the chart or use the chart when rewriting the instructions. (See How to Read Charts, chapter 5, page 147.)

## Example 1: Basic K1, P1 Ribbing

**Flat**

Cast on an odd number of stitches.

Row 1: *K1, P1; repeat from * until 1 stitch remains, K1.

Row 2: P1, *K1, P1; repeat from *.

**KEY**

☐ knit on right side, purl on wrong side

⊟ purl on right side, knit on wrong side

**Circular**

To make this rib work circularly, delete the single edge stitch that is used to center the ribbing and reverse the knits and purls on row 2.

Cast on an even number of stitches.

Round 1: *K1, P1; repeat from *.

Round 2: *K1, P1; repeat from *.

You'll notice that round 2 is identical to round 1, so you just repeat round 1 to make the ribbing. Using a chart makes this very clear.

**KEY**

☐ knit

⊟ purl

## Example 2: Mistake Stitch Rib

There are times when a pattern stitch that has just 1 row of instructions when worked flat must be described with 2 rounds of instructions when worked circularly. Mistake Stitch Rib is a good example. It's worked like plain K2, P2 ribbing, but on a multiple of 4 stitches plus 3. (This is 1 stitch too few for K2, P2 ribbing to line up properly, which is why it's called Mistake Stitch). Both sides of the fabric look identical.

### Flat

Cast on a multiple of 4 stitches plus 3.

Row 1 (right side and wrong side): *K2, P2;
   repeat from * until 3 stitches remain, K2, P1.

Repeat this 1 row for pattern.

### Circular

To convert this to circular knitting, first omit the 3 edge stitches, then rewrite the instructions for the wrong-side rows, swapping knits and purls and starting from the end of the row and working back to the beginning.

Cast on a multiple of 4 stitches.

Round 1: *K2, P2; repeat from *.

Round 2: *K1, P2, K1; repeat from *.

   Or, round 2 could be written this way, if it's easier to understand: K1, P2, *K2, P2; repeat from * until 1 stitch remains at end of round, K1.

   Repeat these 2 rounds for pattern. Again, using a chart makes this much clearer.

**KEY**

(flat)
▢ knit on right side, purl on wrong side
⊟ purl on right, knit on wrong side

**KEY**

(circular)
▢ knit
⊟ purl

# Converting Garment Instructions from Flat to Circular

Once you have figured out how to work any required pattern stitches in the round, you're ready to begin revising the garment instructions. Begin by deciding what order you're going to work it in, then take the flat schematics for the garment and sketch your own circular schematics. If you put enough shaping detail on the circular version of the schematics, you may be able to knit directly from them. If you're not comfortable with this, or if the garment is too complex, you'll need to rewrite the instructions based on the original instructions and your circular schematics.

## Determining the Order of Construction

The diagrams in Order of Construction (chapter 2, page 38) illustrate various ways circular sweaters and vests can be constructed. For guidance, choose the one that looks the most like the garment you plan to make. Remember that pattern revisions will be simpler if you work in the same direction as the original flat garment.

Decide whether some sections will be worked flat or whether all will be knit in the round. Note that some garment architectures require that you add steeks and cut them open to make the armholes and neck openings if you choose to knit the entire garment

in the round (see The Hows and Whys of Steeks, page 88).

Also decide whether the sleeves will be picked up and knit down, knit from the bottom up and joined to the body at a yoke, or sewn on later. Remember that if the body is knit from the bottom up and the sleeves are knit from the top down, any pattern stitch will reverse direction on the sleeves. Consider whether this will look odd. If not, then you can avoid seaming by picking up the stitches for the sleeves around the armholes and working circularly down to the cuff.

Take a look at the sleeve cap: is it shaped? It's easiest to pick up the sleeves and work them down if there is no sleeve-cap shaping, but you can, with a little extra effort, introduce short rows to shape the sleeve cap, and you will still be able to avoid sewing the armhole seam (see Case Studies #3-2, page 78, and #3-3, page 80).

## Making Circular Schematics

Create a schematic for your garment, including measurements, stitch counts, and row counts. If a single schematic gets too crowded with notes, put measurements on one and the stitch counts and shaping details on a second. If you are working from the top

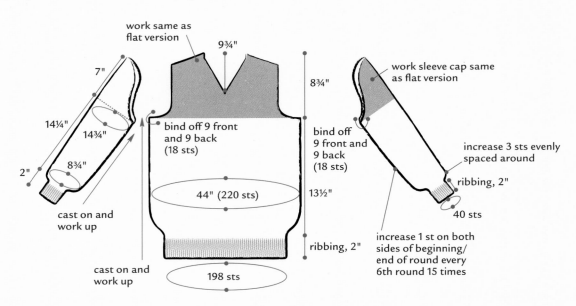

work same as flat version

9¾"

7"

8¾"

14¼"

14¾"

2"

8¾"

cast on and work up

cast on and work up

bind off 9 front and 9 back (18 sts)

44" (220 sts)

198 sts

bind off 9 front and 9 back (18 sts)

13½"

ribbing, 2"

work sleeve cap same as flat version

increase 3 sts evenly spaced around

ribbing, 2"

40 sts

increase 1 st on both sides of beginning/ end of round every 6th round 15 times down and need to be certain that shaping is placed correctly, you may need to include row/round counts. Also add arrows to indicate the direction of knitting, which will help you stay oriented.

Stitch counts will be for the whole round. For example, a round of the body includes the stitches for the front plus the stitches for the back. If there are selvedge stitches used to make the pattern stitch look continuous across seams, you'll need to delete those stitches from the instructions and from your stitch counts. If a close fit is important or the yarn is bulky, you may want to delete the seam stitches even if they don't affect the pattern stitch.

For example, at a gauge of 5 stitches per inch, the 4 stitches that would be lost in sewing the side seams are equal to ⅘ inch. Will a garment this much bigger in circumference still fit okay? In sport-weight yarn,

the difference will be smaller, but in bulkier yarn, at 2½ stitches per inch, the garment would be 1⅗ inches bigger around. Will this be too big? If you think so, then deduct 2 stitches from the back and 2 stitches from the front (1 at each edge) to allow for the lack of seams.

In practice, the only time you would not omit the seam stitches when working in the round is if the garment is worked in stockinette or a very simple pattern stitch like Seed Stitch and the difference in fit because of the slightly larger circumference doesn't matter to you.

## Rewriting the Garment Instructions

Work your way through the instructions, beginning with the cast on, combining the instructions for the front and the back.

## Instructions for Body

| Original Flat | Your New Circular |
|---|---|
| Cast on 99 stitches for back. | Cast on 198 stitches for back and front. *Note:* If you are adjusting for the lack of seams, subtract 4 stitches (2 for the front and 2 for the back) from this and cast on just 194 stitches. Make sure the number you cast on is an even multiple of the border pattern. Join the beginning and end of the round. Place markers at the beginning of the round and the halfway point. |
| Work K1, P1 ribbing for 2 inches. | Work ribbing circularly for 2 inches. |
| Increase 11 stitches evenly spaced across (110 stitches). | Increase 22 stitches evenly spaced around (11 for the front and 11 for the back, total is 220 stitches; 216 if you've omitted the selvedge stitches). |
| Work even until piece measures 15½ inches, ending with a wrong-side row. | Work circularly until body is 15½ inches. *Note:* If you are working a pattern stitch, end after completing what would be a right-side row when working flat. You will work the following bind-off round (which would be a wrong-side row when working flat), and then will be oriented correctly to work the flat sections, starting with a right-side row. |

| Original Flat | Your New Circular |
|---|---|
| **Underarm.** At the beginning of the next 2 rows, bind off 9 stitches (92 stitches remain). | **Underarm.** As you work the next round, bind off 9 stitches immediately before the marker at the halfway point, remove the marker, and bind off 9 more stitches. If you omitted the selvedge stitches for the body, you'll need to get them back again for the front and back above the underarms, which are worked flat. To do this, bind off just 8 stitches before and after the marker (total of 16 stitches). You've made one continuous bind off of 18 (or 16) stitches for the back and the front for one underarm. Continue around and do the same thing as you approach the marker at the end of round, binding off 18 (or 16) stitches for the other underarm. |
| Work the back, shaping the armholes, back neck, and shoulders. | You'll now work flat on just half of the tube at a time. The yarn is still connected at the point where you finished the last bind off. Work across on the right side, beginning the armhole shaping exactly as directed in the original flat instructions. At the end of this row you'll turn and work back on the wrong side. Continue to work the armhole, neck, and shoulder shaping until the back is complete. While you're doing this, you can leave the stitches for the front on the cable of your circular needle, or you can transfer them to another needle or a piece of waste yarn to get them out of your way. |
| Cast on 99 stitches for the front. Work the front the same as the back up to the neck opening. | You've already worked the front up to the underarms, so ignore these instructions. Put the front stitches back on a needle, if necessary; attach the yarn to the front; and prepare to begin working with a right-side row. |
| Work the front, shaping the armholes, neck, and shoulders. | Follow the original directions for the front armhole, neck, and shoulder shaping. |
| Sew the shoulder seams and work the neck border. | Sew the shoulder seams and work the neck border. If the flat instructions call for you to seam one shoulder, then work the neck border flat, you may want to seam both of them and work the border circularly. |

## Instructions for Sleeves*

| Original Flat from the Bottom Up | Your New Circular from the Bottom Up |
|---|---|
| Cast on 41 stitches for sleeve. | Cast on 40 stitches for sleeve (or, if you are omitting the selvedge stitches, cast on 38 stitches), join the beginning and end of the round, and place marker at this point. |
| Work K1, P1 ribbing for 2 inches. | Work K1, P1 ribbing circularly for 2 inches (number of stitches to cast on was adjusted so ribbing is an even repeat of total). |
| Increase 3 stitches evenly spaced across (44 stitches). | Increase 4 stitches evenly spaced around (44 or 42 stitches). The additional increase stitch adjusts the total to the correct number. |
| Work 5 rows even in pattern. | Work 5 rounds even in pattern. |
| Increase 1 stitch at each edge every 6th row 15 times (74 stitches). | Increase 1 stitch at beginning and at end of round every 6th row 15 times (74 or 72 stitches). For neatness, you should leave 1 or 2 stitches in stockinette between the increases at the beginning/end of round. If you are working in a pattern stitch, there may not be a full repeat of the pattern across the beginning/end of round, both because of the seam stitches and because of the increases. |
| Work even in pattern until sleeve measures 16¼ inches, ending with a wrong-side row. | Work even in pattern until sleeve measures 16¼ inches. Stop after you have completed what would be a right-side row if you were working flat. |
| At the beginning of the next 2 rows, bind off 9 stitches (56 stitches). | Stop 9 stitches before the end of the round. Bind off those 9 stitches, remove marker, then continue binding off 9 more stitches (or, if you have omitted the selvedge stitches, bind off 8 stitches before and after the marker). In both cases, you'll have 56 stitches total, which allows you to work the sleeve cap flat according to the original directions.) |
| Shape sleeve cap. | Work sleeve cap shaping flat, following the original instructions. |
| **Finishing.** Sew sleeves to armholes. Sew side and sleeve seams. | **Finishing.** Sew sleeve to armhole. |

*Note: If you prefer to pick up for the sleeves around the armholes and knit down, see Case Study #3-2, page 78, for reversing the shaping, and Case Study #3-3, page 80, for working short-row shaping to form the sleeve cap.

87

# The Whys and Hows of Steeks

Case Study #3-5 assumes that your garment is in a colored or textured pattern that is worked as easily on the wrong side of the fabric as the right side. There will be times when this is not the case, where it's much easier to work your pattern only on the right side, such as when working stranded color patterns. In a situation like this, you may want to work circularly throughout the armhole and neck region of the sweater. To do this, you'll need to cut your knitting.

One option is to do no preparation for these openings and work a straight tube all the way up to the shoulders (see Working a No-Stitch Steek, page 92). A second option is to cast on extra stitches that form a bridge across the neck and armhole openings in the sweater. These stitches are then worked in a different pattern stitch, to distinguish them from the main fabric of the garment. In this chapter, I'll discuss beginning and working several kinds of steeks. Preparing, cutting, and finishing the narrow three- and five-stitch steeks, which each require specialized techniques, is covered on pages 89–91. Finishing cut edges in general, which includes the no-stitch steek and wider steeks, is detailed in Cutting Your Knitting (chapter 6, page 186).

In the discussion that follows, I assume that the garment is being worked from bottom to top, because in most cases that's what makes the most sense. When working circularly in a stranded or textured pattern, it's simplest to begin the tube for the body and then to place the armholes and neck opening where they look most pleasing in relation to the patterns. I'm sure, however, that there will be occasions when you want to work a top-down garment with steeks. When that comes to pass, begin at the shoulders, being sure to cast on stitches for steeks at the front neck opening (and the back neck, if it's shaped). Also cast on stitches at the top of both of the armholes for those steeks. From this point to the bottom of these openings, the steeks are made identically to those worked in the opposite direction. Work whatever shaping is required on either side of the steek. When you get to the bottom of each opening, bind off the steek, then cast on for the underarms or center neck stitches. Continue working in a tube to the bottom of the garment. If the ribbing at the bottom is plain, not stranded, and the garment is a cardigan, you may want to bind off the center front steek and then work the ribbing flat.

## How Many Stitches in a Steek?

I usually work with an odd number of stitches and prefer to make my steeks 9 stitches wide. This gives me a center stitch, which disappears when cut, leaving 4 stitches as a seam allowance on either side. Usually, one of these stitches will unravel, and I'll trim the loose ends before sewing it down, leaving a margin of 3 stitches.

Some knitters cast on more stitches, others as few as 3 stitches. Some prefer to work with an even number of stitches, and to cut between the 2 stitches on either side of the center line. More stitches in the steek mean more work to complete the garment, but using only a few stitches requires you to take extra measures to secure the steek before cutting.

**Steeked vest** inside out with finishing in progress

# Three-Stitch Steek

THIS NARROWER STEEK was described by Eleanor Elizabeth Bernard in an article that appeared in *Knitter's Magazine* in 1996. She contends that it's a waste of both the knitter's time and of materials to make a steek any wider than this.

1. **Cast on 3 stitches** at the opening for your steek.

2. **Work the three-stitch steek** in stockinette stitch. If you are working stranded knitting with two colors, there are two ways you can handle colors at the steek. If the same color is used on both sides of the steek, use one in the 2 outside stitches and the other for the center stitch. If you need to change colors in the steek, work the first stitch in the old color, work the center stitch with both colors, and work the third stitch with the new color. This way, when you crochet your reinforcement, you'll be sure to catch both colors as you work though the outside and center stitches.

3. **Bind off the 3 stitches** when you reach the top of the opening.

4. **Secure one side of the steek** by working single crochet (see appendix, page 270) through the center of the right-hand stitch and the center of the center stitch, catching half of each of these stitches within the single crochet. Cut the yarn and pull the end through the final stitch. Secure the other side of the steek the same way, working through the center of the left-hand stitch and the center of the center stitch. Be careful not to split the stitches as you work and to leave a clear channel up the center stitch.

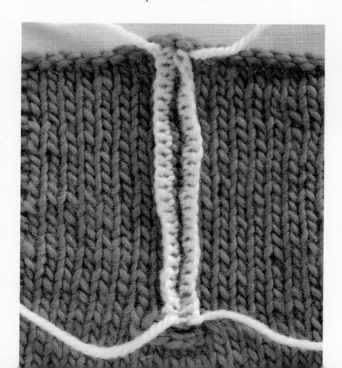

5. Use sharp scissors to cut up the center between the 2 rows of crochet.

6. **Pick up and knit** (see appendix, page 277) stitches in half of each of the outer stitches that remain of the steek, then work borders or add a sleeve.

Ms. Bernard notes that the crochet reinforcement should be worked firmly with a firmly spun, thin yarn and a small crochet hook. When using thinner yarn, it may be necessary to work 2 single crochets in each stitch of the steek so that the edges of the opening don't pull in. Because there is no excess knitting to turn under or be sewn down, this steek is less bulky than other methods.

# Five-Stitch Steek

I LEARNED THIS TECHNIQUE from Rick Mondragon, editor of *Knitter's Magazine*. It allows you not only to cut an armhole or a cardigan front but also to add a slit opening to a knitted fabric after it has been completed, for example, for a polo neck or to make a vertical opening for a pocket. You can plan ahead for this steek by casting on 5 additional stitches at the opening, or you can work a plain tube and then prepare and cut the steek wherever you like, making a wider opening, as shown step by step below.

1 **Determine** where your cut will be: you may want to mark the bottom and top stitch with a safety pin or split marker, or baste a strand of contrasting yarn or thread down that column of stitches.

2 **Unravel** a column of stitches 2 to the right of where the cut will be.

3 **Using** a crochet hook, hook this column of stitches back up, twisting each stitch as you go.

4 **Repeat** steps 2 and 3 for the column of stitches to the left of where the cut will be.

5 **Using** another strand of yarn, insert your crochet hook through the stitch immediately below the bottom twisted stitch of one of these columns, and hook a loop of yarn through from the back. Continue chaining a stitch through each twisted stitch all the way up to the top of the fabric. Break off the yarn and pull it through the last stitch. Repeat for the other column of stitches.

The stitches are already secured on the inside by twisting and crocheting, so there is no need to sew them down or cover them up. The unraveled strands may be trimmed some, but be careful not to trim too close to the crocheted chain or they may unravel completely. I find the fringes created by the unraveled cut ends to be so attractive that they could be used as an embellishment on the outside of a garment.

⑥ **Cut carefully** down the center stitch until you are even with the bottom of the crocheted stitches.

If you plan ahead for your steek, twist the 2 stitches on either side of the cutting line by working into the back of them on every row. Then you can skip steps 2 through 4 and reduce your preparation time significantly. You can also work the center stitch as a purl to make it easy to see the cutting line, so there is no need to baste down the center or to use safety pins or split markers to identify it.

⑦ **The cut edges** will fold naturally to the inside. Pick up stitches down one side, across the bottom, and up the other side. Unless the knitting is very loose, you should be able to pick up and knit under just a half stitch to reduce the bulk at the edge. Work the border.

## Working a No-Stitch Steek

Mary Scott Huff, in *The New Stranded Colorwork,* uses the traditional Norwegian method: She doesn't add any stitches for steeks, and doesn't do any armhole shaping or neck shaping. Instead, the sweater just proceeds in a straight tube up to the shoulders. For each armhole, she sets aside 6 of these stitches, works 2 rows of machine-stitching on either side of the steek (see Cutting Your Knitting, chapter 6, page 186), then cuts it up the center. This is a good idea for sleeves, because it results in a 6-stitch-wide, squared opening at the bottom of the cut. For neck openings, she also works no shaping, but sews the outline and cuts them to the desired size and shape after the knitting is completed.

## Working a Wrapped Steek

In *Alice Starmore's Book of Fair Isle Knitting,* she describes a "wound steek." After the opening for the neck or armhole has been started, instead of casting on stitches for a steek and then knitting them on every row, a quicker method is to wrap the yarns a few times around the point of the needle. On the following round, let these wraps fall off, and then wrap again. When it's time to finish the sweater, cut up the center of all the loose strands. Starmore says that the ends are "eventually darned in on the wrong side"; however, you could, perhaps more easily, secure the edge of the fabric with crochet or sewing or secure the ends by knotting them together in pairs, and then enclose the edge in a binding.

Wound or wrapped steek

## When and Where to Start a Steek

If you're making a cardigan, the center-front steek will run the full length of the garment, and the beginning/end of round will fall at the center of this steek. Whether you're making a pullover or a cardigan, the steeks for the armhole and neck opening are cast on immediately after you start those openings and are bound off just before you end the openings.

## For a Cardigan Front

▷ If the bottom border of your sweater is easily worked back and forth, you may want to go ahead and complete it before beginning to work in the round. To do this, complete the flat bottom border, then cast on the additional stitches needed for the steek, join the knitting into a round, and begin working circularly, as shown on facing page, column one.

▷ You may prefer to work in the round from the very beginning. In this case, add the number of stitches you need for the steek when you initially cast on, join the beginning and end of round, being careful not to twist the cast on, and go to work in the round.

## On Armholes

Work until you reach the armhole shaping. Place markers at the center of the armhole positions.

▷ For a cardigan, the center front is the beginning of the round, so the armhole markers will be placed at the one-quarter and three-quarter points of the round.

▷ For a pullover, the beginning of the round is at the center of one armhole, where there should already be a marker for the beginning of round. The other armhole marker belongs at the halfway point.

At each of the armhole markers, bind off half of the underarm stitches before the marker and half after. On the following round, when you reach the two points where you bound off stitches, cast on the number needed for your steek. You will now have what looks like two buttonholes at the armpits of the sweater. Note that you will almost never cast on the same number of stitches that you bound off, because the width of the steek will not be the same as the width of the underarm shaping.

## For the Neck Opening

Exactly how you handle a steek at the neck opening will depend on the shape of the neck and whether you're working a cardigan or a pullover.

▷ If the sweater is a V-necked cardigan, with a steek already established at the center front, you will simply continue to work that same steek up through the neck opening. To shape the neck, work the required decreases in the fabric of the sweater on either side of the steek. Remember to work them at least 1 stitch away from the steek to make picking up the borders easier. Continue shaping the neck on either side of the steek all the way up to the shoulders.

**Place the center stitch** of a V-neck pullover on a holder when starting a steek on an odd number of stitches.

**Cardigan front steek example** with V-neck shaping on either side of the steek

▷ If you're making a V-necked pullover, how you begin the neck opening depends on whether the front has an even number of stitches or an odd number of stitches.

   ▷ *Even number of stitches.* Work the first decrease before the neck opening and the edge stitch(es) next to it, cast on for the steek, then work the edge stitch and the decrease on the other side of the opening.

   ▷ *Odd number of stitches.* Place the center stitch on a safety pin or split marker, then cast on for the steek and continue around. You can work the first decreases at the same time, or you can begin the decreases a few rounds later.

▷ If you're making a round-necked pullover, the neck opening will begin with binding off stitches at the center front or putting the center front stitches on a holder. On the following round, cast on the steek stitches over the opening to bridge the gap.

▷ If the sweater is a round-necked cardigan, you already have a steek established at the center front. When you begin the neck opening by binding off at the center front, bind off half of the steek, and then bind off half of the front neck stitches following the steek. Work to the end of the round, bind

**Bind off at the beginning and end of round** for a round-necked cardigan, then cast on above it to restart the steek.

off the front neck stitches and the rest of the steek. When you come to this large bound-off section on the following round, cast on the steek stitches again to bridge the gap (photo, page 93, bottom). See Shaping around the Steeks (page 95) for tips on working decreases for a round neck opening.

## Casting On for a Steek

When beginning a steek in the middle of your work, you can use any cast on you like; remember that it won't show once the knitting is finished. If you're working with a single color, use one of the single-strand cast ons, like the knitted or half-hitch cast on (see appendix, page 265). If you are working stranded knitting, then you'll need to cast on with all of the colors in use on the current round. How you manage this will depend on the situation at the point where you start the steek:

▷ If there are two colors in use and you know the long-tail cast on, place one color on your thumb and the other on your index finger and work the cast on.

▷ If you are working with more than two colors, work the long-tail cast on with one color on your index finger and all the others on your thumb.

▷ If you aren't comfortable with the long-tail cast on, work the half-hitch, knitted, or cable cast on, changing colors between each stitch so that all of the yarns are used across the steek, or just hold all the strands together while you cast on.

▷ If you are creating a steek at the beginning of the round and need to change colors for the following round, change to the new color at the center of the steek while you're casting on.

▷ If you forget to use all the colors or forget to change colors at the center of the steek, don't worry about it — you can secure any loose ends when you finish the sweater.

## Working the Steeks

First be sure you know where the beginning of the round is, because that's where you'll be changing colors in stranded knitting or starting the next pattern round in textured knitting. In a cardigan, the steek is at the center front and the beginning/end of round is at the center of the steek. In a pullover, the beginning/end of round is at one of the side "seams." After you begin the armhole opening on that side, the beginning/end of round will be at the center of the steek in that armhole.

You may want to place a marker at the center of this steek as a reminder to help you stay oriented.

Begin every round in the center of the designated steek. Change colors or change to the next pattern round, then continue around working in pattern across the front and back of the sweater, working any required shaping before and after each steek, and working the stitches of each steek so that they are distinctly different than the pattern of the garment.

What do I meant by "distinctly different"? In color patterns, the steek is traditionally worked in a seeded or striped pattern so that it's visually obvious where the garment ends and the steek begins. My preference is for stripes, because that gives me a clear line to follow when cutting. In single-color textured patterns, the steek can be worked in either plain stockinette or a different knit-purl pattern. A vertical pattern, like ribbing, works nicely, but its horizontal elasticity will make the steek shrink to half its width, which can make finishing challenging unless you make the steek much wider. Instead, you can indicate the first, last, and center steek stitches by purling them, while knitting the rest of the steek. If you choose to use a textured pattern across the steek, remember that steeks are best worked firmly, so avoid patterns, like Seed Stitch, that tend to be looser than stockinette.

You could delineate the steek stitches using markers, but I find that my knitting tends to be just a little looser wherever there is a marker on the needle between stitches. You don't want any looseness at the edges of the steek, because that's where you'll be picking up borders to finish your garment, so avoid placing markers on your needles at these points if you suspect the markers might affect your tension. If you find yourself getting confused, you could instead place a split marker or safety pin in the fabric just below the needle to help identify the steek. You might even want to "color code" the markers, using the same color before and after the first steek, a second color before and after the second steek, and so on.

When working stranded color patterns, it's not necessary to cut the unused yarns. If they reappear soon in the pattern, you can just leave them attached and carry the yarn up to the next round where it's needed. If you're using lots of balls of yarn and you leave them all attached, they will get tangled, so cutting at color changes may be less annoying. If you do cut the yarns between rounds, don't bother to leave a long tail, because you'll be cutting it, not weaving it in later. If looseness in the steek at the color changes bothers you, just knot the yarns together, leaving short ends, or let a tail hang down just long enough that it won't unravel. Remember that it doesn't matter how the ends look — they'll all be trimmed off when the steek is finished — so do whatever is easiest and uses the least amount of yarn.

## Shaping around the Steeks

Shaping of the neck and armhole openings is worked in the fabric of the garment, while you maintain the same number of steek stitches throughout. As described in Planning for Increases and Decreases (chapter 2,

**Original Neckline**

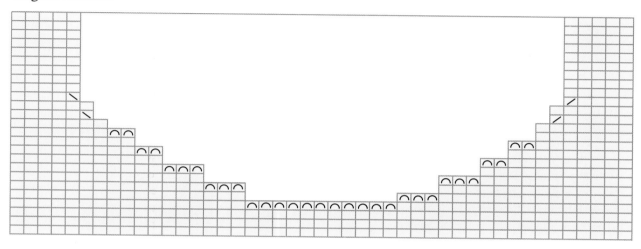

**Redesigned Neckline**

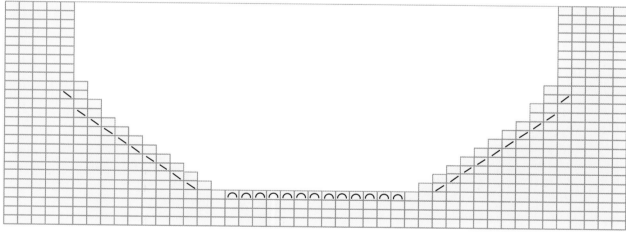

A series of bind offs was used to shape the curve of the original neckline (above). The redesigned neckline is an almost identical curve, but it is worked beginning with decreases on every round, followed by decreases every other round.

| KEY | | |
|---|---|---|
| | ☐ | knit |
| | ╱ | knit 2 together |
| | ╲ | slip, slip, knit 2 together |
| | ⌒ | bind off |

page 59), you'll probably want to work your shaping at least 1 stitch away from the steek, and you'll want the left and right halves of the garment to mirror each other, so you'll need to choose increases and decreases that look symmetrical. When working stranded knitting, using the ssk decrease before a steek and the K2tog decrease after a steek will keep the color pattern intact all the away to the edge of the knitting when it's completed. Placing these decreases in the opposing positions (K2tog before a steek and ssk after a steek) places angled stitches along the finished edge and may interrupt the color pattern, placing the wrong color on top in the decreased stitches. On the other hand, the angled stitches paralleling the steek can make it easier to pick up stitches and sew seams consistently along a steek.

If there is no armhole shaping, then the steek and the garment on both sides are just worked straight, in whatever patterns you've chosen.

V-necks and shaped armholes usually have a series of regularly spaced single decreases (or increases if you're working top to bottom), which must be worked in the garment stitches adjacent to the steek.

Round-neck openings are sometimes designed with more complicated curves and call for a series of bind offs. Working more than one set of bound-off stitches along an edge doesn't integrate well with a steek (because you'll need to bind off and cast on again for the steek each time). It's best to redesign your neck opening so that there is no more than one decrease at the neck edge on each round after the initial bind off at the center front. See the charts on page 95 for an example.

## Binding Off the Steeks

When you get to the top of the opening, work around one last time, binding off just the steek stitches. If two colors are in use, alternate the two across the bind off. Once you have bound off the neck and armhole steeks, you can join the shoulders using three-needle bind off (see appendix, page 261), or bind off the shoulders and then sew them together.

## Finishing the Steeks

After you've bound off the steeks, prepare them to ensure that they don't unravel. You can then cut them, add borders, and finish the cut edges. This is explained in detail in Cutting Your Knitting (chapter 6, page 186).

# Converting Circular Garment Instructions to Flat

There may be times when you want to modify instructions for a circular garment so that you can knit it flat instead. This could be because you want the support of seams, because you want to use intarsia or a pattern stitch that is more easily worked flat, or because you don't have access to the required circular or double-pointed needles. To accomplish this, you'll need to reverse the process described for converting flat to circular (page 74).

① **Review the instructions.** First read through the original pattern and make sure you understand it completely, including all shaping and finishing.

② **Convert the pattern stitches.** If some sections of the original garment are worked flat, you may already have both flat and circular instructions for the pattern stitch. If not, then convert the pattern stitch to flat knitting. Evaluate the pattern to decide whether it will be easier to work the even-numbered rounds or the odd-numbered rounds on the wrong side of the fabric. If plain knit rounds alternate with more complicated pattern rounds, then just change all the knit rounds to purl rows and work them on the wrong side. Once you've decided which will be wrong-side rows, rewrite them, reversing knits and purls and reversing the order of the row, because you work in the opposite direction on wrong-side rows. See Case Study #3-4 (page 82) to compare the circular and flat versions of pattern stitches. Make a flat swatch to test the new instructions as well as to check the gauge. If the pattern stitch looks bad or is difficult to work at the beginning or end of the row, you may need to add edge stitches to center the pattern on the fabric or to provide a smooth edge for sewing seams and picking up borders. Add 1 stitch at each edge to form a selvedge. Because these stitches will disappear into the seams, if you don't add selvedge stitches, the finished garment will be smaller than originally designed.

③ **Make a circular schematic.** If the pattern doesn't provide complete labeled schematics, create your own, including stitch counts, lengths, and notes on shaping for all the garment sections. Indicate the beginning of round for each section as well. While you can skip this step, I find that diagramming the garment helps prevent a good deal of confusion and mistakes as I work out stitch counts for the flat instructions and schematics. For an example of a circular schematic with notations, see Case Study #3-5 (page 84).

4) **Locate the seams.** Decide where each garment piece will begin and end. Usually the beginning of the round in the original garment will be at one of the side seams, and you can divide the body in half starting there. On sleeves, the beginning of round is normally where the sleeve seam should be placed, and runs from the inside of the cuff up to the center of the underarm.

5) **Determine the order of construction.** Flat sweaters can be constructed in several ways. Review Order of Construction in chapter 2 (page 38) and choose the method that best matches what you plan to make. Decide whether the sleeves will be worked separately or picked up and knit down. Remember that if the sleeves are knit in the opposite direction from the body, the pattern stitches may look noticeably different in the two sections of the garment. Also keep in mind that working the garment in the same direction as the original will make it easier to rewrite the instructions; however, if you want to reverse the direction of knitting, you may.

6) **Plan the finishing details.** Consider how you will shape and join the shoulders, whether you will sew all the seams or whether some pieces will be picked up and knitted onto others, and whether the borders will be knit as part of the garment pieces or picked up and added later. See Planning Ahead for Perfect Finishing in chapter 2 (page 50) for finishing options.

7) **Make flat schematics.** Sketch a simple schematic for each piece of your garment, including lengths, stitch counts, row counts, and direction of knitting. See Case Studies #3-1 (page 76) and #3-2 (page 78) for examples.

8) **Rewrite the garment instructions.** Convert the instructions from rounds to rows. Review Case Study #3-5 (page 84). Your original instructions will be similar to the circular instructions in the right column. Your revised instructions will look more like the flat instructions in the left column.

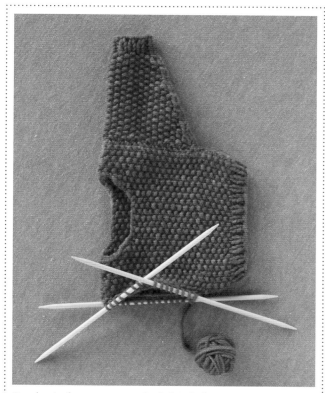

Seed stitch sweater **worked circularly**

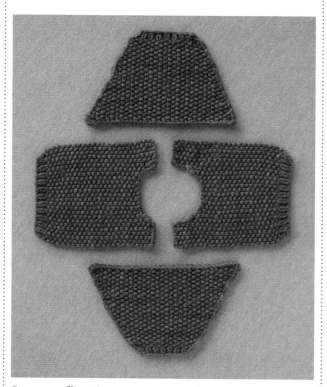

Separate flat pieces **to construct the same sweater**

## chapter four

*Forethought:*

# Shaping and Fitting

S HAPING YOUR GARMENT IS important on two levels. On the stitch level, you need to control how increases and decreases interact with any pattern stitches, as well as their impact on the edges of the garment pieces. Looking at the big picture, you also need to shape your garment so that it fits. In chapter 2, we discussed placement of increases and decreases, how they affect the edge of your knitting, and why this matters. In this chapter, we'll focus first on the technical issues of shaping at the same time as working pattern stitches, then move on to how you can make adjustments to the fit and style of your garment by changing the length or width; adding darts, pleats, or gathers; and modifying the sleeve and armhole styling, the neckline, and shoulder shaping.

# Shaping Your Knitting

Although some shaping is accomplished by casting on and binding off, for the most part shaping your knitting requires the use of increases, decreases, or short rows. How you handle the shaping will have major impacts on how the knitting looks and will influence how neatly and efficiently you can complete seaming and add borders to your garment. I discussed placement and slant of increases and decreases in chapter 2. In this chapter, we'll explore how best to integrate shaping in a variety of pattern stitches and situations.

Working "in pattern as established" while shaping the garment at the same time can be a challenge. This is one of the reasons that many patterns are written to begin at the bottom edge and work straight in pattern up to the underarm — it gives you a chance to learn the pattern stitch before adding the complication of shaping. When you begin a garment at the neck and work down, you must start the shaping immediately after completing the neck border, along with the added difficulty of placing the pattern stitch on each shoulder so that it will be centered and seamless at the center front and back, and when you reach the underarm, the pattern will be continuous where the body meets at the side seam. Unless you are already very comfortable with the pattern stitch, all this can be daunting. The best solution is to chart the shape of each piece and the pattern stitch, increases, and decreases within that shape.

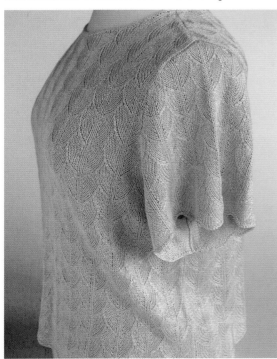

**Integrating the pattern stitch** with the shaping makes for perfect finishing.

You have many choices of *how* to work both increases and decreases, which are investigated in detail in the case studies that follow.

▷ **Single decreases** include K2tog, P2tog, ssk, and ssp. Which you use depends on the effect you want. K2tog and P2tog slant to the right, while ssk and ssp slant to the left. Choose between the knit and purl versions depending on whether you are working on the right or the wrong side of the fabric, and whether you want a smooth knit stitch or a bumpy purl to show on the right side of the garment. Knitters sometimes substitute K2tog-tbl for ssk and P2tog-tbl for ssp. These decreases result in a left-slanting decrease, but they twist the stitches. This drives some perfectionist knitters (like myself) crazy, but it is perfectly acceptable if it's not noticeable. The twisted stitches are usually invisible in dark or textured yarns.

▷ **Double decreases** include even more numerous choices, but I limit this discussion to K3tog, P3tog, sk2p, and s2kp2. The first two slant to the right, sk2p slants to the left, and s2kp2 is centered. Sssk or sssp (worked the same as ssk and ssp, but with 3 slipped stitches) may also be used if you need left-slanting double decreases. Again, choose among these based on how you want the decrease to look and which side of the fabric is facing you. Purled double decreases are seldom worked — usually P3tog is used — but it's possible with some slipping back and forth to work a purled version of the s2kp2. You may see P3tog-tbl specified in pattern stitch instructions to serve as the purl-side equivalent of sk2p, even though it results in twisted stitches and can be difficult to work. For better results, you can substitute sssp for P3tog-tbl. See the appendix (page 271) for how to work the various double decreases.

▷ **Single increases** include M1 (which can be executed in numerous ways), Kfb, lifted increase, and yarnover (yo). There are methods of working all of these so that they look symmetrical on opposite edges of the knitting.

▷ **Double increases** can be accomplished by working a pair of single increases, in addition to the true double increases, which include the double yarnover and K-yo-K or K-P-K into a single stitch.

In the case studies that follow, rather than referring repeatedly to "increases and/or decreases" I just say "shaping" to indicate either.

## Shaping a Garment at the Edge

Let's say you need to decrease at the edge of a garment, which frequently happens at the underarm and at the neck. You begin by binding off some stitches, and then you decrease 1 stitch every other row to make a slanted edge. The result, when the knitting stretches, is a curve. The challenge is to make sure that, as you remove stitches at the beginning of the row, you work the pattern stitch so that it lines up with the rows you've already completed. You also need to make sure that the opposite sides of the garment mirror each other; if they are obviously asymmetrical, it can be ugly. Two things that may help you stay oriented are charting out the pattern stitch with the decreases and marking the repeats of the pattern in the area where decreases will occur. Case Studies #4-1 through #4-5 include a variety of situations, such as ribbing, a textured pattern, lace, and cables that illustrate some of the challenges you may face when shaping at the edge.

## Shaping a Garment in the Center

There will be times when you need to increase or decrease in the center of the fabric, to make a circular yoke or round collar, or to work mitered corners for a raglan sleeve or a square collar.

Mitered corners are worked just like shaping at the edges of the knitting, but with a pair of decreases for each corner. Depending on whether you are increasing or decreasing, what kind of increase/decrease you are using, and what looks best to you, you may want to place one or more stitches between the decreases or increases at the center of the miter. Case Studies #4-6 to #4-8 explore center shaping.

## Quick Reference for Abbreviations

| | |
|---|---|
| K2tog | Knit 2 together |
| K2tog-tbl | Knit 2 together through back loops |
| K3tog | Knit 3 together |
| Kfb | Knit-front-back |
| M1 | Make 1 |
| P2tog | Purl 2 together |
| P2tog-tbl | Purl 2 together through back loops |
| P3tog | Purl 3 together |
| P3tog-tbl | Purl 3 together through back loops |
| ssk | Slip, slip, K2tog |
| ssp | Slip, slip, P2tog |
| sk2p | Slip 1, knit 2 together, pass slipped stitch over |
| s2kp2 | Slip 2 together knitwise, knit 1, pass 2 slipped stitches over |
| sssk | Slip, slip, slip, knit 3 together |
| sssp | Slip, slip, slip, purl 3 together |
| yo | yarnover |

## Quick Reference to Chart Keys

| | |
|---|---|
| ☐ | knit on RS, purl on WS |
| ⊟ | purl on RS, knit on WS |
| ◉ | yarnover |
| ⌢ | bind off |
| ╱ | K2tog on RS, P2tog on WS |
| ╲ | ssk on RS, ssp on WS |
| 🆈 | right-slanting increase |
| 🆈 | left-slanting increase |
| 🆇 | cast on |
| 🆇 | left-slanting double decrease |
| ✗ | delete symbol |

*See How to Read Charts, chapter 5, page 147.*

*Note: These abbreviations and symbols are used in Case Studies #4-1 to #4-5 that follow.*

# Shaping in a Textured Pattern (Diamond Brocade)

The purled stitches in Diamond Brocade don't line up with the previous row; they are always offset 1 stitch to the left or to the right. You can use your knitting as a guide, but there is always the danger that you will accidentally shift the purled stitches in the wrong direction, so "read" your knitting carefully as you work, or make a chart of the pattern stitch and include the bind offs and decreases as shown in blue on the chart below to help yourself stay oriented.

Cast on a multiple of 8 stitches plus 1.

**Swatch to test bottom-up shaping**

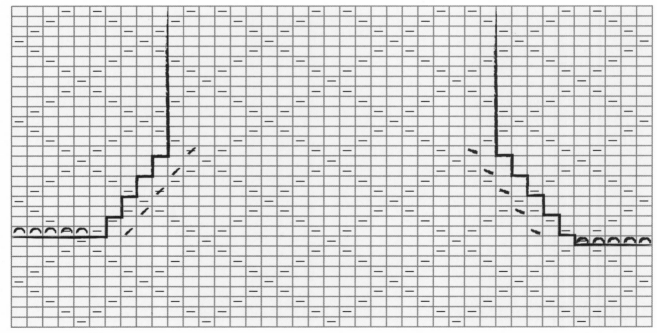

**Bottom-up pattern stitch chart** with bind offs and decreases marked

Row 1 (right side): K4, *P1, K7; repeat from * until 5 stitches remain, P1, K4.

Row 2: P3, *K1, P1, K1, P5; repeat from * ending last repeat P3 instead of P5.

Row 3: K2, *P1, K3; repeat from *, ending last repeat K2 instead of K3.

Row 4: P1, *K1, P5, K1, P1; repeat from *.

Row 5: *P1, K7; repeat from *, ending P1.

Row 6: Repeat row 4.

Row 7: Repeat row 3.

Row 8: Repeat row 2.

Repeat rows 1–8 for pattern.

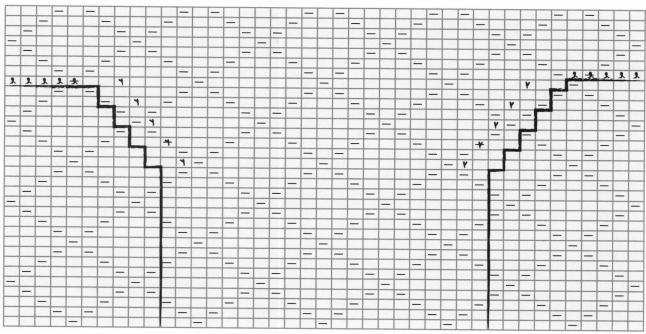

**Top-down pattern stitch chart** with cast ons and increases marked

**Swatch to test top-down shaping**

**KEY**

| | |
|---|---|
| ☐ | knit on right side, purl on wrong side |
| — | purl on right side, knit on wrong side |
| Y | right-slanting increase |
| Y | left-slanting increase |
| 오 | cast on |
| ╱ | knit 2 together |
| ╲ | slip, slip, knit |
| ◠ | bind off |

# Shaping in a Lace Pattern (Razor Shell)

Lace patterns are worked by making yarnovers to form the eyelets and then decreasing to bring the resulting stitches back to the original number. The decreases may happen on the same row as the increases, or on later rows. Razor Shell is a good first example, because the increases and decreases occur on the same row, making it easier to analyze how to maintain the pattern while decreasing. Notice that the increases are worked as 2 separate yarnovers on either side of a knitted stitch. The decreases are worked by slipping a stitch, knitting 2 together, then passing the slipped stitch over (sk2p), which is a double decrease. The challenge is that whenever one of the yarnovers disappears at the beginning or end of the row, you must work a single decrease (K2tog or ssk) instead of the original double decrease so that you don't end up with too few stitches. To make the pattern look consistent, choose between K2tog or ssk based on the direction that it leans, so that it

matches the original pattern stitch. In this case, the double decrease leans to the left, so it's best to use the ssk as your single decrease because it also leans to the left. On the other hand, you may want to use a K2tog when the armhole shaping intersects with the pattern stitch's shaping along the left edge, so that the line of decreases along the edge is continuous.

As with textured stitches, it can be easier to cope with the changing number of stitches if you plot out the decreases and the pattern in a chart and if you place markers in your knitting to indicate the beginning of each pattern repeat in the area where you're decreasing.

Cast on a multiple of 6 stitches plus 1.

Row 1 (wrong side): Purl.

Row 2: K1, *yo, K1, sk2p, K1, yo, K1; repeat from *.

Repeat rows 1 and 2 for pattern.

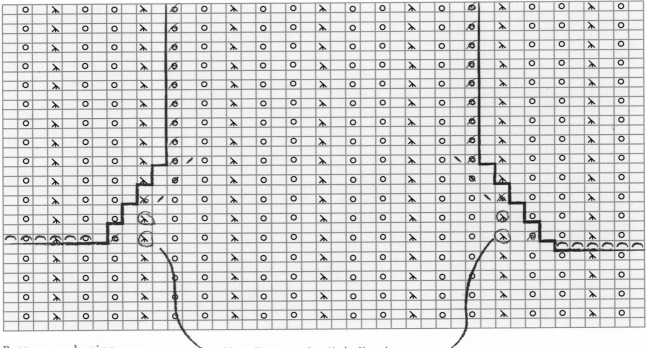

**Bottom-up shaping in lace pattern**

— *Keep this ⋏ — it will do the shaping.* —

**Bottom-up:** testing shaping from the chart

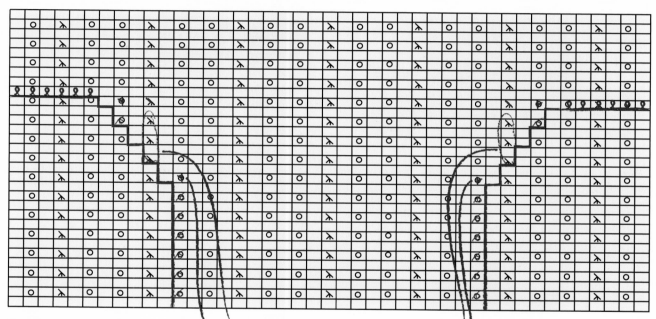

**Top-down** shaping in lace pattern

*Delete ⋏— YO will do the shaping*

*Closed increase instead of YO*

**Top-down:** testing shaping from the chart

**KEY**

| | |
|---|---|
| ☐ | knit on right side, purl on wrong side |
| ─ | purl on right side, knit on wrong side |
| ╱ | knit 2 together |
| ╲ | slip, slip, knit |
| ⋏ | slip one, knit 2 together, psso |
| Y | left-slanting increase |
| ⅄ | right-slanting increase |
| O | yarnover |
| ℒ | cast on |
| ⬦ | delete yarn over or decrease |

# Shaping in Ribbing

Working increases or decreases while maintaining a simple ribbed pattern is easy because once the pattern is established, it can be seen clearly, and it's obvious how to continue in pattern: when you see a knit stitch, knit it; when you see a purl stitch, purl it.

**Bottom-Up Decreases in K2, P2 ribbing.** This example was worked exactly like the K1, P1 version at left, but with the decreases 2 stitches away from the edge, so that there appear to be 3 knit stitches at each edge. When the border is picked up, 2 knit stitches remain, integrating perfectly with the K2, P2 pattern. Just like K1, P1 ribbing, K2, P2 ribbing can be shaped by increasing, taking care to place the increases so that there are 3 distinct knitted stitches at each edge. One of these will disappear into the seam or behind the border, leaving 2 knit stitches to form a full rib.

**Bottom-Up Decreases in K1, P1 ribbing.** This example, with shaping like small armholes at both sides, was worked with the decreases 1 stitch away from the edge, using an ssk at the beginning of the row and K2tog at the end of the row. The result appears to be 2 knit stitches at the edge (see left edge). When the borders are picked up, 1 knit stitch remains, which integrates perfectly with the ribbed pattern (right edge).

**Top-Down Increases in K1, P1 ribbing.** This example was worked from the top down, increasing to make the same shape as the swatch shown above. The increases (M1s, twisted in opposite directions on the two sides) are worked 2 stitches away from the edge (see left edge). When the border is picked up, 1 knit stitch remains, which integrates perfectly with the ribbed pattern (right edge).

# Shaping in a Lace Pattern (Fan Shell)

Fan Shell can be difficult to maintain in pattern while shaping is worked, because two decreases are worked on rows 3, 4, and 5, but the six increases that replace these stitches occur suddenly on row 6. The key to maintaining the pattern stitch is to understand how many stitches per repeat there should be when you complete each row, and to adjust the increases and decreases to match this at the beginning and end of every row, allowing for narrower panels of the pattern at the edges. As soon as the shaping starts, you may also simply maintain the narrower sections at the edges in plain stockinette. Or you can work the areas where shaping will happen in stockinette from the very beginning, keeping the more complicated pattern stitch in a panel at the center of the garment.

Charting, in a case like this, may not clarify things for you. With the varying number of stitches on each row, there will be a lot of "no stitch" squares in the chart that may make it even more confusing. An easy solution is to do the best you can with the work on your needles, to decrease or increase and maintain the

pattern. Then, the next time you work row 1, make sure you have the correct number of stitches in the repeats at the edge. If you don't, increase or decrease a stitch unobtrusively near the edge to correct the problem.

Cast on a multiple of 15 stitches plus 4.

Row 1 (wrong side): P4, *K11, P4; repeat from *. (15 stitches per repeat)

Row 2: K4, *P11, K4; repeat from*. (15 stitches per repeat)

Row 3: P2, *P2tog, P11, ssp; repeat from * until 2 stitches remain, P2. (13 stitches per repeat)

Row 4: K2, *ssk, K9, K2tog; repeat from *, until 2 stitches remain, K2. (11 stitches per repeat)

Row 5: P2, *P2tog, P7, ssp; repeat from * until 2 stitches remain, P2. (9 stitches per repeat)

Row 6: K4, *[yo, K1] five times, yo, K4; repeat from *. (15 stitches per repeat)

Repeat rows 1–6 for pattern.

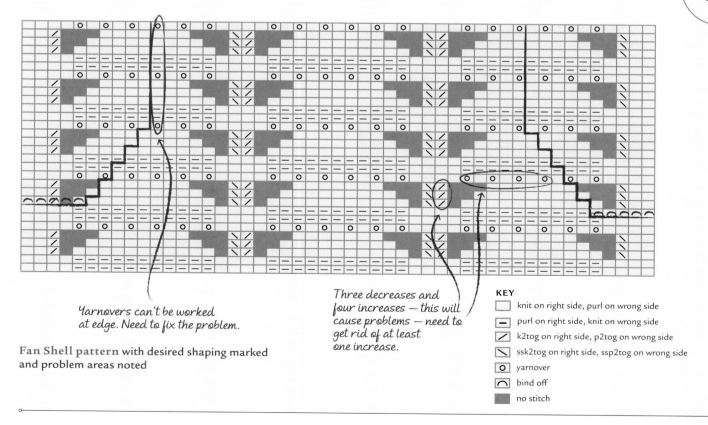

Yarnovers can't be worked at edge. Need to fix the problem.

Three decreases and four increases — this will cause problems — need to get rid of at least one increase.

**Fan Shell pattern** with desired shaping marked and problem areas noted

**KEY**

| | |
|---|---|
| ☐ | knit on right side, purl on wrong side |
| ▬ | purl on right side, knit on wrong side |
| ╱ | k2tog on right side, p2tog on wrong side |
| ╲ | ssk2tog on right side, ssp2tog on wrong side |
| ⊙ | yarnover |
| ⌒ | bind off |
| ▨ | no stitch |

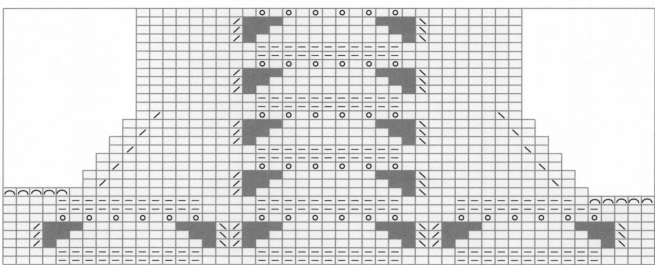

**Fan Shell showing shaping revisions** from original chart and eliminating partial repeats of the pattern on both sides

**KEY**

| | |
|---|---|
| ☐ | knit on right side, purl on wrong side |
| − | purl on right side, knit on wrong side |
| ╱ | knit 2 together on right side, purl 2 together on wrong side |
| ╲ | slip, slip, knit 2 together on right side; slip, slip, purl 2 together on wrong side |
| ○ | yarnover |
| ⌒ | bind off |
| ▉ | no stitch |

**Swatch to test shaping from chart.** Plain stockinette at both sides of the shaped area, which looks awkward, although it might look fine in a full-size garment

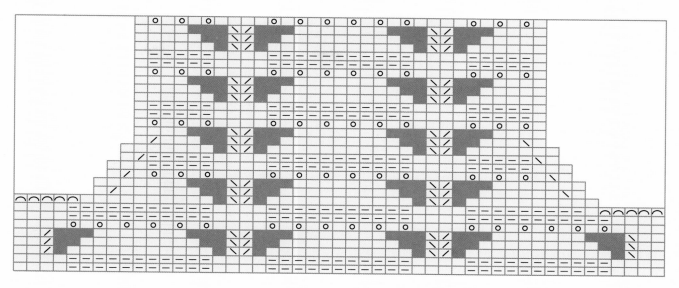

Fan Shell with shaping revisions and incorporating half a pattern repeat on both sides

Swatch to test the half repeats of Fan Shell at both sides of shaped area carrying the pattern out to the edge of the fabric

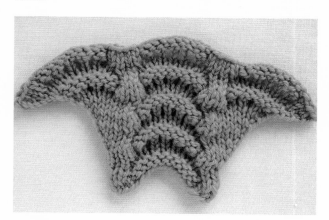

Increasing in Fan Shell

## Increasing in Fan Shell

It's rare that you'd work a sweater in Fan Shell from the top down, because the scalloped cast-on edge makes such a nice embellishment at the bottom of a sweater (the bound-off edge usually doesn't have as deep a scallop). In the swatch shown, the upper edge scallops because it is not constrained by the bind off, and the upside-down armhole-like shaping at either side allows the whole top of the swatch to flare. There are other cases, however, where you'd need to increase in this pattern, for example to taper a sleeve from bottom to top. Just reverse the process described above. While increasing, work the extra stitches in stockinette until you have at least enough to work half of the pattern repeat, then begin working the additional stitches in pattern. When you have enough for a full repeat, work the full repeat.

# Shaping in a Cabled Pattern

Stitches with manipulations that all go in one direction, like cables, can present difficulties when trying to achieve symmetry between the two edges of the garment. One edge may look fine, while the other looks awkward. When the decreases cut off part of a cable, you can end up with wide plain areas that look unplanned. There are several ways to improve the appearance of cables interrupted by shaping:

▷ Reverse the twist of the cables on the left half of the garment so they are symmetrical with the right half.

▷ When only some of the cable stitches remain, work narrower cables on the remaining stitches, crossing them more frequently if this improves their proportions.

▷ Make the cables look more symmetrical by working the stitch manipulation on part of the stitches rather than on the full number called for in the instructions.

**Decreases in cable pattern** with stockinette filler stitches at edges

**Decreases in cable pattern,** with narrower cables at edges. It can help to work narrower cables on the remaining stitches. In this case, it might have looked even better to cross the 2-stitch cables at both edges every 4th row instead of every 8th row. In this swatch the edge stitches were maintained in reverse stockinette, but they could also be worked in stockinette for a more finished transition to the border.

# Mitered Decreases to Make Corners

Mitered corners can be worked using either a double decrease (one that turns 3 stitches into 1 stitch) at each corner or two single decreases at each corner. When two single decreases are used, it's important to make them symmetrical, for example, pairing each K2tog with an ssk.

**Symmetrical decreases with 1 stitch between.** In the corner on the right, the K2tog is followed by the ssk. In the corner on the left, the two are reversed.

**Asymmetrical decreases.** If you use the same decrease on both sides of a corner, it will look unbalanced. This swatch shows two corners: the one on the right is made with two K2tog decreases, the one on the left with two ssks.

**For a more decorative effect,** you can put a small design element between the two decreases at the corner. Here, a cable highlights the corner. On the right, the K2tog precedes the corner with the ssk following it, making two columns of stitches that clearly parallel the cable. At the left, the two are reversed for a more subtle effect.

**Symmetrical decreases with no stitches between.** To make the corners look balanced, each was formed by a K2tog and an ssk. In the corner on the right, the K2tog is followed by the ssk, creating two parallel columns of stitches that clearly define the corner. In the corner on the left, the two are reversed, making the grain of the knitted columns appear to meet at the corner itself.

**Double decreases can appear either centered or leaning,** depending on which one you use. The s2kp2 in the middle is a centered decrease, slightly more difficult to work than the left-leaning sk2p at right or the right-leaning K3tog at left.

# Mitered Increases to Make Corners

Like decreases, mitered increases can be worked as a pair of single increases on either side of the corner or as a double increase in the corner stitch.

Kfb increases must be worked so that the tiny bumps are arranged symmetrically around the corner. So that the corner stitch falls between the two bumps, work a Kfb increase in the stitch before the corner stitch and one in the corner stitch itself (right). If you like, you can place more stitches between them (left).

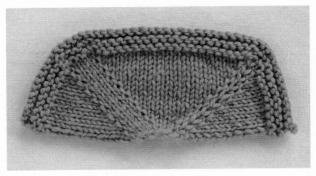

M1 increases worked on either side of corner stitches should be twisted in opposite directions to make them symmetrical. At left, there are 3 stitches between the increases, at right, only 1 stitch.

With yarnovers, there's no need to worry about symmetry. Just place one or more corner stitches between them.

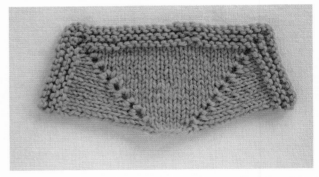

The double increase K-P-K into a stitch (left) is slightly bumpier because of the extra wraps for the purl, but still very similar to K-yo-K into a stitch (right).

# Circular Shaping in Pattern Stitches

Shaping curved structures, like a collar or a sweater yoke, while working in pattern can be challenging because you must fully integrate the pattern stitch with the decreases. This means that as the knitting gets wider, you must either add more pattern repeats or each pattern repeat must get wider. The examples below illustrate ways of doing this when working in ribbing, cables, and a lace pattern.

To make a flat circle, you need to decrease or increase 8 stitches every other round in garter stitch, 9 stitches every other round in stockinette, less than this in ribbing (because it is tall in proportion to its width), and more than this in lace because open patterns tend to be wider in proportion to their height. To calculate the shaping of a curve in any pattern stitch, see the instructions for Creating a Curved Border (chapter 8, page 225). Because knitting stretches, deforms, and can be blocked more easily the more loosely it's knit, working loosely will make it easier to get good results.

Integrating decreases to make a circle for the yoke or collar of a sweater when working in ribbing requires that you reduce the number of stitches in each repeat of the ribbing. In this example, the swatch begins at the outer edge with K3, P3 ribbing. The first set of decreases reduces the purled stitches by one, so it becomes K3, P2 ribbing. Maintaining the 3 knit stitches makes the first set of decreases unnoticeable; you can see that the purled ribs are narrower, but

you can't tell how it was done. The second round of decreases reduces the purled stitches again, so it is now K3, P1 ribbing. The third set of decreases removes the final purled stitch, so it is no longer ribbing, just plain stockinette at the center.

Another approach to the same shaping in K3, P3 ribbing is to alternately reduce the number of purl stitches and the number of knit stitches, so that the ribbing gets narrower as you approach the center. Just like the previous example, the swatch begins at the outer edge with K3, P3 ribbing and the first set of decreases reduces the purled stitches in each repeat by one. The second round of decreases reduces the knitted stitches in each repeat, so it becomes K2, P2 ribbing. The decreases could have continued in this manner to the center, decreasing another purl stitch to make K2, P1 ribbing, then a knit stitch, making it K1, P1 ribbing. A final set of decreases would make the last purl stitch disappear, turning it into plain stockinette at the very center.

**Circular swatch in K3, P3 ribbing,** making both knit and purl ribs gradually narrower

To work ribbing while increasing, you can reverse the progression of decreases described in the previous two examples. In the example on the following page, K-yo-K was first worked in the center of the purled ribs to create new knit ribs, then in the resulting 1-stitch purled ribs to bring them back to 3 stitches each. This increase is characterized by a small eyelet (which

**Circular swatch in K3, P3 ribbing,** getting rid of all the purl stitches

makes the increases easy to see in this photograph), but the effect will be different depending on what increase you choose to use.

**Increasing in K3, P3 ribbing** by adding new ribs

Round collars or sweater yokes are worked from the top down along these same lines by leaving a hole at the center for the neck opening. The example below began in stockinette, with purled ribs created by Kfb and Pfb increases, which are practically invisible.

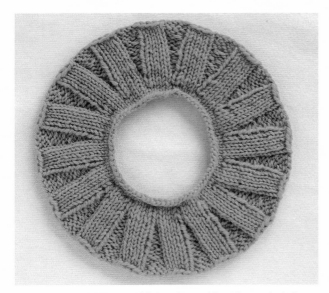

**Increasing in K4,P4 ribbing** by making the purled ribs gradually wider

When working a cabled pattern, the same approaches can be used as for plain ribs. Either get rid of all the purled stitches first, then the knit stitches that make up the cables, or gradually reduce both the purled stitches and the cable stitches. In both cases, you can still cross the cables to continue the pattern stitch for as long as possible. The swatch below began at the bottom with 6-stitch cables separated by 2 purls. After a few rows, decreases were worked to reduce the purled stitches to just 1 between each cable, and then the cables themselves were gradually made more narrow, until the swatch ends at the top with K1, P1 ribbing.

**Decreasing by making both the purls** and the cables narrower

Working cables while increasing reverses the process. You can effectively hide the increases in the knit stitches by making them at the center of the cable, because they are obscured each time the cable is crossed.

**Increasing by making both the purls** and the cables wider

114

This example was worked by beginning with a 12-stitch pattern repeat, then decreasing 2 stitches in each repeat until only 4 stitches remain in each repeat.

Lace pattern where size of each repeat is reduced

The fan shape of the swatch below was achieved by increasing to add pattern repeats. It begins with five repeats of 6 stitches each. K-yo-K and yarnovers are used to add stitches at the knit rib that falls between the 2 yarnovers in each pattern repeat. Until there are enough stitches to form a new rib, the new stitches are worked in stockinette. Once enough stitches have accumulated, the pattern stitch is worked continuously across the whole piece. This achieves a foliated effect, rather than the crisp angularity of the same pattern stitch in the previous example.

The same lace pattern, adding whole repeats to make it wider

# Fitting Your Garment

Fitting your garment means analyzing it, section by section, to determine whether it will actually fit *you*, and making adjustments so that it will. Garments that really fit are more comfortable to wear and look better. You may also want to change the shape for aesthetic reasons — you just want a slightly different style. Keep in mind, however, that changing the shape of the garment may affect the way it drapes and will change its proportions, so it may not end up looking or behaving the way it was originally conceived by the designer.

The changes you may want to make are covered in detail in this chapter, working from the bottom to the top of a sweater, which is the order in which you'll most likely encounter them. (If you're working top down, of course you'll encounter them in the opposite order.) The material below assumes that you followed the advice in chapter 2 on selecting the size that fits you in the shoulder and neck area. This being so, you shouldn't need to adjust the shoulder width, but just in case, I've included that, too.

I've found two very helpful tools in fitting garments. One is a pad of large sheets of 1-inch grid paper used for flip charts, which is very handy for charting out complex areas like armholes, sleeve caps, and necklines at full size. You can find pads of this paper at office supply stores. The second is knitter's graph paper. You can use standard graph paper with square cells for working out row-by-row shaping for curves and diagonals like darts, armholes, shoulders, and neck openings, but knitter's graph paper will give you a better feel for the actual proportions of the shaping because the width and height of each rectangle are in the same proportion as the shape of your actual stitches. An Internet search for "knitter's graph paper" will come up with many options for creating it using a spreadsheet program (such as Excel) or downloading files you can print yourself. For the highest level of accuracy, match the proportions of the rectangles to the stitches and rows in the gauge for your project. It's not necessary to print knitter's graph paper at full size, unless you want to.

## Changing Body Shaping

To determine the actual measurements of the sweater you plan to make, see chapter 1, and then decide whether the measurement of the body below the underarms needs to be adjusted.

## Making the Body Wider

Assuming that you've selected the size where the shoulder area fits, but you need the body below the underarm to be larger, there are several approaches you can take. If the hip area is the widest dimension, then you can taper gradually (see illustration, page 117) along the side seams or with vertical darts from the hip to the narrower area at the armhole (see illustrations, pages 118–19). If the bust area is larger than the hips, you can create a gradual taper from the narrower

**Decreasing Methods for Yoke**

*The additional width* in the body of this sweater front was decreased across 1 row at the bottom of the garter stitch yoke, resulting in soft gathers.

*The same shaping* as in the example above was accomplished by using a slipped-stitch pattern for the yoke that is narrower in gauge. This assumes that the slipped-stitch pattern matches the stitch and row gauge of your original pattern instructions so that you don't need to redesign the shaping of the armholes, shoulder, or neckline.

hip circumference to the larger bust circumference, then quickly reduce to the correct number of stitches at the underarm, either by tapering at the side seams or by working decreases across the entire front to form a gather with a narrower yoke above. Depending on the required measurements of the back versus the front, both halves of the garment may be the same, or they may be different widths depending on where the alteration is needed.

In knitting you have the flexibility of decreasing to make the gathers, or of working a different pattern stitch that pulls in the fabric horizontally. To gather by decreasing, just decide how many stitches you need after decreasing, and decrease that number of stitches spaced evenly across the row. To use a pattern stitch, you'll need to test out the difference in width between the two patterns in swatches. Some adjustment to the number of stitches may be necessary immediately before beginning the new pattern, to make it come out the correct width and to have the correct multiple of stitches to work the pattern stitch.

## Making the Body Narrower

Again assuming that you're making the size where the shoulder area fits, if the body needs to be narrower, you can reduce the number of stitches below the underarms by planning a gradual taper from the larger number of stitches at the underarm to the smaller number of stitches at the waist. The shaping can be worked at the side seams (opposite, top), with vertical darts (pages 118–19), or both. Be sure to allow enough ease in the bust or chest so that the garment fits comfortably, and begin making the body smaller below the widest point in the body you're fitting.

## Tapering the Body

To make a body that tapers from the underarm or bust-line to the waist, you need to know three things:

▷ Width or circumference at the widest point (most likely the bust or chest) in stitches

▷ Width or circumference at the narrowest point (most likely the waist or bottom edge) in stitches

▷ Distance between the two measurements (the bust-to-waist length) in rows.

Subtract the number of stitches at the narrowest point from the number of stitches at the widest point to find the difference between the two. In most cases you'll be shaping along the side seams (or, if you're working circularly, where the side seams would fall), so assume

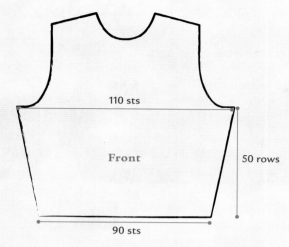

110 sts

Front

50 rows

90 sts

**Tapering the body gradually** from underarm to waist

place over 46 rows, leaving 4 rows to work even at the end.

▷ Assuming you are working from the bottom up, work the shaping every 6th row four times, and then work the shaping every 4th row six times. For top-down construction, reverse this, working the shaping every 4th row, followed by every 6th row. The shaping will take place over 48 rows. Instead of a straight taper, it will start more gradually at the waist and then become more pronounced as it nears the bust.

▷ If you are working circularly, there are no wrong-side rows to be navigated, so you can just alternate working the shaping every 4th round and every 5th round, for a total of 45 rounds.

The frequency of shaping rounds rarely comes out to be a whole number, so you need to plan your shaping to spread it out more or less evenly over the rows available, as demonstrated in these examples. It's best not to place a shaping row right at the underarm, so plan the placement of the shaping to leave a few rows or rounds plain between the underarm and the highest shaping row.

## Creating a Trapeze or Swing Shape

Shaping a garment that gets wider from the bustline or underarm to the bottom edge is done exactly like tapering the body. You need to know the number of stitches in the widest measurement and the narrowest measurement, and the number of rows between them.

Work out a plan for shaping just as in Tapering the Body (opposite).

that you'll be working half of your shaping at each side seam and divide the number of stitches by two (when working flat) or four (when working circularly) to give you the number of shaping rows. Then divide the total number of rows by the number of shaping rows plus one. This will tell you how often to work increases (if working from the bottom up) or decreases (if working from the top down).

For example, the schematic (above) shows a width of 110 stitches at the bust and 90 stitches at the waist. The difference between these two is 20 stitches. Divide 20 stitches by two (assuming you will be shaping at both sides of the garment piece) to get 10 shaping rows. The distance between the waist and the bust is 50 rows. Divide 50 by 11 (1 more than the number of shaping rows) and round the result to discover that you need to work the shaping every 4½ rows. Since this isn't possible, you'll need to work the shaping every 4 or 5 rows. It's awkward to work some shaping on right-side rows and some on wrong-side rows, so shaping on right-side rows only is going to be easier. Here are a couple of examples of how to space the shaping out more or less evenly just on right-side rows.

▷ Alternate working the shaping on the 4th row, then on the 6th row. Over the course of 50 rows you will have worked 10 shaping rows, which is what you need to accomplish. By decreasing (or increasing) at both edges on each shaping row, you will have removed (or added) the required total of 20 stitches by the time your 50 rows have been completed. The last of these shaping rows will fall on the final row of the 50, which is not optimum: you want to be able to work a few rows even at the end. To adjust for this, work the first 3 shaping rows on the 4th row and the last 2 on the 4th row, alternating between 4 and 6 rows in the middle of the shaping. This way the shaping will take

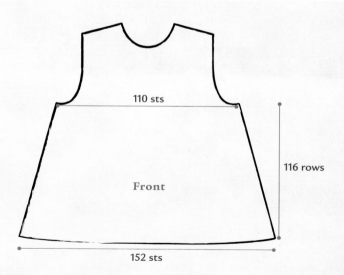

110 sts

Front

116 rows

152 sts

**Tapering the body gradually** from hip to underarm

## Fashioning a Fitted Waist

Fitting the waist requires the same sort of planning as the previous two examples. A garment with a fitted waist gets smaller from the hips to the waist and then larger again from the waist to the bust (or vice versa, if you are working from the top down). You'll need three width or circumference measurements and two lengths:

▷ Stitches at hips

▷ Stitches at waist

▷ Stitches at bust

▷ Rows between hips and waist

▷ Rows between waist and bust

You'll need to plan how to taper from the hips to the waist within the number of rows between those two measurements and how to taper from the waist to the bust within the number of rows between those two

measurements, just as described in Tapering the Body. It's best to allow at least a short area at the waist without any shaping, rather than decreasing to the waist and immediately beginning to increase again.

## Making Waist Darts and Princess Seams

Princess seams and waist darts are planned out exactly like the side-seam shaping for a fitted waist described (at left), but the increases and decreases occur at several other points around the garment, rather than just at the side seams.

Using the same example of a fitted garment, but working the shaping at both side seams and at two waist darts or princess seams, there are six decreases or increases on each shaping row: there is a single increase/decrease at each of the two edges and a double increase/decrease at each of the two darts. The shaping rows will be spaced much farther apart than when contours are worked only at the side seams.

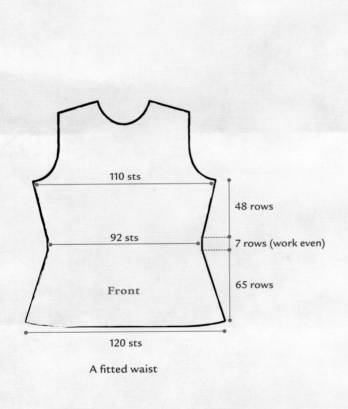

A fitted waist

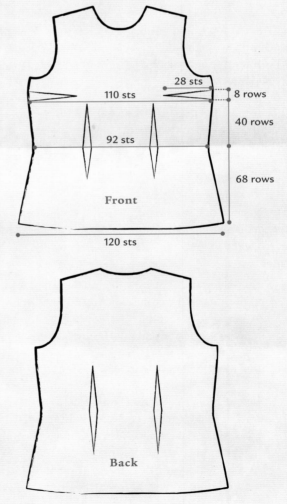

Vertical darts and bust darts for shaping

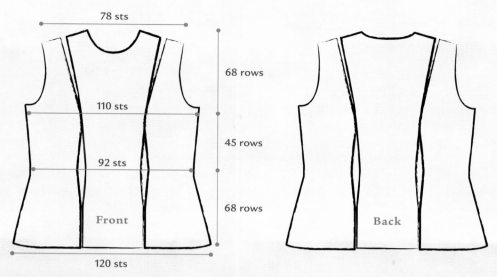

78 sts

68 rows

110 sts

45 rows

92 sts

68 rows

Front

120 sts

Back

Princess seams for shaping

Shaping for waist darts and princess seams can be worked using double decreases and increases, so that they appear narrow.

Working the same shaping with symmetrical single decreases and increases a few stitches apart produces a wider, but smoother effect.

## Adding Short-Row Bust Darts

Women who are well-endowed in the bust area frequently have the problem that the bottom edge at the front of their sweaters and vests hangs higher than the back. Bust darts prevent this problem by making the front longer using short rows. If a person has very rounded shoulders or a rounded back, the opposite may occur; the bottom back of the sweater may hang higher than the front. In this case, a few short rows scattered through the back shoulder area (not necessarily lined up to form a dart) will lengthen the back so that it hangs evenly. See the appendix (pages 279–80) for complete instructions on how to work short rows.

## Measuring for Bust Darts

Everyone's body is different, so bust-dart shaping is highly individual. Proper fit is very important. To ensure accurate measurements, wear whatever garments you normally would under the sweater or vest, fasten a belt or tie a piece of yarn snugly around your waist, and get a helper to take the following measurements with a flexible dressmaker's tape measure.

▷ **Front measurement.** From the top point of the shoulder to the top of the belt or piece of yarn. Measure straight down over the point of the bust in the front.

▷ **Back measurement.** From the same point at the top of the shoulder straight down to the top of the belt or piece of yarn in the back.

The front measurement should be longer than the back. If it's not, you don't need a bust dart. The difference between the two measurements is the height of the dart. Multiply this times your row gauge to get the height in rows. For example, if the front measurement is 22 inches and the back measurement is 19¾ inches, then the difference is 2¼ inches. At a gauge of 7 rows per inch, 7 rows × 2.25 inches = 16 rows (rounded to the nearest row). Divide this number in half, because each short-row turning is worked on a pair of rows: 16 ÷ 2 = 8 pairs of short rows. (If you end up with a fraction, just round off to the nearest whole number.) This is the number of short-row pairs you'll work to make your dart.

Holding your arm out to the side, have your helper measure horizontally from the side seam out to the point of your bust.

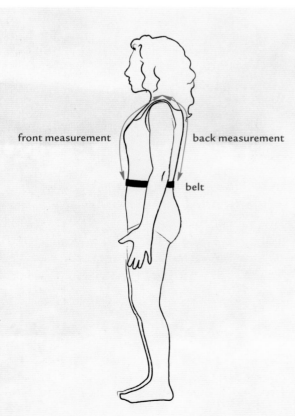

front measurement     back measurement

belt

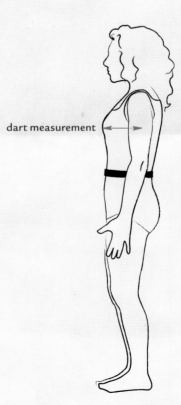

dart measurement

Because it should stop a bit short of the point, subtract ½ to 1 inch from this measurement. Multiply this times the stitch gauge to find the width of your dart in stitches. For example, at 5 stitches per inch, a 4-inch dart would be 20 stitches wide.

## Planning the Dart

In our example there are 8 turning rows, and you need to figure out how to distribute 20 stitches across them. Divide the number of stitches (20) by the number of turning rows (8). You'll probably end up with a fraction, as in this example where 20 stitches ÷ 8 rows = 2½ stitches. You can't work a half a stitch, so you're going to need to do a little more work to figure out how to handle this. Here are three different solutions that will get you close enough for a good fit:

**Quick-and-easy solution.** Just round off the number of stitches to 3: 3 stitches × 8 rows = a dart 24 stitches wide. In this example, that's more than ½ inch wider than desired. This may be okay if your dart will still stop at least ½ inch short of the bust point. On the other hand, if this would bring the end of the dart out past the point of the bust, don't do it!

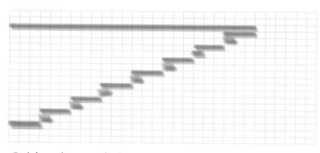

Quick-and-easy solution

**Exact solution.** Since 2½ falls halfway between 2 and 3, you can alternate 2 stitches and 3 stitches. If you do this four times, you get exactly 20 stitches. (2 + 3) × 4 = 20 stitches over 8 turning rows.

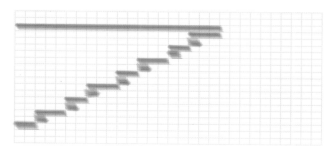

Exact solution

**Compromise solution.** Reduce your dart to 7 short rows and work 3 stitches on each, for a total of 7 rows × 3 stitches = 21 stitches. This will make your dart 2 rows shorter (about ¼ inch) and 1 stitch wider (about ⅛ inch), neither of which should make much difference in fit.

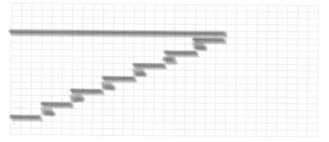

Compromise solution

If all these calculations make you uncomfortable, just sketch out a plan on a piece of graph paper, which will show you the actual shape of your dart.

1. Draw a horizontal line as wide as the dart should be, allowing one square per stitch.
2. Mark a point as many squares below one end of the line as there are rows in your dart.
3. Draw a diagonal line from this point to the other end of the dart.
4. Draw in stair steps 2 rows high to match the slope of the diagonal line, because short rows are always worked in pairs. Each step is the ending point of a short row.

## Working the Darts

Now how do you put your plan for the dart into effect? Let's use the "exact solution" at left as an example and assume we are working a cardigan front from the bottom up. Figure out how far below the underarm the point of the dart should fall, allow for the total number of rows in the dart, and start that much below the underarm. Work the front until you get to this point.

Looking at the chart and the plan at left, you'll be leaving 2 stitches unworked at the end of the first row. As you are approaching the side seam working across the front, stop when 2 stitches remain at the end of the row, wrap and turn, then work back to the center front. Looking at the chart and the plan at left, you'll be leaving 3 more stitches unworked at the end of the 2nd short row. So, on the next row when you are once again approaching the side seam, stop when 5 stitches remain before the end of the row, wrap and turn. Continue this way, stopping 2 or 3 stitches farther away from the side seam until a total of 20 stitches remain unworked at the end of the row. On the next row, as you approach the side seam, work across all of these stitches, picking up the wraps and working them together with their stitches. See the appendix for complete instructions on how to wrap and turn and how to pick up the wraps (pages 279–80).

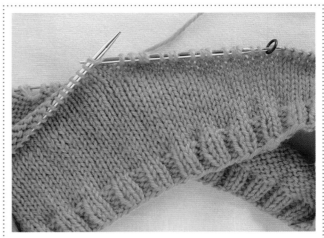

**Placing a marker** at each of the "side seams" helps you stay oriented when working bust darts on a circular sweater.

**Dart with short rows completed,** before picking up the wraps

**If you are working a pullover,** you'll be working the short rows at both edges. To do this, work a short row stopping 2 or 3 stitches before the side seam at one edge, wrap and turn, and then work a short row stopping the same number of stitches before the side seam at the other edge. You'll be alternately working short rows on the right side and on the wrong side.

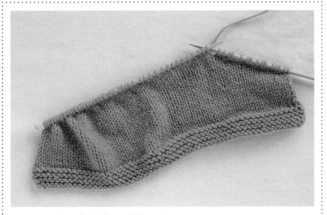

**Darts at both sides of front in progress**

**If you are working circularly,** you'll make the short rows just as for a pullover, but instead of working them at the edge of the fabric, you'll be working up to the point where the front meets the back of the sweater on one side, and then on the other.

**If you are working from the top down,** rather than from the bottom up, start the dart below the underarm, at the level where you want the point of the dart to fall. Work the short rows in reverse of the process described — turn the chart upside down to see what this will look like. On the first short row, stop 20 stitches away from the side seam. On the next short row, work past the original turning point (picking up the wrap and knitting or purling it together with its stitch) and stop 3 stitches closer to the side seam (17 stitches from the seam). Continue working 2 or 3 stitches closer to the seam on each short row and picking up the wrap at the previous turning point until you reach the seam.

## Planning for Level Darts

The instructions on page 121 produce a slanted dart that is very flattering for larger figures. If you prefer a dart that is horizontal rather than diagonal, you'll need to plan it a little differently. Let's take the same example as above, a dart 20 stitches wide and 16 rows high. First, divide the total number of rows by four, which gives you just 4 short rows. You'll work these 4 short rows twice in the course of the dart, first working gradually away from the side seam, then back toward it. Divide the 20 stitches by the 4 short rows and you get 5 stitches. This is the number of stitches more (or fewer) that you'll work on each short row. As you work the second half of the dart, you'll be wrapping the same stitch that you wrapped during the first half of the dart. Be careful to pick up both the wraps from these turning points when you come to them. You'll also be doing this on the same rows where you are wrapping and turning for another short row.

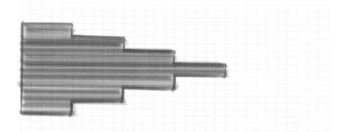

Chart of level dart 20 stitches wide and 14 rows tall

The same fit can be achieved by working either a level dart (*bottom*) or a slanted dart (*above*).

You'll notice that this makes a dart only 14 rows high. If you want the height to be taller, then divide the total number of stitches by five instead of four. This will result in a dart that is 18 rows tall, with 4-stitch increments. Because the longest row of the dart is worked only once, you can't make it exactly 16 rows tall. In a situation such as this, choose whichever option will work best for you — shorter or taller.

## Working Darts in Pattern Stitches

When planning your garment, you may want to work side panels in a very simple pattern stitch, garter stitch, or stockinette stitch, to make the dart easier to work, relegating more complicated patterns to the center front where there will be no shaping.

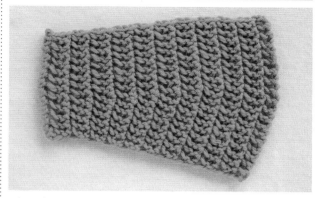

This dart is worked in **faggoting rib**, which has a 3-stitch repeat. The short rows were worked in 3-stitch increments with no wraps, making it easy to maintain the pattern stitch. Eliminating the wrapped stitches leaves holes at the turning points, but they integrate with the lace pattern.

In **garter stitch**, wrap when turning to prevent holes from forming, but don't bother to pick up the wraps later because they'll disappear into the garter ridges.

In a **knit-purl textured pattern**, wrap the stitches when you turn to prevent holes from forming. When you pick up the wraps, knit or purl them together with their base stitches to match the pattern stitch.

If you do decide to work a dart in a more complex pattern stitch, involving cables, twisted stitches, or increases and decreases, try it out in a swatch before working it in the garment itself, especially if the stitch count is different on different pattern rows. Charting it along with the pattern stitch could help. Experiment to see whether the dart is easier to work or looks better if begun on a particular row of the pattern stitch. The pattern repeat should also be a factor in planning your dart; for example, if you are working a pattern with a 4-stitch repeat, you may want to work the dart in 2- or 4-stitch increments on each short row, making it easier to keep track of the pattern stitch as you work. Always take care on the first complete row above the dart to work the next pattern row all the way across so that the pattern is continuous at center front, even though it has been interrupted at the dart.

## Changing the Armhole Depth

If the rest of the shoulder area fits but the armhole is too tight or too loose, you'll need to change the armhole. Exactly how you do this depends on what kind of armhole you're working with. When you change the armhole, you must also change the sleeve cap to fit it.

### Adjustments for a Drop Shoulder

Drop shoulder sweaters have no armhole shaping. To make the armhole bigger, just make the sleeve wider at the upper edge. You'll need to adjust the sleeve tapering to get a smooth line from cuff to underarm.

### Adjustments for a Square Armhole

These are just drop shoulders, but with a square armhole cut into the body of the sweater so that the shoulder line falls closer to the natural shoulder of the wearer. To make the square armhole larger, work the armhole bind off lower on the body of the sweater, assuming you're working from the bottom up. When working

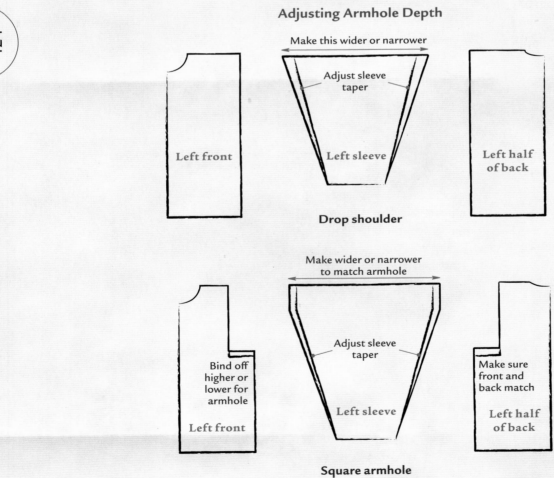

**Adjusting Armhole Depth**

Make this wider or narrower

Adjust sleeve taper

Left front     Left sleeve     Left half of back

**Drop shoulder**

Make wider or narrower to match armhole

Adjust sleeve taper

Bind off higher or lower for armhole

Left front     Left sleeve

Make sure front and back match

Left half of back

**Square armhole**

Forethought: Shaping and Fitting

from the top down, make the armhole longer before you cast on for the underarm. Make sure the front and back match, and make the top of the sleeve wide enough to fit the new armhole. You'll need to adjust the sleeve tapering to get a smooth line from cuff to underarm. Be sure to work the upper section of the sleeve straight to match the depth of the cut-in armhole, as shown in the schematic (opposite).

## Adjustments for a Round Armhole

To make a round armhole taller, assuming the shoulder width of the sweater fits correctly, just make the straight section of the armhole above the underarm shaping longer; don't make any changes to the underarm bind off or diagonal shaping. The same number of stitches should be bound off at the underarm of the sweater and the underarm of the sleeve. The diagonal shaping immediately after the bind off of both should also be the same. This means that these two sections will automatically match each other.

To fit properly, the curved section of the sleeve cap between the diagonal shaping and the center top of the sleeve cap must be the same length as, or a little longer than, the straight, unshaped front and back sections of the armhole. If the edge of the sleeve cap is longer than the armhole edge, it will need to be eased in or gathered a bit when joining the seam. When this is the case, the extra space in the sleeve cap allows a little more room in the shoulder area at the top of the sleeve for ease of motion.

To design the new sleeve cap, figure out how tall the armhole opening is from the end of the shaping up to the shoulder. Design the sleeve cap at full size on 1-inch gridded flip-chart paper. First draw the sleeve the correct width, with the underarm bind off and the diagonal shaping on both sides of the sleeve (shown in solid black). Mark the center line of the sleeve up through the sleeve cap area (shown in black dashes). Using a flexible ruler or a piece of yarn cut to the correct length (shown in green yarn), create a curve that reaches from the top of the diagonal shaping to the center point of the sleeve. Draw this curve on the paper (shown in black dots), then duplicate it for the other half of the sleeve.

Now translate your full-size drawing into knitting instructions. If you've drawn it on 1-inch grid paper and you know your stitch and row gauge, this is easy to do. You can write it out in row-by-row instructions, you can knit it to match the full-size pattern you drew (lay it down frequently on the pattern to make sure the shaping matches), or you can make a chart of the shaping on graph paper.

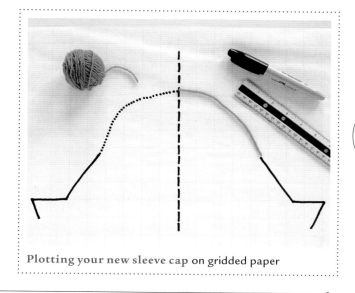

Plotting your new sleeve cap on gridded paper

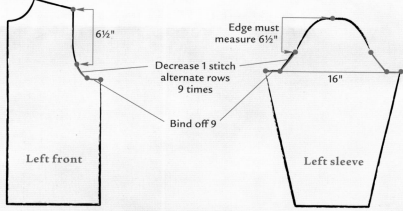

## Changing the Armhole and Sleeve-Cap Style

There are times when you may want a more fitted armhole or a change to a more casual look. If you change the armhole style, you'll need to change the sleeve cap to fit it.

### Creating a Drop Shoulder

To create a drop shoulder, get rid of all armhole shaping and work the body straight up to the shoulder. Taper the sleeve to make the top of it whatever width you like, then bind off straight across. Center the sleeve on the shoulder seam and sew it to the body, then sew the side and sleeve seams together. The width at the top of the sleeve determines the size of the armhole. (See drop-shoulder schematic, page 124.)

### Designing a Square Armhole

A sweater with a square armhole is shaped identically to a drop-shoulder sweater, but the point where the top of the sleeve meets the armhole falls at the natural shoulder, so the sweater appears to fit better. First determine how wide you want the shoulders to be, based on your full shoulder width measurement. Note how much narrower the shoulders are than the body of the sweater (the body width will be the circumference divided in half, if you are working circularly) and divide this difference in half to figure out the width of the bind off at the underarm. After binding off for the underarm, you'll work straight up to the shoulder without any additional shaping. Design the sleeve as described in Creating a Drop Shoulder (above). The width of the top of the sleeve, divided in half, gives you the depth of the armhole. The sleeve is tapered up to the point where it meets the body of the garment, then worked straight for the same length as the width of the armhole bind off. (See square armhole schematic, page 124.)

### Designing a Round Armhole

Determine how wide the shoulders should be based on your full shoulder width and how deep the armhole should be based on your armhole depth measurement. The difference between the width of the body and the width of the shoulders, divided in half, gives you the width of each armhole. Figure out how many stitches will give you this armhole width. Bind off half of these stitches at the underarm, then decrease the rest of them, 1 stitch every other row, to make a diagonal. From this point, the armhole is worked straight up to the shoulder without additional shaping. See Adjustments for a Round Armhole (page 125) for how to design the sleeve cap to fit this armhole.

### Designing Dolman Sleeves

A dolman sleeve is very wide at the armhole, which can extend all the way down to the waistline or to the bottom of the garment, and very tight at the wrist. Dolman sleeves can be worked separately and joined to the body (opposite, center), but they are frequently worked in one piece with the body (opposite, bottom).

To design a separate dolman sleeve to fit the oversize armhole, decide how deep and wide you want the armhole to be, just as for a round armhole. Draw the armhole on 1-inch grid paper, then design the sleeve cap to fit this as described in Adjustments for a Round Armhole (page 125).

If you make dolman sleeves in one piece with the body, the transition from body to sleeve can be a corner or a curve, and the easiest way to design this curve is to draw it actual size on 1-inch grid paper. To fit the sleeve length properly, you'll need to measure the length from the back neck bone to the wrist, with the arm slightly bent. (See drawing, opposite, top.)

## MEASURING FOR DOLMAN SLEEVES

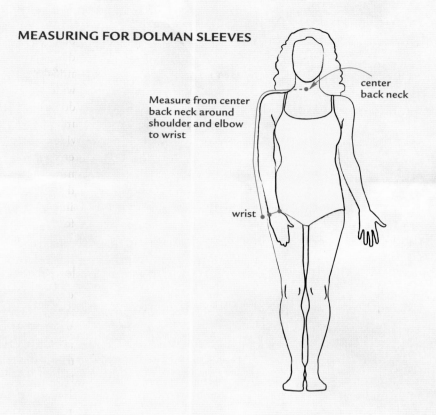

center back neck

Measure from center back neck around shoulder and elbow to wrist

wrist

## TWO APPROACHES TO DOLMAN SLEEVES

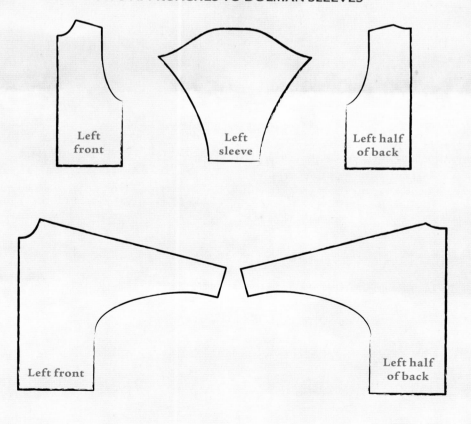

Left front

Left sleeve

Left half of back

Left front

Left half of back

## Changing the Shoulder Width for Better Fit

In order to change the full shoulder width without changing the width of the body, you have to make up the difference either in the armhole shaping or by adding shaping somewhere between the two armholes. Whenever you change the armhole shaping, it affects the shape of the sleeve cap that must fit into it. Because it's so complicated to change the shoulders, armholes, and sleeves of the sweater, I recommended in chapter 1 that you select the size you'll make based on the fit at the shoulder (see Choosing the Right Size, page 18). Then, all you have to do is to adjust the size of the body relative to the shoulder.

On the other hand, if you can find a size where the sleeves, armholes, and neckline are going to be a perfect fit without any adjustments, but the shoulder is just a little bit off, it may actually be easier to adjust the width of the shoulder alone, by working increases or decreases in a targeted area just below the shoulder seam.

To shape the garment adjusting only the width of the shoulder, you can work gathers (decreasing rapidly along a single row), vertical darts (decreasing or increasing along a column of stitches up to the shoulder), or pleats at the shoulder seam (folding and overlapping sections of the shoulder as you bind it off). You can also unobtrusively decrease or increase a few stitches here and there to adjust the shoulder without it being obvious how you did it.

### Gathers to Make a Narrower Shoulder

Gathering the shoulder at the bind off is the simplest method of making a shoulder narrower and requires the least planning. You can decrease evenly spaced across the final row to get down to the correct number of stitches, or you can decrease while binding off, and you don't need to worry about integrating your shaping with any pattern stitch.

### Working Pleats for a Narrower Shoulder

To work pleats all the way across the shoulder, you would need to have three times the width in the shoulder area than you want at the shoulder seam itself (see How to Knit a Pleat (opposite). You can also work just one pleat at the armhole edge to reduce the number of stitches as needed. The pleat will look good only if it's reasonably wide — about ¾ to 1 inch, so you'll need to have about double that width (1½ to 2 inches) of excess stitches for a pleat to be practical.

Stop 1 row short of the completed length of your shoulder. Position the pleat so that at least 1 stitch remains beyond the pleat at the armhole edge, to allow for seaming. Following the directions in How to Knit a Pleat, slip half of the stitches you want to get rid of to the first double-pointed needle, and the other half to the second double-pointed needle.

Note that pleats make the fabric very bulky because they are three layers thick, so are most practical in garments worked in thinner yarns to make a stretchy fabric. Bulky yarns worked firmly should be avoided unless you want to make a very strong statement at the shoulder.

**Pleat at shoulder.** Like the other examples in this section, the width of this shoulder has been adjusted by 8 stitches, overlapped to form a pleat at the armhole edge.

**Shoulder gathered by decreasing** on the last row before binding off.

# How to Knit a Pleat

START WITH THREE TIMES the number of stitches you want to end with. For example, a pleat 4 stitches wide requires 12 stitches to start; after the pleat is completed, you'll end up with 4 stitches. So, to make a piece of knitting with pleats all the way across that ends up 16 stitches wide, you'd need to start with three times that number of stitches (48), plus at least 1 stitch at each edge to allow for seaming or picking up a border, for a total of 50 stitches.

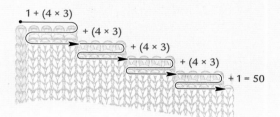

(2) **Hold all three needles** together, then work across, knitting through all three layers to join them.

(1) **Slip the first third** of the stitches onto a double-pointed needle. Slip the second third onto a second double-pointed needle. Fold the pleat to the back or to the front.

(3) **Completed pleats** make the fabric one-third the width and triple the thickness where they overlap.

## Scattered Decreases or Increases to Adjust the Shoulder Width

Scattering the shaping across multiple rows makes it less noticeable than working it all on one row and provides a smooth transition in the shoulder area. You can easily work decreases to make the shoulder narrower or increases to make it wider. Decide how many rows you have available to spread out the shaping and work out a plan for scattering them regularly across the available area. For example, if you want to get rid of 16 stitches over an area 32 rows long, you could decrease 1 stitch every other row. To render them less noticeable, be sure to stagger the decreases so they don't line up.

**Scattered Decreases and Increases**

**Narrower shoulder** with scattered decreases

**Wider shoulder** with scattered increases

## Vertical Darts to Adjust the Shoulder Width

Like darts worked at the waist, darts at the shoulder reduce or increase the width of the fabric along a vertical column of stitches. You'll need to know the length (the number of rows from top to bottom) and the width (the number of stitches you want to get rid of or add) of

the proposed dart. Divide the stitches by the number of rows to figure out how often to decrease or increase. Remember that you can use single or double increases or decreases.

**Vertical Darts**

**Double decreases** were worked every 4th row to reduce the width of this shoulder.

**Pairs of M1 increases** on either side of a center stitch were worked every 4th row to increase the width of this shoulder.

## Changing the Length and Width of Sleeves

You can resize the sleeves if, for example, they won't fit properly or because you like more (or less) ease than the pattern calls for. Changing the length can be accomplished without affecting the sleeve cap. Keep in mind, however, that changing the width at the top of the sleeve cap may require you to modify the armhole as well.

### Altering the Sleeve Length

In the unlikely event that the sleeve is straight, with no increases or decreases along the seam from cuff to underarm, then just make it whatever length you like.

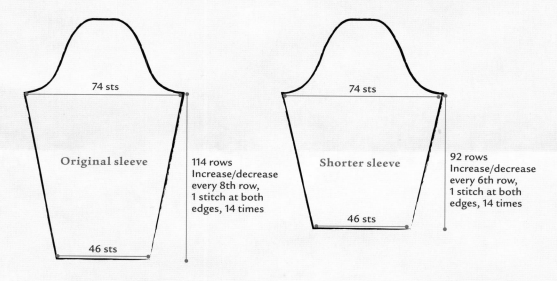

Original sleeve — 74 sts, 46 sts — 114 rows Increase/decrease every 8th row, 1 stitch at both edges, 14 times

Shorter sleeve — 74 sts, 46 sts — 92 rows Increase/decrease every 6th row, 1 stitch at both edges, 14 times

**ALTERING SLEEVE WIDTH**

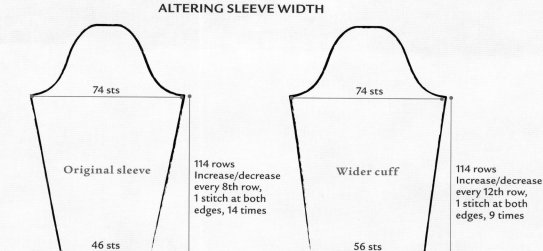

Original sleeve — 74 sts, 46 sts — 114 rows Increase/decrease every 8th row, 1 stitch at both edges, 14 times

Wider cuff — 74 sts, 56 sts — 114 rows Increase/decrease every 12th row, 1 stitch at both edges, 9 times

131

To adjust the length of a tapered sleeve, you'll need to figure out how often to work the required increases and decreases within the desired length. To do this you'll need to know the following:

▷ Width or circumference at the underarm (the widest point) in stitches

▷ Width or circumference at the wrist (the narrowest point) in stitches

▷ Distance between the two measurements in rows. To determine the exact sleeve length, it's best to complete the front and back of the garment, join them at the shoulders, and complete the neck border, then try on the incomplete garment and measure, over a slightly bent elbow, from the edge of the shoulder down to your wrist.

Once you've collected this information, calculate how often you need to work the shaping exactly as described in Tapering the Body (page 116).

## Changing the Sleeve Width

First determine exactly where the sleeve needs to be wider or narrower. Is it at the cuff? At the underarm? In the sleeve cap? Or along the entire length? What you need to do to fix the problem depends on your answer.

If the only adjustment is to make the cuff smaller, it's easiest just to cast on fewer stitches for the ribbed band, then increase to the specified number of stitches at the top of the cuff (or, if you are working from the top down, decrease to the number desired for the cuff when you arrive at that point).

If the cuff needs to be larger in circumference, but the sleeve cap is fine, if the sleeve needs to be wider at the underarm but the cuff is fine, or if the whole sleeve needs to be adjusted, you'll need to know the same stitch and row counts as listed in Altering the Sleeve Length (page 131). Then you can plan to taper the sleeve as described in Tapering the Body (page 116). If this results in a change in the width at the underarm and in the sleeve cap area, you'll also need to redesign the sleeve cap so that it still fits the armhole opening, as described in Adjustments for a Round Armhole (page 125).

## Tapering the Sleeve at the Center

When working either a drop-shoulder sleeve or a square armhole and its corresponding sleeve, you can improve the fit by working the sleeve tapers at the center of the sleeve rather than at the outer edges. This naturally creates an angled sleeve cap for a better fit. How far apart you space the pair of increases (or decreases) will determine how wide the cap is at the top of the sleeve.

**Increase placement.** These two sleeves were shaped identically, but the increases on the sleeve at left were worked at the edges, and the ones on the sleeve at right were placed in the center.

## Changing the Neckline

You may need to change the neck shaping to make a garment fit properly, to make a neckline higher or lower, or you may want a different type of neck opening altogether.

## Designing a V-Neck

You'll need to know how wide the neck opening should be in stitches (see Getting the Back Neck Shaping Right, page 134) and how deep you want the V to be in rows. Once you have this information, figure out a shaping plan exactly as described in Tapering the Body (page 116). For a good fit in a V-neck, so that it doesn't shift from side to side, make sure the back neck fits close to the wearer's neck and employ sloped shoulders that fit well. Be sure to allow for the width of any neck border you plan to add.

Rather than calculating the neck shaping, you also have the option of charting it (see opposite page). Mark the width and length of the neck opening, and then draw diagonal lines from the center front at the bottom to the outer edges of the neck at the top. Draw in stair steps following the line to indicate decreases (shown in blue).

**Designing a V-Neck**

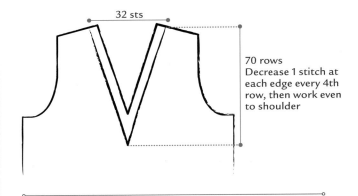

32 sts

70 rows
Decrease 1 stitch at each edge every 4th row, then work even to shoulder

## CHARTING A V-NECK

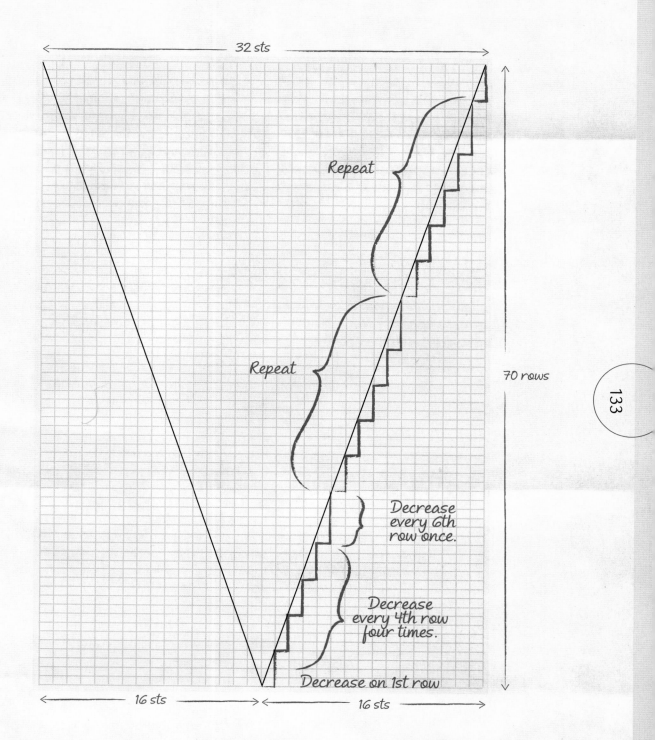

32 sts

Repeat

Repeat

70 rows

Decrease every 6th row once.

Decrease every 4th row four times.

Decrease on 1st row

16 sts

16 sts

## Designing Round Necks

Again, you'll need to know how wide the neck opening should be in stitches (see Getting the Back Neck Shaping Right, following) and how deep you want the neck to be in rows. Once you have this information, plot the neckline on knitter's graph paper. First draw a rectangle that represents the width and depth of the neck opening, then sketch a nice curve within that rectangle. Finally, draw stair steps along the edges of the rectangles that represent stitches, remembering that the shaping will normally be done on alternate rows, not on every row (shown in blue on the chart). Like V-necks,

round necks lie better if the back neck opening fits properly and the shoulders are sloped.

## Getting the Back Neck Shaping Right

Many simple sweaters have no back neck shaping. If the fabric and neck border are stretchy, it will droop at the back neck to form a curve, but if the fabric doesn't stretch, the sweater will sit too far back on the shoulders, the sleeves will rotate so that the top of the sleeve cap is too far back, the sleeve seam is too far forward, and the bottom of the front will fall higher than the bottom of the back. Considering all the problems that

**DESIGNING ROUNDED NECKS**

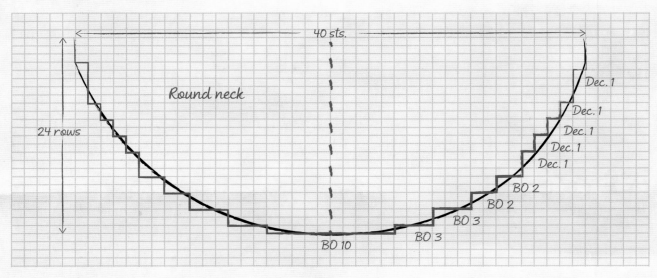

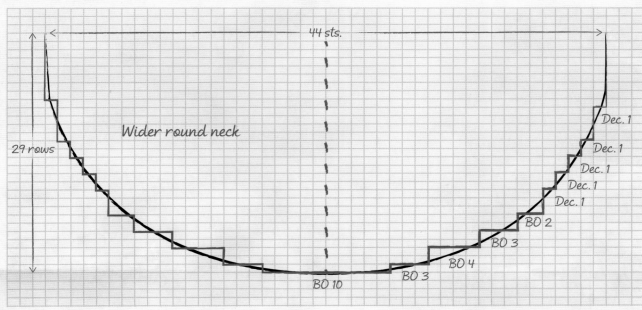

a lack of back neck shaping can cause, it's clear that taking the time to carve out a back neck can make a very significant difference in fit, even if you change nothing else about a sweater.

The width of the back neck opening must match the width of the front neck opening and the actual width of the wearer's neck. This can be difficult to measure directly, but you can calculate it by measuring the cross-shoulder width and the individual shoulder widths. Subtract the two individual shoulders from the full width and what's left is the width of the neck opening (see How to Take Body Measurements, page 20).

The back neck opening should fall at the bone at the top of your spine where your neck meets your back, unless of course you want it lower. To figure out how deep this is, measure from your waist up to that bone, and from the waist up to your high shoulder (the point where your shoulder meets your neck). The difference between these two measurements is the depth of your back neck opening (see How to Take Body Measurements, page 20).

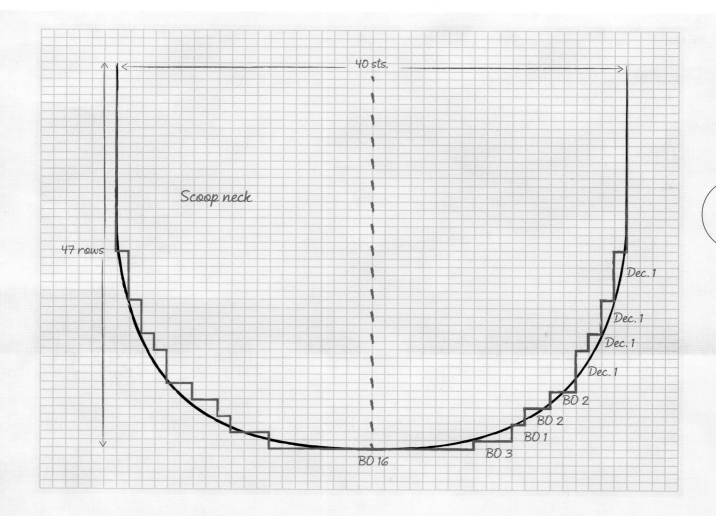

## DESIGNING BOAT NECKS

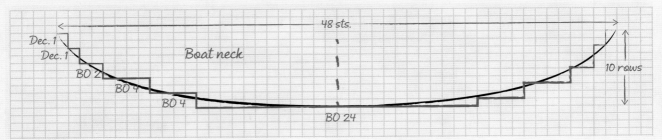

Design the actual back neck opening as described for round front necks (page 132 and chart, top left). The back neck will be much shallower than the front, but it should still have a nice smooth curve. Be sure to allow for the back neck border.

### Designing Boat Necks

Again, you'll need to know how wide the neck opening should be in stitches. Boat necks can be made straight across, or they can be slightly curved. If the fabric is stretchy and the neck border also stretches, it will naturally drape into a curve without any additional shaping. If the fabric is firmer, you will want a slightly curved neck opening: Follow the same procedure as for round necks (page 132) to plan and chart your neck opening. Boat necks fit best when the garment is closely fitted to the body, because a sweater that has both a loose body and a wide neck opening will tend to shift back and forth on the shoulders. A slightly curved boat neck is shown above, enlarged to allow for a narrow border.

### Adding Shoulder Shaping

Simple sweaters frequently don't include shoulder shaping, but, like back neck shaping, shoulder shaping can improve fit a great deal. If we stood with our arms straight out to the side all the time, unshaped shoulders would be fine. When we lower our arms and our shoulders return to their natural slope, it's better that sweaters be shaped to fit them. When your arms are lowered, both sides of the front and back droop, distorting horizontal stripes and making the bottom edge hang lower at the side seam than in the center. In a thin drapey fabric, this may look and feel just fine. In a thicker stiffer fabric, it may look (and feel) dreadful. To work out a plan for shoulder shaping, you need to know:

▷ Width of the sweater's shoulder in stitches

▷ Shoulder depth in rows (measured at the armhole edge of the sweater). This is easiest to determine as the difference between the length from the waist to

**Adding Shoulder Shaping: Round Armholes**

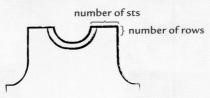

Round armholes without shoulder shaping

Round armholes with shoulder shaping

**Adding Shoulder Shaping: Drop Shoulders**

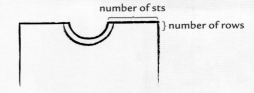

Drop shoulder without shoulder shaping

Drop shoulder with shoulder shaping

These schematics show the sweater fronts in black, with the shape of the body indicated in green.

the high shoulder and from the waist to the outer shoulder at the armhole. If the armhole is shaped and falls at the natural shoulder line, then this will be the same as the body measurement for shoulder depth. If you are working on a drop-shoulder sweater, then this measurement is going to be larger.

Once you have these two numbers, divide the number of rows in half, then divide the number of stitches by the result. For example, if the shoulder is 25 stitches wide and the shoulder depth is 10 rows, divide 10 in half to get 5, then divide 25 stitches by 5 rows to get 5 stitches.

The shaping can be worked either by binding off or by making short rows (see appendix, pages 279–80). Based on our example, you would bind off 5 stitches at the shoulder on each of the next 5 rows that start at the armhole edge.

To work short rows, you'd work 5 stitches fewer on each short row as you approach the shoulder edge, just as if you were working a bust dart (see Working the Darts, page 121).

You'll need to start working short-row shoulder shaping 1 or 2 rows earlier than bound-off shaping to ensure that the overall length is correct when the shoulder shaping is completed. The advantage of working short-row shaping for your shoulders is that you can then join the front and back using a three-needle bind off instead of sewing.

Keep in mind that shoulder shaping is not appropriate with all armhole and sleeve types. Introducing sloped shoulders into a drop shoulder or square armhole sweater may not work well unless the fabric is very stretchy, or unless you combine it with at least a shallow cap on the sleeve.

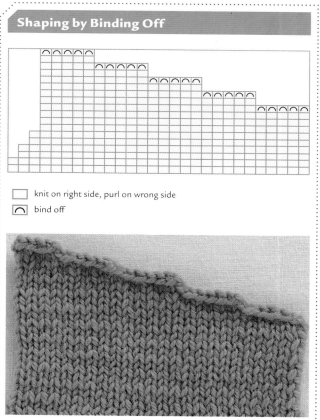

## Shaping by Binding Off

| | knit on right side, purl on wrong side |
| | bind off |

In this example of a bound-off sloped shoulder, 5 stitches were bound off at the beginning of the right-side rows five times.

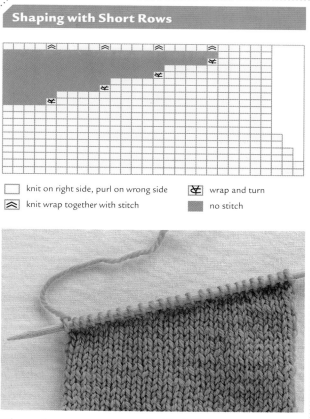

## Shaping with Short Rows

| | knit on right side, purl on wrong side | | wrap and turn |
| | knit wrap together with stitch | | no stitch |

These short rows were worked by knitting across 20 stitches, turning and purling back on the wrong side, then knitting across 15 stitches, turning and working back, and so on, working 5 fewer stitches on each pair of short rows. Working short rows in 5-stitch increments forms the same shape as binding off 5 stitches repeatedly.

# Work in Progress

## chapter five

AFTER YOU'VE MADE your initial choices of yarn, pattern, and needles, and planned your cast on, edge stitches, how to handle shaping, whether you want to change the order of construction from flat to circular (or vice versa) and whether you need to make alterations so the garment will fit better, at last it's time to start knitting. In chapters 1 through 4, I covered things that you need to consider before you begin to work on your garment (or at least before you get very far into it). So here we are, halfway through the book, and *finally* you're ready to cast on and get started.

This chapter addresses things you should pay attention to while you're actively knitting the sweater. In the course of making a garment there are so many points where your judgment is required that it's important for you to take stock of your knitting frequently. I've tried to highlight the moments when you'll need to analyze the situation and decide what to do about it. Some of these will be in response to problems you'll encounter, while others are simply opportunities to fine-tune your knitting and make it better.

# Understanding Knitting Instructions

For lots of reasons, knitting instructions can be difficult to interpret. One of the problems we encounter is that there are so many different ways to say the same thing. And then there are the abbreviations. It's simple enough to remember that K1 means "knit 1" and P1 means "purl 1," but keeping track of what sk2p or 2/2 RC mean can be daunting. (In case you're curious, the first is a double decrease worked "slip 1 knitwise, K2tog, pass slipped stitch over," and the second is a cable where you slip 2 stitches to a cable needle, hold it behind your work, K2, and K2 from the cable needle.) The Craft Yarn Council has published a list of standard knitting abbreviations (see Online References in appendix, page 284, for their website). For stitch manipulations not included in this list, or for variations specific to individual designers and publishers, refer to the list of abbreviations in the individual pattern, magazine, or book.

The same knitting techniques may be called by several different names; if you run across an unfamiliar technique, you may just know it by a different name. And sometimes different techniques are called by the same name; the one you know may be different from what the designer meant. If you don't understand the instructions, they may be poorly written, or you might be misinterpreting them. Unfortunately, it doesn't always work for the designer to add more detailed explanations — sometimes it puts people off because it makes the project seem complicated, or the additional detail is actually more confusing.

The best thing to do, when you're not sure you understand the instructions, or the results are not what you expected, is to use common sense. Compare all the information the pattern provides (text, photos, charts, schematics) to see if they are consistent. There may be a mistake in the text that's correct in the chart, or vice versa. Review the abbreviations to see if you are misinterpreting what they mean. Check the publisher's website for errata, where they post corrections to patterns. Contact the designer. Search for the pattern at the online knit and crochet community website Ravelry.com to see if anyone else has commented on the problem. In many cases, there may not be a mistake, but you may be misinterpreting the pattern directions — it's easy to do! If you discover there really is an undocumented problem in a pattern, let the designer or the publisher know, and be sure to post it on Ravelry for the benefit of others who will run into the same problem.

## Interpreting Written Instructions

Like all specialized disciplines, knitting has its own jargon, which you must learn to be able to follow the instructions. One of the best ways to learn the jargon is to find a knitting mentor — an experienced knitter who can answer your questions. In the absence of such an advisor, knitting reference books and online resources like Ravelry and YouTube are invaluable. With online images, you can see what to do step by step, even when there's not enough room in the pattern to include so much detailed information. Online video lets you watch demonstrations of techniques over and over until you understand them.

### Deciphering Pattern Repeats

Instructions for pattern stitches that repeat can be as confusing as algebraic equations, especially when groups of repeating instructions are nested within other repeating instructions. Parentheses, square brackets, and asterisks are all indicators of sections of the row that are repeated. How do you interpret this, for example?

> **Abbreviated Instructions for Row 2**
> K2, *[(P1, K1-tbl) three times, P1, 2/2 RC] twice, (P1, K1-tbl) three times; repeat from * until 3 stitches remain, P1, K2.

First let's look at the asterisk (*). The asterisk is the beginning of the main repeating section of the pattern. The semicolon (;) is the end of this main pattern repeat. This means that you'll knit the first 2 stitches, then repeat the instructions between the asterisk and the semicolon until there are only 3 stitches left at the end of the row. On the last 3 stitches you'll work purl 1, knit 2.

Next let's look at the square brackets. They enclose a series of directions, and after the brackets it says to work everything inside the brackets twice.

Now let's look *inside* the square brackets to what it is that you're supposed to do twice. At first glance it's fairly obvious that you work some purls and some knits into the back loop, and then you work a cable. The instruction "P1, K1-tbl" is inside its own set of parentheses, meaning that this instruction all by itself is repeated, and it says to work it three times, after which you purl 1, and then get to work the cable just once.

When you complete the square-bracketed section for the second time, you have that familiar P1, K1-tbl in parentheses to repeat three more times. After you've done this, you come to the semicolon and, assuming there are more stitches on your needle, you go back to the asterisk before the square brackets and repeat the whole thing all over again, until you have only 3 stitches left at the end of the row. What a relief to just work P1, K2 at the end of the row!

Writing it all out in order doesn't really make it clearer. This is what it would look like:

**Expanded Instructions for Row 2**
Knit 2
*purl 1, knit 1 through the back loop
purl 1, knit 1 through the back loop
purl 1, knit 1 through the back loop
purl 1, cable 4 holding the first 2 stitches in back
purl 1, knit 1 through the back loop
purl 1, knit 1 through the back loop
purl 1, knit 1 through the back loop
purl 1, cable 4 holding the first 2 stitches in back
purl 1, knit 1 through the back loop
purl 1, knit 1 through the back loop
purl 1, knit 1 through the back loop
repeat from * until only 3 stitches remain at the end of the row
purl 1, knit 2

When you consider that this is *just 1 row* of a pattern stitch, you can see why knitting instructions are abbreviated.

Luckily, you won't often find instructions that are this convoluted. A good pattern writer will take pity on the poor knitter and make the instructions easier to comprehend, simplifying it by explaining the different pattern stitches and referring to them. For example, this pattern uses two main elements: Twisted Rib and a 4-stitch cable, shown in the photo and chart below.

▷ Twisted Rib: *P1, K1-tbl; repeat from *. If 1 stitch remains, P1.

▷ Cable: Slip 2 stitches to cable needle, hold it in back, K2, K2 from cable needle.

▷ Pattern panel (11 stitches): Work Twisted Rib over 7 stitches; work cable over next 4 stitches.

Now it's possible to write an understandable instruction, referring back to the explanations of the pattern stitches:

**Ideal Instructions for Row 2**
K2, *work pattern panel twice, work Twisted Rib over next 6 stitches; repeat from * until 3 stitches remain, P1, K2.

## Ending Where?

You'll frequently run across instructions that tell you where to end one section of the garment, in preparation for beginning the next. These are intended to provide information that will make the knitting less confusing, but many knitters misinterpret them, so here are explanations of what they really mean.

**Ending with a wrong-side/right-side row.** This means that the last row you actually complete will be on the side specified.

**End ready to begin with a wrong-side/right-side row.** This means that the last row you complete before continuing will be on the opposite of the side specified, so that when you turn to begin the following row you're in the correct place.

**Ending with row x.** This assumes that you are working a series of numbered rows repeatedly, for example to make a pattern or to complete a series of increases or decreases. Work until you've completed the row specified, and then move on to the next instruction.

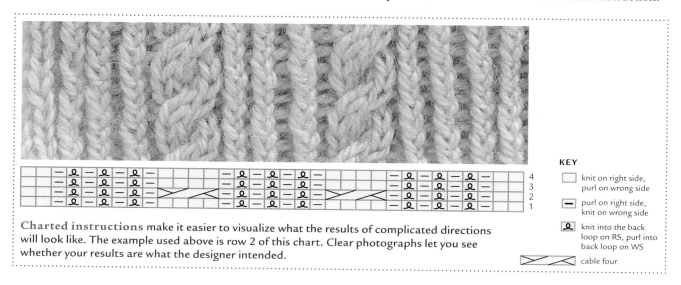

**Charted instructions** make it easier to visualize what the results of complicated directions will look like. The example used above is row 2 of this chart. Clear photographs let you see whether your results are what the designer intended.

**KEY**

☐ knit on right side, purl on wrong side

— purl on right side, knit on wrong side

&#x2640; knit into the back loop on RS, purl into back loop on WS

✕ cable four

## Ending How?

There are also instructions for pattern stitches that specify exactly how a row should end. There are many ways to write these instructions, and I've found that knitters are prone to misinterpreting the subtle differences between the various instructions.

**Ending ___.** This usually specifies what to do with the stitches at the end of the row that fall outside of the pattern repeat. For example, if you are working a slipped-stitch pattern on an odd number of stitches, the instructions might say:

> *K1, slip 1 with yarn in front; repeat from * across, ending K1.

This means that you repeat the 2-stitch pattern until you get to the last stitch, and then you knit it. The end-of-row instructions could be stated more explicitly like this:

> *K1, slip 1 with yarn in front; repeat from * until 1 stitch remains, K1.

And the following instruction would create exactly the same pattern as the last two examples:

> K1, *slip 1 with yarn in front, K1; repeat from * across.

The difference in the third version is that the extra edge stitch is described as being at the beginning of the row instead of at the end.

**Ending the last repeat ___ instead of ___.** This type of instruction is used when the last repeat of a pattern row is slightly different in order to center the pattern on the fabric or because there aren't enough stitches left for a full repeat at the end of the row. Let's take the same example used at left, but put 2 knitted stitches at each end of the row instead of 1. One could write the instructions any of these ways to obtain the same results:

> K1, *K1, slip 1 with yarn in front; repeat from * across, ending K2.

> K2, *slip 1 with yarn in front, K1; repeat from * until 1 stitch remains, K1.

> K2, *slip 1 with yarn in front, K1; repeat from * across, ending the last repeat K2 instead of K1.

KEY

☐ knit on right side, purl on wrong side

Ⴤ slip with yarn on right side

**Chart and swatch** for knitting instructions with edge stitches above

## Evenly Spaced

When a series of increases or decreases is worked on a single row or round, you'll see the instructions to increase (or decrease) a number of stitches *evenly spaced* across or around. This happens frequently at the top of ribbing, where the transition is made to the body of the garment. Sometimes the designer will give explicit instructions how to space the increases. If these are not provided, you'll need to figure out the spacing for yourself. There are two approaches you can take: mathematical calculation and eyeball estimates.

If you are mathematically inclined, calculate the positions of the increases/decreases by dividing the total number of stitches by the number of stitches to be increased/decreased. For flat knitting, you then adjust the position of the decreases to leave a few stitches at each edge.

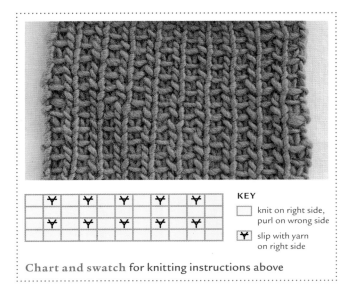

KEY

☐ knit on right side, purl on wrong side

Ⴤ slip with yarn on right side

**Chart and swatch** for knitting instructions above

For example, if you are working circularly on 80 stitches and you need to decrease 9 stitches evenly spaced, 80 stitches divided by 9 decreases = 8.888 . . . , which means it's almost 9 stitches, so you'd knit around decreasing every 9th stitch (except that there will be 1 fewer stitch between the last decrease and the end of the round). But you must remember that each decrease uses 2 stitches out of the 9, so you'll need to work (K2tog, K7) around in order to decrease every 9th stitch, and at the end of the round you'll work K2tog, K6.

If you were working flat on 80 stitches and needed to decrease 9, you'd divide 80 by 9 and get 8.88 . . . , but you'd then make the first decrease after only half of the calculated stitches, to center the decreases and prevent any from falling at the edge of the fabric. So, you'd begin by working K3, then repeat (K2tog, K7) eight times, and end the row K2tog, K3.

But what if the answer is somewhere in the middle? For example, if you needed to decrease 7 stitches, 80 divided by 7 = 11.43. You need to decrease about every 11½ stitches, and 2 of these will be used by the decrease, so there will be 9½ stitches between each decrease. To accomplish this you'll alternate between 9 stitches and 10 stitches, repeating (K2tog, K9, K2tog, K10) until you get to the end of the round. You won't be able to complete the last repeat at the end of the round, but you will end up with 7 stitches decreased and they will be spaced out as evenly as possible.

If you were working flat and needed to decrease 7 stitches, you could just work fewer stitches at the beginning and end of the row and 10 stitches between each decrease like this: K3, (K2tog, K10) six times, K2tog, K3.

For increases, the calculation is worked the same way, but the adjustment for the number of stitches between increases differs depending on the increase you use. Some increases (M1, lifted increase, and yo) fall between stitches, so you don't make any adjustment. Others (Kfb, Pfb, and knit and purl into a single stitch) use 1 stitch, so you adjust by 1 stitch. For example, if you have 70 stitches and need to increase 10, 70 stitches divided by 10 increases = 7; you need to increase every 7 stitches. To do this using M1 increases, repeat (K7, M1) around. Using Kfb increases, repeat (K6, Kfb) around. If you're working flat, adjust so that no increases fall at the edge of the fabric by working about half of the knit stitches before the first and after the last increase.

If you dislike even the idea of calculating the stitches between increases or decreases, then it's just as effective to estimate the spacing. You'll need as many split markers or safety pins as the desired number of increases or decreases. Fold the knitting into halves (or quarters if it's wide). Place a marker at the beginning and end of each half or quarter and then spread out the rest of the markers more or less evenly between these. You don't need to count stitches, just eyeball it. Adjust the positions of any markers that look noticeably closer together or farther apart. On the next row or round, work a decrease (or an increase) at each of the marked points. So long as they're spaced more or less evenly, it will look just fine.

## Every ___ Row/Round

Instructions for how often to work increases and decreases are usually given using this phrase, especially for something tapered like a sleeve. For example:

Increase 1 stitch at each edge every 4th row.

This is frequently interpreted wrongly as meaning, work 4 rows, and then increase. If you work 4 rows between increases, you're doing the increases every 5th row, which will result in a taper that is significantly longer. Your garment will be too long by the time you get to the correct width. Instead, you should work 3 rows even, then increase on the 4th row.

### Repeating Based on a Number of Rows or Rounds

Increasing every 5th row (*left*) means that you reach the desired width more slowly than if you increase every 4th row (*right*).

Sometimes you'll run across similar directions for working pattern stitches. For example, when knitting in the round, the instruction to purl every 5th round makes a fabric with evenly spaced ridges.

When working flat knitting, rather than in the round, instructions to work shaping every other row are easy to follow because all of the shaping will happen on the same side of the fabric; if you increase for the first time on the right side, then you'll always increase on the right side.

## In Pattern as Established/Maintain Pattern

This means to continue working the pattern stitch you are already working, regardless of any increases, decreases, bind offs, or cast ons you may also be instructed to work. To do this, you must figure out how to execute each row of the pattern stitch so that it lines up properly with the row below, so that the pattern looks continuous, regardless of shaping. Shaping while working a pattern stitch is discussed in Shaping Your Knitting, chapter 4, page 100.

## At the Same Time

This little phrase strikes fear into the hearts of many knitters. It's used when two things must happen concurrently. It may be that you need to continue a pattern stitch while working shaping.

Or it may be that you need to shape two different areas at once, for example, the neck opening and the armhole opening, or the neck and the shoulder slope. Keep in mind that you are shaping each of these at different edges of the garment.

The instructions will read something like this:

> Bind off 7 stitches for underarm at the armhole edge on the next wrong-side row. Beginning on next right-side row, decrease 1 stitch at neck edge, then continue decreasing 1 stitch at neck edge every 4th row 10 more times. *At the same time*, at armhole edge decrease 1 stitch every right-side row eight times, then work armhole even until it measures 5¾ inches from bind off and 17 stitches remain, ending with a right-side row. Continuing neck decreases until complete, bind off 4 stitches at armhole edge every wrong-side row four times. This shaping is illustrated in the chart and photo opposite.

In other words, after you've bound off the stitches at the underarm, you'll be shaping both the neck edge and the armhole edge. Written out row by row, this is how you proceed after binding off 7 stitches:

> Row 1 (right side): Decrease 1 stitch at the beginning and end of the row.
>
> Row 2 (wrong side): Work even.
>
> Row 3: Decrease 1 stitch at the end of the row.
>
> Row 4: Work even.

Each time you repeat rows 1 through 4, 1 stitch is decreased at the beginning of the row for the neck and 2 stitches are decreased at the end of the row for the armhole. After you've repeated the 4 rows four times, a total of 8 stitches will have been decreased at the armhole. It's time to stop decreasing at the end of the row, but you must continue decreasing at the beginning of the row. Written out row by row, this is how you do it:

> Row 1 (right side): Decrease 1 stitch at the beginning of the row.
>
> Rows 2–4: Work even.

When you've worked these 4 rows five times and then worked row 1 once more, the armhole should measure 5¾ inches and there will be only 17 stitches left, so it's time to start the shoulder shaping. Notice that you begin on the very next row, which is a wrong-side row. Here it is, row by row:

> Row 1 (wrong side): Bind off 4, work to end of row.
>
> Row 2 (right side): Work even.
>
> Row 3: Bind off 4, work to end of row.
>
> Row 4: Decrease 1 stitch at the beginning of the row.
>
> Repeat rows 1–3 once more, and all the stitches will be bound off.

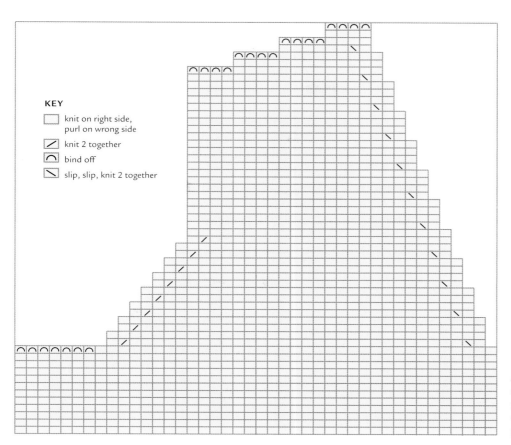

## KEY

⬜ knit on right side,
purl on wrong side

◹ knit 2 together

⌒ bind off

◺ slip, slip, knit 2 together

**At the same time,** this chart shows the armhole, neck, and shoulder shaping described on the opposite page.

**Following the instructions** results in the armhole, neck, and shoulder shaping in this sample.

## Place Marker/Slip Marker

Most of the time, working with markers is very straightforward, but sometimes confusion happens because some instructions tell you in excruciating detail what to do with the markers and others tell you almost nothing. When the instructions tell you to "place marker," then stick it on the needle tip after the stitch you just worked. Whenever you come to the marker in the future, slip it to the working needle, unless the instructions say to do otherwise. When there is an increase to be worked immediately before or after the marker, be careful to work the increase in the correct position (either before or after slipping the marker). If the increase happens to be a yarnover, the yarnover and the marker may swap positions while you're working the rest of the row or round. Note the correct position and fix it if necessary the next time you come to that marker.

## Reversing the Shaping

You'll see this expression used in the neck and shoulder area of a sweater, especially in older patterns. There will be complete instructions for working the first side, whether it be left or right, then it will say to work the opposite side, "reversing the shaping." If you're making a cardigan, this may comprise the complete instructions for the second front! To do this, work all the edge shaping at the opposite side. For example, if decreases were worked at the *end* of each right-side row on the first piece, they will be worked at the *beginning* of the right-side rows on the second piece. Bind offs and cast ons are reversed by working them with the opposite side of the fabric facing you. For example, if the first piece was finished off by binding off 4 stitches at the beginning of 4 *wrong-side* rows, working the same bind offs at the beginning of 4 *right-side* rows will create a mirror image of the original. Note that bind-off and cast-on shaping will start 1 row earlier or later on the second piece than on the first.

### Work Even

Usually found in the form "Work even until . . . ," this means to continue in whatever pattern is in progress without working any increases or decreases, so that the sides of the piece stay even.

### Work to . . .

I find the following instruction confusing because it's imprecise: "Work to *x* stitches before the end of row" or "Work to *x* stitches before the next marker." For example, if you are to work "to 10 stitches before the next marker," do you leave 10 stitches unworked, or do you work that 10th stitch and leave 9 unworked? What you're supposed to do is to leave all 10 stitches unworked.

### Work to within . . .

Recently I've noticed a lot of patterns that say, "Work to within *x* stitches of the end of row" or "Work to within *x* stitches of next marker." The instruction then tells you what to do with those stitches. If you try to interpret this instruction logically, it seems to indicate that as long as you have fewer stitches than are specified at the end of the row or before the marker, you're good to go. This is not in fact the case. If it says to work until you are within 5 stitches of anything, you'd better darn well stop with exactly 5 stitches left or you'll run into problems! What this instruction should say is, "Work until *x* stitches remain at the end of the row/before the next marker."

### Right Front/Left Front

Instructions for sweaters contain frequent references to the right and left front and to the right and left shoulders. These don't refer to the right (or left) as you look at it, but to the right (or left) when the garment is worn. Hold the sweater front up to your own body, with the public side facing out, to identify which side is which and avoid confusion. This problem doesn't come up when working with the back of the sweater, because the right shoulder of the back is on the right-hand side as you look at it.

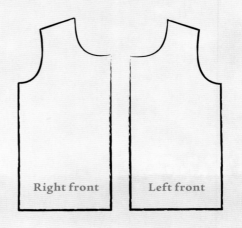

**Identifying Right and Left Garment Sections**

Right front        Left front

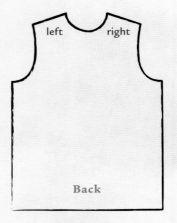

left        right

Back

## With Right Side/Wrong Side Facing

For some reason, many knitters find this instruction confusing. You'll see it most frequently as part of the instructions for picking up stitches, as in "With right side facing you, pick up 78 stitches along neck edge." It really means just what it says. Hold the fabric with the side indicated toward you, then begin the action described.

## Pick Up *versus* Pick Up and Knit

Usually this is shortened to "pick up," as in "Pick up 78 stitches along neck edge." In reality, what this almost always means is to use the working yarn to pick up and knit the stitches, not to try somehow to place stitches that are part of the existing fabric onto a needle. You will very occasionally run across the instruction to pick up in one step and then to knit across the stitches in a separate step. The instructions may make this clear by saying, "pick up (but do not knit)." Picking up without knitting only works well with slipped edge stitches, which are larger and looser than regular stitches at the edge of the fabric. For a lot more detail on this, see Planning for the Best Edges and Seams in chapter 2 (page 53), Neck, Armhole, and Front Borders in chapter 8 (pages 220–31), and Pick Up/Pick Up and Knit in the appendix (page 277).

## How to Read Charts

Charts make it easy to work pattern stitches and color patterns flat or circularly, without having to refer to the instructions in words. Charts are laid out in a grid, with one square representing each stitch. They portray textured pattern stitches using individual symbols for the various stitch manipulations, such as purls and slipped stitches. Color charts may show the actual color of each stitch, or may use a symbol for each color so that it's easy to substitute colors to create different colorways. The Craft Yarn Council has developed standard symbols for these charts (see Online References in the appendix, page 284, for the website).

When representing flat knitting, charts usually show a single pattern repeat plus any additional stitches that serve to center the pattern on the fabric. In circular knitting there are usually no centering stitches because the stitch count is generally an exact multiple of the pattern repeat, so the pattern stitch repeats around perfectly. The repeating section of the chart is usually indicated by a wide bracket across the bottom or heavy vertical lines (sometimes in a contrasting color) on each side of the repeat. If there are no special markings,

check for supporting text instructions that clarify which stitches are in the repeating section of the pattern. Each horizontal row of a chart represents a row of your knitting. Each square across the row represents an individual stitch. Because the first row hangs at the bottom of your knitting, the first row of a chart is the bottom row. For the same reason, if you are making a sweater from the top down, the images on the chart will be upside down, because your sweater is upside down as you work it.

In very rare cases, knitting charts are not based on a grid, for example, when they represent circular or swirled knitting. In these cases the designer must invent a new system, which will be explained in the supporting text.

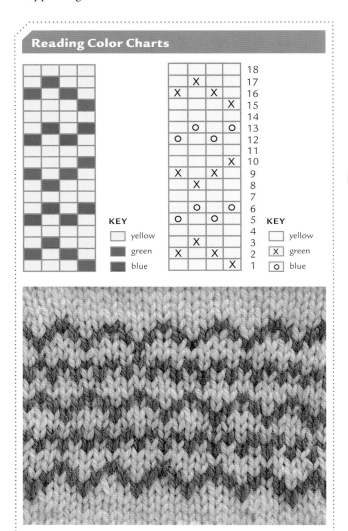

**Both charts** result in this same knitted fabric.

## Following Charts When Working Flat

When working flat, read the right-side rows from right to left, because that's the direction standard knitting is worked. Work any edge stitches at the beginning of the row, work the pattern repeat over and over until you approach the end of the row, and end with any edge stitches at the end of the row. Turn your knitting.

## Charts and Mirror-Image Knitting

Some knitters work in the opposite direction, holding the working needle in the left hand and proceeding across each row from left to right. Many other knitters who normally work in the standard direction have learned to "knit to and fro," which allows them to reverse direction across the row for convenience when working short rows or entrelac (for Knit To and Fro, see appendix, page 276).

The explanations for charts assume that you are a standard knitter. If you are working in the opposite direction, then read the chart in the opposite direction to match your knitting. When the wrong side is facing you, be sure to substitute knits for purls and vice versa.

Be aware, though, that this may not work in every case. For example, if there are Kfb increases at both edges of the knitting, to make them appear symmetrical they are worked 1 stitch farther away from the end of the row than from the beginning of the row, because the bump caused by knitting into the back of the stitch always follows the stitch itself. A mirror-image knitter would also need to work a Kfb increase at the beginning of the row 1 stitch closer to the edge than at the end of the row, but this would be at the left side of the chart (and the knitting) rather than at the right.

Decreases are also reversed for mirror knitters. K2tog slants to the left, and ssk slants to the right. Chart symbols, however, indicate the slant of the decrease, so if you use a decrease to match the slant shown on the chart (rather than that designated in the key), the results should be perfect.

When you work the next row across the wrong side of your knitting, you must read across the next higher row of the chart in the opposite direction, from left to right. First work any edge stitches at the left edge of the chart, then work the pattern repeat across, and finish by working any edge stitches at the right edge of the chart. At the same time, you need to realize that the chart shows what you will *see* on the *right* side of the knitting, not what you will *do* on the *wrong* side. If you knit a stitch on the wrong side, it will look like a purl on the right side. On the wrong-side rows you must, therefore, reverse all the knits that you see in the chart for purls, and substitute purls for knits. The key to your chart probably will have a reminder that the symbol for a knit stitch means to "knit on the right side and purl on the wrong side" and that the symbol for a purl stitch means to "purl on the right side and knit on the wrong side."

Continue moving up 1 row on the chart each time you complete a row of your knitting. Remember to read all the right-side rows from right to left and the wrong-side rows from left to right, and to reverse the knits and purls when you are working on the wrong side.

## Following Charts When Working Circularly

Assuming you always work with the right side facing you in circular knitting, begin reading the chart at the bottom row from right to left, just like flat knitting. Work the pattern repeatedly until you get to the end of the round. Then, move up 1 row on the chart and follow it from right to left, working the pattern repeat in the new row until you again reach the end of the round. Always read from right to left and always move up 1 row in the chart each time you begin a new round.

## Working Part of Row or Round from a Chart

Sometimes a chart will be provided just for a panel that is worked on part of each row. For example, a complex cabled pattern may be charted, while the stitches on either side are worked in something simple, such as Seed Stitch. In these cases, the section that the chart represents is usually designated by markers, and the instructions tell you to work in Seed Stitch up to the first marker, work the center panel based on the chart to the following marker, then work to the end of the row or round in Seed Stitch.

## Working Charts Showing Every Other Round

Occasionally, only every other row or round will be included in a chart. For example, wrong-side rows or plain rounds may be eliminated to reduce the size of large lace charts. In flat knitting, the right-side rows are the pattern rows and the wrong-side rows (that do not appear) are simply purled, or the stitches are worked "as established," knitting the knits and purling the purls. When knitting in the round, the plain rounds would be either knitted or worked "as established." If every other row is omitted from the chart, it will explain this in the instructions. The row numbers will increase by increments of two on these charts, and you'll need to remember to work the wrong-side rows or plain rounds before moving up to the next row of the chart.

### Same Chart, Different Notation

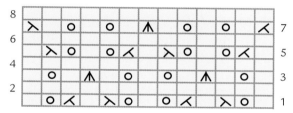

Chart showing all rows

Chart showing only pattern rows

## Deconstructing Chart Symbols

Knits are usually shown as an empty square. On right-side rows, knit these stitches. On wrong-side rows, purl them (so that when you turn to the right side they look like knits). Each pattern should include a key to the symbols, which provides guidance such as "knit on the right side, purl on the wrong side." Purls are usually shown as dashes, shaded squares, or dots. On right-side rows, purl these stitches. On wrong-side rows, knit them (so that when you turn to the right side they look like purls).

If the pattern has a different number of stitches on some rows, you may see a black or dark gray square mysteriously labeled "no stitch." This seeming contradiction means that, while there's a placeholder in the chart for a stitch that has disappeared or will appear on a subsequent row, there's currently no corresponding

stitch on your needle. When you come to "no stitch" in the chart, ignore that square on the chart, skip to the next square on the chart that represents a real stitch, and continue working with the next stitch on your needle. (For a list of symbols commonly used in charts, see the appendix, page 282.)

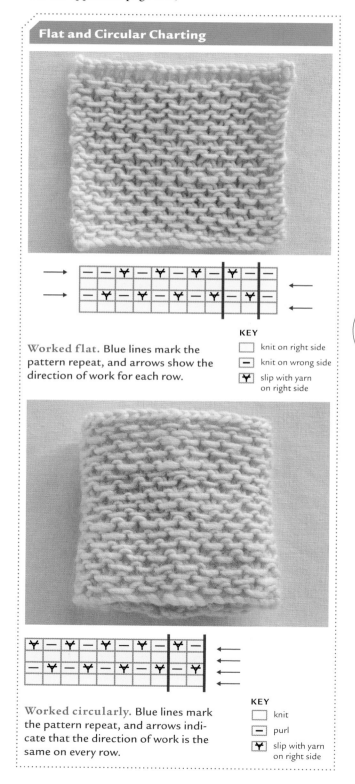

**Flat and Circular Charting**

Worked flat. Blue lines mark the pattern repeat, and arrows show the direction of work for each row.

KEY
☐ knit on right side
— knit on wrong side
Ⴟ slip with yarn on right side

Worked circularly. Blue lines mark the pattern repeat, and arrows indicate that the direction of work is the same on every row.

KEY
☐ knit
— purl
Ⴟ slip with yarn on right side

# Reality Checks

There's a tendency, when happily knitting from someone else's instructions, to get the project underway and then shift to automatic pilot, knitting along without paying much attention to how things are going. Even though I'm a designer and write knitting patterns, when I'm working from someone else's pattern, I tend to do exactly that, suspending my judgment and blindly following the instructions. There are a lot of reasons why this is a bad idea. It's easy to misinterpret the instructions and to blissfully knit several sections of a garment before you realize that something is radically wrong — like it's three sizes too small. This can happen if your gauge changes in the course of the project, and, as a result, part of the garment may end up significantly different in size than the rest. Or you may drop a stitch or make a mistake in a pattern stitch and not notice until much, much later, when it's much, much more work to correct the problem. Or you may misinterpret instructions for decreasing to shape the armhole or neck, for example working them every other row when they should have occurred every fourth row. For all these reasons, it's important to stop fairly frequently and evaluate your knitting. Here are the questions you should be asking yourself.

## Is Your Gauge Consistent?

Is the full-scale knitted piece consistent with your swatch? Does it look looser or tighter than the swatch? Measure a larger area than you could in your swatch to see if it's the correct gauge.

If there are any problems, decide how disastrous the predicament is. Will it be just a tiny bit off in size, or will it be much too big or too small? If it's not going to fit, stop and take action right away. You might try changing needle size in midstream. If changing needles doesn't look too bad, continue on, keeping an eye on things to see whether they continue to look good. If changing needles looks bad, you may need to unravel back to the border and work from there, or you may just need to cut your losses and start over.

## Is Your Piece the Right Size and Shape?

Measure the dimension of the piece you're working and check it against the schematic to see if it's coming out the right size and shape overall. Eyeball it and think about whether it looks the right size *to you*. If you're partway through a section, estimate what the length and width should be at this point, and whether it will end up the right size when completed. If it seems to be getting too wide too quickly or too slowly, you can adjust the spacing of any increases or decreases as you go, to make it come out just right. See chapter 4, for modifying the length and width of various garment pieces.

If you're working from the top down, be sure to check the fit of the neck opening, armholes, and shoulders when you complete them, before continuing with the body and sleeves. These are difficult and time consuming to correct after the rest of the sweater has been completed. Place the stitches on a long circular needle, two circulars, or a piece of yarn, so that you can actually try it on for fit. Circular needles are the most efficient choice, because you can knit the stitches onto them (instead of wasting time slipping them back and forth), and then keep right on working on the circular needle(s).

## Do You Like the Fabric?

Take a good look at the fabric. Stop and fondle it often. Do you like the way it looks and feels? Does it seem appropriate for what you're making? If it's stiff and thick or very soft and stretchy, will it behave the way it should in the finished garment? A stiff, thick fabric must be fitted very carefully to make a comfortable sweater. A very stretchy fabric tends to stretch out of shape. If you think there's a problem, try to figure out why it's happening. Did you substitute a thicker or thinner yarn that's causing the problem? Are you really getting the correct gauge? Try swatching again with a different needle size (larger to loosen up the fabric; smaller to tighten it) and see whether you can get a fabric you like at the correct gauge. If you can, you'll need to start the project over. If you can't, it may be that this isn't a good project to finish — perhaps you should do something else with this yarn.

Does the pattern stitch look right? Compare it to any photos of the garment. If it looks like the pictures, all's well. If it doesn't, but you like it anyway, that's fine, too. If it looks awful, you need to do something about that before you go any further.

Be sure to take a look at it from a distance to see whether the pattern and the yarn work together. Does the pattern disappear at a distance? If a textured pattern doesn't show up, you can sometimes improve the stitch definition by knitting it more tightly, but occasionally it's just a matter of the yarn structure; see chapter 2, page 23, on how to select the best yarn for your project. If a color pattern doesn't show up, it may be that you need more contrast between the colors. If they are all light, all medium, or all dark, they will tend to blend together from a distance. This is a problem you can detect ahead of time, if you make a point of evaluating your swatch at a distance and in dim light.

## Is There a Problem with the Instructions?

If the project isn't coming out at all as expected, try to figure out why. Is there a mistake in the instructions? Did you perhaps misinterpret or miss something you should have done? Check the publisher's website and Ravelry.com for notes of any errors, or notes on what you find confusing. Contact the publisher and those on Ravelry who have completed this project to see whether they had a similar problem or can shed any light on your difficulties. If you bought the pattern and yarn at a local store, take it to the store to ask for advice.

## When Your Yarn Causes Problems

One factor that is entirely out of your control, assuming you purchase yarn rather than spinning and dyeing your own, are inconsistencies and problems with the yarn itself. You may encounter annoyingly frequent knots, colors that rub off on your hands and clothes, inconsistencies in color, twist, and thickness, dyes that run, and shrinkage. The best way to avoid these problems is to be critically discerning when you buy yarn — look for problems in the balls and skeins. If you find any, decide whether you can live with them before you complete the purchase. Learn as much as you can about yarn by asking other knitters to share their experiences, checking Ravelry for comments, and reading the reviews at the online newsletter *Knitter's Review*. (For websites, see Online References in the appendix, page 284.)

### Dye Lot Differences and Color Variations

While you should always try to purchase enough yarn for your project from one dye lot, this is not always possible. Skeins of handpainted or handdyed yarns may vary in color even if they are from the same batch.

   If there is a difference in color, you can disguise the transition from one to another by alternating rows or rounds of each yarn. When you're working circularly, just knit around once with one yarn, then knit around with the second yarn. When you change yarns, be careful not to twist them and not to pull the yarn so firmly that the last stitch made with it collapses to form a tight column of stitches that looks like a seam. Follow these guidelines, and the change of yarns at the beginning of the round will be unnoticeable.

   When working flat, use a circular needle or two double-pointed needles so you can work from either

**Coping with Dye Lot Problems**

It's amazing how obvious a small variation in color can be in the knitted fabric.

Ready to purl across with the first yarn at right. You can see the tail from the new yarn, and the second strand of working yarn waiting at left.

In circular knitting, you can alternate the two skeins to blend two dye lots together. This is called helix knitting.

end of the row. Knit across once with the first yarn, then slide the stitches back to the other end of the needle and knit across again with the second yarn. Turn your work and purl across with the first yarn, slide the knitting back to the other end of the needle, and purl across with the second yarn. Repeat these 4 rows to alternate the two yarns in stockinette stitch (see photos on previous page).

If you are working a pattern stitch, try to alternate balls by working 2 pattern rows on the right side followed by 2 on the wrong side. If you find this confusing, just work 2 rows (right side, then wrong side) with one ball, followed by 2 rows with the other. You're really just working 2-row stripes. Carry the yarns up the edge of the fabric loosely enough so that it stays stretchy.

## When You Run Across Knots in the Yarn

Whether you run out of yarn at an inconvenient moment or unexpectedly encounter a knot, you need to treat them the same way. The general rules are don't tie a knot and don't knit past a knot. Instead, cut the yarn when you run across a knot in your yarn, and proceed as if you're starting a new ball of yarn. In a garment with a wrong side where the ends can be hidden later, just leave 4 to 6 inches of both ends dangling and weave them in later. If the resulting loose spot bothers you, go ahead and weave the ends in right away. See Weaving in Ends as You Go in the appendix (page 281) for instructions on how to weave in the ends as you knit.

If your garment is reversible or is openwork, it's going to be more difficult to deal with the ends. Areas such as lapels, collars, and cuffs, which may be turned back, need to look good on both sides. My preference is to splice the yarn ends, which involves overlapping and twisting the two ends together, and then knitting past the join. Once it is knitted, it won't come apart. Another approach is to use the "Russian join," where the ends of the two yarns are looped together. This has two advantages: if you are changing colors, there's a very neat transition because they don't overlap, and you don't need to worry about the join pulling apart before you have a chance to knit it. The Russian join is easiest to work in plied yarn. See Russian Join (page 278) and Splicing Yarn (pages 280–81) in the appendix for complete instructions.

Another option is hiding the ends while sewing them in, called duplicate stitch. When you come to the break in the yarn, overlap the two ends for about 8 to 10 inches and work just 1 stitch with the doubled yarn at the center of the overlap. You may be tempted to secure the new yarn by knitting a whole section of a row with

Overlap the yarn at the break and knit just 1 stitch. On the following row, work the double strand as a single stitch.

the doubled strand, but this usually results in noticeably larger stitches. For this reason, it's best to sew the ends in later. When you do, follow the path of the yarn exactly across the row for an inch or two before clipping the excess close to the fabric (see Duplicate Stitch Purl Side in the appendix, page 272). For slippery yarn, you may use a tiny dab of Fray Check (available at fabric stores) to anchor the ends so they won't pop out.

When working in lace or an eyelet pattern, if splicing the ends together won't work for some reason, plan ahead to make your finishing simpler by positioning the break where it will be easier to sew in the ends. If there will be seams, place it at the beginning of a row, where the ends can later be woven in along the seam. If there are solid areas in the pattern, place it at or near one of these. You can then weave in the ends on the wrong side of the solid area, where they will be hidden.

## Other Yarn Inconsistencies

Sometimes yarn will have a few quality problems. There may be an area where there is more twist or less twist than the rest of the ball or skein. Or there may be a section that's noticeably thinner or thicker than the rest. Some yarns, of course, are meant to be thick and thin, slubbed, or garneted with contrasting colors. In other yarns, it's simply a sign of poor quality control. Don't just knit past occasional inconsistencies hoping they won't show — they will! Treat them as recommended for knots (above): cut the yarn and discard the bad section.

If you have a whole skein that's different from the rest of the yarn for your project, you may not be able to finish the project without using it. You can sometimes disguise inconsistencies by reserving this yarn for the borders, which are frequently knit at a different gauge and in a different pattern stitch from the rest of the garment. If this won't work, you can also use the technique (described on page 151 for color variations) of alternating rows or rounds to integrate variations in yarn thickness or texture.

## Dealing with Mistakes

Actual mistakes in the knitting are, of course, something you'll also have to cope with. This includes things like dropped stitches, extra stitches created by accident, mistakes in pattern stitches, and variations in gauge.

There are some you'll absolutely need to address: Changes in gauge, for instance, will affect the ultimate utility of the garment — it may come out too big or too small to be comfortable. Losing or adding stitches inadvertently can also change the size of the garment, making it narrower or wider. Some mistakes impair the integrity of the fabric: Dropped stitches, if not secured, will continue to unravel, creating holes in the garment. A mistake that affects the stitch count will also make things more difficult for you when you get to future shaping in the garment, because you won't be able to follow the instructions exactly; it may be possible to adjust for this, but it's frustrating and will slow you down.

On the other hand, there are mistakes that are just aesthetic — they affect the way a garment looks, but don't affect its fit or function. This would include things like accidentally working the same row of a pattern twice, substituting a knit for a purl in a textured pattern, or working the wrong color in stranded knitting. With these sorts of problems you have three choices: leave it as is, disguise it, or fix it. You'll need to decide how much time you want to spend on these "nonessentials." Unfortunately, these are sometimes the mistakes that are most visible and may drive you crazy. If you're not sure, you can always leave the problem alone for now and plan to disguise or fix it later if it continues to bother you.

In the following sections I offer specific prescriptions for ways to cope with a wide variety of mistakes. Some fixes are easier and take less time than others. Before you jump in and start working on the more complex ones, take a little while to inspect your knitting carefully, diagnose and analyze what's really wrong, then plan the best way to fix it. You may be very uncomfortable with some of the suggestions (like cutting or unraveling a section in the middle of the work and reknitting it). It can also be difficult to predict how long a specific

solution will take; sometimes it's actually quicker to just rip out and do it over than it is to spend hours correcting one small problem in the middle of the fabric.

In light of the annoyance that even aesthetic mistakes can cause, I have also provided some suggestions for detecting these mistakes as soon as possible, when they're easier to fix.

If the mistake is of too great a magnitude or the suggested fix seems overwhelming to you, then the bottom line is that you can always unravel back to the point of the mistake and knit that section over. This can be a painful exercise if you've sweated over the section to be removed, but it's really best to cut your losses and do it over if necessary in order to save the sweater. You may want to set it aside for a time, to contemplate whether this is really the only option and to consult with other knitters who may have found another way to cope with the same problem or who'll offer moral and technical support during the process. It's possible that letting the project age, like fine wine, will give your imagination time to come up with a novel solution.

Some mistakes elude even the most vigilant of knitters and are discovered after the garment is finished. If this happens to you, consult Fixing Mistakes (chapter 6, page 174) and The Elusive Pursuit of Perfection (chapter 8, page 253).

## What to Do about Dropped Stitches

If you notice a dropped stitch within a row or two, it's easy to hook it back up with a crochet hook. If the dropped stitch occurred more than a few rows earlier, however, the knitting will become very tight when you try to do this, so it's better to unravel the whole piece back to the mistake to fix the problem. This may not be practical if you discover the dropped stitch much later. See the appendix for how to hook up individual stitches (pages 271–72) and chapter 6 for how to deal with dropped stitches discovered after binding off (page 175).

## When You Discover You Have Extra Stitches

Unravel to the point where the stitch appeared. Work the extra yarn into the stitches on either side until the knitting looks even. If this will make a large loose area, it may be better to just decrease to get rid of the stitch when you discover it. Be sure to hide the decrease in an unobtrusive place. Usually there will be a hole where the stitch was created. Use a piece of yarn to close up the hole and weave in the ends on the back. (See Closing Up Holes, chapter 6, page 174.)

# Fixing a Mistake in Cable

① **Second cable crossing** below needle twists the wrong way.

② **Knit to the beginning of the cable.** Unravel the cable stitches to mistake.

③ **Use double-pointed needles** to work back up to the top correctly.

## When You Made Incorrect Stitches in the Pattern

If the problem is limited to a few stitches, work the current row until you are above the mistake. To correct the previous row, unravel the one section that is a problem and rework it, then continue with the current row. For a mistake farther down in the knitting, unravel the stitches directly above it down to the problem. If there are just a few stitches to be corrected, use a crochet hook to work up the column of stitches correctly.

If there are more stitches, use short double-pointed needles the same size as those for your project to knit the unraveled area back up. These are especially convenient because they allow you to work from either end. In a complicated pattern, it may be least confusing to unravel and reknit one complete repeat of the pattern. Be sure to work each loose strand of yarn in order from bottom to top.

Try to keep the tension of the yarn consistent with the rest of the fabric, so that you don't end up with a tight area at one side of the correction and a loose area at the other. If you do, simply slip the stitches one at a time to another needle, beginning at the loose end, tightening up the first stitches you come to and loosening up the later ones. When the correction has been completed, use the tip of a needle to tease the yarn from any loose areas into tighter ones.

## When You Worked a Whole Row Incorrectly

If the problem is a whole row worked incorrectly, you can either rip your knitting back to that point and reknit it, or (if it's a long way down) you can replace the row (see photos on facing page). Snip 1 stitch in the row with the mistake. Make your cut about 6 stitches from the end of the row to ensure that you have a long enough tail at the end of the row to weave in after your correction is complete.

Unravel the whole row and slip knitting needles into the active stitches you've created above and below the row to be corrected. If it's difficult to insert the size needle you've been using, then use slimmer needles. Using a yarn needle and Kitchener stitch (see appendix, page 276), replace the row correctly. You can use the unraveled yarn, but it won't be quite long enough to complete the repair. It also may be difficult to work neatly if the yarn is kinky from having been knitted. You can wet it and lay it out flat to dry or steam it very lightly with a steam iron to straighten out the kinks. When there are only 4 to 6 inches of yarn left, start an additional piece of yarn to complete the join.

# Correcting a Whole Row

① **Mistake to be corrected:** Here, an entire purl row was worked in stockinette fabric.

② **Snip a stitch** near the beginning of the row.

③ **Use a blunt-tipped needle** to pick out the row stitch by stitch.

④ **Place the stitches** above and below the opening on needles, and work Kitchener stitch to replace the purled row.

It can be very confusing to work Kitchener stitch in pattern. If there are any plain knit or purl rows in the pattern immediately above the mistake, snip and pick out the plain row, then unravel until the row with the mistake has been removed. Place the knitting on needles and rework the section you removed until you are ready to replace the plain row. Use Kitchener stitch to reinsert the plain row, which is much easier than trying to work Kitchener in pattern.

If there are no plain rows, you may want to practice Kitchener stitch in pattern on a swatch before you cut your knitting. Work the swatch in pattern, making one pattern row (the one you will need to duplicate later) in a contrasting color. Snip and remove the same pattern row from the swatch in a section above the contrasting row. While you are working Kitchener stitch, refer to the contrast-color row as a guide. If you find yourself making errors while doing this, practice the pattern row by working duplicate stitch along the contrasting row, following the path of the original yarn exactly.

## Disguising the Jog

In flat knitting, you can perfectly match pattern stitches and stripes at the seams when you join pieces together. One of the few drawbacks of circular knitting is that some patterns cannot be matched perfectly where the end of one round meets the beginning of the next. There are, however, techniques to disguise the jog or stair-step effect that is integral to circular knitting.

The "jog" is the place where the pattern is noticeably discontinuous when you begin a new round. When you change to the next round of a pattern stitch or a new color at the beginning of the round, it's obvious where you made the change. The jog occurs because circular knitting is really a spiral, where each round lies above the previous one. Most of the tube doesn't appear to be spiraling: only when there's a discontinuity where one round ends and the next begins is its true structure apparent.

# Preventing Pattern Stitch Errors

Attempting to correct errors can be very frustrating and time consuming, especially if your best efforts fail and you end up unraveling and starting over. If you realize that a particular pattern stitch is causing you difficulties, so that you need to correct more than a few mistakes or you find it impossible to correct the mistakes efficiently, take steps to prevent the mistakes from occurring and to make fixing them easier.

**If you keep losing your place in the instructions, try one of these:**

▷ Place a sticky note just above the line you are working.

▷ Use a highlighter or check mark to keep track of each line or row as you complete it.

▷ Use removable highlighter tape, which can be moved down the page as you work and doesn't mark the paper permanently.

▷ Use a document holder and magnetic straight edge to keep your place.

▷ Write each row of the pattern on a separate file card, punch a hole in the corner, and place them all on a metal ring or a piece of yarn. As you complete each row, flip the card for that row to the back.

▷ If you are working from complicated and confusing text, try charting the instructions for clarity and working from the chart.

**If you keep losing your place in the knitting on your needle, here are some suggestions:**

▷ Track individual repeats across the row by placing a marker between each repeat.

▷ Track the first row of each repeat by placing a split marker or safety pin in the first stitch of that row. To determine which row you are on, just count rows beginning with the marked row.

▷ If you can't tell the right side from the wrong side, place a split marker or safety pin on the right side of the fabric, near the beginning of the row.

If you find it difficult to make corrections without unraveling, especially if it's almost impossible to get the stitches back on the needle afterward, place "lifelines" in your knitting periodically (see appendix, page 277). Choose a pattern row you can recognize (for example, the first or last row of the pattern stitch), or perhaps the row immediately below the one on which you tend to make mistakes. Whenever you complete that row of your pattern, take a thin, smooth, strong thread or yarn and run it through all the stitches using a yarn needle. (I like to use crochet cotton.) Leave long tails at both ends of the lifeline so there's no danger of any stitches falling off or the thread pulling out. If you need to backtrack, you can easily unravel back to the lifeline and slip your needle back in. In fact, you can first slip a needle into the fabric following the path of the lifeline, and then unravel down to it. This is most easily accomplished if you use a thinner needle. Work the stitches back onto the proper size needle on the first row you rework.

**Inserting a lifeline** through the stitches on the needle, using crochet cotton and tapestry needle

The jog is most noticeable when the pattern is strongly horizontal.

Garter stitch

Purled ridges

Stripes

## Working Pattern Stitches without the Jog

There are a variety of ways to make the jog less visible. Which you choose will depend on the situation.

### When Working Vertical Patterns

Make the total number of stitches an exact multiple of the pattern repeat when working a vertical pattern such as ribbing or cables, and the pattern will repeat seamlessly around.

**Planning Vertical Patterns**

K2, P2 ribbing in the round

Two-stitch colored stripes in the round

157

### Adjusting Stitch Counts to Avoid the Jog

**Working Seed Stitch** on an even number of stitches (*bottom*) makes a noticeable jog. On an odd number of stitches (*top*) the pattern flows from round to round with no jog.

**Like Seed Stitch,** Salt and Pepper can be worked on an odd number of stitches (*top*) to eliminate the jog.

**Patterns that reverse every other round** can be made to appear seamless by adjusting the number of stitches to allow for half of a pattern repeat at the end of the round rather than a full repeat. This Broken Garter Stitch has a pattern repeat of 6 stitches. In the bottom half, an even multiple of 6 results in the end of round 1 running into the beginning of round 2, because 3 stitches on either side are all knitted or all purled. Decreasing 3 stitches to remove half a repeat means that the pattern always switches from knit to purl, or vice versa, at the end of the round, continuing the pattern seamlessly in the top half.

## Patterns that Reverse on Every Round

Patterns like Seed Stitch and the two-color checkerboard known as Salt and Pepper can be coaxed to repeat seamlessly by adjusting the number of stitches. If you work them on an even number of stitches, the jog is obvious; if you add or subtract 1 stitch to make the total odd, they repeat joglessly.

## Working with Strongly Horizontal Patterns

It's not quite as easy to disguise the point where the end of one round meets the beginning of the next if the pattern is strongly horizontal.

**Single pattern rounds (see facing page).** If there is just one round to be dealt with, for example, one ridge of purl stitches or a round of eyelets, work the single round, then slip the first stitch of the following round. This will pull the first stitch of the pattern round up next to the last stitch (see facing page).

**Two-round patterns.** For patterns that have a 2-round repeat, like garter stitch or alternating rounds of two colors, you can use helix knitting (see appendix, pages 272–73) to hide the jog. For jogless garter stitch, use two balls of the same color — one for the knit rounds and one for the purl rounds. For alternating stripes just 1 round wide, use one ball of each color.

**Patterns more than 2 rounds long.** If you have a horizontal pattern more than 2 rounds long, the most efficient solution is to introduce seam stitches. These are a small number of stitches at the beginning of the round that are worked in stockinette, garter, or some other simple pattern stitch. They serve to separate the beginning and end of the round of more complex patterns so that their misalignment is not so noticeable. On sleeves, you will want just one set of seam stitches at the beginning/end of round, which will run along the inside of the sleeve. Make the bodies of sweaters and vests symmetrical by introducing a second set of seam stitches halfway around.

**Single-round stripes,** unless they lend themselves to helix knitting, can be made to look continuous only if you cut all the yarns at every color change. Leave 6-inch tails, long enough to sew with easily. When you have finished the project, turn it inside out and duplicate stitch these ends across the end of the round, directly behind the stitches of the same color. As you work, take care to adjust the tension of the stitches attached to the tails so they are the same size as their neighbors. The photos on page 160 show how to proceed step by step. (See Duplicate Stitch, Purl Side in the appendix, page 272.)

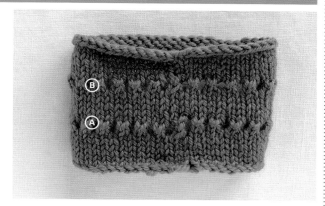

**Single pattern rounds.** In each of the two examples (*above*), nothing has been done to disguise the jog in the pattern round at the bottom Ⓐ. At the top Ⓑ, the jog has been made less obvious by slipping the first stitch of the following round.

**Two-round patterns.** At the left, garter stitch in helix knitting; at the right helix knitting makes the beginning/end of round disappear in one-round stripes.

**Patterns more than 2 rounds long.** Double garter stitch with and without seam stitches

# Jogless Single-Round Stripes

Leave ends long to work with when changing colors.

① Duplicate stitch the contrast color from right to left across the end of the round behind stitches of the same color (one green strand woven in, three strands left to go).

② Duplicate stitch the contrast color from left to right across the end of the round behind stitches of the same color (two green strands woven in, two yellow strands to go).

③ Duplicate stitch the main color from right to left above the stripe (one yellow strand left to go).

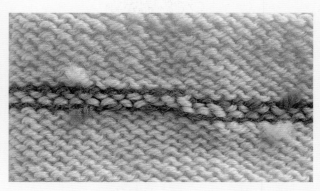

④ Duplicate stitch the main color from left to right below the stripe (finished, wrong side).

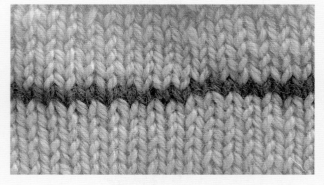

⑤ The ends of the single-round stripes in the finished knitting (right side) line up when you take the time to weave in the yarn properly.

**Multi-round stripes.** You can disguise the jog at the beginning and end of multi-round stripes by adding seam stitches as described in the hints on page 158 for Patterns More than 2 Rounds Long.

**More Ways to Disguise Jogs**

Cable at color change

One-stitch stripe at beginning/end of round in color not used

▷ One disguise that works especially well is to make a small cable using the final 1 or 2 stitches of the round crossed over the first 1 or 2 stitches of the round. The cable twists effectively distract the eye from the color changes and from any distorted stitches caused by carrying the yarn up the back of the fabric between stripes.

▷ You could also disguise the jog, and carry colors up for use on future rounds, by working a 1-stitch stripe in each color on any round where it is not used (see photo at below left).

If you're working in stockinette and don't want to add seam stitches, but still want to smooth the transition between colors, the first step is to cut the ends of the yarn each time you change colors. Next, slip the first stitch of the second round of each color. Finally, duplicate stitch all the ends on the back to align the colors properly at the color changes, as described for Single-Round Stripes (opposite).

# Binding Off and Casting On in the Middle

Shaping armholes, necklines, shoulders, and buttonholes will frequently require you to bind off or cast on while the work is still in progress.

## Binding Off at the Beginning of a Row

When the instructions say to bind off 5 stitches at the beginning of the row, you need to actually work the 6th stitch so you can pass the 5th one over it, binding it off. You'll always need to work 1 more stitch than the instructions call for in order to bind off the right number. Count the remaining stitches afterward to ensure that you've done it correctly.

The standard bind off will usually work just fine, either for shaping at the edge of a garment piece or to make an opening like a buttonhole. Just be sure you don't bind off too tightly. If binding off tightly is a problem for you, try the suspended bind off or one of the decrease bind offs (see appendix, page 259 and 261) to loosen it up. If you're working in stockinette or another pattern stitch with a tendency to curl, reduce the curling by binding off in K1, P1 ribbing.

## Casting Onto Work in Progress

Casting on at the edge of your work, over an opening like a buttonhole, or when starting a steek requires a single-strand cast on. The long-tail cast on, which requires two strands, won't work in these situations (unless you're working with two colors), so if this is the only cast on you know, you'll need to learn another one. Choose one of the single-strand cast ons based on how you want the edge to behave.

▷ For a stretchy edge, like the thumb opening of fingerless mittens, use the knitted or half-hitch cast on.

▷ For a less stretchy edge, like you'd need on a buttonhole, use the cable cast on.

▷ To prevent curling, try the ribbed cable cast on. You can expect this one to be moderately stretchy.

The instructions for all of these single-strand cast ons are in the appendix (pages 264–67).

## Closing Up Holes at the Cast On or Bind Off

Casting on or binding off in the middle of your work tends to leave a loose strand or a little hole at the beginning or end. To tighten it up, when you come to the loose strand on the next row or round, pick it up, twist it, and put it on the left needle as you would an M1 increase. Knit or purl this twisted stitch together with the next stitch, as your pattern dictates.

Or, when casting on, you can plan ahead and cast on 1 fewer stitch than specified. When you come to it on the next row, pick up the long strand between the stitches, twist it, and put it on the left needle. This provides the additional stitch needed, and no decreasing is necessary.

If a small hole remains, close it up using a nearby tail of yarn when you weave in the ends, or use a separate piece of yarn if there's none in the neighborhood.

## Fixing Holes in Cast On or Bind Off

When you cast on or bind off mid-row, you are likely to get a small hole.

① When you come to the strand on the next row, pick it up, give it a twist, and put it on left needle.

② Knit or purl this twisted stitch together with the next stitch, keeping to pattern.

Hole is now closed.

## Bottom Borders on a Top-Down Sweater

If you're working the major garment pieces from the top down, whether in separate flat pieces or joined together in the round, you'll usually continue through the bottom border on the body and the sleeves, and then bind off. The general advice for bottom borders given in Beginning with the Very Best Borders (chapter 2, page 50) also applies in this situation.

If you're working a ribbing attached to stockinette stitch in a wool or wool-blend yarn, you'll need to reduce the number of stitches by about 10 percent and move to a needle about two sizes smaller to produce a bottom border that pulls in a bit and retains its shape under tension. For other types of borders and in other combinations of base fabric and border stitches, you'll need to adjust the number of stitches and the needle size so that the border is correctly proportioned to the body or sleeve.

## Binding Off at the End

Generally, the final bind off on shoulders should be firm to support the sweater. On the other hand, if you're working top down, the bottom edge of the body and sleeves must be stretchy enough to be pulled on without straining the knitting (or the wearer), but appear neat and tidy when relaxed.

When choosing your bind off, think about how it needs to behave. Does it need to stretch or should it be firm and supportive? Should it be decorative? Does it need to maintain the pattern stitch or can it be plain? Do you want the bind-off chain to show along the edge, or would you prefer it to be more understated? The examples at right show a range of options for binding off, appropriate for a variety of situations.

### Working the Basic Bind Off

The standard bind off, where you knit 2 stitches and pass the first one worked over the second one and off the needle, will be the obvious choice for most situations. Even this very basic technique has several variations.

First consider how it will look.

Second, consider the tension of your bind off. Many knitters bind off a little too tightly. If you need a firm bind off, this can be helpful. On the other hand, if you need a bind off that is reasonably stretchy or must be loose enough not to pull in the edge of the fabric, try these alternative methods to see which works best for you. You may find that all of them are useful in different situations. Instructions for all are in the appendix.

**Bind Off Variations**

The knitted version (worked knitting all the stitches, with the right side of the fabric facing you) makes a very prominent chain along the edge of the fabric. If you want your bind off to look this way, but need to work it from the wrong side of the fabric, just purl all the stitches instead of knitting.

The purled version (worked either from the wrong side, knitting all the stitches, or from the right side, purling all the stitches) makes a neat purled ridge at the edge of the fabric, perfect for making garter stitch look continuous all the way to the very end Ⓐ, and makes a pleasant contrast to ribbing Ⓑ.

The K1, P1 ribbed version of the basic bind off, which is made by alternately knitting and purling the stitches as you bind off, makes the signature chain of stitches lie along the very edge of the knitting, rather than on the knitted face of the fabric.

- ▷ **Decrease bind offs (ssk version, purl version, and Russian bind off).** In each of these a decrease is used to work 2 stitches together with the next, rather than passing one over the other (page 259).

- ▷ **Suspended bind off.** Instead of dropping the stitch you pass over, leave it on the left needle until it is pushed off by working the next stitch (page 261).

Properly tensioned bind off (*above*) and tight bind off (*below*)

## When You Need a Stretchy Bind Off

Sometimes you need a bind off that has more stretch than you can achieve with the standard bind off. It may be for an area that is around the outside of a curve, along the edge of a ruffle, or on an edge that needs to stretch enormously to prevent the yarn from breaking.

The bind offs described here are just the tip of the iceberg — there are so many ways to bind off that it helps to have a comprehensive reference on hand so you can choose just the right one.

**Sewn bind off.** I learned this bind off from Elizabeth Zimmermann's *Knitting Without Tears*. It's especially good when you don't want the thicker edge that a bind-off chain makes. Because its tension depends entirely on how tightly or loosely you sew it, you can control it completely (see appendix, page 260).

**Picot bind off** creates a little bit of embellishment while adding stitches to the edge. This makes the edge longer, so it can stretch (see appendix, page 260).

**Yarnover bind off.** I like to use this along the edge of ruffles, because it's easily worked along long edges and requires no special knowledge. A regular bind off will act as a restraint, but the yarnover bind off is stretchy enough so the ruffle can ruffle to its full potential. This bind off can look a little messy when it's relaxed, but it's nice and neat when stretched (see appendix, page 261).

**Tubular bind off.** This bind off (see appendix, page 261) is an exact match for tubular cast on (page 43), so you can make the beginning and ending edges of your garment match. It integrates perfectly with K1, P1 ribbing, and it wraps around the edge of the fabric without the bulky edge characteristic of the basic bind off (see appendix, page 261).

## Bind-Off Embellishments

Like the picot bind off, many embellishments at the bound-off edge are both decorative and add stitches that result in a stretchy edge. One exception to this is the I-cord bind off, which tends to have less stretch instead of more. These embellishments can be very feminine and frilly, or tailored and restrained.

### How to Create a Ruffled Edge

A ruffle worked at the edge of the knitting is going to have plenty of stretch. To make a ruffle, all that's required is to increase substantially, at least doubling the number of stitches, and then work until the ruffle is as deep as you like. Within that framework, you have lots of options.

▷ Work closed (M1 with the working yarn) or open (yo) increases, which are preferable to Kfb increases. The M1 and yo use the working yarn to create the new stitch, resulting in a looser fabric. Kfb should be avoided, because it tends to tighten the fabric when worked many times on the same row.

▷ Work all the increases on 1 row, spread them out over several rows, or work them gradually throughout the ruffle.

▷ Make a curly-edged ruffle by working in stockinette, a more restrained flat ruffle in garter stitch, or use any other simple noncurling pattern stitch.

▷ Finish off your ruffle with a stretchy bind off, either the yarnover bind off or a decorative bind off like the picot bind off.

**Variations on ruffles are limitless** (*top to bottom*): gradual increases using eyelets in stockinette stitch; increases only at the base of a garter stitch ruffle; doubling the stitches on every row in stockinette.

## Exploring the Possibilities of Applied Edgings

You can work a strip of noncurling knitting, plain or fancy, perpendicular to the main fabric, joining it to the base fabric at the end of every other row, and thus binding off. One side of this strip becomes the finished outer edge of your knitting, replacing the less stretchy chain of the standard bind off. If you decide to finish a garment with an applied edging, remember to allow for the width of the edging. For example, if you plan to add an edging that's 2 inches wide, stop working 2 inches before you would normally bind off. You may want to put the stitches on pieces of yarn or spare circular needles, join the garment pieces together, and then work the edging seamlessly across all the pieces to bind them off. (General instructions for working applied edgings are in the appendix, page 259.)

### Several Applied Edgings

**Simple garter stitch edging**

**One repeat of Faggotting Rib** is used here to create an openwork edging while binding off.

**A simple lace** edging

## Shaping Finesse for Curves and Slopes

Necklines and shoulders often require a series of stepped bind offs for proper shaping. This type of shaping is sometimes used on armholes as well. Shoulder instructions will say something like, "Bind off 5 stitches at the beginning of the next 6 right-side rows." At necklines and armholes, where a gradual curve is desirable, the instructions will read more like this: "Bind off 8 stitches at the beginning of the next right-side row. Bind off 4 stitches at the beginning of the next 2 right-side rows. Bind off 2 stitches at the beginning of the next 3 right-side rows," and then instructions for decreasing 1 stitch at the edge for a number of rows will follow.

If you follow these instructions exactly, you'll end up with an edge with pronounced corners or "stair steps" where each of the subsequent bind offs begin as in the photo below. These can be difficult to pick up stitches along or to seam neatly.

**To smooth the transition between each group of bound-off stitches,** slip the first stitch of each bind off (except the first), instead of knitting it. For example, instead of following the instructions above for the shoulder shaping, do this:

▷ Bind off 5 stitches at the beginning of the next right-side row, then work to the end of the row. Work 1 wrong-side row. *At the beginning of the next right-side row, slip 1 knitwise, knit 1, pass slipped stitch over, then bind off 4 more stitches. Work to the end of the row. Work 1 wrong-side row. Repeat from * four more times, at which point all the shoulder stitches will have been bound off.

**To work the same shaping on the wrong side of stockinette,** do this:

▷ Bind off 5 stitches in purl at the beginning of the next wrong-side row, then work to the end of the row. Work 1 right-side row. *At the beginning of the next wrong-side row, P2tog, then bind off 4 more stitches. Work to the end of the row. Work 1 right-side row. Repeat from * four more times.

**Shoulders, armholes, and necks** shaped with a series of bind offs have pronounced stair steps.

**When the additional groups of bind offs** begin with a slipped stitch or decrease, the sloped and curved edges are much smoother and easier to work with when finishing the sweater.

**For an even smoother edge,** you can incorporate slipped stitches on every row of the shaping, for example:

▷ Bind off 5 stitches at the beginning of the next right-side row, then work to the end of the row. *On the following wrong-side row, work until 1 stitch remains, slip 1 purlwise. At the beginning of the next right-side row, slip 1 knitwise, knit 1, pass slipped stitch over, then bind off 4 stitches. Work to the end of the row. Repeat from * four more times, at which point all the shoulder stitches will have been bound off.

If the unworked slipped stitches make you uncomfortable, you can accomplish the same smoothing effect by working a decrease at the end of each row where no stitches are bound off, and at the beginning of the group of bound-off stitches on the following row. The two decreases take the place of 2 bound-off stitches in each group of 5, leaving only 3 stitches to actually bind off. Note that you can substitute ssk for skp, if you like.

**To work the bind off on the right-side rows:** Bind off 5 stitches at the beginning of the next right-side row, then work to the end of the row. *Work the next wrong-side row until 2 stitches remain, ssp. At the beginning of the following right-side row, skp, bind off 3, then work to the end of the row. Repeat from * until all stitches have been bound off.

**To work the bind off on the wrong-side rows:** Bind off 5 stitches in purl at the beginning of the next wrong-side row, then work to the end of the row. *Work the following right-side row until 2 stitches remain, K2tog. At the beginning of the next wrong-side row, P2tog, bind off 3 in purl, then work to the end of the row. Repeat from * until all stitches have been bound off.

**Slipping the first stitch** of the bind off and the last stitch of the row before each bind off makes an even smoother edge.

## Creating Hems and Casings

Hems can be created when you bind off, if an elastic border isn't required. All you need to do is to continue knitting beyond where you want the fabric to end, then fold the additional length to the inside and secure it to the back of the fabric. A casing is just a hem big enough to run a drawstring or a piece of elastic through. This is another embellishment that offers several options:

▷ At the point where you want the edge of the fabric to fall, you may work a fold line by working 1 or 2 rows in reverse stockinette, create a picot edge by repeating (K2tog, yo) all the way across, or make a rolled edge by doing nothing special at all.

▷ The additional length for the inside of the hem should be worked as flat as possible to reduce bulk, so stockinette stitch is the best choice, even if the outer layer is worked in some other pattern stitch.

▷ The inner layer of a hem can sometimes be too bulky and will cause the outer layer to bulge. For this reason, you may want to work the inner layer with thinner yarn, fewer stitches, or a smaller needle.

▷ When joining the hem on the inside, you can sew it down (either binding off first, or being careful to sew through every stitch so it can't unravel); pick up stitches across the back of the fabric and then join using the three-needle bind off; or pick up 1 stitch at a time on the back of the fabric and knit this stitch together with the next stitch while you bind off. (See Joining Bind-Off Hems, appendix, page 273.)

## Firm and Supportive Bind Offs

You may want the bind off to prevent a piece of knitting from stretching or even to gather the edge. If you find yourself in this situation, there are several techniques you can employ, depending on how you want the edge to look.

You can make a firm edge by using a smaller needle while binding off. If this doesn't make the edge short enough, try the 1-over-2 bind off. It's worked similarly to the standard bind off, except that you start with 3 stitches instead of 2. Passing 1 stitch off the needle over the other 2 each time you bind off firmly gathers the edge (see appendix, page 260).

**Hem Styles**

*Top to bottom:* rolled hem, folded hem, and picot hem

Three ways to join (*top to bottom*): sewn without binding off, three-needle bind off, and picking up while binding off

1-over-2 bind off results in a very firm gathered edge.

The I-cord bind off makes a cord along the edge as you bind off, providing support with a very slight stretch. This can be worked in the same or a contrasting color. If the I-cord needs to be either a little tighter or looser, you can easily adjust it by changing the size of the working needle (see appendix, pages 259–60). The I-cord can also be made longer to fit the edge by working an occasional unattached round (work just the cord stitches with no decrease to bind off a stitch) or shorter by decreasing periodically in the main fabric stitches while joining the I-cord (which requires that you K2tog on the main fabric before passing the slipped stitch over to join the cord).

I-cord bind off in a contrasting color

## Integrating the Bind Off with the Pattern Stitch

When it's going to be hidden in a seam or a picked-up border, it doesn't really matter what the bind off looks like, so you might as well use the basic bind off. What is more important in these cases is how the hidden bind off behaves: make sure it's elastic if it will need to stretch or firm if it's required to support the garment.

When the bound-off edge will be seen, however, you should consider binding off in pattern. If you've been working a pattern stitch based on knits and purls, binding off in pattern is just a matter of continuing to work the knits and purls of the pattern stitch as you bind off. More complicated patterns, especially those that have a different number of stitches on different rows or that are much wider or narrower than plain old stockinette stitch, may require additional adjustments when binding off. Sometimes, you can get away with binding off on a plain row of the pattern. Other times, you may need to work increases, decreases, or short rows while binding off to avoid distorting the fabric.

### Binding Off for Chevron Patterns

Plain bind off on a chevron pattern like Razor Shell makes a slightly scalloped edge.

Including all the increases and decreases of the pattern row while you bind off creates an excellent exposed edge of points that mirrors the cast-on edge.

## Binding Off Scalloped Patterns

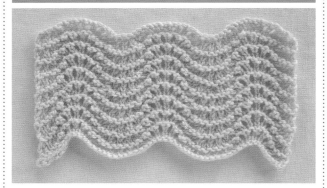

**Row 4 of Old Shale** is a plain knit row on the wrong side. Binding off on this row makes the pattern stitch look finished to the very edge, and working the bind off loosely allows the edge to ripple so that it matches the rest of the fabric.

**If you need a straight edge for seaming** or picking up a border, shift the decreases to the sections where increases occur in the pattern stitch when you work the final row and eliminate all the increases. This counteracts the curves and shortens the bound-off edge so it's the same width as the rest of the fabric. Unfortunately, it also distorts the fabric so that the pattern is stretched out of shape at the top and must be blocked to encourage it to lie flat.

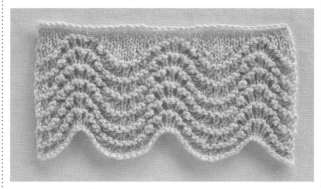

**A more complicated solution**, that makes the transition from a scalloped pattern to a straight edge without distortion, is to fill in the areas over the decreases with short rows, as well as decreasing to shorten the bound-off edge.

## Binding Off Cabled Patterns

**Cables pull the fabric in horizontally.** Binding off without adjusting for this means that the edge will flare above each cable, especially the wide ones.

**Decreasing above each cable** as you bind off pulls the edge in. Decrease just 1 stitch on narrow cables, more on the wide ones.

**Bind off on a row** where you cross the cables to take the pattern all the way to the edge.

The traditional Fan Shell pattern is similar to Old Shale, except that, while all the yarnovers occur on a single row, the decreases happen gradually, so that the number of stitches varies from row to row. If you bind off on a row with the smallest number of stitches, you get a nice, straight edge.

This example was bound off in knitting on the wrong side on a row with the maximum number of stitches. It looks loose and messy.

Since the most noticeable pattern element is a ridge formed by 2 reverse stockinette rows, work until the first of these has been completed, then bind off on the following row in pattern to make the pattern continue to the edge of the fabric. Blocking is required to make the scalloped top edge neat.

The double wraps worked on every row of Horizontal Brioche cause the edge to ruffle if you bind off all those stitches normally.

To make the upper edge behave, work single wraps on the last row, reducing the stitches by half, then bind off.

## What Comes Next?

When you've completed the front and the back, consider blocking those pieces, joining the shoulders, and adding the neck border before moving on to the sleeves. This will allow you to check the fit in the neck and shoulder area and to determine exactly how long the sleeves should be from cuff to armhole. (See chapter 2, pages 38–39 for more details.) To get an even better idea of the fit, baste the side seams together and try on the body of the sweater.

You may want to block all the pieces as you complete them, just to check their actual measurements and to make finishing quicker and easier. Each piece can be drying while you knit the next. (See chapter 7, page 194, for blocking methods.) This also gives you a chance to admire your work with justified pride.

# Evaluation and Adjustments

## chapter six

WHEN YOU'RE DONE knitting the major garment pieces, before you put anything together or pick up any borders, stop and evaluate what you've completed so far. Ask all the same questions as you did while the work was in progress. Lay the pieces out and look at them up close and from a distance to see whether there are any problems. If you don't discover any, be very proud of yourself for a job well done! If you do, this is your chance to fix them before moving on.

## Honest Assessments, Practical Solutions

▷ Is it the right size and shape? Compare each of the finished pieces to the schematic and measurements.

▷ Will the sweater fit the person it's intended for?

▷ Are matching pieces the same size? Hold the pieces up against each other. Do the sides, shoulders, and any other edges that will be seamed together match in length? If there are two fronts, are they the same size (assuming the front isn't asymmetrical)?

▷ Are there any obvious problems, like mistakes in the pattern stitch, holes, or variations in yarn color? You might want to take the knitting out into daylight, where it's much easier to see problems of this sort.

▷ Does the fabric look the same on all the pieces, or is it noticeably looser or tighter in some areas?

How you deal with problems at this point depends upon their severity. Each of these solutions is discussed in detail following this summary:

▷ Blocking will take care of minor discrepancies in the size of the pieces (see chapter 7, page 194).

▷ Major problems in size or shaping may require reknitting, but you don't necessarily need to reknit the whole piece — you can detach a section, add or remove what's required, then put the sections of a piece back together. See Size and Fit Adjustments (page 177) for details.

▷ If the garment is too small overall, you may be able to pick up stitches and add to the length or width, rather than reworking the whole garment.

▷ If the garment is too big overall, consider cutting the pieces down to size or sewing wider seams.

▷ Hide small mistakes in the pattern stitch by embroidering over the problem area with yarn to create what looks like the correct stitches. If this doesn't work or for larger areas, snip a stitch, unravel, and rework correctly.

▷ Holes and dropped stitches are easily secured using a piece of yarn on the back of the fabric, then weaving in the ends.

▷ If the color or quality of the yarn changes abruptly at some point, you can sometimes camouflage this using duplicate stitch.

▷ If you've added steeks or planned to cut your garment, this is also the time to prepare the future openings. Then you'll be ready to cut, add borders, and finish the edges.

## Fixing Mistakes

Mistakes in the knitted fabric can range from a stitch that was knitted instead of purled, to a dropped stitch or a cable crossed the wrong way or not at all. Depending on how big the problem, there are several different approaches you can take to disguise or fix stitch-level mistakes. Keep in mind that the main purpose of fixing a dropped stitch is to prevent it from unraveling, and that all the other corrections are cosmetic — your goal is just to make them look as good as possible. Some of the fixes below are made using a new piece of yarn, but if there is a long enough end waiting to be woven in nearby, you can always use it instead.

### Closing Up Holes

It is easy to close up holes that are caused either by an incorrectly formed stitch or an accidental yarnover, as well as those that are located at the corner of a neckline or armhole. Cut a piece of yarn about 10 inches long; on the back of the fabric, use a yarn needle to sew around the hole, close it up, and then weave in the two ends on the back of the fabric.

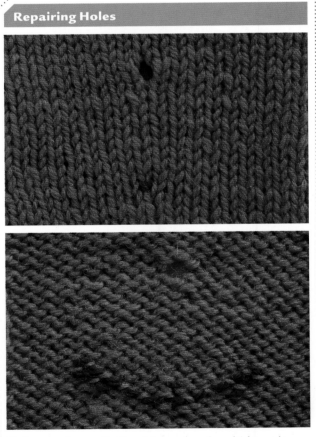

**Repairing Holes**

**Holes can be easily fixed** by sewing closed (shown in contrasting yarn for clarity).

## Capturing Dropped Stitches

Dropped stitches may have unraveled a few rows, so first hook the dropped stitch up as described in Dropped Stitch (appendix, pages 271–72). When you've hooked up all the loose rows, you'll need to secure the top stitch on the back of the fabric. Using a piece of yarn 6 to 8 inches long and a yarn needle, weave the yarn in for a few stitches before the dropped stitch and 1 row above it, work through the loose stitch, and then continue weaving it in for a few more stitches.

## Dealing with Problem Rows

If the problem is a whole row worked incorrectly, you can remove that row and replace it as described in When You Worked a Whole Row Incorrectly (chapter 5, page 154). If the problem is only in one part of the row, you may unravel just that section of the row, rather than taking out the whole row.

## Small Mistakes in Pattern Stitch

When just a couple of stitches were worked incorrectly, try hiding the mistake using embroidery. If a stitch was worked in the wrong color, use duplicate stitch (appendix, page 272) to work the correct color over it. For problems with texture, like a cable that wasn't crossed correctly or a missing purled stitch, you can sew over the mistake so that it looks correct (see photos, page 176).

### A Duplicate Stitch Fix

One row of this pattern was worked with brown a stitch to the left of where it should have been. On the right half, this has been fixed by duplicate stitching in pink over the brown, and in brown over the pink where they should have been in the first place.

### Fixing a Dropped Stitch

Dropped stitches will usually unravel a few rows.

Hook up the loose rows with a crochet hook.

Secure the stitch with a separate piece of yarn on the wrong side (shown in contrasting color for clarity).

Right side when completed

Cable at left was corrected using matching yarn, so the mistake is almost undetectable; the center cable has not been corrected. Cable at right is corrected in contrasting yarn for clarity. To make a correction like this, first sew the stitch that's underneath the cable crossing, then the stitch that crosses on top of it. The outer edges of the original stitches will stick out to either side, so sew across the back of the fabric, pulling those 2 stitches closer together.

Embroider over the stitch to make a knit look like a purl.

## Larger Mistakes in Pattern Stitch

Mistakes that are more than a few stitches wide can be difficult to disguise, especially when worked in bulky yarns or in an open pattern of eyelets or lace. In cases like these, it may be easiest to take out the bind off, unravel the width of just a single pattern repeat, and then work that section back up, perhaps using a pair of double-pointed needles if you find that more comfortable or convenient than using regular needles. For an example of using this method to correct a mis-crossed cable, see When You Made Incorrect Stitches in the Pattern (chapter 5, page 154).

If the problem is a long way down in the knitting, it may actually be less work to snip a stitch on a simple row (one with all knits or all purls) directly above the center of the problem area, unravel just a few rows down the problem, knit just this pattern repeat back up to the row you cut, then use a new piece of yarn to replace that row using Kitchener stitch (see appendix, page 276).

## Opportunities for Embellishment

Mistakes also offer an opportunity for embellishment of the fabric. If there are several small mistakes to be dealt with, consider adding a bead, braid, button, or small area of embroidery to cover up the mistake. Then add a few more of the same embellishment scattered over the fabric to make it look intentional. This is especially useful if you're working in a yarn that is difficult to manage, something that tends to cause more errors overall. Small clear glass beads are very nice for this, because they take on the color of the yarn. If there are only a few errors that need to be hidden, add a few extra beads strategically placed to balance the embellishment.

Sew on beads to hide holes and incorrectly formed stitches.

## Variations in Dye Lot, Color, and Yarn Quality

When you're holding your knitting close enough to work on it, you may not notice that the color has changed just a little in a new ball of yarn. From across the room or out in daylight, it may be very obvious that a row is a little lighter than the one next to it. You can camouflage the variation by working duplicate stitch every other stitch above and below the color change. Use each of the yarns originally knit on one side of the color change to duplicate stitch on the other side. This will blend the two shades together over 2 rows, eliminating the abrupt change in color and making it less noticeable.

When working with some yarns, whether spun by hand or at a commercial mill, you may find an area that varies in thickness, twist, or surface texture. If you don't notice this until the garment is finished, you can try to hide the problem using the same duplicate stitching technique recommended for color variations. If this doesn't work, it may be necessary to replace the problem section with yarn that better matches the rest of the garment.

**Duplicate stitches** may help disguise dye lot problems.

## Size and Fit Adjustments

Before you do anything to fix a problem with the way a garment fits, make sure you understand exactly what the problem is. Lay the garment pieces out on top of a sweater that fits to see what the difference is in length and width. Make notes and sketches, with measurements, to show the size of the pieces now and the size they need to be. Refer to these notes often as you make adjustments.

The kinds of changes you can make at this point, without actually starting the whole garment over, fall into three categories: changing the length, changing the width, and changing the shape of an opening.

## Changing the Length

The easiest change to make is in length. To make a piece longer or shorter, you could just undo the bind off, slip the stitches back onto the needle and knit some more, or unravel to the correct length, and bind off again. In circular knitting, plain stockinette stitch may be unraveled in either direction. In flat knitting, if necessary, you may unravel a few rows of stockinette or garter stitch toward the bind off, but at the end of each row of flat knitting you must pull all the yarn through the final stitch, which quickly becomes cumbersome as the loose yarn grows to be yards long. In pattern stitches that include knits and purls on a single row, you can only unravel from the bind off toward the cast on, the direction opposite from that of the original knitting.

If you change the length at the shoulder, it will probably make the neckline and the armhole the wrong size. You may want to unravel from the shoulder to the point where the armhole and neck shaping began, work the body a little longer, and then reknit the armhole, neck, and shoulder area. If this seems like too much work, read on to the end of this section. Note that proponents of top-down knitting cite this situation as the best reason for knitting from the top down — you can easily adjust the length before you bind off at the bottom.

**At the cast on.** To add length at the cast-on edge, pick up stitches along that edge and just knit down. If it was originally worked in garter stitch or stockinette, the transition to the added length may look seamless, assuming your tension is consistent, but a row with different tension may make the beginning of the addition obvious.

For a smooth transition to the new section, instead of picking up stitches, remove the cast on. Starting with the tail attached at one end of it, pick it out stitch by stitch, placing the resulting loops on a needle. If you have sufficient courage, it's less work to cut the bottom strand of yarn every few stitches across the edge and just pull out the short pieces. If you prefer not to cut the bottom edge, cutting off the yarn you're unraveling whenever it becomes too long to easily work with will make the process go faster. Slip the resulting loops onto a needle, and then work the added length from that point.

**Adding to ribbing.** If the bottom edge is a ribbing, the addition will be noticeable because the ribbed pattern won't match up when you add to it in the opposite direction. You can attempt to disguise this by working a couple of rows of reverse stockinette at the transition, but it will look better if you remove the ribbing entirely and then work down to avoid this problem.

**In the middle.** The best solution frequently is to adjust the length in the middle of the piece. First take it apart at a point where there is no shaping; if possible, do this where there also is no pattern stitch. If you are working in a pattern, select the simplest row and remove it as described in Divide and Conquer, opposite.

If the main section of the body is in stockinette or garter stitch, then detach the ribbing, put the stitches of the upper section on a needle, and work down from there to make the piece the desired length (A, opposite).

If you want to add length but don't want to work the bottom border again, remove a row above any increases at the top of the ribbing. Slip the stitches of both sections back onto a needle. Work up from the bottom section to add whatever length you like. If the garment was worked in a pattern stitch, be sure to add full pattern repeats so the pattern looks continuous. Use Kitchener stitch to rejoin the upper and lower sections (B, opposite).

If you want to make the piece shorter, remove a wider section. Put the body stitches back on a needle and work the bottom border from the top down. Or, if you don't want to work the border again, you can unravel the bottom section down to the ribbing and use Kitchener stitch to rejoin the upper and lower sections. Again, if there is a pattern stitch, you'll need to remove full repeats of the pattern (C, opposite).

**Garter stitch can be extended** by picking up along the cast on and working down. It may appear seamless if the cast on is loose enough, but there may be a variation in tension along the original cast on. The addition is shown here in contrasting yarn for clarity.

**Ribbing cannot be added seamlessly.** When working in the opposite direction there will always be a half-stitch jog.

**Two ridges of garter stitch** after picking up help to disguise the jog in ribbing.

# Divide and Conquer

To add or remove length in the middle of the knitting, first take it apart where you want to make the adjustment. Snip 1 stitch at the center of the row and pick out that row across to both edges.

Slip the live stitches onto a needle. This will be easier if you use a thinner needle. To prevent the knitting from unraveling, be careful not to stretch it in width. Instead, gather it up into your hand and pinch the base of each stitch as you gently slip the needle into it, just as shown in Taking Out the Bind Off (page 180).

Depending on what you plan to do next, you may want to put both of the detached sections onto needles, or you may want to unravel one of them to reuse the yarn.

**Snip a stitch** at center and pick out the row to the edges.

## STRATEGIES FOR LENGTHENING OR SHORTENING PIECES

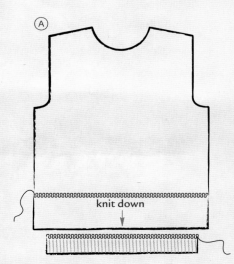

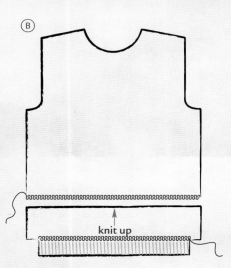

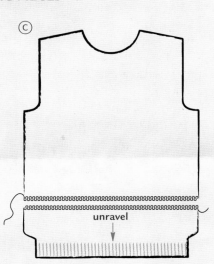

**To make the body longer:**

①  Detach the ribbing.

②  Place the body stitches on a needle.

③  Work down to make body longer.

④  Add ribbing either by working it down and binding off or use Kitchener stitch to rejoin the original ribbing.

**To add length if your pattern stitch looks funny upside down:**

①  Detach the ribbing.

②  Put the ribbing stitches on a needle.

③  Work up from the ribbing.

④  Attach the new section to the body using Kitchener stitch.

**To shorten the body:**

①  Detach the lower section at the top of the area you want to remove.

②  Unravel down to the top of the ribbing and then rejoin using Kitchener stitch.

OR  Place the body stitches on a needle and work the ribbing down.

## Taking Out the Bind Off

FIRST, TEASE THE CUT END OF YARN OUT through the last stitch. Pull on the yarn to undo 1 stitch at a time, and slip them onto a knitting needle. Pinch the fabric just below the stitch you are removing to prevent it from unraveling. A needle thinner than the size you originally used will be easier to slide into the stitches. Many yarns will felt or tangle together — use a pair of sharp-pointed scissors or snips to cut just the fibers that refuse to let go.

(1) **Pull out the yarn tail** to free the last stitch, then undo the stitches one at a time.

(2) **Pinch the fabric** just below the stitch you are unraveling and place it on the needle.

## Changing the Width

If the body or the sleeves come out too tight or too loose, it's possible to adjust for this without unraveling.

### Making Your Piece Wider

To make the knitting wider, you can

▷ Pick up stitches along the edge and knit a section at right angles to the original knitting.

▷ Knit a parallel section onto the original section (See Knitting On, page 182.)

▷ Knit a section and sew it on.

While each of these methods does make the piece wider, it will also change the overall shape. For example, adding width to the side of a sweater this way will make the armhole wider at the underarm, so the sleeve will require a corresponding adjustment in order to fit the armhole properly. If you add width to the sleeve, the armhole must be adjusted to fit it. If both are too narrow, then a single strip can be added that runs up the side seam and down the sleeve seam. If only one must be enlarged, then a gusset must be added to the adjoining underarm, to taper the addition neatly down to nothing. (See facing page.)

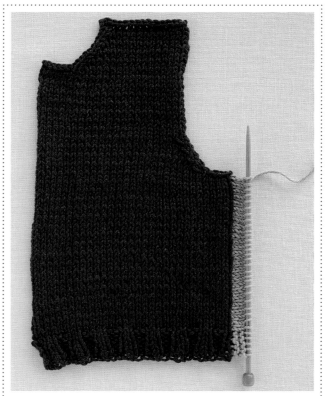

**Adding width** to the body by picking up stitches and working perpendicular to the original knitting

# STRATEGIES FOR ADDING WIDTH TO A GARMENT

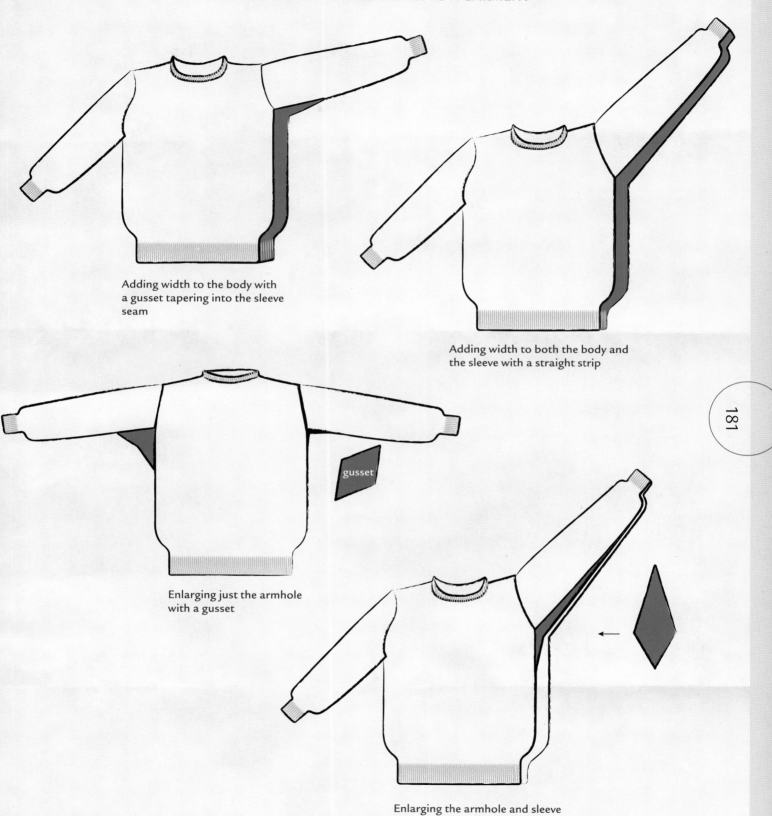

Adding width to the body with a gusset tapering into the sleeve seam

Adding width to both the body and the sleeve with a straight strip

gusset

Enlarging just the armhole with a gusset

Enlarging the armhole and sleeve

# Knitting On

ALSO CALLED "STRIP KNITTING," this technique allows you to join whatever you're knitting to the side of another piece that's already finished.

## Method 1: Pick Up as You Go

**Setup:** Cast on 1 stitch more than the desired width for the new section. If the first row will be on the wrong side, work that row.

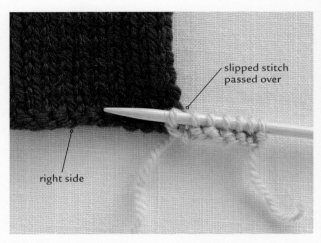

① Work across on the right side of the new section until 1 stitch remains, slip it knitwise. Insert the tip of the needle into the first stitch of the corresponding row on the existing piece of knitting, pick up and knit a stitch, pass the slipped stitch over.

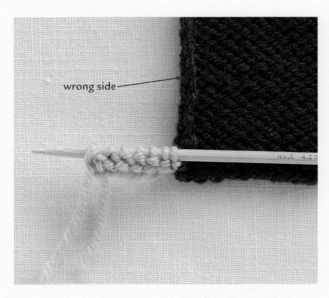

② Turn to the wrong side and work to end of row.

Repeat steps 1 and 2 until the new section is the same length as the original piece of knitting. Notice that you are attaching the two strips of knitting only at the end of the right-side rows, which is every other row. Be careful to pick up the stitches in every other row of the original fabric, not every row, so that the new section won't ruffle or pucker. When the two sections are the same length, bind off.

To knit a strip onto the left side of an existing piece, *work to the end of the row on the wrong side of the new strip; with the wrong side of the existing strip facing you, pick up and purl 1 stitch in the edge of the fabric, turn to the right side, K2tog, knit to the end of the row; repeat from * until the new strip is the same length as the old. Bind off. (For pick up and purl, see appendix, page 278.)

## Method 2: Pick Up First

If you find it difficult to pick up consistently in every other row along the edge at the end of the right-side rows, you may find it easier to prepare for joining the new section by picking up all the stitches along the existing piece of knitting before you begin attaching the new section.

**Setup:** With the right side facing you, pick up and knit 1 stitch in every other row. Knit across on the wrong side. You can continue with the same working yarn, or change to a contrasting color (as shown here for clarity). Cast on the desired stitches for the new section.

① Work across on the right side of the new section until 1 stitch of it remains, slip 1 knitwise, K1 (this is one of the picked-up stitches), pass slipped stitch over.

② Turn and work to the end of the row on the wrong side.

Repeat steps 1 and 2 until all of the stitches you picked up along the edge of the knitting are gone and the new section is the same length as the original section. Bind off.

To knit a strip onto the left side of an existing piece, work Setup as described above, then work from top to bottom to form the new strip.

## Making Your Piece Narrower

To make the knitting narrower after it's completed, you have two options. You can unravel and knit it again, or you can cut it. The latter is a daunting prospect, because once you've cut you can't unravel and reknit, so be very sure you've evaluated the situation and determined that cutting is really the best solution before you put scissors to fabric. You might want to baste the pieces together along the proposed seams using a sewing needle and thread to make sure that the finished size will be exactly what you want. You'll need to prepare the section to be cut and then finish the edges after cutting to prevent them from unraveling. (See Cutting Your Knitting, page 186.)

## Reshaping the Openings

If your armhole or neck openings came out the wrong size or shape, you can correct them by unraveling from the shoulder down to the beginning of the opening and reknitting. If they are too big, you can pick up stitches around or along the edge of the opening and add to them, just like making a border, until they are the correct size. If these openings are too small and you choose not to unravel, then the only alternative is to cut.

Regardless of which method you end up using, it's important to plan the new shape of the opening completely before you begin making the changes. Draw the new shape at life size on a piece of 1-inch gridded flip-chart paper to make a pattern you can follow. (See photo, below.)

### Reknitting May Be the Best Solution

Assuming that you worked the sweater from the bottom up, the best method of correcting problems in the neck

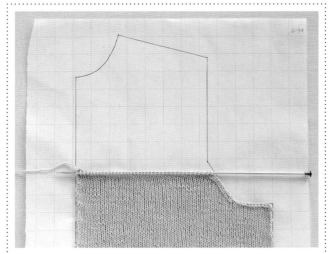
Work shaping to match the outline.

and shoulder area is to take out the bind off, unravel to the beginning of the opening that's the problem, and then work it again to the right shape. Lay it down frequently on your pattern and work bind offs and decreases to match the outline.

If you need to rework the top of a top-down sweater, you can use any of the methods described in the following photographs. Another option is to snip a stitch just below the problem area and pick out 1 row or round of knitting, as described in Divide and Conquer (page 179). From this point you can start over again from the top down correcting the shaping. When you reach the point where you separated the knitting, rejoin the new top to the body using Kitchener stitch. Or you can put the stitches of the bottom section on a needle and work up in the opposite direction, reversing the shaping.

## Reshaping to Make an Opening Smaller

**If a sleeveless armhole or the neck opening is too big all the way around,** just make the border wider to fill in the opening. You may need to decrease in the curved sections of the openings to prevent them from flaring. See The Special Challenge of Shaped Borders in chapter 8 (page 224) and the discussion of designing borders in chapter 3 (pages 70–73) for ways to do this. Use the paper pattern to determine when you've built up the border to the additional width needed.

**If there will be a sleeve and the armhole opening is too big all the way around,** join the shoulder seams and use a circular needle to pick up stitches as you would for a border. Pick up 1 stitch for every stitch across the bound-off sections of the underarm. Measure the rest of the armhole edge and multiply the measurement by your stitch gauge to determine how many stitches to pick up along the rest of the armhole. Work in stockinette or in a pattern stitch that suits the garment, decreasing in the underarm area to maintain the shape of the armhole (A, on facing page). How much you need to decrease will depend on what pattern stitch you are working. In stockinette, decrease 4 or 5 stitches every other row, with the stitches concentrated in the curved sections of the underarm. If the shoulders of the garment are sloped, you should also decrease occasionally at the shoulder seam in the middle of the row to continue the shaping. You can work circularly, if you prefer, by joining the side seams, picking up stitches, and then working the addition in the round. As you work, compare the shape of the opening to your paper pattern.

If the opening is too wide but the correct depth, or if it is too low but the correct width, you'll need to fill in sections with additional fabric. This is worth a try if for some reason you can't unravel and rework the problem area, but it may look a little strange. It won't take long to add the section, however, and if you don't like it you can easily unravel it and try a different solution. Use the paper pattern to determine where the section you're adding begins and ends (B). Mark both ends and the center point with safety pins or split markers.

Use a tape measure to measure along this edge between the end points and multiply this by your stitch gauge to determine how many stitches to pick up. Also measure at the center point of the area you plan to add to determine how deep the addition needs to be. Multiply this by the row gauge to determine how many rows you need to add.

You'll need to work short rows to gradually fill in the space. Divide the number of stitches by the number of rows you want to add. For example, if the section you're adding is 30 stitches wide and needs to be 7 rows tall, first subtract 1 from the number of rows (to allow for the pickup row); this leaves 6 rows to work with. Divide 30 stitches by the remaining 6 rows to get 5 stitches per short row. This tells you that you need to work the short rows in 5-stitch increments.

Using a circular needle, with the right side facing you, pick up and knit the total number of stitches (30 in our example) between the two markers. Turn and work back to the center point, and then work 5 additional stitches. Wrap and turn, then work until you are 5 stitches past the center point in the other direction. Wrap and turn, then work until you reach the wrap on your first short row. Pick it up, knit or purl it together with the stitch it wrapped, and continue until you are 10 stitches past the center point. Continue working short rows, working 5 additional stitches on each row and picking up the wraps as you pass them, until you reach the two end markers. At this point, you can bind off, picking up the last of the wraps as you do so. (For complete instructions on short rows, see the appendix, pages 279–80). As you work, compare the shape of the opening with your paper pattern to make sure it's working out as planned, and make adjustments as you go, if necessary.

You have the option of filling in this area with stockinette stitch, garter stitch, a pattern stitch, or the ribbing you'll use for the border around the opening. If the next step will be to work the border, then there's no need to bind off; you can work the new section in ribbing, pick up stitches along the rest of the opening, and continue straight up into the ribbing.

## Reshaping Armholes and Neck

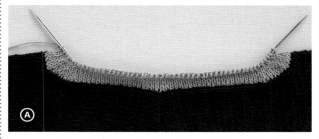

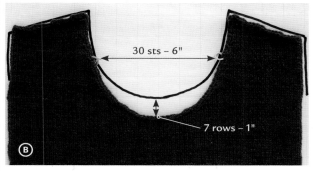

Front and back of armhole, with additional stitches on needle picked up around armhole in contrasting yarn

**The black line** indicates the desired neckline. Place markers at the end points and center to stay oriented while you're picking up stitches. Measure width and depth to determine how many stitches and rows are required.

Completed addition to make the neck higher

## Cutting to Make an Opening Larger

On your paper pattern that shows the neck and armhole openings the correct size (see introduction to Reshaping the Openings, page 184), mark a seam allowance about ½ to ¾ inch beyond the edge of the opening and trim the pattern along this line. This is the cutting line you'll use to adjust the shape of the opening.

Lay the pattern out on the knitting and use a textile marker or felt-tipped pen to mark the knitting along the edge of the pattern. Any kind of marker will do, as long as you can see it on the knitting. You may want to use a washable marker so that any accidental marks will be easier to remove from the garment. Using contrasting sewing thread, baste along the line where you want the actual edge of the opening to fall. Use sewing thread for this rather than yarn, because sewing thread can easily be pulled out later.

You'll use the basting thread as a guide later when picking up stitches for the border or sleeve, or when sewing in a sleeve. Follow the guidelines in Cutting Your Knitting (at right) to secure and cut the edge. Other finishes for cut edges are covered in Bindings and Facings to Enclose Edges (chapter 8, pages 235–37).

---

**Enlarging an Opening**

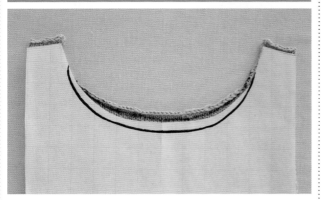

Use the pattern as a guide to mark the cutting line.

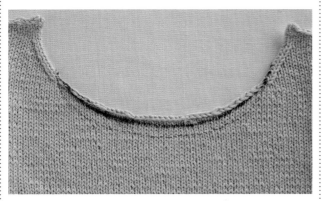

While the amount cut off looks very small on this neckline, the results will be 1 inch lower.

---

# Cutting Your Knitting

You may have planned to work your garment circularly and then cut the front, armholes, and neck openings, or you may have ended up with a sweater that's too big or an opening that's too high and now are considering cutting to correct the problem.

If you did plan ahead, you may or may not have added stitches to form steeks (see chapter 3, page 88). If you worked one of the three- or five-stitch steeks described in chapter 3, secure the edges as specified in those instructions. For all other steeks or knitting you plan to cut, use the directions below.

The steps are really very straightforward:

① Secure the knitting so it won't unravel when cut.

② Cut.

③ Finish the edge so it won't unravel when worn.

## Preparing to Cut

Put the knitting aside for a few days to let it set. If you don't want to wait, then speed the process by blocking the steeks. The purpose of this is to set the yarn so it's less likely to unravel. You can mist the steeks with cool water from a spray bottle and lay them out neatly to dry; steam them by hovering with an iron; or wash the whole garment, roll it in a towel to remove excess moisture, and then lay it out to dry. (For more information on blocking, see chapter 7, page 194.)

If you are working with natural wool or other animal fibers with a tendency to felt, you don't need to secure the knitting before you cut. If the fiber is superwash wool; an animal fiber that you suspect might not felt; silk; a plant fiber like linen, cotton, or hemp; or a slippery remanufactured fiber like rayon or bamboo, you need to stitch along both sides of the cutting line before you cut. The purpose of this is to keep the fabric from unraveling during the lifetime of the garment. You can do this by hand or by machine.

▷ **With a sewing machine,** set the stitch length small enough to catch every row of knitting. Sew along both sides of the center of the steek at least 1 stitch from the column of stitches that will be cut. Some folks advocate sewing again parallel to this, but I haven't found that to be necessary. Many people say to use a straight machine stitch, but straight stitches don't stretch and knitting does, so I prefer to use a narrow zigzag stitch.

Zigzag machine stitching on both sides of the center where the steek will be cut. Notice that the stitching catches both the brown and the pink stitches, ensuring that neither color will unravel.

▷ **By hand,** use a sharp sewing needle and thread to sew through each row of knitting so that every strand of yarn will be secured. Use a whipstitch (ensuring that the stitching will stretch with the knitting), and work through the 3rd and 4th stitches from each edge of the steek (ensuring that both colors are secured). Don't worry about how the sewing looks. Once you're done, it won't show on the outside of the garment. Depending on how you finish the cut edge, it may not even show on the inside. (For an illustration of whipstitch, see the appendix, page 281.)

Hand sewing. Steek prepared by hand for cutting

## The Cutting Procedure

Place a folded newspaper or magazine inside the garment so that you don't accidentally snip a strand on the back of the fabric elsewhere in the garment.

Use a pair of sharp sewing shears. Larger, sharp scissors make the cutting quicker, easier, and more accurate. Short, dull scissors will pull on the edge, causing more unraveling, and will require more cuts, resulting in a jagged edge.

Cut just one steek at a time, add the border, and finish that one opening before you move on to cutting the next steek. If you cut all the steeks at once, there is nothing to support the other openings, which can result in stretching and distortion at corners and perhaps a bit more unraveling than is desirable. Waiting to cut them keeps them neat and secure until you're ready to work with them.

Cutting the steek. Use sharp sewing shears to cut the steek neatly.

## Finishing the Cut Edges

The next step is to add a border and then to either enclose or sew down the cut edge. If you didn't sew along both sides of the steek before cutting, enclosing or sewing down the cut edges *must* be done to prevent them from unraveling in the future. If you did sew before cutting, the finishing described here will make the inside of the garment neater and protect the cut edges from excessive wear.

First pick up stitches for the border. Picking up stitches along a cut edge is a little different from picking up along the normal edge of a piece of knitting. For one thing, you'll be working farther away from the edge. For another, the type of border that you plan to add will dictate how you pick up stitches.

## Picking Up for a Single Layer

As soon as it's cut, a steek worked in stockinette will naturally roll to the inside. Pinch the fabric to make a fold, with the first stitch of the garment at the very edge and all the steek stitches to the inside. The steek stitches should be easy to identify because you worked them in a striped or checkered pattern to distinguish them from the body of the garment, or you identified the outer stitch of the steek by purling it. The pinched stitch just outside the steek is your edge stitch. Pick up and knit stitches for the border by inserting the needle under both strands of this edge stitch, wrapping the yarn, and knitting up a stitch.

Pick up and knit stitches under both strands of the edge stitch.

When the border is completed, the steek is hidden on the inside of the garment.

**Around an armhole,** start picking up stitches at the center of the underarm and work around the armhole until you get back to the center of the underarm. If the armhole was shaped, pick up 1 stitch in each stitch across the bottom. Work up the side of the armhole, picking up 3 stitches for every 4 rows along any diagonal shaping and up the unshaped vertical edge to the shoulder. If you were careful to work the diagonal shaping at least 1 stitch from the edge, there will be a neat, easy-to-follow column of edge stitches running all the way from the bottom of the armhole to the shoulder seam. When you get to the shoulder seam, continue down the other side and complete the circuit. You can use the live stitches to make an armhole border or a top-down sleeve.

**For a neck opening,** start at one of the shoulder seams and pick up stitches exactly as described for the armhole. Along the vertical and diagonal side edges, pick up 3 stitches for every 4 rows. Along the horizontal center front and back edges, pick up 1 stitch in every stitch.

## Finishing the Edge

You have several options once you've completed a single-layer border.

▷ **If the fabric is thick,** trim the raveled cut edge of the knitting, and then sew it down with yarn on the inside of the garment. Whipstitch along the cut edge in one direction, carefully sewing through the strands of yarn on the back of the garment so it won't show on the outside, then whipstitch around again in the other direction, which will make crosses covering the cut edge (opposite, top left).

▷ **If the fabric is thinner,** trim the raveled cut edge of the knitting, fold it under, and then sew the folded edge down with yarn on the inside of the garment. Whipstitch along the folded edge just once, carefully sewing through the strands of yarn on the back of the garment so it won't show on the outside (opposite, bottom left).

▷ **Purchase bias binding,** unfold it at the center, then sew it over the cut edge of the knitting using a sewing needle and thread. Work carefully, sewing through the strands of yarn on the back of the garment so it won't show on the outside.

## Enclosing the Cut Edge in a Folded Border

You can also work the border in a single layer, but make it twice as deep as its finished dimension, then fold it to the inside, enclosing the cut edge. This is best reserved for thinner fabrics because the result will be a border three layers thick (the outer layer of the border, the cut edge of the fabric, and the inner layer of the border). This may be an advantage around the neck or armholes of a sweater, providing extra warmth for the wearer.

## Sewing Down Steeked Edges

Whipstitching the cut edge in place

Whipstitching the folded edge in place

## Enclosing a Steeked Edge

Picking up through fabric to begin a border that will enclose the cut edge

Folded border with purled row to make a neat edge

Weaving the stitches to the pickup row, instead of binding off, makes a smooth, neat finish.

Instead of folding the steek to the inside, hold the fabric flat and insert your knitting needle from the right side of the fabric between the last 2 stitches of the body (this will be a whole stitch away from the steek). On the back of the fabric, wrap the yarn around the needle, and then use it to pull the new stitch through to the right side. Pick up 3 stitches for every 4 rows along the side of the steek and 1 stitch in every stitch along the top or bottom edge of the knitted fabric (top right).

Now, work a border twice as deep as the one you want to end up with. You can work this in ribbing, stockinette, or another pattern stitch, but keep in mind that a thinner fabric is preferable to a thick one. You may want to add 1 or 2 rows of reverse stockinette at the halfway point, to make a neat fold at the outer edge of the border. When the knitting is completed, trim the raveled cut edge, fold the border to the inside and sew it down with yarn along the pickup row, just as you would finish a hem (see appendix, page 274). The cut edge will be encased neatly inside the border (center and bottom right).

## Enclosing the Cut Edge in a Binding

When the border is one that can be worked in flat knitting (like the neck, front opening, or bottom edge of a cardigan), you can work both the inner and outer layer of the binding at the same time and then join the two layers together to make a very neat border with the cut edge hidden inside. Like the folded border above, this binding also results in three layers of fabric — the two layers of the binding plus the cut edge — so it can be very thick. It's best employed when working with thinner yarns.

You'll need two circular needles. It's easiest to work this if the needles are longer than the edge to be finished so the stitches aren't compressed on the needles. First pick up stitches from the right side of the fabric, as described for the folded border above. Pick up very, very loosely or you won't be able to complete the next step. You could even use a larger needle size to ensure that your picked-up stitches are consistently larger than usual, then change to the normal needle size when picking up is complete. (Using a set of interchangeable circular needles makes this easy. Initially put a larger tip on one end of the needle and use it to pick up the stitches, then just replace that tip with the correct size.) When you've worked all the way across the edge, picking up stitches on the first needle, increase 1 stitch by working a M1 with the working yarn at the end of the needle.

Turn to the wrong side. Continuing with the same working yarn and using the second circular needle, pick up and knit a stitch in the strand that runs across the back of the fabric between each of the stitches you picked up with the first needle. When you've worked all the way across, work another M1 at the end of the second needle. You should end up with 1 fewer stitch on the second needle than on the first.

You'll now work circularly on the two needles, enclosing the cut edge. See Creating a Binding to Enclose an Edge (chapter 8, page 235) and the appendix (page 268) for more discussion of this technique of working on two circular needles. When your border is wide enough to enclose the cut edge, trim any raveled ends (being careful not to cut your machine- or hand-sewing) and then join the two layers of the border to enclose it completely, using either three-needle bind off for a supported edge (page 261) or Kitchener stitch for a stretchy edge (page 276). You also have the option of joining the two layers without binding off, allowing you to add a single-thickness collar or buttonband (see page 286, bottom right).

# Enclosing Cut Edges in Binding

strands between stitches

① Pick up for the inner layer of the binding through the strands between the stitches in the outer layer.

② Pickup on both sides completed

③ Joining the layers with three-needle bind off

④ Completed binding, right side

⑤ This type of binding makes a very neat finish on the wrong side, and no sewing is required.

191

# Putting It
# All Together

## chapter seven

BEFORE YOU PUT THE pieces together, you'll need to make some final decisions on what order to do the finishing in. When should you block? Should you weave in loose ends and add embellishments before or after seaming? When should you add the borders?

Many of the answers are common sense. For example, block your pieces before sewing to make sure they're the correct size and to minimize curling so sewing up is easier. Add embellishments that cross more than one garment piece after they have been joined. Other considerations are far more subtle, and are sometimes just a matter of personal preference.

# Best Finishing Practices

How you put your sweater together depends, of course, on your personal preferences, but here's my take on best practices for finishing any sweater:

▷ Weave in any loose ends in the middle of the fabric to get them out of the way before blocking, seaming, and bordering, especially if you've been using a technique like intarsia that produces a lot of cut ends. Avoid weaving in ends along edges that will be seamed or where a border will be picked up, because they will make it more difficult to work the seams or the pickup consistently, and it's easier to weave them in along the seam or the picked-up edge of the border later.

▷ Block the pieces before you seam to check the final size; it also makes them easier to work with.

▷ Borders or embellishments that are attached to just one piece of the garment should be added before you sew the seams, because it's easier to work with a smaller, lighter piece of knitting. One exception to this is afterthought pockets (see page 249), where you may want to wait until all the other finishing steps are completed before trying on the garment and deciding on the placement of the pockets.

▷ Additions that cross from one piece of the garment to another (for example, collars, ruffles, or I-cord embellishments) must be worked after the pieces are joined together.

## Blocking Knitted Pieces

Instructions for knitted garments rarely tell you that you need to block the pieces before assembling or the finished garment afterward. If your pattern doesn't mention blocking, you'll need to use your own judgment. Blocking before assembly is *always* the best practice; however, *if* the pieces you've made are nice and neat, *if* they are just the right size, and *if* you are positive from working with your swatch that they won't end up a different size after washing or blocking, you *may* skip straight to sewing up and weaving in ends. On the other hand, blocking will make the rest of the finishing process far more pleasant and efficient.

Blocking should also be done after the finishing is completed. Blocking the entire garment may not be necessary at that point, but selected blocking of the seams to flatten and smooth them, and of key sections like front corners, the curved edge of the neckline, or collars will perfect the final look of the garment.

▷ Garments worked in stockinette stitch can be annoying to put together, because the pieces curl at all the edges. Blocking helps to eliminate much of the curling so they are easier to manage.

▷ Careful blocking smooths shaped edges, making it easier to sew seams and pick up stitches along them. Blocking also gives you a chance to make any corners come to nice, crisp points.

▷ Ribbed or cabled fabrics are very elastic. They must frequently be stretched horizontally during blocking so that they drape properly and to show off the pattern stitch. It's important to block them to the correct size before seaming or adding borders, so that the seams and borders are worked across the finished width and length of the fabric and don't end up too tight.

▷ Stranded colorwork pulls the knitting in horizontally and tends to look puckered. Blocking stretches it in width and smooths the surface of the fabric.

▷ Lacy fabrics generally must be blocked fairly firmly in both dimensions to open up the holes, smooth the fabric, and stretch it to its final dimensions. Just as for ribbed and cabled fabrics, it's important to do this before seaming and picking up borders so that they don't end up too tight.

▷ If the sweater is worked in intarsia, blocking after the ends have been woven in will reduce inconsistencies in tension, smooth the fabric, and make the edges more even, which is a boon when seaming.

▷ If you plan to cut your knitting, blocking helps to set the stitches so they are less likely to unravel after cutting.

▷ Blocking can also be used to solve minor problems in size. Use a yardstick or pin pieces out on a gridded board to ensure they are the correct size and shape. If they are too small, they can be stretched some during blocking. If they don't easily stretch far enough, then blocking isn't the answer. If the pieces are slightly too large, you may be able to pat them into a smaller shape during blocking. If they are inconsistent (for example, one front is longer than the other), blocking can be the solution, unless stretching the smaller piece makes it look noticeably different from its mate.

Don't block the completed pieces or the finished garment unless you've already blocked your swatch. We all know that the swatch should be blocked before you begin working on the garment, because then you'll know whether to expect the fabric to stretch or shrink, but sometimes we don't always do it. In particular, knitted alpaca fabric has a reputation for stretching significantly when blocked (and even after blocking!), and knitted cotton fabric frequently becomes wider and shorter.

Ribbed front before blocking

### Blocking Sweater Pieces

Garment pieces before blocking

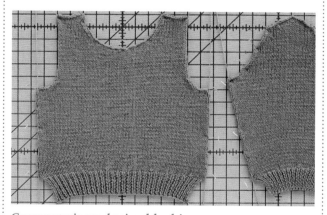

Garment pieces during blocking

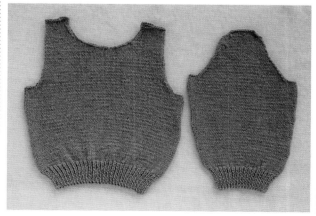

After blocking, the pieces curl less, and the curves and corners are nice and neat.

The same front after blocking, with light stretching

195

Most yarns can be washed, even when the label indicates otherwise. Yarns are frequently marked "dry clean only" if the dye is expected to run or if there will be significant shrinkage. Hand-washing and blocking your swatch will provide valuable information on both of these issues, which is yet another reason to wash and block your swatch before working a garment. If you end up in a situation where you do not want to wash the garment pieces but still would like to block them, try the cool-mist method or very gentle steaming (facing page).

There are three approaches to blocking. The first, wet blocking, is to soak the knitting or to wash it as you would the finished garment, then lay or pin out the pieces and let them dry. The other two methods involve pinning out the dry pieces, then either steaming them or misting them with cool water and letting them dry.

## Blocking Stranded Knits

**Before blocking**, stranded knitting curls and puckers.

**After blocking**, it's smoother and better behaved.

## Blocking Lace

**Before blocking**, Turkish Stitch curls diagonally.

**After blocking**, the fabric lies flat, and the structure of the lace is easy to see. (See page 199 for blocking in process.)

## Blocking Aids

Blocking should be done on a flat surface, large enough to fit the garment or pieces to be blocked.

▷ You can use a bed, the rug, or anything else that's flat that you can stick pins in. It's best if the surface doesn't absorb water (because the knitting will dry faster) and if it's colorfast (so it doesn't stain your knitting). Lay a thin towel or sheet over it (especially the rug) to keep your knitting clean and to protect the surface from staining if the yarn runs.

▷ You can purchase blocking mats conveniently marked in a grid or interlocking foam squares that let you build a surface the size you need.

▷ You can also make your own blocking mats out of foam-core board, rubber floor mats, or anything else that's soft enough to accept pins and doesn't absorb water. You can cover it with 1-inch checked gingham or windowpane-plaid fabric to make a gridded guide.

▷ A gridded pattern cutting board is an excellent blocking surface, which you can waterproof by covering with clear contact paper. Add another layer of contact paper when the first one becomes too holey from being stuck with pins.

▷ If you need a larger surface, place two blocking boards side by side. Smaller items can be blocked on a towel or on an ironing board.

A rigid yardstick works better than a flexible tape measure to verify that the knitting is blocked to exactly the right size. Square grids on a blocking mat are very helpful to ensure that corners are actually square and that sides are parallel to each other.

Pins that don't rust are essential to the process. Purchase stainless steel T-pins, which are widely available from knitting suppliers. Other types of pins may rust and mark your knitting permanently.

Blocking wires make the process of pinning out much more efficient. Sets of blocking wires usually include straight stiff wires in long and short lengths and flexible curved wires (for armholes and neck edges). These can be woven regularly through the edge of the knitting and then pinned out to make a nice even edge with just a few pins. To deal with an edge longer than your blocking wires, overlap two (or more) of them.

## Misting

COOL-MIST BLOCKING is a good choice when the item doesn't need severe stretching, as well as for all delicate fibers like silk, synthetic fibers (such as acrylic and nylon), and cellulose fibers (rayon, bamboo, SeaCell, etc.). You can expect it to dry much more quickly than wet blocking, but not quite as fast as steaming. Dense fibers that do not absorb water well, such as linen and cotton, may require you to spray on quite a lot of moisture for good results. They really respond best to wet-blocking, but misting instead means they'll dry more quickly.

1. Pin the finished pieces or garment out on your blocking surface, using blocking wires if desired.

2. Using a spray bottle of cool water, mist the entire surface until it feels moist. It's important that the knitting absorb enough moisture so that the underside of the fabric is damp. Sometimes pressing it with the flat of your hand will help absorption.

3. Leave the item pinned in place until it is dry.

4. Remove the pins and wires gently, being careful not to stretch the knitting.

## Steaming

STEAM BLOCKING is a good choice when the item doesn't need severe stretching or when you need to block a few specific areas of the garment. You can expect it to dry much more quickly than wet blocking. Steam should be avoided for silk, synthetic fibers (such as acrylic and nylon), and cellulose fibers (rayon, bamboo, SeaCell, etc.), because heat may damage them.

1. Pin the finished pieces or garment out on your blocking surface, using blocking wires if desired. Be sure to use a surface that can withstand heat.

2. Using a steam iron or a steamer, hover it over the surface of the fabric without touching it. If your iron has a steam button, use it to apply the steam evenly and more quickly to the surface. Start with the lowest temperature that produces steam to see if the fabric responds by relaxing to its pinned-out dimensions. If not, you can increase the temperature up to the setting for the fiber content of the yarn.

3. Leave the item pinned in place until it is cool and dry.

4. Remove the pins and wires gently, being careful not to stretch the knitting.

# Wet Blocking

WET-BLOCKING IS BEST for situations where you want to make the biggest difference in the appearance and behavior of the fabric. It's appropriate for all types of fibers as long as you treat them gently. Wool, for example, absorbs enough water in the process that the weight of the water can stretch and damage the garment if not supported properly. Silk and rayon become very fragile when wet and must be treated gently to protect the yarn from breakage. Linen, a very strong fiber, is an exception to this rule — you don't need to worry about the fiber becoming more fragile when wet; however, you do still need to support it if you don't want to risk undesired stretching. Like stretching, wringing the fabric may damage the yarn, so rather than wringing, squeeze gently and roll it in a towel to remove excess water. Wool and other animal fibers are more likely to shrink and become felted when subjected to agitation and changes in water temperature. For both these reasons, keep the water consistently lukewarm and avoid doing anything but gently squeezing the knitting — don't stroke or rub it.

① **Run a basin or tub** of lukewarm water large enough that the knitting barely floats in it. There's no need to use a huge amount of water for a small garment.

② **If you think the project** could use cleansing (a definite possibility after being handled and carried around while in progress), add a small amount of liquid dish detergent, laundry detergent, or wool wash to it. Do not use anything with additives such as brighteners, color enhancers, or bleach, such as Woolite and many laundry detergents. Swish the water around to mix in the cleaning agent. Avoid using too much or agitating it so much that it becomes foamy. Too much soap can be difficult to rinse out.

③ **Put the knitting in the water** and gently press it down to help it absorb the water. Never run water directly on wool or other animal fibers, because it might initiate the process of fulling (known commonly as felting), causing the fabric to shrink, lose stitch definition, and become thick and stiff. Leave the knitting in the water for 20 to 30 minutes, if you have the patience and you're not worried about the colors running, so that it absorbs as much water as possible. If it floats, turn it over and give it a gentle squeeze to get the air out.

④ **Open the drain** and let the water run out. Squeeze as much moisture as you can out of the knitting by pressing it against the side of the basin. Lift it up, supporting all of it so that the weight of the water still held in the fibers doesn't stretch it out of shape, and set it to one side.

⑤ **If you used any soap or detergent,** refill the basin (or tub) with clear lukewarm water and put the knitting back into the water. Adding a glug of white vinegar to the water will neutralize any alkalinity from the soap and thus extend the life of the fibers. Squeeze the knitting gently a few times to rinse out any soap or dirt that may still cling to the yarn. Empty the water again and squeeze out the excess against the sides. Repeat this step, without the vinegar, until the water is clear, so you know you've removed all the soap, dirt, and excess dye.

⑥ **Lay the knitting neatly** on a large thick towel. Roll the towel up and then squeeze it firmly (you can even walk on it) to get as much water out as possible. If the towel becomes saturated, repeat with a dry towel.

⑦ **Unroll the knitting** and continue to support it as you lay it out on your blocking surface (see Blocking Aids, page 197). Shape the knitting to the correct size, smooth the surface of the fabric with your hands, and pinch up any surface features (like cables or bobbles) that you'd like to emphasize. Stretch ribbed bands in the direction of the ribbing and let them dry in a relaxed position to improve their appearance, shape, and performance.

**Stretch ribbed bands** in direction of ribbing.

8. **Reshape any decorative edges,** pulling points or scallops into shape. You can shape the knitting and leave it lying unpinned to dry, or you can pin out just a few points to improve their shape. For a smoother surface or if the knitting must be stretched, pin it out to the correct shape and size. Blocking wires make it possible to get better results with fewer pins. Weave the wires in and out along the edge every stitch or two in solid fabric, through all the loops along a yarnover edge, or through each point along a chevroned edge. When the wires are in place, pin to your blocking surface.

9. **Leave the item pinned** until it is completely dry. You can shorten drying time by increasing airflow using a fan, or blocking near a heating vent or in a sheltered area outside.

10. **Remove the pins gently,** being careful not to stretch the knitting.

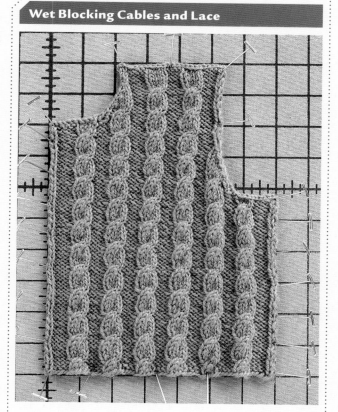

## Wet Blocking Cables and Lace

**If cables are blocked too severely,** they end up flat and boring. Here, the fabric has been patted out so that the cables are easy to see, and key corner points have been pinned out square.

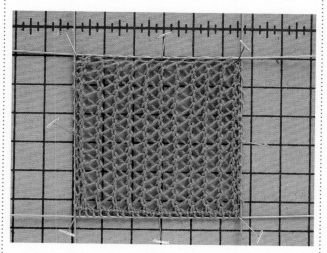

**Blocking wires ensure the lace** is stretched evenly in both dimensions.

# Dealing with Ends

In chapter 2, I discussed planning for how the cut ends of yarn will be handled when there are lots of color changes. Planning ahead allows you to weave them in as you go (reducing the number to be dealt with later) or to leave the ends long enough to sew, braid, or incorporate into fringe.

If there is just the normal number of ends, at the beginning and end of each piece, and at a few points where you needed to start a new ball or deal with a knot, you can wait until after the separate pieces have been joined together.

On the other hand, if you've been working intarsia, where there are ends all over the back of the fabric, it's easiest and best to weave them in and block the pieces before you start putting them together.

If you've been working stripes or color patterns that require you to regularly change colors at the beginning of rows, all your ends will be at the edge. It's usually better not to weave these in until *after* you've completed the seaming and picking up borders. Weaving in these ends can make it difficult to see the structure of the edge stitches. This makes it hard to sew or pick up stitches consistently. If the edge is loose because of all the color changes, tighten it up to the right tension and tie the ends together temporarily to secure them while you take care of the other finishing tasks. Then go back, untie the knots, and weave in the ends.

## A Strand at a Time

There are lots of ways to weave in the ends on the back of solid fabrics where they won't show. Thread each end through a yarn or tapestry needle to work it in on the back of the fabric. You should always leave ends 4 to 6 inches long to make this possible. If the ends are too short, however, here are a few suggestions:

▷ Use a crochet hook to work the yarn through.

▷ Use the yarn needle backward, sewing with the blunt eye instead of the pointy end.

▷ Sew with the empty needle, threading it with the short yarn end just before pulling it through the fabric.

When you finish weaving in the end, stretch the fabric a bit to ensure that the end was woven in loosely enough, then trim the excess.

In all of the illustrations at right and opposite, I've used contrasting yarn to make it easier to see how the ends were handled. When the ends are the same color as the base fabric, they will, of course, be much less visible.

In stockinette or garter stitch, pick a row of purl bumps on the back of the fabric and weave a serpentine path through them.

Ribbing. Weave in ends vertically on ribbing, following a single rib. To distribute the bulk, alternate between the two sides of the rib, if you like. If you reach a nonribbed area, switch to one of the other methods.

## When Ends Call for Special Care

On garments that are reversible, loosely knit, or lace, special care is required so that the ends don't show. I discussed this in chapter 2 (Planning for Ends, page 65) and in chapter 5 (When Your Yarn Causes Problems, page 151), because most of the time it's easier to take care of them by splicing them together while you're working, so that you don't need to hide them later. You'll still have a few ends to cope with (the tails at the cast on and bind off, for instance) when the knitting is finished. Choose the least noticeable method that works with your yarn in your particular project. The photos opposite illustrate possible choices for these situations. Note that the "end" is shown in contrasting yarn for clarity. (For how to weave in along a seam, see Working Ends in Along Seams on page 202.)

Reversible fabrics. Duplicate stitch is your best bet if you need to weave in an end in the middle of the fabric when both sides will show. For stockinette and reverse stockinette stitch, you'll find directions in the appendix (page 272). For other pattern stitches, just follow the line of the yarn along the row, as shown here.

Lace or eyelets. Find a solid spot and weave in the end on the back of it. You may need to duplicate stitch to get to that point.

Along a cast on. You will need to adapt your sewing method to match your cast on. Some cast ons make the end difficult to hide. In this photo, the tail has been woven in every other stitch, being careful to follow the diagonal slant of the yarn in the original cast-on edge.

Along a bind off. Work in and out of the fabric just below the chain of stitches.

When weaving the ends horizontally, use a darning needle (which has a sharp point). Weave the end in normally, then reverse direction and cross the path of the strand you just wove in two or three times, intentionally sewing *through* the strand itself.

When weaving diagonally, reverse direction to make a shape like a fish hook.

**When there are lots of ends** in one area, weaving diagonally (see photo on previous page) instead of (or in addition to) horizontally allows you to spread out the ends to reduce the bulk. You can also weave in the first batch of ends, than weave the rest on top of those in layers.

**Contrasting colors may show through** the fabric when woven under a whole strand of yarn on the back. Try to sew the ends in behind a matching color. If this is not possible, use a darning needle (which has a sharp point) and sew through just a tiny bit of the yarn in the base fabric, rather than under a whole strand, as shown in diagonal weaving on previous page.

**Slippery yarns,** such as silk, rayon, and cotton, may simply slide back out when the ends are woven in conventionally, but there are a couple of ways to lock them in. (See bottom of page 201.)

## Working Ends in Along Seams

Ends left at the edge of the fabric where there's a seam can be woven along the selvedge on the inside and will not show on the outside of the garment. Be careful to adjust the tension of the end to match the knitting by stretching the fabric a little before you trim the end.

When there are ends spaced regularly along a seam, leave longer ends (6 inches) so that you can French braid them. This is quicker than weaving the ends in separately. Start at the top or bottom of the seam and begin braiding the strands parallel to the seam. As you work, pick up all the ends you come to and add them to the braid. At the end of the seam, spread out the remaining ends and weave them in separately on the back of the fabric. If there are too many ends, this can become quite thick, so is not a good option.

## Enclosing Ends in a Border

Along the exposed front, neck, or armhole edges and along cut openings of a striped or stranded garment, you can achieve a very clean finish by enclosing the edges completely, but first you must secure the ends. If they are long enough, you can knot pairs of them together. If there are lots of them, or they are cut short, use sewing thread to stitch along the edge by hand or machine, being careful to sew through every strand, just as you would to secure the fabric before cutting your knitting (see chapter 6, page 186). After you have applied the border, but before you close it up, trim the ends neatly to reduce bulk (but don't cut the sewing thread!). Enclose the entire edge by making a doubled border, a binding, or a facing (see chapter 6, pages 188–91 and chapter 8, pages 235–37). For less bulk, you can also sew on bias binding to cover the ends (Finishing the Edge, page 188).

Before you decide to finish the edges with an enclosed border, take into account that the edge will be a double or triple thickness. If the edge has been cut, then the original fabric will extend into the double thickness of the border, making three layers. If the edge has not been cut, there will still be the double layer of the border plus the added bulk of the cut ends. A double thickness may be okay in worsted-weight yarn, but a triple thickness in worsted-weight yarn is very bulky. Because of this, enclosed edges are really best reserved for garments made from thinner yarns and avoided when using thicker yarns.

**Weaving in Along Seams**

At the end of the lavender stripe there were four ends to be woven in: two purple and two lavender. The lavender ones were woven in every other stitch along the left-hand side of the seam, one up and the other down. The purple ends were woven in the same way along the right-hand side of the seam, distributing the bulk.

French braiding the ends secures them without sewing all the individual strands.

## Decorative Uses for Ends

Braids and fringes are not appropriate for all garments. I would hesitate to put braids or fringes along the side seam of a sweater, for example, but they might be nice along the sleeve seam of a child's garment (reminiscent of a fringed buckskin jacket), around the neck of a sweater knit side to side, or along a striped bottom edging when there are lots of ends to be secured for an ethnic or exotic look. Braids are a better choice than fringes on garments that will be worn and washed frequently, because they hold up better and look neater after drying.

Plan ahead for incorporating cut ends in fringes and braids by leaving them long enough (at least 6 inches) to work with. If they seem sparse, supplement with additional cut pieces of yarn. You may want to reserve yarn for this purpose before you begin your sweater, to make sure you don't run out during finishing. And remember that fringes and braids present great opportunities for beading.

### Some Fringe Options for Ends

Before sewing the seams, knot the existing ends together so that they won't pull loose. While sewing the seam, make sure the ends are left hanging on the outside of the garment. After the seam is completed, use a crochet hook to pull additional strands of yarn through the seam line and knot them to match the existing ends. When you complete the fringe, shake it out and give it a haircut to even up the ends. If you have a rotary cutter, you can use it in combination with a ruler to ensure a neat cut.

The fringe on this sleeve was actually used to join the seam. One strand from each stripe was pulled through the opposite edge of the sleeve seam, then knotted together with an end of the same color. The cuff was seamed using a long tail intentionally left when casting on.

Cutting individual pieces of fringe can be time consuming. To cut a lot of fringe quickly, find a stiff object (like a book) that is slightly wider than the desired length of the fringe. Wrap the yarn around it repeatedly, then cut all the strands along one edge and you'll end up with a quantity of pieces all the same length. Remember that the pieces must be twice the desired length because they will be doubled and pulled through the fabric, leaving them half the original length.

### Making Braids with Ends

Arrange the ends in groups of three and braid them. Secure each braid by tying one strand around all the rest and trim them neatly. If you like, you can include more strands in a single braid by doubling some of the strands. If you end up with too few strands to complete the final braid, cut a piece of yarn double the length of the existing strands. Pull it through the fabric at the base of the planned braid, even up the ends, then include the new strands in your braid.

Braids of doubled strands ornament the neckline of this sweater with a striped garter-stitch yoke so that none had to be woven in on the inside.

## Joining the Pieces

Although this discussion of putting your sweater together falls near the end of the book, if you paid attention to some of the hints in earlier chapters, you may have already joined some of the seams while the work was in progress.

For example, if you're working conventional bottom-up or top-down sweater construction with all the garment sections in separate pieces, you'll almost always want to begin by joining the front to the back at the shoulders. I find it helpful when fitting a sweater to then immediately complete the neck border, so I can try on the garment and check for the proper sleeve length before I make the sleeves. If the shoulder is a little wider than you expect, or the shoulder seam or neck opening stretch a bit under the weight of the knitting, you can then adjust the sleeve length so that the sleeves don't end up too long.

The next step is to join the sleeves to the body at the armhole. After this is completed, join the side and sleeve seams. I like to start at the bottom edge of each of these and work toward the underarm. This ensures that the edges are properly aligned. If the underarm seam doesn't match exactly at the underarm, no one will be able to see it.

If there are any other borders or embellishments to be added, this may be done either while the pieces are still separate or after they are joined. Pockets and embellishments that are attached to just one piece are most easily worked while the pieces are separate. On the other hand, waiting until everything else is completed allows you to try on the garment and ensure that the pockets and other additions are placed in exactly the right locations. Work additions like ruffles, collars, or I-cord that cross more than one piece after they are joined.

In the sections below, you'll find a discussion of the various methods of joining knitting, including sewing, crocheting, and knitting together. In the accompanying photos, the yarn used for joining is shown in a contrasting color so it can be seen clearly, but, of course, you will be using matching yarn, which will be much less noticeable. Instructions for working the most common of these seaming techniques are in the appendix (page 278–79).

## Perfecting Sewn Seams

Sewing is the most conventional method to join your knitted pieces together, but many knitters find it difficult to sew knitting neatly and consistently. The key to being able to do so is preparation — your edges need to be neat and consistent, and then your sewing will follow suit. How you sew them together is dictated by whether you are joining two side edges together (as for a side or sleeve seam), the tops or bottoms of pieces (as for shoulder seams), or the side of one piece to the top or bottom of another (as for armhole seams). Your approach may also vary depending on whether the stitches you need to seam are in stockinette stitch, garter stitch, ribbing, or some other pattern.

## Choosing the Right Sewing Needle

To sew your seams, you'll need a yarn or tapestry needle. Both have blunt tips, so they are less likely to split the yarn as you sew. Yarn needles have eyes large enough for worsted- or bulky-weight yarn. They can be made of metal or plastic, with or without bent tips. Tapestry needles come in several sizes, smaller than yarn needles, but with larger eyes than regular sewing needles. They should be used with finer yarns, such as sport or fingering weight. You may pick whatever style needle you like, as long as the eye is large enough for your yarn to slide through freely. Darning needles have large eyes and sharp points like sewing needles. If the item is very tightly knit, you may find that the sharp point makes it easier to sew up.

## Joining Side Edges with Mattress Stitch

Mattress stitch is your best bet when joining the side edges of two pieces of knitting, like the side or sleeve seams of a sweater. When sewn consistently and at the correct tension, the pieces will appear seamless unless the garment is stretched horizontally.

Use safety pins to attach the sides of a long seam before sewing them together. While you work, make sure the pins stay horizontal.

The single most important factor that affects perfect seams in this situation is how the edge stitches and any increases or decreases were worked. As I discussed in chapter 2 (in Planning for the Best Edges and Seams, page 53, and Planning for Increases and Decreases, page 59), if you plan to join the seams using mattress stitch, maintain the edge stitches in stockinette and work all increases, decreases, or pattern stitches at least 1 or 2 stitches away from the edge. This ensures that at least one column of stockinette stitch runs along the edges of the knitting, so that it's easy to see where to sew. When you prepare for it this way, mattress stitch is a neat and efficient means of joining the side seams.

You'll find instructions for mattress stitch in the appendix (page 278). Be sure to work with the public side of the knitting facing you and to sew a whole stitch away from the edge consistently for the best-looking seams. If this makes a bulky seam and the edges are neat and fairly tight, you may be able to get away with working just a half stitch away from the edges. To do this, work through the center of the edge stitches, rather than between the edge stitch and the next stitch in.

On long seams, attach the two pieces together periodically using safety pins or split markers. Keep an eye on them as you work to make sure the points that you've connected line up properly. If they don't, occasionally work under two strands (2 rows) on the side that's longer and under just one strand (1 row) on the side that's shorter to bring them back into line.

### Starting the Seam Right

To prevent a small gap from forming at the bottom of the seam, work a figure 8 across between the two corners before working up along the seam. First sew through one corner from the back to the front, then the other corner from the back to the front. If it still looks a little thin across the bottom edge, do it once more.

Beginning a seam with a figure 8 can make the cast on look continuous along the bottom edge.

### The Challenge of Seaming Ribbed Borders

Making seams look good in ribbed borders is a particular challenge. I discussed this at length in Making Borders Look Continuous across Seams (chapter 2, page 52). If you set up your ribbing as described there, you'll be able to seam the borders together neatly. These are your options:

▷ **K1, P1 ribbing on an odd number of stitches.** Place a knit stitch at each edge on the right-side rows. Sew the seam a half stitch in from the edge so that the 2 remaining half stitches on either side of the seam come together to form what looks like a single knit rib. When you reach the top of the ribbing, you can transition to sewing a full stitch from the edge for the rest of the seam, or you can stick with a half stitch if it looks better.

Seam sewn a half stitch from the edge throughout

▷ **K1, P1 ribbing on an even number of stitches.** Place 2 knit stitches at one end and 1 knit stitch at the other on the right-side rows. Sew a whole stitch from the edge in the ribbing. The remaining stitches on either side of the seam consist of a purl on one side and a knit on the other, so the ribbing looks continuous. When you get to the top of the ribbing, continue to sew a whole stitch from the edge.

▷ **K2, P2 ribbing.** Work on a multiple of 4 stitches plus 2 and place 2 knit stitches on each end on the right-side rows. Sew a full stitch in from the edge. This leaves 1 knit stitch on each side of the seam, which, when pulled together in seaming, looks like a 2-stitch knit rib. Continue sewing a whole stitch from the edge in the stockinette section above.

**K1, P1 ribbing.** Seam sewn a whole stitch from the edge throughout

**K2, P2 ribbing.** Seam sewn a whole stitch from the edge throughout

Sewing through the "smiles"

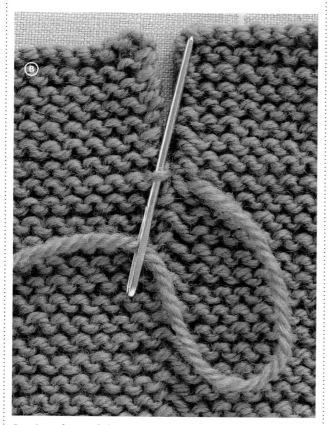

Sewing through bumps at the end of each ridge

## Seaming Garter Stitch

Garter stitch side seams are a special case where you don't always need to use mattress stitch. For a strong neat seam, you can, of course, keep the edge stitches in stockinette and sew a mattress stitch seam just as you would in stockinette stitch. Garter stitch, however, has a different proportion than stockinette stitch. It's a little shorter (there are more rows per inch) and a little wider (there are fewer stitches per inch), which means that the seam will end up a little longer than the garter stitch fabric on either side. If the garter stitch was worked firmly, this may look pretty bad; if it was worked loosely so that the fabric stretches, the longer seam may be just fine.

To avoid this potential problem, it's easy to make a neat, nonbulky seam simply by sewing into the little curved "smiles" at the end of each garter stitch ridge, alternating between the two sides (see Smiles, appendix, page 280, A). For a seam that's reversible and has no bulk at all, sew through the bump at the very edge of the fabric instead (B). Adjust the tension of the seam so that the strands running between the two edges are the same size as the stitches on either side.

## Joining Top and Bottom Edges by Weaving

Weaving is a way of joining knitting where you sew in a new row of stitches. It's normally used to join shoulders or other top and bottom edges of knitting to each other. The basic instructions given in the appendix (page 279) are for working it on "dead" stitches — those that are at the cast-on or bound-off edge — but it can also be used to join a combination of live and dead stitches. When worked on all live stitches, this is called Kitchener stitch. I use the term *weaving* if at least one of the pieces to be joined does not have live stitches, in order to distinguish it from Kitchener stitch.

Although it takes a little more effort, weaving dead stitches together at the shoulders is sometimes preferable to joining live shoulder stitches using three-needle bind off. Because there are two bound-off edges plus the sewn seam, the shoulder seam will both wear and hold its shape better. It will also appear more perfect, with the additional row of stitches making a smooth transition between the front and back shoulder, rather than the more obvious seam created by three-needle bind off.

Weaving a seam when at least one set of stitches is live is useful to reduce the bulk of a seam. This makes a seam allowance (the bind off or cast on) on one side, but no seam allowance on the other side.

Weaving makes a very neat seam, but patterns like this beaded rib won't match exactly at the shoulder.

Weaving to join a shaped shoulder

### Weaving with Pattern Stitch or Sloped Shoulder

It can be a little confusing to work weaving when the fabric has a pattern stitch or the shoulder has been sloped with a series of bound-off stitches.

When joining the tops of two pieces with pattern stitches, be aware that they will not match perfectly — they will be a half stitch out of alignment. This will be less obvious if you end each piece with a plain row of stockinette. If you don't like the way that weaving looks in a particular pattern stitch, it may be one of the times when three-needle bind off is preferable, because the stitches on both sides of the seam will align perfectly.

When joining shoulders with shaping, work the weaving straight across until you come to the end of a bound-off section. On the next stitch, shift 1 row up or down to follow the diagonal slope of the edge. Do this at the same time on both sides of the seam so it will look symmetrical. On the following stitch, shift again, then work straight across until you come to the end of the current group of bound-off stitches. Shifting 1 row twice makes a smoother transition than suddenly jumping 2 rows to the next level of bound-off stitches.

# Live Stitches to Dead Stitches

WEAVING CAN BE USED to join the shoulder when one of the shoulders has been bound off but the other has not. The bound-off edge will provide support so that the shoulder won't stretch out of shape, while weaving live stitches from the other shoulder will reduce the bulk of the seam.

Finish the second shoulder with a wrong-side row if you are right-handed and want to sew right to left while joining; end with a right-side row if you are left-handed and prefer weaving in the opposite direction. Cut the working yarn, leaving a tail with about ¾ to 1 inch for each stitch in the shoulder. This should be fine for worsted-weight yarn, but you may need a little more for bulkier yarns, and less for thinner yarns. In the photos, I've used contrasting yarn for clarity, but you'd normally use the working yarn, which will match the piece with the live stitches.

(1) Lay the pieces out so that the live stitches are at the top of one piece and the edge to be joined on other piece is above this. The right sides of both will be facing you.

(2) Using a yarn needle, look for the first stitch to be joined on the bound-off edge. The two halves of this stitch will make a V pointing toward the bound-off edge. Sew underneath these two strands.

③ **Sew into the first live stitch** from the right side of the fabric, remove it from the knitting needle, and come out through the second live stitch from the back of the fabric. This is identical to what you'd do in Kitchener stitch, so you can think of it as going into the first stitch knitwise and out through the second stitch purlwise. Notice that you've sewn under two strands, just as you did on the other shoulder.

⑥ **Sew through the following stitch** purlwise. Repeat steps 4 – 6 until you complete the seam. As you work, adjust the tension so that the row of stitches you're creating is the same size as the row of stitches immediately below it.

④ **Sew through the next stitch** to be joined on the bound-off edge. This is easy to identify once you've begun, because you'll always sew back into the last stitch you came out of and under two strands that make a V toward the edge of the fabric.

Weaving live to dead stitches completed

*Note:* If you are working from left to right, the procedure is identical, but your needle will always come out of the fabric two strands to the right of where it went in.

⑤ **Sew through the next stitch** to be joined on the live edge knitwise, removing it from the knitting needle.

## Weaving versus Kitchener Stitch

When making conventionally constructed sweaters, there are few times when Kitchener stitch would be appropriate. The only time it would be possible in the traditional bottom-up sweater is to join the shoulder seams, but because it makes a seamless join, there will be nothing to support the shoulders, and they'll stretch out of shape, compromising the fit.

On the other hand, Kitchener stitch is very useful for sweaters worked from cuff to cuff. Instead of working across the whole sweater, reversing the shaping on the second half, you can make two pieces from cuff to center, reversing the shaping for the neck opening, and then use Kitchener stitch to join them at the center back. Leave the front open for a cardigan, or Kitchener it together to make a pullover. This is a real advantage when making large, heavy, side-to-side sweaters, where the weight and bulk of the sweater can be very annoying while you are working the final sleeve.

Kitchener stitch is also absolutely necessary if you need to make changes in the length of a garment after the pieces have been completed (see Changing the Length, chapter 6, page 177) or to correct a mistake in a pattern stitch (see Larger Mistakes in Pattern Stitch, chapter 6, page 176).

The key to making a good-looking combination seam is to remember that you are making a new row of stitches and to adjust the tension on the working yarn so that the seam stitches you are creating are the same size as the stitches in the top row of the piece you're seaming. You may be tempted to pull the yarn very tight to try to hide it — don't! This will make a very firm, unyielding seam. Because the armhole has to stretch whenever you move your arms, the seam must stretch along with your body, or the yarn might break.

Straight sleeve cap attached to a drop shoulder body

### Setting in a Sleeve

Joining two shaped edges, in order to ease a fitted sleeve cap into a shaped armhole, for example, is more challenging than joining two straight edges. But, if you know how to weave the horizontal ends of two pieces together, how to join the vertical sides using mattress stitch, and how to sew an end to a side with a combination of the two, you have all the tools you need to manage a set-in sleeve.

First, let's look at the structure of these pieces, which will make it easier to understand what you're doing when it comes time to sew them together. The armhole for a set-in sleeve is shaped with a short bound-off edge at the underarm, followed by a slanted section of decreases, and then a straight edge up to the shoulder. The sleeve cap is shaped in the same way, bound off at the underarm, and sloped using a series of decreases, but then ends with a series of bind offs.

To join them, match the bound-off section of the sleeve underarm to the bound-off section of the armhole and pin both ends of these sections in place. When you seam this section, you'll be joining the tops of two pieces of knitting, so use weaving. Match the sloped section of each as well and pin them in place. On these sloped sections, use mattress stitch because you'll be

## Joining Top or Bottom Edges to Side Edges

To join the end of a piece of knitted fabric (like the top of a sleeve) to the side of another piece of knitting (like the armhole of a garment), use a combination of mattress stitch and weaving. This is what I call a *combination seam*, and the instructions are in the appendix (page 279). The basic concept is that you work identical to mattress stitch along the side edge of the knitting, and you work exactly like weaving along the top or bottom of the knitting on the opposite side of the seam, so it's a combination of the two. Joining two straight edges is fairly straightforward, except that you need to adjust for the fact that knitted stitches are wider than they are tall. In stockinette, this means that as you sew you'll join about 3 stitches to every 4 rows.

joining two side edges. Match the center of the sleeve to the shoulder seam, then distribute any fullness in the sleeve cap evenly along the straight edge of the armhole and pin every couple of inches. Sew this section using a combination of mattress stitch and weaving, because you'll be joining the top of the sleeve to the side of the body.

Stop frequently as you work to check that the two edges are still aligned properly. Lay out the garment and make sure the points joined by safety pins are still even with each other. If necessary, adjust by working under two strands more frequently (or less frequently) as you work into the armhole edge. Keep the safety pins level, and your seam will work out fine.

## Setting in a Sleeve

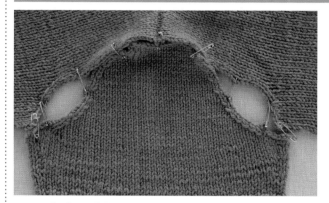

**Pinned.** Shaped sleeve cap pinned to armhole ready to seam

**Combination seaming.** Where the top of the sleeve meets the side of the armhole, use combination seaming. Remember that in stockinette, stitches are wider than they are tall, so you'll need to adjust for this by occasionally working under two strands on the armhole side of the seam.

**Weaving.** Along the straight section of the underarm, use weaving.

**Completed sleeve seam**

**Mattress stitch.** Along the diagonal side of the sleeve cap, which is matched to the diagonal and vertical side of the armhole, use mattress stitch, sewing between the 2 edge stitches on both sides of the seam.

# Live Stitches to Edge Stitches

**YOU CAN ALSO USE A COMBINATION** of weaving and mattress stitch to join live stitches at the top of a piece to the side of another piece of knitting, for example, when joining the top of a sleeve to the body of a drop-shoulder sweater.

Finish the sleeve with a wrong-side row if you are right-handed and want to sew right to left while joining; end with a right-side row if you are left-handed and prefer weaving in the opposite direction. Cut the working yarn, leaving a tail with about ¾ to 1 inch for each stitch in the top of the sleeve. This should be fine for worsted-weight yarn, but you may need a little more for bulkier yarns, and less for thinner yarns. In the photos, I've used contrasting yarn for clarity, but you'd normally use the working yarn, which will match the sleeve.

① **Lay out the pieces** with their right sides facing you. The live stitches of the sleeve will be at the top and the body of the sweater will be above it, with the shoulder seam aligned with the center of the sleeve. Use safety pins or split markers to mark the center of the sleeve and the points on the body where the corners of the sleeve should be attached.

② **Using a yarn needle,** sew under just one strand between the first and second stitch at the edge of the body where the corner of the sleeve should be attached.

③ **Sew into the first live stitch** on the sleeve knitwise and slip the stitch off the needle, then work into the second live stitch purlwise and leave it on the needle.

④ **Sew through the edge of the body again,** working between the first and second stitches just as before. Insert the needle in the same spot you came out of the last time, and under one strand. Occasionally, you will need to sew under two strands in order to keep the sleeve aligned properly with the body (see Stitches versus Rows, opposite).

(5) Sew through the next 2 stitches to be joined on the live sleeve edge. Always sew into the last stitch you came out of knitwise (and slip it off the needle) and out through the next stitch purlwise (leaving it on the needle).

Repeat steps 4 and 5 until you complete the seam. As you work, adjust the tension of your working yarn so that the row of stitches you're creating is the same size as the row of stitches immediately below it.

Completed seam joining live sleeve stitches to the side of the body. Note that this shoulder seam was joined using three-needle bind off, so the edge stitches align perfectly. If the shoulder seam had been woven together, the seam would be a half stitch off at the outer edge, and the armhole seam would have had to shift a half stitch over on the body of the garment at this point.

## Stitches versus Rows

In stockinette, there are more rows in any given length of knitting than there are stitches in the same length. This means that when you're joining the top of something (like a sleeve) to the side of something (like the body), there will frequently be fewer stitches than there are rows. You'll need to adjust for this by occasionally working under two strands (2 rows) of the body as you sew. You can plan for this ahead of time by counting the rows in the body and the stitches in the sleeve and working out how often you'll need to skip a row by working under two strands rather than one. If both of the edges are straight, you can usually match them up by sewing 3 stitches for every 4 rows or 5 stitches for every 7 rows.

▷ For 3 stitches to 4 rows: Every time you work under a strand on the armhole side of the seam, you've worked 1 row. So work under a single strand after the first stitch, a single strand after the second stitch, and then under a double strand. This is easy to keep track of by muttering "single, single, double" to yourself repeatedly.

▷ For 5 stitches to 7 rows: Work "single, single, double, single, double" repeatedly.

In other pattern stitches there may be a different proportion of rows to stitches. For example, in garter stitch, 2 rows are the same length as 1 stitch, so you can easily join stitches to rows by attaching 1 stitch to each garter ridge.

You can also place safety pins or markers periodically along the seam to align the two edges properly. Keep an eye on them to make sure the points that you've connected line up properly. If they don't, work under two strands more frequently (or less frequently) to bring them back into line.

## Options for Seaming without Sewing

There will be times when sewing isn't an option, because the color of the yarn (think of sewing up a black, very fuzzy mohair sweater), the texture of the yarn (if it's too bumpy you won't be able to sew with it), or the pattern stitch makes it too difficult. In these cases, joining by some other means can be a great relief. Your options are either to find a way to knit the pieces together or to crochet them together. Both of these methods are, in fact, inferior to sewing, because they add more bulk to the seams and can be very noticeable. In a dark or textured yarn, however, they are much less likely to be unsightly than in a smooth, light-colored yarn.

### Joining with a Knitted Seam

You can also easily join a sleeve that has not been bound off using the three-needle bind off (appendix, page 261). If it's a drop-shoulder sweater, with no defined armhole, first mark the beginning and end of the armhole area with safety pins. Pick up exactly the same number of stitches along the armhole edge as there are in the sleeve, and then use the three-needle bind off to join the two pieces (on the inside or the outside).

To join two pieces without live stitches, pick up the same number of stitches along both edges and then work three-needle bind off to join the two together. Be sure to pick up the correct number of stitches along each edge so your bound-off seam doesn't ripple or pucker the fabric. Use the same guidelines as for picking up stitches to add a border (1 stitch for each stitch across a cast-on or bound-off edge, and 3 stitches for every 4 rows along the side edge). If you bind off tightly, you may need to pick up more stitches along the edges because the bind off will compress them, but keep in mind that the more stitches you pick up and the more tightly you bind off, the bulkier and less stretchy your seam will be.

As you can see from the photo (top right), these joins really do make a significant addition to the knitting, adding 1 or 2 rows from picking up stitches in addition to binding off. On the other hand, they also offer the opportunity for embellishments. Instead of binding off as you join, you can knit the two layers together and then add a ruffle, a cord, or a mock tuck or pleat that will cover up the awkward join. See Knitted Embellishments (chapter 8, page 250) for ideas.

**Two straight edges joined** (with contrasting yarn) by picking up and using three-needle bind off

**Joining and adding a cord**

**Decorative three-needle rickrack.** Picking up stitches along both edges and joining them on the outside using three-needle bind off and alternating knit and purl stitches will make a rickrack effect for a decorative seam. You may want to use a larger needle for the bind off to prevent it from being too tight. Also be careful to work your knits and your purls with the same tension to keep the rickrack balanced.

### Joining with Crocheted Seams

Slipstitch crochet and single crochet (see instructions in appendix, page 270) are extremely useful when you need to join two pieces of knitting with a yarn that makes it difficult to sew. Yarn that falls into this category might be textured so it doesn't pass easily through the fabric, the plies could stretch at different rates and create snarls, or it might be so softly spun that it falls apart. Keep in mind

**Single crochet** worked on the wrong side encloses the selvedge, so although it adds bulk, it can be useful for securing or enclosing cut edges and ends (left, wrong side; right, right side).

**From the wrong side, slipstitch crochet** can be worked through the two layers of fabric without wrapping around the selvedge, so it is less bulky (*left*, wrong side; *right*, right side).

**Slipstitch crochet** worked from the right side, alternating between the two sides of the seam, isn't bulky because the seam falls between the two pieces of knitting. In this example, the crochet was worked into the knitting every other row, but it could also be done every row to create a firmer, more substantial join.

**Single crochet** can also be worked from the right side, alternating between the two sides of the seam. Like slipstitch crochet, this adds very little bulk.

that in all these cases you could substitute a smooth yarn in the same color and sew the seams conventionally. (See Joining with Difficult Yarns, page 217.)

Some crocheted seams are much bulkier than sewn seams; for example, single crochet through the edge of two layers of knitting will result in a seam allowance that's almost four times the thickness of the base fabric. This is one case where slipped edge stitches are an advantage; they reduce the bulk and make it easy to crochet into the edge consistently. Other crocheted seams are much less bulky, and some, when worked decoratively between the two pieces of knitting, can actually serve as embellishments. You can reduce the bulk by substituting a thinner yarn in a matching color and fiber.

## Seaming in Difficult Situations

There will be times when seaming is extremely difficult, whether it's because the knitting is physically challenging to sew through, because the yarn is difficult to sew with, or the pattern stitch makes it difficult to sew neatly. In these cases, you can join the seams without sewing or substitute a different yarn for sewing up.

## Joining Lace or Loose Knitting

Sewing together pieces of very loose or openwork knitting requires different techniques than sewing solid pieces. The seams tend to look messy and much more solid than the rest of the fabric. Luckily, there are a lot of approaches you can take to this problem.

▷ Plan a garment with fewer seams. Work it circularly, for example, or in one piece below the underarms.

▷ Pick up and knit pieces together rather than sewing up later. For example, pick up the sleeve at the shoulder and knit it down to the cuff.

▷ If you do need to seam, test out the edge stitches on your swatch. Try to pick up stitches along the edge. If it's easy to pick up stitches neatly and consistently, then it will also be easy to sew a seam neatly and consistently.

▷ Make solid stockinette or garter stitch edges a few stitches wide on the pieces and sew them the same way you would knitting that is solid throughout. Note that the seams will be very noticeable if they are much more solid than the rest of the fabric.

▷ Work a single edge stitch in garter. This can be seamed flat and reversible by sewing through the bump at the end of each ridge (see Seaming Garter Stitch, page 206). It's easy to adjust the tension on

this type of seam so you can make it as loose as you like just by stretching the fabric. This may be the most unobtrusive and easiest seam you can make in lace or loose knitting.

▷ In lace, use yarnover edges to make a more open or decorative join (see Add a Yarnover Edge, chapter 2, page 58). Yarnover edges can be joined with decorative crocheted seams (bottom), or by picking up stitches through the loops along both edges and working a decorative three-needle bind off (page 214).

▷ For a less bulky seam, work a half stitch, rather than a whole stitch, from the edge in mattress stitch. Depending on the evenness and tension of your edge stitches, this may look messy, or it may look just fine.

### Joining Yarnover Edges

Working a yarnover edge (see chapter 2, page 58) creates a series of loops at the edge of the knitting. They can be sewn, crocheted, or laced together. If they are loose enough, the loops themselves can be chained alternately from side to side with a crochet hook to join the pieces. Depending on how you handle it, the seam can become a decorative element. If you don't crochet, you can achieve almost the same effect by picking up stitches through the yarnovers along both edges and working a decorative three-needle bind off (page 214).

The lace cast on (see appendix, page 265) mimics the yarnover edge and can be used to join in the same fashion, either to a yarnover edge or to another cast-on edge.

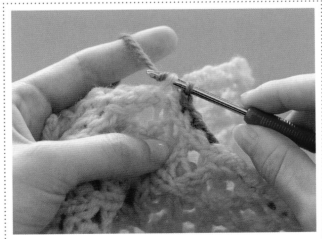

**Yarnover edges, crocheted together** using slipstitch crochet and contrasting yarn

### *Picking Up Sections of a Garment*

Picking up a sleeve and working it down, even with short rows as shown (below), can appear much neater and easier to work than seaming in this very noticeable area of a sweater. See Working Darts in Pattern Stitches (chapter 4, page 123) for tips on integrating short rows into pattern stitches, as well as Case Study #3-3, Short-Row Sleeve Caps (page 80).

**Picking up instead of seaming.** The sleeve stitches were picked up all the way along the armhole, and then short rows were worked beginning from the shoulder seam with one additional pattern repeat on each row. (Shown in contrasting yarn for clarity.)

## Joining Very Tight Knitting

Very tight, sturdy knitting presents other challenges when it's time to join the seams. Pulling the yarn repeatedly through the fabric can abrade it so that it becomes weak and may break before the seam is completed. Crocheting the seams could be a good (but bulky) option, assuming the edge is loose enough to work through with a crochet hook. You can plan ahead for easier seaming in a tight fabric by working

**While slipped-stitch edges can be a disadvantage** in looser knitting, they can make it easier to sew or crochet together more tightly knit pieces.

slipped-stitch edges. Another option is to substitute a strong, thin yarn or thread for sewing up.

## Joining with Difficult Yarns

Fragile, fuzzy, or textured yarns can be difficult to sew with. If it's not possible to redesign the garment to eliminate seams, try crocheting the edges together. If crocheted seams are too bulky, sew the seams using a strong smooth yarn in a matching color. Try to match the fiber content of the original yarn. For example, use wool-blend sock yarns with wool, wool blends, or other animal fibers, and embroidery floss with cotton or other plant fibers. Both come in a wide range of colors, making it easy to match the color of your yarn.

## Joining Bulky Knitting

Seams in bulky knitting can be very bulky themselves. Avoid crocheted seams worked from the wrong side, which will just add more bulk. You could crochet a decorative seam between the two pieces of knitting (see Joining with Crocheted Seams, page 214) without adding significantly to the thickness. You could also use mattress stitch and reduce the bulk of the seam by sewing a half stitch from the edge and under 2 rows with each stitch, rather than a full stitch from the edge and under every row; this may look messy if the edge stitches are too loose. You can also use a thinner yarn or split your plies to make a thinner yarn for sewing up, assuming the resulting yarn is strong enough. When joining sleeves in a bulky drop-shoulder sweater, consider picking up stitches along the body and working the sleeve down, or work the sleeve from bottom to top and use weaving to join the live stitches to the side of the sweater (see Live Stitches to Dead Stitches, page 208, and Live Stitches to Edge Stitches, page 212).

### Joining Bulky Knits

**Working a half stitch from the edge** (*left*) makes a much less bulky seam than working a whole stitch from the edge (*right*). On the right side, both methods look almost identical.

# Borders, Bindings, and Embellishments

AFTER THE SEWING up is finished, there are still plenty of things to do on a sweater. While you may not be interested in adding unnecessary embellishments, borders deserve your attention because of the important roles they play in supporting the garment and in making its edges behave the way they should. You also have the opportunity to add collars, pockets, cords, and ruffles. Then, for the final detailing, block the seams and anything else you want to look particularly good.

## chapter eight

# Neck, Armhole, and Front Borders

Conventional bottom-up and top-down garments knit with shaped armholes and necklines usually are finished off by adding borders around the neck and around sleeveless armholes. Cardigans require borders along both sides of the front, frequently with buttons and buttonholes. All of these borders are very, very noticeable. Poorly executed borders can make a garment that is otherwise perfect look vile.

There are several challenges in adding borders:

▷ Picking up the stitches

▷ Determining the correct number of stitches

▷ Shaping the border to make it better behaved

▷ Binding off at exactly the right tension

To better understand the important role of borders, especially the neck border, take a look at Changing the Borders in chapter 3 (page 70). Well-made neck and armhole borders are essential to the structure and fit of sweaters and vests, and are in such prominent positions that any failings in proportion or execution will be immediately noticeable. It may require several attempts, but it's worth the effort to unravel and do them over until they are exactly right.

## How and Where to Pick Up the Border Stitches

This section covers picking up stitches along the straight or shaped edge of the knitting, but assumes that it's just a normal edge. If you're working with a cut edge, because of adjustments for size or because you've steeked the garment, see Finishing the Cut Edges in chapter 6 (page 187).

In stockinette or a stockinette-based fabric, always work 1 full stitch in from the edge — this will be easy because you kept 1 or 2 edge stitches in stockinette and did any increasing, decreasing, and patterning farther away from the edge, so they won't get in the way of picking up the stitches (see Planning for the Best Edges and Seams in chapter 2, page 53). Always pick up stitches by inserting the needle through the fabric and knitting up a new stitch through the edge of the fabric using your working yarn.

If you worked the garment in garter stitch, you may have worked the garter stitch all the way to the edge, or you may have worked slipped-stitch edges to make it easy to pick up 1 stitch in every other row. Depending on how you handled your edge stitches, you have several pickup options.

**Picking up a whole stitch from the edge in stockinette.** In this photo, the knitter is working from the bound-off edge toward the cast on. When working in either direction, you can be sure you're picking up a whole stitch from the edge by inserting the tip of the needle underneath both of the strands that make up the stitch.

**Picking up a whole stitch from the edge in garter stitch.** Pick up under the stitches between the ridges.

**Picking up half a stitch from the edge in garter stitch.** If the edge is loose, pick up in the little knot at the end of each ridge; otherwise, pick up in the long, loose stitch between each ridge.

Picking up a whole stitch along a slipped edge in garter stitch. This can sometimes look loose.

Picking up a half stitch from the edge along a slipped edge in garter stitch. Picking up under the back half of the stitch creates a neat ropelike detail. Picking up under the front half of the stitch hides the edge stitch completely.

## Picking Up Just the Right Number of Stitches

Your pattern may tell you how many stitches to pick up, but this isn't necessarily the number *you* need to pick up along the edge of *your* sweater. Rather, it's the number that the designer estimates will fit along the edge of the size you're making, assuming you didn't make any changes (intentional or unintentional) in the length or width. Alternatively, the pattern may tell you how often to pick up along the edge (for example, 3 stitches for every 4 rows) and what multiple of stitches you need to end up with (for example, a multiple of 4 stitches plus 2 to work K2, P2 ribbing). This is much more likely to result in a successful border (and it's what I recommend that you actually do), because it takes into account any changes that may have been made in your particular sweater. What neither of these instructions allows for is significant differences in tension between the original designer and the knitter. For example, if you work ribbing much looser than the designer expects, your ribbing will end up the wrong size. (If you think you might have this problem, see Needle Size Makes a Difference, page 224.) These factors could make your sweater different enough from the designer's concept that the instructions might not work for you.

You should be familiar with the basic proportions for picking up the right number of stitches along the edge of the basic fabrics (stockinette and garter) to make standard ribbed or garter stitch borders. In most cases, you can substitute these for pattern instructions that tell you to pick up a certain number of stitches, to make a border that neither flares out nor gathers the edge of the fabric.

**For ribbed borders attached to stockinette stitch,** pick up about 3 stitches for every 4 rows along the side and diagonal edges of an opening, and 1 stitch in every stitch along a bound-off or cast-on edge. To pick up along a curved edge like an armhole or neckline, you'll need to pick up along all three types of edges: horizontal (along a bound-off or cast-on edge), diagonal (along increases and decreases), and vertical (along the side). (See photos page 222.)

**For garter stitch borders attached to a garter stitch base fabric,** pick up 1 stitch for every 2 rows (which is the same as picking up 1 stitch for every ridge) along the side of the fabric, as shown in photos at left.

**For other pattern stitches.** The proportions above are designed to work when you are adding a ribbed border to a stockinette garment or a garter stitch border to a garter stitch garment. In other situations, they most likely will not work properly. You can figure out the correct number of stitches for your border by working a separate gauge swatch in the border pattern. See Getting Neck Borders Right in chapter 3 (page 71) for how to plan a border with exactly the right number of stitches.

A final consideration is that you need to adjust the number of stitches to fit the border pattern. If you find it difficult to pick up the correct number of stitches, it's best to pick up a few more than you need, and then decrease to the correct stitch count on the first row or round of your border. If you come up just 1 or 2 stitches short when picking up, you can increase to make the adjustment.

▷ If you're working the border circularly, make sure that the total number of stitches is an exact multiple of your pattern stitch, so that it repeats seamlessly. For example, use an even number of stitches for K1, P1 ribbing and a multiple of 4 stitches for K2, P2 ribbing.

▷ If you are working a flat border that will later be joined using a seam, be sure to add edge stitches so that the seam will look neat in the finished border (see Making Borders Look Continuous across Seams in chapter 2, page 52).

## Picking Up along a Curved Edge

① Pick up and knit 1 stitch in each stitch just below the bound-off edge, knitting directly into each stitch so the bind off is hidden.

③ Pick up and knit 3 stitches for every 4 rows along the diagonal edge. To do this, work a stitch in each row for 3 rows, then skip over the 4th row.

② Skip over the stretched corner stitch. Picking up on both sides of this loose corner pulls it together so there won't be a hole.

④ Pick up and knit 3 stitches for every 4 rows along the vertical edge.

▷ If you are working a flat border that will not be seamed, be sure to allow for edge stitches that will make the finished border look neat. See Making the End Stitches Look Good (page 228).

## Fiber Makes a Difference in Borders

I have commented in several places within this book that other fibers just don't behave the same as wool or wool-blend yarns. This is especially noticeable in borders. Because they are inelastic and have less "memory" than wool, borders in other fibers tend to stretch out of shape. See Fiber Content and the Finished Fabric (chapter 1, page 24) for a discussion of this problem. If your borders don't seem to be behaving the way they should, especially if they are lethargic and enervated, try some of the suggestions in Beginning with the Very Best Borders (chapter 2, page 50), Changing the Borders (chapter 3, page 70), or in the following pages.

**A curved edge with ribbing in a variety of fibers** (*top to bottom*): silk, a mohair/wool blend, a cotton/wool blend, wool, and a silk/wool blend. The more wool in the yarn, the more the border pulls in naturally.

**The same curved edge in wool with four different borders** (*top to bottom*): K2, P2 ribbing; K1, P1 ribbing; Open Star Stitch; Baby Cable Ribbing. Open Star Stitch flares beyond the edge of the swatch, a sign that a few stitches need to be decreased at the upper edge to shape it properly. Notice also how the K2, P2 ribbing naturally pulls in more than K1, P1 ribbing.

## Pattern Stitch Makes a Difference, Too

Some pattern stitches are more elastic and have more memory than others. Ribbing will stretch and tends to return to its original width; K2, P2 and K3, P3 ribbings are better at this than K1, P1. Ribbing with stitches twisted by working into the back loop will have more memory than standard ribbing. Pattern stitches that are not ribbed tend to be less elastic (don't stretch as much as ribbing) and to have poorer memory (so they stretch out of shape). Because of these inherent properties, it's easier to make a ribbed border that looks good and behaves well. If you're working in anything other than a basic ribbing, you'll need to size your border carefully, plan for it to stretch, and, if it's along a curved edge, you may need to shape it for best results. (See photos, page 223, right.)

**Borders worked with different-size needles.** In this silk yarn, the border at the top was worked on needles the same size as the base fabric. The one in the center was worked on needles two sizes smaller, and the one on the bottom was worked on needles four sizes smaller. Notice that the border stitches on the bottom are a little tighter and neater and that the border pulls in just a little at both ends (which is what you want in a perfect border), rather than flaring at one end like the border at the top.

## Needle Size Makes a Difference

You may have picked up exactly the right number of stitches but still run into a problem if your ribbing tends to be looser or tighter than the norm. You can deal with this by adjusting the needle size. Use a smaller needle to make the ribbing just a bit tighter, and a larger one to make it just a bit looser. You can tell you've got the right needle size when the knit stitches in K1, P1 ribbing look the same size as your knit stitches in stockinette.

Remember that most ribbed borders are worked on needles two sizes smaller than the body of a stockinette stitch garment. This serves two purposes: it makes the stitches a little smaller so they look neater, and it makes the border a little firmer so it retains its shape. Even if the instructions don't say to do so, you can go ahead and work the border on smaller needles to improve the look and behavior of your border.

When working in any fiber other than wool or a wool blend, you can significantly improve the behavior of ribbed borders by using needles three or four sizes smaller. They'll hold their shape better and look neater.

## The Special Challenge of Shaped Borders

Borders along a straight edge (like the bottom of a sweater) are very straightforward — you need to make sure only that they are worked on the correct number of stitches and with the correct needle size and they'll come out fine. Borders along shaped edges like necklines and armholes have the added challenge that they need to fit around the inside of a circle, square, or V. Shaped bottom edges, like a curved shirt tail or a pointed vest detail, require the border to fit properly around the outside of a curve or corner.

### Working a Border with Corners

V- and square-necked openings have corners, and your border needs to fit perfectly into those corners or it won't lie flat. You can work these as mitered corners, making decreases at the corner points, or you can work each of the straight sections flat, overlap them, and sew down the ends. For examples of these two treatments, see the photos of V-Neck borders in chapter 3 (page 72).

Mitered corners on a neckline require that you decrease 2 stitches at each corner on each decrease row or round. You can do this with a double decrease like s2kp2, or you can work a pair of symmetrical decreases on either side of the corner stitch (see Symmetrical Increases and Decreases in chapter 2, page 61). To match the angle of the corner, you'll need to decrease at

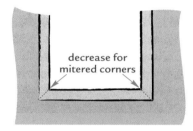

**Outside corner border.** Borders worked on outside corners, using the K-yo-K increase (*left*) and paired M1 increases on either side of corner stitch (*right*).

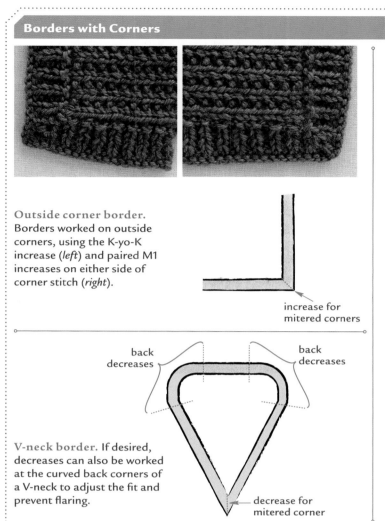

increase for mitered corners

back decreases

back decreases

**V-neck border.** If desired, decreases can also be worked at the curved back corners of a V-neck to adjust the fit and prevent flaring.

decrease for mitered corner

decrease for mitered corners

**Square neck border.** The corner at left was worked using two separate but symmetrical decreases. The corner at right was worked with the double decrease s2kp2.

exactly the right rate. How often you work the decreases will depend on the angle of the corner and the pattern stitch in your border. For a low V-neck, you may need to decrease on 2 out of 3 rows or rounds, or on 3 out of 4. For a higher V-neck or a right-angle corner, you may need to decrease on every other row or round.

If you need to add a border to an outside corner, for example on a squared shirt tail, a collar, or at the top or bottom corner of a cardigan front, you can work a double increase (such as K-yo-K in a single stitch) or a pair of symmetrical increases on either side of the corner stitch (see Symmetrical Increases and Decreases in chapter 2, page 61). If the border is worked in garter stitch, then work the increases every other row or round. In other pattern stitches, you'll need to increase a little more often to make the corner lie flat — try increasing on 2 out of 3 rows or 3 out of 4 rows. Be sure to bind off loosely, perhaps working your final corner increase while binding off, so that the edge lies flat.

## Creating a Curved Border

You can ensure that the border fits perfectly in a round neck opening, an armhole opening, or around a curved shirt tail by shaping it, planning for a smaller number of stitches around the inner edge of the curve and a larger number of stitches around the outer edge of the curve.

To make a shaped border you need to know how many stitches there should be where the border meets the edge of the garment and the number of stitches at the outer edge of the border. For a neck border, make sure that the measurement at the outer edge will be long enough to fit over the wearer's head. You also need to integrate the shaping with the pattern stitch for your border, and place the shaping to fit the curved sections of the edge the border is attached to. See Case Study #8-1, page 226, for details.

# Adding a Curved Border

① Work a gauge swatch in your border pattern about 5 to 6 inches wide and as tall as you want your border to be, block it under tension, and then measure the gauge in stitches and in rows. For this example, the gauge is 4½ stitches and 6 rows per inch.

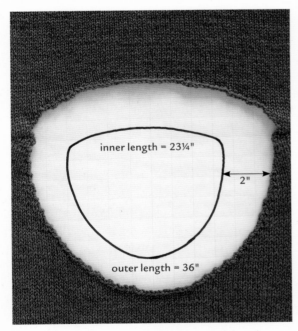

inner length = 23¼"

2"

outer length = 36"

② To measure the outer edge of the neck border, lay the garment out flat and use a flexible tape measure to measure along the edge where the border will be applied, then measure along an imaginary line where you want the outer edge of the border to fall.

③ Based on the inner length and the outer length, calculate how many stitches you need to pick up for your border and how many you need when you bind it off. The difference between these two numbers is the total number of decreases or increases you need to work while completing your border. Remember to adjust the number to accommodate your pattern stitch. On a neck opening, which gets smaller as you work it, you'll decrease. On a shirt tail or collar, where the curve gets larger as you work out, you'll need to increase so that the border gets wider.

Stitches to pick up = 36" × 4½ stitches per inch = 162 stitches

Decrease to: 23¼" × 4½ stitches per inch = 105

How many stitches to decrease = 162 – 105 = 57 (about ⅓)

④ Figure out which rows of the border you can work the shaping on without messing up the pattern stitch. In garter stitch borders, you can work shaping throughout the border. With other patterns, you may be able to incorporate shaping only in the first few and the last few rows. If this is the case, consider working 1 or 2 rows of plain stockinette or reverse stockinette immediately after picking up the stitches and immediately before binding off.

⑤ Plan where you will place the shaping. On a round neck opening, the decreases can be spread evenly around. On other curved edges, the shaping should be placed where the curve occurs. If you have two curved areas (say, two corners of a shirt tail or the front and back of a scooped neck), divide the shaping evenly between the two. (See drawings, facing page, top.)

## WHERE TO PLACE THE SHAPING ON CURVED BORDERS

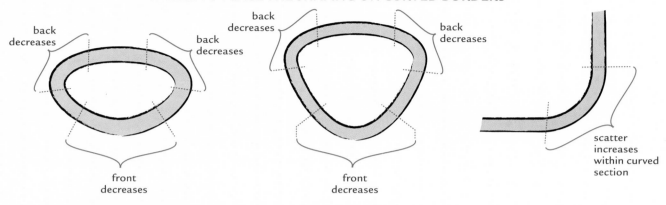

back
decreases

back
decreases

back
decreases

back
decreases

back
decreases

front
decreases

front
decreases

scatter
increases
within curved
section

**Round neck border**

**Scoop neck border**

**Outside curved border**

(6) You now know how many stitches to increase or decrease in each section of the border, and you know how many rows you have to do it in. Make a plan! In our example, we need to decrease 57 stitches to get from 162 stitches at the pickup to 105 at the bind off. Because the border will be worked in a pattern stitch, we won't be able to decrease in the pattern stitch without messing it up, so we'll need to decrease before starting the pattern and after finishing it. To allow for this, after picking up we'll work a purl round, then work another purl round while decreasing some of the shaping stitches. We'll then work the border

pattern. Immediately before binding off, we'll work 2 more purled rounds, decreasing the rest of the shaping stitches. If you wish, you can bind off while working some of the decreases.

Garter stitch borders are easier to shape because you can decrease throughout and still maintain the pattern. Note that if you bind off firmly, you may be able to make a shorter outer edge without doing all of the planned decreases. If you're making an outer curved edge, like on a shirt tail or collar, be careful to bind off loosely instead.

On the scoop neck from our example, 9 decreases were worked in the front section of the border on the 2nd purled round, and 48 were worked in the purled round following the pattern stitch to reach our total of 57 decreases. The bind off was worked in purl to mirror the 2 purled rounds at the beginning of the border.

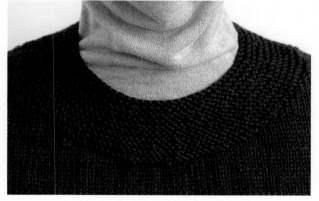

On this round neck, the border was worked flat, because that's easier in garter stitch, and then seamed at one shoulder. On the first right-side row, 6 stitches were decreased evenly spaced to reduce the total number to an even multiple of eight. On all the subsequent right-side rows, 8 stitches were decreased, staggering the decreases so they never lined up with earlier decreases. Staggering the decreases ensures that the border will be curved.

## Options for Front Borders

The front borders of cardigans, which can be plain or can provide space for buttons, buttonholes, and other fastenings, support the front edges. They need to be exactly the correct length and to lie flat. Blocking is required to ensure that the fronts are indeed the correct length, their corners are square, and they are perfectly flat. Buttonholes present their own problems — it's hard to make holes just the right size for the buttons.

Front borders can most easily be worked perpendicular to the fronts, by picking up stitches all along the front edge and then working out. Or, they can be worked in a long strip from top to bottom, either sewing this strip to the front after it is complete, or by Knitting On (chapter 6, page 182).

### Choosing the Correct Size Needle

Assuming you are applying a ribbed border to a stockinette stitch garment, you'll usually use a needle two sizes smaller than that used for the body of the garment when you work the border. This makes the ribbed stitches look neater (loose ribbing can look sloppy) and helps the border retain its shape when worn and stretched.

Remember, though, that all knitters are individuals, and the knitting that comes off their needles can vary a great deal. If your ribbing tends to be very loose, you might need an even smaller needle. If your ribbing always tends to be tight, you might need a larger needle. And, if you're making a border that's not ribbed on a garment that's not stockinette, you may need to adjust for the difference in gauge produced by whatever knitted fabrics you are using instead. The best way to determine the needle size for the borders in your particular situation is to test it out on your swatch as described in Swatching to Refine the Details (page 34).

### How to Get the Right Number of Border Stitches

Before making a border worked perpendicular to the front, work a swatch in the ribbed (or other) pattern you plan to use for the front borders. Be sure to use the size needle you plan to use for the actual border. Measure the border swatch slightly stretched to determine the stitch gauge. Measure the front edge and multiply by the stitch gauge to determine the number of stitches you need to pick up for the border. Adjust the number of stitches to center your pattern and to make both ends look good.

## What Does "Slightly Stretched" Mean?

When ribbing is at rest, it naturally scrunches up so that the knit ribs hide the purl ribs. When blocking your swatch, stretch it sideways just enough so that the purl ribs show in nice proportion to the knit ribs. Don't stretch it to its maximum possible length, which will remove all its elasticity. You want it to still be elastic after blocking so that it can stretch and rebound as ribbing naturally does. If your border isn't ribbed, then stretch it just enough during blocking so that the pattern stitch looks its best. To do this, you may need to stretch it a bit in both dimensions. As with ribbed borders, you don't want to max out the stretch; treat your border gently.

### How to Get the Right Number of Border Rows

If you'll be working your border in a long strip with the side attached to the front of your garment, you'll need to be sure it's the correct length. Work a swatch in the ribbed (or other) pattern you want to use for the front borders. It should be the same width you plan for the finished border and at least 6 inches long. Be sure to use the size needle you'll use for the actual border; usually this will be two sizes smaller than that used for the body of the garment. Measure the border swatch slightly stretched to determine the row gauge. Measure the front edge and multiply by the row gauge to determine the total number of rows for the border. If you plan to attach the border to the body as you go, count the number of rows in the front to determine how often you'll knit up a stitch along the edge to attach the border smoothly to the garment.

### Making the End Stitches Look Good

How you handle the end stitches of a border worked perpendicular to the body depends on what will happen next to these stitches. Consider whether they will be the finished edge of the knitting, or whether a neck or bottom border will be picked up along them.

If the ends of the borders will be hidden by another border, you don't need to worry about how they look, so long as you can pick up neatly across them. You may, however, want to consider how the border will look once

Ribbed border with slipped-stitch edge

K1, P1 border with an extra knit stitch at the end

K2, P2 border with 3 knit stitches at the edge

Ribbed bottom border with 1 stitch in garter stitch at each end to prevent curling. Notice that where this border crosses the ends of the two side borders, a knit stitch neatly abuts it. The side borders were worked with an extra knit stitch at each end, which disappeared to the wrong side when the bottom border was added.

2-stitch corded edge

the end stitch disappears behind the adjacent border. When the ends of the border will be exposed, you'll want to make those edge stitches look as good as you possibly can. You have lots of options for this tiny detail.

▷ If your edge stitches are neat, you can continue the ribbing (or other pattern) all the way to the edge of the fabric.

▷ If your edge stitches are loose or sloppy, try working a slipped stitch at the beginning of each row, allowing an extra stitch for this purpose if you like the look of it (A).

▷ Because stockinette curls toward the purl side along the side edges, you can allow for this by adding an extra knit stitch at both ends — this will curl to the back so that the knit rib at each end still looks complete after curling. If you need to pick up another border across this end (for the neck, for example), then the extra stitch disappears behind the pickup row (B, C, D).

▷ You can create a more substantial edge at the end of the border by working a slipped cord at the end of the row (E). See Corded Edges in chapter 2 (page 57) for instructions.

▷ You can place an additional stitch at the end, but work it in garter stitch (knitting it on every row), so the edge doesn't curl (D, page 229).

▷ If you make the front, neck, and bottom borders all in one piece, by picking up stitches all the way around the outer edge of the cardigan, you can work mitered corners and will have no exposed edge stitches. (See Working a Border with Corners, page 224.)

## Starting Double, Ending Single

There will be times when you want the inside of the front borders to look just as good as the outside. All cardigans will flop open sometimes when they aren't buttoned shut, or you may want to make a garment that's fully reversible. To accomplish this, pick up and begin your border exactly as described for Creating a Binding to Enclose an Edge (page 235). After working just 1 or 2 rounds, join the two layers together and continue in a single layer.

**The picked-up edge of the border** looks the same on the inside and the outside.

## Yarnover Pickup

ANOTHER OPTION for covering the edge inside and out is to work a yarnover between each stitch as you pick up along the edge, then create a 1-row binding using tubular knitting. The pickup row tends to look loose and messy unless you control the tension while picking up, but you can easily do this by changing needle sizes.

① Using a needle two sizes smaller than you plan to use for your border, pick up and knit the stitches for the border, adding a yarnover after each stitch (except at the end of the row).

② Work tubular purling for 1 round to make a binding 1 row wide. To do this, work across the first row as follows: With yarn in front, *slip 1 purlwise, P1 (you'll be purling the yarnovers from your pickup row); repeat from * until 1 stitch remains, slip 1 purlwise. On the following row, with yarn in front, *P1, slip 1 purlwise; repeat from * until 1 stitch remains, P1. You'll be purling the stitches you picked up on your pickup row. If you wish, you may work this step in tubular knitting, but to do so you must move the yarn forward and back between every stitch, so purling is quicker and easier.

③ Join the two layers: P2tog all the way across, until 1 stitch remains, P1. This will reduce the number of stitches by almost half, getting rid of all those extra yarnovers from your pickup row.

④ Make a gradual transition to the desired needle size for your border. Work the first row with needles one size larger, then change up once more, to the size you want to use for your border.

The finish on the wrong side will not be as neat as working a full binding (see Starting Double, Ending Single, above), but this is quicker and easier to execute and you don't need a second needle to do it. While shown here on a collar, this is also a great technique for making the pickup row on sweater fronts reversible.

**This collar was picked up** with the inside of the garment facing the knitter, so the "right side" is shown where the collar joins the garment at the left and around the back neck. The "wrong side" is shown under the collar at right.

Borders, Bindings, and Embellishments

## Doubled Front Borders

Double-thickness borders along the fronts of a cardigan will keep their shape better and look and feel more substantial. If you want to make borders that are plain stockinette, doubled borders will allow you to do this without the borders curling. On the other hand, a double-thickness border can be very bulky if worked in worsted-weight or heavier yarns. To make a double-thickness border, use any of the options in Bindings and Facings for Enclosing Edges (page 235). Remember to work any buttonholes in both layers of the border.

## Buttons and Buttonholes for Front Borders

Buttons (and their holes) can be problematic in knitting. It can be so difficult to find the perfect button to match a garment that it's sometimes best to choose the buttons first, then buy the yarn. When you purchase buttons, choose those that can be cleaned the same way as the yarn. For dry-clean-only yarn, choose buttons that can be dry cleaned. For washable yarn, choose buttons that can be washed.

Making holes that actually fit the buttons, so the garment can be closed easily and will *stay* closed, can also be tricky. Spacing the holes evenly along the front presents an additional challenge. You can work the buttonholes while making the front band, or you can add them later. In all cases, however, before you begin working the holes, you need to plan how they will be made and where they will be placed.

A final difficulty — one that rears its ugly head even when the buttonholes are perfectly placed and executed — is that knitting stretches. This can cause the front to stretch between the buttonholes, making curved gaps all along the center front. The only way to avoid this is to sew some nonstretchy material (like grosgrain ribbon) along the inside to stabilize the fronts, but it can also be mitigated by using more buttons and placing them closer together.

### Where to Put Buttons and Buttonholes

It's best to work the button border first; based on that, figure out where the buttonholes will fall on the opposite front.

▷ Lay a ruler or tape measure on the finished border and place a split marker or safety pin in the border to mark the location of each button. Count the stitches between the markers and between the markers and the ends of the band. If the number of stitches isn't consistent between the markers, adjust the positions of the markers. Note these and use them as a guide for placement of the holes.

▷ Plan to place the top button (assuming it buttons all the way to the neckline) at the center of the neck band.

▷ To make the spacing work out evenly, you can adjust the space between the bottom button and edge of the bottom border.

**On horizontal borders** (worked perpendicular to the body of the garment), determine ahead of time what row or rows of the border the buttonholes will be worked on.

▷ Work until you've completed the row before the beginning of the buttonholes, then place markers to indicate where each buttonhole will be worked.

▷ When you work the buttonholes, be sure to center them on the points you marked. For example, if the buttonhole is worked across 3 stitches, begin working it 1 stitch before the marked stitch so it will be centered at the correct point when completed.

**On vertical borders,** you'll work a narrow strip from end to end, adding one buttonhole at a time.

▷ If the vertical border is knitted onto the front as you go, place a marker in the edge of the front at each point where there will be a buttonhole. As you work the border, when you come to each marker, center the buttonhole horizontally on the border. You may need to begin a multirow buttonhole a row before the marker so it will be centered vertically in the correct position.

▷ If the vertical border will be sewn on later, stop and measure frequently so you'll know when it's time to start each buttonhole. You can lay the border in progress down on the button band (which already has markers indicating the position of each button) to see exactly where the buttonholes should go. When you center the hole horizontally on the band, allow for 1 stitch to disappear into the seam allowance when the border is sewn to the front.

## Choosing the Type of Buttonhole

There are many different kinds of buttonholes to choose from. Make your selection based on how they look and whether they fit your button. Test your buttonholes by adding a button band to your swatch. This gives you the opportunity to try several different buttonholes and to make them different sizes. Make sure the hole is barely big enough for the button to pass through. The instructions for all the buttonholes shown here are in the appendix (pages 262–63).

The most basic buttonhole is a simple eyelet, which will work anywhere. This is the smallest hole you can make, and it is especially good for bulky yarns or for tiny buttons on baby clothes. It looks great placed in a purled rib of K1, P1 ribbing (B).

Vertical buttonholes are least noticeable in ribbing when placed in a purl rib. You can choose versions that integrate well with both K1, P1 ribbing and K2, P2 ribbing (A, C).

Horizontal buttonholes are especially good in garter stitch, where they can be hidden in the valley between two ridges. These include the afterthought buttonhole (D), the one-row buttonhole (E), and the three-row buttonhole (F). The first is very convenient

## Buttonhole Options

Buttonholes for K1, P1 ribbing. Vertical buttonhole Ⓐ, eyelet buttonhole Ⓑ

Vertical buttonhole for K2, P2 ribbing

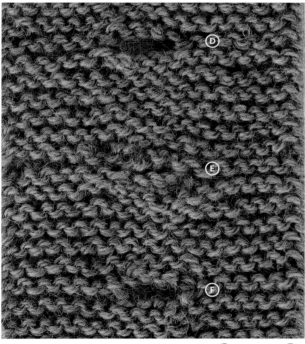

Horizontal buttonholes. Afterthought Ⓓ, one-row Ⓔ, three-row Ⓕ

Loop and slit buttonholes made with applied I-cord. First the burgundy cord was attached, then the buttonholes were made while attaching the pink cord.

if you discover you didn't make a buttonhole when you should have, or if you just don't want to worry about the buttonholes while working your bands. The second is a little more complicated than most buttonholes, because the yarn is woven in and out between the stitches to prevent the buttonhole from stretching.

I-cord buttonholes are very versatile, easy to position, and are added when cording is applied to the edge of the garment. They work best when you first work a plain cord along the edge, then make the buttonholes while attaching a second cord. To make a slit buttonhole, when you reach the point where the buttonhole should start, stop attaching the cord. Instead, just work plain I-cord for the length of the buttonhole, then begin attaching it again. To make a loop buttonhole, do the same, but work a longer section of detached cord, and when you are ready to attach it, pick up your next stitch in the same spot you picked up the last stitch before starting the loop. (For applied I-cord instructions, see appendix, page 274.)

## Adjusting Too-Loose Buttonholes

If you end up with a buttonhole that's too loose, use matching yarn to sew across one or both ends to make the buttonhole shorter and weave the yarn in and out along both sides of the opening to prevent stretching. You can also work buttonhole stitch (appendix, page 262) around the buttonhole using yarn or sewing thread.

## Attaching the Buttons

Sew the buttons on along the front, positioned so they line up with your buttonholes.

If the holes in the buttons are large enough, use a tapestry needle and the yarn from the project to attach them. As you work along the front, don't cut the yarn between each button; instead, weave the yarn in and out on the back of the fabric (just as if you were weaving in an end), until you get to the position for the next button. This ultimately is less work than weaving in two ends of yarn for every button. (See photo on following page.)

If the hole in the button is too small for a tapestry needle threaded with yarn to pass through, use a sewing needle and thread.

Shank buttons (with a loop attached to the back) allow you to button up thick knitted fabric without compressing the fabric. If you are attaching buttons with holes through them to a thick fabric, create a sewn shank between the button and the fabric. Using thin yarn or sewing thread, sew the button on loosely,

**Make a shank** with sewing thread to accommodate the thickness of the knitted fabric.

leaving space between the button and the fabric; wrap around the strands between the button and the fabric a few times, then pull through to the back and secure.

If the knitted fabric is loose, so that any tension on the buttons pulls the strands of yarn leaving gaps, you can provide reinforcement by sewing a small flat button to the back of the fabric. When you attach your buttons, sew through the one on the back, the fabric, and the button on the front all at the same time.

If you have been unable to purchase buttons that can be laundered or dry cleaned with the sweater, plan to remove and replace them every time the sweater gets dirty and needs to be cleaned. This can be annoying and time consuming if you have to cut off and re-sew the buttons each time, but there are a few alternatives.

▷ A neat trick is to use the little plastic clips that sometimes secure buttons with shanks on their display cards in the store. Hold the button in place on the right side of the fabric and slide one of these clips into the back of the shank. This allows you to pull it out to remove the button before cleaning the sweater and quickly replace it afterward. A substitute for this is R-clip cotter pins that you can find at hardware stores. Unfortunately, even if the buttons look good on the outside of the sweater, you'll have to keep the sweater buttoned all the time, or the clips will show when the front flaps open.

▷ You can also use button pins, which are safety pins with a little bump at the center to accommodate a button with a shank, but these tend to shift around unless the fabric is very thick and stiff.

▷ The best option, which will look good on both the inside and the outside of the garment, is to make buttonholes on both sides of the front, then make your own double buttons by sewing two buttons

233

together. These work like the buttons for French cuffs, holding the two layers together. The back button should be flat, so it's comfortable to wear. If two flat buttons the same size are used, they can be two different colors or styles, allowing you to wear either side out to change the look of the sweater. If the back button is smaller than the front, then the buttonhole on the inner layer of the front band must be smaller to match it.

**Sewn-On Buttons**

Buttons sewn on with yarn

Buttons attached with button pins

On the right side, you shouldn't be able to tell how the buttons were attached.

## Perfecting Transitions from Garment to Border

Even if you pick up exactly the right number of stitches as described previously (see How and Where to Pick Up the Border Stitches, page 220), the point where the border meets the garment may still look messy and inconsistent.

When picking up stitches along an edge, especially a curved edge, one issue is that you need to pick up unevenly. For example, when picking up for ribbing along the side of stockinette stitch, you'll usually pick up 3 stitches for every 4 rows of the base fabric. In some yarns, the skipped rows will stand out like a sore thumb, and it will look like you didn't know how to pick up evenly. To avoid this problem, pick up 1 stitch consistently in every stitch and every row around an opening or along an edge, then decrease to the correct number of stitches on the first row or round of your border. The picked-up stitches will look even, and you'll end up with the correct number of stitches for your border. If the picked-up stitches or the whole picked-up row looks looser than the rest of the border, you can make it look neater by using a needle one size smaller for the pickup row than for the border itself.

A second issue is that, especially along a curved edge, there are variations in how you pick up stitches. Some will be in the top of columns of stitches, some between stitches, and some along the diagonals formed by shaping a neckline or armhole. Any variation like this immediately attracts our attention. To camouflage these variations, after you pick up for the border, work reverse stockinette for 1 or 2 rows or rounds before beginning the pattern stitch for your border. The even ridge of purled stitches will then be what people notice, rather than the uneven picked-up stitches. You can frame your border with reverse stockinette by working reverse stockinette to match at the outer edge.

# Bindings and Facings to Enclose Edges

Take into account, before you decide to finish the edges with an enclosed border, that the edge will be a double or triple thickness. If the edge has been cut, then the original fabric will extend into the double thickness of the border, making three layers. If the edge has not been cut, there will still be the double layer of the border. A double thickness may be okay in worsted-weight yarn, but a triple thickness in worsted-weight yarn is very bulky. This may be an advantage around a neckline or cuffs, providing extra stability and warmth. In other locations, like the front opening or around armholes, it may be less comfortable and less attractive. Because of this, enclosed edges are really best reserved for garments made from thinner yarns and avoided when using thicker yarns.

## Making a Doubled Border

To make a doubled border, pick up stitches along the edge as usual and work the border as usual. When it is the width you want, make a fold line by working 1 or 2 rows or rounds in reverse stockinette. This will make a ridge that, when folded, forms a neat edge. Work either in stockinette or ribbing until the second half of the border is the same width as the first. Attach the edge to the inside just as for a hem (see appendix, page 273).

If you need buttonholes in a doubled border, you must work the opening twice for each buttonhole: once

**Sewing down a doubled border**

in the first half and then in the identical position in the second half, so that the two openings line up when the border is folded. You can leave the two layers separate and just slip the button through both, or you can use buttonhole stitch to join the two layers. Another option is to make matching afterthought buttonholes in each layer, and then instead of the sewn bind off, use Kitchener stitch around the opening to join the two layers. (For all of these techniques, see the appendix.)

## Creating a Binding to Enclose an Edge

Bindings achieve the same end as doubled borders, but both layers are worked at the same time and then joined when you bind off. To begin a binding, pick up and knit stitches along the edge as usual, using a circular needle. Be sure to work loosely while picking up, or use a larger needle to ensure that the picked-up stitches are loose enough. At the end of the first side, work an M1 with the working yarn. (See photo 1, following page.)

Turn the garment over so the wrong side is facing you. Using a second circular needle, pick up and knit 1 stitch under the strand between each of the stitches you picked up on the right side. After you've picked up all the stitches on the wrong side, work another M1 at the end of this second needle. You should end up with 1 fewer stitch than on the first side. (See photo 2, following page.)

Work around on the two circular needles (see the instructions for working on two circular needles in the appendix, page 268) until the border is the desired width. If there are any cut ends along the edge to be enclosed, trim them, then hold the two layers together and work three-needle bind off (see appendix, page 261) to secure the live stitches and join the two layers at the same time. (See photo 3, following page.)

If desired, you can join the two layers together without binding off, and continue in a single layer. (See photo 4, following page.) This is an excellent way to join a decorative panel with lots of ends to another section of a sweater, producing a clean finish on both the inside and the outside of the garment. Before starting the binding, be sure to knot the ends securely or hand- or machine-stitch along the edge so there's no chance they'll unravel. When the binding is wide enough, hold the two needles together as if you were going to work three-needle bind off, but just knit the front and back layers together. For a reversible binding, alternately knit and purl as you work across joining the layers.

As for a doubled border, if you need buttonholes in a binding, you'll have to work the opening twice for each buttonhole: once on the outer layer and once in the identical position in the inner layer so that the two openings line up. You can use buttonhole stitch to join the two layers, or leave the two layers separate and just slip the button through both. Note that if a doubled border is covering a lot of cut ends or a cut edge, the presence of the yarn or knitted fabric between the two layers will make it difficult, if not impossible, to pass a button through.

## Using a Facing to Enclose an Edge

Facings differ from borders in that they are located on the inside of the garment. For example, a facing can be worked at the top of a sleeve to completely enclose the cut edge of a steeked armhole opening, or it can cover the inside of a neckline that has been cut after the knitting is finished (rather than shaped during the knitting). Using a facing ensures that the garment is finished on the inside as neatly as on the outside. Facings can also be useful along cardigan fronts, providing extra support to keep the front from stretching out of shape, covering up yarn ends from color changes, or hiding zipper tapes.

Like bindings, facings can be bulky. When they cover a cut edge, there will be three layers of fabric: the finished outer layer of the garment, the cut edge folded to the inside, and the facing covering the cut edge. When they cover an edge where there are lots of tails of yarn from color changes, there will be two layers (the outer layer of the garment and the facing), plus any bulk added by the tails. The advantage of a facing over a binding is that the bulk is moved farther away from the edge of the garment, and the facing can be worked in a thinner yarn than the rest of the project to reduce the additional bulk.

Along curved edges, like armholes and necklines, facings must be shaped to prevent the garment from puckering when the facing is sewn to it. When sewing onto the back of a knitted fabric, use matching yarn

## Enclosing an Edge with Binding

① Pickup for binding completed on right side

② Pickup for binding in progress on the wrong side

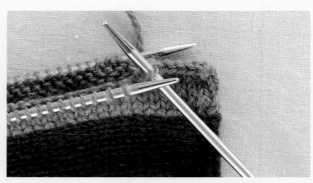

③ Joining the two layers using three-needle bind off

④ This binding encloses the cut ends from multiple stripes. Joining the layers without binding off allows you to continue with another section of the garment.

or sewing thread, being careful not to sew all the way through; the join should be invisible from the outside of the garment. When sewing a facing down over a zipper tape, use sewing thread and a sharp sewing needle, rather than a yarn or tapestry needle.

In the example shown below, a neckline was cut from an unshaped piece of knitting. The burgundy border was picked up through the fabric a short distance from the cut edge, just as for a binding. The first row of the border was purled on the wrong side, leaving a row of bumps to be used for picking up the facing. After the ribbed border was completed, the facing was picked up in pink yarn through the purled row at the base of the ribbing. Increases were worked so that the stockinette stitch facing would mimic the curve of the neckline. (These increases were 2 stitches every other row for this example of half of a front neck opening; for a complete round neck opening, about 8 stitches every other row would be needed.) The facing was bound off and then sewn down to the back of the green fabric.

In her book *The New Stranded Colorwork*, Mary Scott Huff uses a very clever traditional Norwegian technique for facing the cut edge of an armhole. It requires that the sleeve be knit from the bottom up with no sleeve cap shaping. At the top of the sleeve, a few rounds of reverse stockinette are worked to make a facing before binding off. The sleeve is sewn to the armhole below the section of reverse stockinette, and then the facing is sewn down on the inside to cover the cut edge of the armhole. When working the facing rounds, you must increase at the seam line so that the facing will lie smoothly against the body below the underarm.

## The Zipper Controversy

Zippers are a source of much dispute within the knitting community. The major difficulty, which cannot be overcome, is that knitted fabric stretches, but the zipper tape does not. This makes it difficult to sew the two together without stretching the knitted fabric either too much or too little. Zippers do not work well on loose, stretchy fabrics, which tend to sag on either side of the zipper, so they are best attached to firmly knit garments. If the zipper is not sewn onto the garment properly, it will look appalling and will be impossible to ignore because of its prominent position at the center front.

Unfortunately, there is little agreement on the best way to attach zippers to sweaters. Some recommend that you get a zipper longer than the opening, so that you can turn under and sew down the zipper tapes at the neck edge to make them the correct length. Others feel that the doubled sections of the zipper tape are too bulky and advocate using a zipper shorter than the opening, asserting that knitting tends to get shorter and wider over time and many washings, so the shorter

### Covering an Edge with a Facing

Sewing down the facing to cover the cut edge

Facings make a very smooth finish on the right side of the fabric.

tape is better in the long run as well as in the short run. This is true of some fibers (cotton sweaters tend to get shorter and wider), but not of others (garments made from alpaca and slippery fibers tend to grow longer). Some people dislike the way the zipper tape looks on the inside of the garment and prefer to cover it with a knitted facing, while others feel that the additional layer of knitting makes the sweater front much too bulky.

My own opinion is that you should suit yourself on all of these issues, and that all of the opinions expressed in the preceding paragraph will probably apply, at one time or other, to some garment or other. The most important thing is to place and attach the zipper so that the yarn at the front edge doesn't get caught in the zipper teeth when you zip and unzip the sweater. The second most important consideration is to attach the zipper neatly and evenly so that it looks good.

Sewing on the zipper is a two-step process. First, you need to position it properly and anchor it down so that it won't shift while you perform the second step: actually sewing it in place. Here are some hints to help you achieve that. Don't feel that you need to do everything I suggest — some of the tips below will be more useful than others, depending on your personal inclination and the situation — but do be inspired to invent and implement other methods of your own.

## Preparing to Sew In the Zipper

▷ **Use a separating zipper.** For a cardigan, make sure you purchase a separating zipper (one that comes apart at both ends). It's very frustrating to get home and discover that you've bought the wrong kind of zipper, but it happens to all of us. Separating zippers don't come in as many colors or lengths as regular, non-separating zippers, so you may need to opt for a contrasting color. For a slit-neck opening that doesn't go all the way to the bottom of the front, use a regular zipper that opens only at the top.

▷ **Work flow.** It's easiest to sew the zipper in place while the fronts are still separate from the rest of the sweater, before any of the other seams have been sewn, but this may not be possible if the zipper crosses the neckband. To make the edges nice and even, block the fronts first.

▷ **Stabilizing.** One of the problems you'll encounter is that the sweater front will stretch out of shape while you're trying to apply the zipper. You can stabilize it by sewing on a strip of thin paper all along the front, which will be torn off later. You could

also stick on a piece of masking tape to stabilize the front, and thereby avoid some sewing, but don't do this unless you are ready to sew on the zipper without delay — you must remove the tape as soon as possible to ensure the adhesive doesn't transfer permanently to the yarn. Using Wash Away Wonder Tape (see below) will also stabilize the front while you work with it. If you are comfortable crocheting, you can work 2 rows of crochet (perhaps 1 row single crochet followed by 1 row reverse single crochet) to make a neat corded edge. The 2 rows of crochet make a clear guide to follow when sewing the zipper in place and extend past the center front to cover the zipper.

▷ **Planning for the teeth.** When you attach the zipper, line the teeth up with the edge of the fabric. Decide whether you want the zipper teeth to show when the zipper is closed. If you want the teeth to show, let them extend beyond the edge. If you don't want them to show, they should come exactly to the edge.

▷ **Basting.** Avoid using straight or safety pins to hold the zipper in place while sewing because they stretch and distort the knitting and bend the zipper tape, making it difficult to attach the zipper neatly and evenly. Instead, baste the zipper tape to the knitted fabric so that it won't shift while you're sewing it. Using a sharp sewing needle and thread, make long loose stitches. Baste one side in place, then with the zipper closed, line up the two fronts and baste the other side in place. Once you have basted both sides of the zipper in place, zip it open and closed a few times to make sure it doesn't catch the yarn and that both sides of the front line up correctly when it's closed. If you don't stabilize the fabric first, it's easy to stretch it out of shape during basting, so check for any places that look inconsistent. If you find a problem, snip the basting thread and pick out just that section. Line it up properly and baste just that section again.

▷ **Alternative to stabilizing and basting.** You can stick the zipper to the knitting using a double-sided tape called Wash Away Wonder Tape, which dissolves when the sweater is washed. First lay the sweater front out flat (perhaps pin it down to a blocking surface to ensure that the edge is straight and won't shift). Stick the tape to the sweater, then stick the zipper onto the tape.

▷ **Try it on.** Before you sew the zipper in place, close the zipper and hold the front up by the shoulders to see how it behaves. Does the sweater stretch and sag noticeably on either side of the zipper? Or, on the other hand, does the edge look like it's stretched too much where it's attached to the zipper? If you see a problem, remove the zipper and baste it on again with exactly the right amount of stretch along the front edges.

## Sewing In the Zipper

You can sew the zipper in either by hand or by machine. To make the stitches less noticeable, sew through the center of the edge stitch or sew between the first and second stitch from the edge, using thread that's as close in color to your yarn as possible. If sewing by hand, a back-stitch is preferable, because it's unlikely to break when stretched. If sewing by machine, use a stitch length that produces at least 1 stitch per row of the knitting.

**Installing a Zipper**

**Wrong side.** The zipper has been basted on with aqua thread. At left, the zipper has also been sewn down close to the edge of the knitting in orange thread using a running stitch. The excess length of the tape was folded to the inside, trimmed, and the outer edge whipstitched down in orange thread.

**Right side.** Even with the basting and final sewing worked in contrasting thread for clarity, the sewing is barely visible.

On the wrong side of the fabric, whipstitch the inner edge of the zipper tapes to the back of the knitted fabric by hand, being careful to sew only partially through so that the stitches don't show on the outside. (See appendix, page 281.)

If the zipper tapes extend beyond the ends of the opening, you may trim them or fold them under at an angle so that the ends extend away from the edge of the garment. Either way, whipstitch down the ends with a needle and thread.

After sewing is completed, remove the basting thread.

### Covering Up the Zipper Tape and Teeth

If you don't like the exposed zipper tape that shows on the inside of the garment, you can enclose the zipper in a binding (see Creating a Binding to Enclose an Edge, page 235). Instead of joining the two layers of the binding when it is the width of the zipper tape, bind off the two layers separately, insert the zipper tape between them, baste carefully, and then sew in place.

You can also cover the zipper tape with a facing. You can find complete directions for doing this in "Marilyn H's Hidden Zipper" in the Fall 2012 issue of *Knitter's Magazine*. To accomplish this, she works a column of purled stitches near the front edge of the garment, then picks up along this column of stitches on the wrong side of the garment to start the facing that will enclose the zipper tape.

You can cover up the zipper teeth on the outside of the garment by picking up stitches along either edge to add a flap. If you plan to do so, be careful not to sew the zipper tape too close to the edge, which will make picking up the stitches very difficult. Choose a pattern stitch for the flap that has as little bulk as possible and doesn't curl.

## Collars for a Dressier Look

Usually the neckline of a sweater is finished off with a ribbing or other noncurling border. Much less frequently in handknits, a collar is added for a dressier look. It's best to bind off the neck stitches and then apply the collar to the finished neck opening; the additional support this provides will help the opening retain its shape. If the neck stretches, the collar will not drape properly. The collar itself can be made separately and sewn on, or it can be picked up and worked out from the neckline.

If you decide to add a collar to a garment originally designed to have a ribbed border around the neck, you'll need to either knit the garment pieces with a higher neck to begin with, or add the border before you attach the collar. If you don't adjust for the missing border, the neck opening will be larger, and the collar must be shaped so that it will lie correctly (see Shaping Collars, page 242). Note that the back neck *must* be shaped for the collar to lie properly.

Collars in garments made from woven fabrics are stiffened using interfacing, so that they hold their shape. You could do the same to handknit collars; using fusible interfacing over the whole surface of the collar works very well to make it keep its shape. But the additional thickness may not be desirable, and the interfacing will show on the underside of the collar unless you cover it with a second layer of knitting or with a facing of woven fabric. If you prefer knitted or crocheted finishing on sweaters, as I do, then a reasonable alternative is to work the collar firmly in a noncurling pattern stitch, or to work it in two layers.

Knitted collars can be problematic because their edges and points must be perfect. Collars become the focal point of the sweater, framing the face, and any inconsistencies along the bottom or front edges are extremely noticeable. Take care to bind off at just the right tension so that the outer edge doesn't pull in or flare, especially at the corners. You can also reinforce the edge of the collar with applied I-cord or with a crocheted edging, which will help the collar to hold its shape as well as provide a smooth, perfectly finished edge. (For applied I-cord instructions, see appendix, page 274.)

## Picking Up Stitches for Collars

Picking up for a collar is very similar to picking up for a regular neck border except for a few very important factors. Because collars spread out from the neck opening, it's important to pick up enough stitches for the outer edge of the collar, assuming you are making a collar that's a straight, unshaped strip. Second, because the inside of the garment shows when the front folds back at the lapels, but the outside of the collar shows at the back of the neck if the collar rides up, it can be difficult to decide which is the "right" side to pick up on.

The weight of the sweater can be annoying to support while working the collar and can actually stretch the collar out of shape. Reduce that weight significantly by attaching the collar before you sew the sleeves into the sweater. You can also avoid this problem entirely by working the collar separately and then sewing it on.

## How to Pick Up for a Collar

First you'll need to decide which is the "right" side and which is the "wrong" side.

▷ If the collar will *never* fold open at the center front and show the inside of the garment, then the outside of the sweater is the "right" side for picking up a collar. In this case, hold the right side of the sweater facing you as you pick up for the collar.

▷ If the collar is shaped so that it lies flat all the way around, then the inside of the sweater is the "right" side for picking up a collar. In this case, hold the wrong side of the sweater facing you as you pick up for the collar.

▷ If, as is frequently the case, the inside of the garment will show at the front when it falls open and the outside will show at the back of the neck below

the collar, then the "right" side will change from inside to outside as you work around the neckline picking up stitches. There are two ways to deal with this. The first approach is to proceed across the front of the neck, working the usual "pick up and knit," but with the wrong side of the sweater facing you. When you reach the shoulder seam, switch to working "pick up and purl" across the back, and then return to "pick up and knit" for the second front (see appendix, page 277). The second approach, which can be used for all collars, is to make the edge reversible by enclosing it in a binding (see Starting Double, Ending Single, page 230), by using the Yarnover Pickup (page 230), or by working a collar that is two layers thick so that each layer covers one side of the pickup row (see photo, page 246, top left).

### Picking Up for Different Kinds of Collars

This collar was picked up with the right side of the garment facing the knitter for half of the neckline (*at left*) and with the wrong side of the garment facing for the other half of the neckline (*at right*). With the front folded back to form lapels, the wrong side of the pickup row is exposed at left, while the right side looks nice and neat at right.

At the back of the neck with the collar up, the difference is striking. The neat right-hand side is preferable to the left-hand side, where the wrong side of the pickup row is exposed.

With the front completely closed, the difference between the two sides of the front isn't noticeable because the collar covers up the pickup row. You can tell they are different, but one doesn't look any better or worse than the other.

A shaped collar, like this circular collar, lies flat against the outside of the sweater. Pick up with the wrong side facing you for a shaped collar like this one, because the wrong side of the pickup row will never show.

## How Many Stitches to Pick Up for a Collar

Because a collar flares out from the neck edge, as opposed to a border, which pulls in from the neck edge, you need to pick up more stitches than you would for a border. In my experience, it's best to pick up 1 stitch in every stitch along the horizontal cast-on or bound-off edges and 1 stitch in every row along diagonal or vertical edges. (For illustrations of how to pick up and knit stitches in each of these situations, see page 277.)

If the collar will be shaped to form a circle or square, proceed to shape it accordingly. If the collar will be a straight, unshaped strip, you have several options depending on the type of knitted fabric it's made of. If it's stretchy, no further shaping may be necessary, because it will stretch to fit around the neckline. Stretchy collars should be blocked to the correct shape so that they behave themselves when the sweater is worn. If the fabric is firm, you should increase on the first row to the number of stitches needed for the full width of the collar on its outer edge.

## Working the Collar Separately

Knitting the collar separately and then sewing it on gives you two advantages: you don't have to deal with supporting the weight of the entire sweater while you work, and you can knit the collar in any direction (from end to end, top to bottom, or bottom to top).

To make a collar starting from the top and working down (that is, from the neck edge and working out), follow the directions for the various collar shapes provided below, increasing to make the collar larger at the outer edge.

To make a collar in the opposite direction, from bottom to top, work the shapes, decreasing according to the guidelines for each shape, so that the upper edge is smaller than the lower edge. You can reduce the bulk where the collar is attached to the neck opening by sewing through the live stitches at the neck edge of the collar, rather than binding off and then sewing down.

To make a collar from end to end, it's best to chart the shape on knitter's graph paper, and then follow the chart to determine how to cast on, bind off, increase, or decrease to achieve the desired shape. You can also use short rows to make a collar flare or curve when worked from end to end.

## Pattern Stitches for Collars

The primary consideration for collars is that they should not curl, so avoid stockinette stitch, unless your collar will be two layers thick. To hold their shape, collars should be fairly firm, and ideally the edges should be very neat, so choose a pattern stitch that doesn't curl and that holds its shape well. Garter stitch, worked firmly, is an excellent choice. Seed Stitch, if worked firmly, is also an option. Ribbing will also work well, especially if blocked slightly to flatten the fabric. On the other hand K1, P1 ribbing, if left completely relaxed, can masquerade nicely as stockinette stitch. If you are working a wide collar that you want to drape nicely, then intentionally make the fabric looser and softer so that it will stretch and drape to behave properly.

## Corded and Crocheted Edges

Corded or crocheted edges will make the edges look neat and even, help the whole collar retain its shape, and help prevent the corners from curling, something that happens frequently, even if the rest of the collar is very well behaved.

**Cording along collar.** This garter stitch collar has cording along both ends and the outer edge. The 3-stitch cords at the ends are worked as described in Corded Edges (chapter 2, page 57). The cording along the outer edge is worked as an I-cord bind off (appendix, pages 259–60), starting with the 3 stitches from the cord already established at the edge of the knitting. To make the cord travel smoothly around the corner, 1 row of plain I-cord was worked on these 3 stitches before beginning to bind off. After all the collar stitches were bound off, the I-cord bind off was joined seamlessly to the cord at the other edge using Kitchener stitch.

## Shaping Collars

Collars can be simple rectangular strips that are calmly tailored or exuberantly ruffled, can be shaped into squares or circles, and can have pointed ends. I have provided directions for the simplest of the many possible collar variations. For more in-depth discussions of tailoring collars and lapels, see Deborah Newton's *Designing Knitwear* and Shirley Paden's *Knitwear Design Workshop*.

## Shaping a Straight Collar

As their name implies, straight collars do not actually need to be shaped in knitting. In sewn garments made from woven fabric, they have a very slight curve, so you can ease them neatly onto the neck edge of the garment; the slightly longer outer edge ensures that they lie neatly around the neck without hugging it too tightly. In knitting, which stretches, neither of these is strictly necessary, because you can block the collar to the correct shape. However, especially if you are working the collar firmly or in a non-wool fiber, it's nice to shape it so it's exactly right even before blocking.

Begin the collar by picking up stitches along the neck opening or casting on. If you want to shape the collar a bit, just increase a few stitches (3 or 4) evenly spaced across the row every few rows to create a slight curve. Continue until the collar is the size you want, then bind off, being careful to match the tension of your bind off to the fabric of the collar. The corded collar shown (opposite) was shaped by increasing just 4 stitches on every 8th row to make a very slight curve.

Shaping the points of a straight collar is your choice: leave them straight or make them pointier for emphasis. To create points, increase at both ends of the collar as you work it. The more often you increase, the more pointed the ends will be. (See photo below right.)

## Shaping a Round Collar

Round collars, as the name indicates, are shaped so that they form a circle. To do this, increase 8 stitches every other round in garter stitch while working out from the neck edge. In other pattern stitches, work a gauge swatch to determine the stitches and row gauge. Figure out how long the collar must be at the neck edge and how long the outer circumference will be. Plan to increase to the required number of stitches at the outer edge over the course of the collar. This is exactly the same procedure as for decreasing to shape a curve (see Case Study #8-1, page 226).

To make a circle, rather than a geometric shape with noticeable corners, stagger the increases on each succeeding increase row so that they never line up with prior increases. This can be difficult to accomplish in many pattern stitches, but you may be able to achieve a circle by gradually moving from smaller- to larger-size needles as you work the collar. Gathering the edge of the collar attached to the neck will also help. The stitches will be held close together at the neck edge, flaring out to help produce a curve. To do this, pick up more stitches at the neck than you normally would, or increase significantly on the first row of the collar.

**Shaped collar.** This round collar in garter stitch is designed to lie completely flat. It was shaped by working 8 staggered increases every other row. It also takes advantage of some of the properties of knitting — that you can control how wide the knitting is by changing needle sizes and that stockinette stitch curls. The first few rows of the collar were worked in stockinette stitch, working the knit rows when the outside of the garment was facing the knitter. The stockinette stitch naturally curls to the outside, forcing the fold-over of the collar at the neck edge to be neat and hold its shape. To ensure that the collar doesn't appear gathered where it meets the garment, the first row of the stockinette stitch section was worked on a needle two sizes smaller than the garter stitch section of the collar, the 2nd row on a needle one size larger than that, and finally on the 3rd row the switch was made to the needle size that would be used in the rest of the collar in garter stitch.

**Straight collar.** Note the difference in appearance between a shaped collar and a straight collar. When the garment is laid out flat, the back neck obviously sticks straight up. A shaped collar, in the same position, lies flat. The points of this collar were shaped every 4th row.

## Shaping a Square Collar

To make a square collar, pick up stitches around the neck opening, then mark four corner points. Work a double increase or a pair of symmetrical increases at each corner. Do this every other row (or round) in garter stitch. To determine the correct rate of increase in other pattern stitches, you'll need to work a gauge swatch. Use the stitch and row gauge to work out how many rows will be in your collar and the number of stitches at the outer edge, then make a plan for how to increase over the course of the collar to end with the correct number of stitches. Remember that you'll be increasing 2 stitches at each of the four corners, for a total of 8 stitches on every increase row/round. Notice that this is exactly the same procedure (in reverse) as for decreasing to make a border on a square neck (page 225).

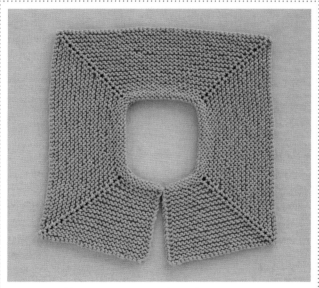

**Square collar in garter stitch**, with K-yo-K increases at each corner

## Shaping a Shawl Collar

Shawl collars are just wide strips of soft fabric that stretch to go comfortably around the neck. They may be set into a squared-off front neck opening, or be applied along the entire front edge of a V-necked cardigan. To add extra width to the collar at the back so it keeps the neck warm while folding over nicely, work short rows to build up that section. These may be worked immediately after picking up the stitches or immediately before binding off the outer edge, but working short rows at the beginning results in a smoother outer edge.

**Shawl collar applied to a squared-off V-neck.** This collar was worked straight, with no short-row shaping. As a result it is fairly low in the back where it folds over. (See schematic below, left.)

**Shawl collar on a cardigan front.** Short rows were worked in upper section (from the lapels up to the shoulder seams) immediately after picking up stitches. This ensures that the overlapping front edges will lie flat while the collar folds back. (See schematic below, right.)

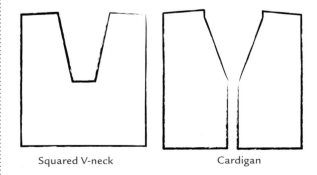

Squared V-neck            Cardigan

# Working Short Rows for a Shawl Collar

**TO FIGURE OUT HOW** to work short rows to make the back neck of the shawl collar wider, you need to know how many extra rows you want to add. In this example, we'll assume you want to make a cardigan with a shawl collar.

(1) Work a swatch in the pattern stitch you plan to use for your collar and measure it to determine the number of rows per inch.

(2) Decide how much higher you want the collar to be at the back neck than at the center front. Multiply this distance by the number of rows per inch to find the number of rows you will work. You'll need as many split markers as the number of rows.

(3) With the right side of the garment facing you, pick up stitches along the whole front and neck edge for your border.

(4) Place two markers a little below the diagonal shaping on both fronts. Place two markers at the shoulder seams. Make sure the number of stitches between both sets of markers is identical. Place the remaining markers spaced evenly between the ones on each front, half on either side.

(5) Work the first row until you pass the center back and come to the second shoulder marker. Take the marker off the needle, *wrap and turn, work in pattern until you reach the first marker; repeat from * until you've worked your way out to the markers below the lapels, and no markers remain on the needle. Each time you pass a wrapped stitch, pick it up and work it together with its base stitch in pattern. Be sure you know which is the right side of the collar: it's the side that's facing you when the wrong side of the garment is toward you. Make sure that the wraps fall to the wrong side of the collar when you pick them up.

*Note:* If you're making a shawl collar on a pullover, the first two markers should be placed at the bottom corners. After that, the short rows are worked exactly the same as for a cardigan.

See the appendix (pages 279–80) for complete instructions on working the wrap and turn and picking up the wraps.

## Facings for Collars

For a collar that holds its shape better, or if you really want a stockinette stitch collar and nothing else will do, you can add a facing, which is simply a second knitted layer, shaped identically to the first, that lies underneath the collar. There are two ways to accomplish this. You can work one layer, followed by the other layer, and then sew it down, or you can work both layers at the same time, then bind them off together at the outer edge. These two methods are identical to working doubled borders or bindings, except that the collar may be shaped while the doubled borders or bindings are rarely shaped.

## Working a Doubled Collar

With the right side facing you, pick up the stitches for the collar around the neck opening. On the first row, increase 1 stitch at both ends so that, when the ends are seamed together, the collar will still be long enough to fit the neck edge. Work the underside of the collar first, shaping it if desired; end with a right-side row. On the following wrong-side row, knit across. This makes a reverse stockinette ridge that ensures a neat fold at the outer edge of the collar. Work the upper side of the collar, exactly reversing the shaping of the first layer. When completed, sew the two ends of the collar together, then fasten down the live stitches along the line where the collar meets the edge of the garment, as you would for a hem (see top of next page and appendix, page 273).

## Binding to Make a Faced Collar

Pick up the stitches for the collar along both the inside and the outside of the neck edge just as you would for a binding. (See Creating a Binding to Enclose an Edge, page 235, for complete details on how to accomplish this.) Be sure to cast on 1 or Make 1 at the end of each needle so the collar won't pull in at the ends.

Doubled collar. The points on this collar were shaped by increasing while working the first layer, and by decreasing at the same rate while working the second layer. The collar was attached to the neckline by weaving the live stitches to the back side of the pickup row, hiding the uneven edge of the neckline for a very clean finish. The outer layer of this collar is 2 rows longer than the inner layer, so that it curves nicely over the under layer without puckering or appearing strained.

Work your collar as for a binding, keeping it on two circular needles, and working circularly first across the one layer and then across the other on each round. Work any shaping on both the upper and lower layers so that they match. If you work the lower layer on a needle one size smaller, it may pull in just the right amount to make the upper layer lie neatly on top of it when worn. You may also work one more row on the top layer before joining.

When the collar is completed, join the two layers using either three-needle bind off or Kitchener stitch (see appendix pages 261 and 276).

## Designing and Working Lapels

Lapels form when the center front edges are folded back to form a V below the round neck opening. Shaping a V-neck removes the lapels completely, so there is nothing to fold back. For a wider lapel, the front must be shaped at the center edge to make it wider in the lapel area.

Because the inside of the garment shows when the lapel is turned back, it's best to use a reversible pattern stitch, or to switch the right and wrong side of the pattern stitch within the V formed by the lapel area so that the right side shows when it is folded back. It's also perfectly acceptable to use a different pattern stitch for the lapels than for the body of the garment.

Notched lapels are formed when the collar doesn't reach all the way to the neck edge at each side.

A notched lapel, with the lapel area and collar worked in Seed Stitch. The collar was picked up with the inside of the garment facing the knitter, using "pick up and knit" on the fronts and "pick up and purl" across back neck.

So that the points don't curl, the lapel area was worked in Seed Stitch to match the collar.

# Practical and Decorative Pockets

Like many embellishments that are standard on woven garments, pockets can be problematic in handknits because of the tendency of the knitted fabric to stretch. Regardless of how you construct your pockets, anything heavy placed inside them will make a sweater stretch out of shape. Despite this problem, they are still helpful for warming hands and transporting mittens.

## Patch Pockets

Patch pockets are usually knitted separately and then sewn in place. This procedure is simple to understand, but can be difficult to execute neatly. To avoid the problem of sewing the pockets in place, you can pick up stitches for them instead and then knit the pocket onto the garment.

## Working Vertical Patch Pockets

Using working yarn and three double-pointed needles, pick up and knit stitches for the two sides and the bottom of the pocket. You can fold the fabric and do this holding the working yarn on the right side, or you can leave the fabric flat and hold the working yarn behind the fabric, using a crochet hook if necessary to pull the new stitches through to the front. Along the bottom, you'll need 1 stitch for each stitch in the width of the pocket. Along the two sides, you'll need 1 stitch for every 2 rows in the length of the pocket. When you finish picking up the required stitches, cut the yarn, leaving a tail to weave in later.

Begin working back and forth in stockinette across the bottom stitches of the pocket. Slip the first stitch of each row purlwise. When 1 stitch remains at the end of each row, work a decrease, joining the last stitch from the pocket and the next available stitch from the side of the pocket. On the knit rows work skp; on the purl rows, work P2tog.

## Making Mitered Patch Pockets

Using working yarn and three double-pointed needles, pick up and knit stitches for the two sides and the bottom of the pocket as described for the vertical patch pocket (above), except you'll need to pick up the same number of stitches along both sides of the pocket as for the bottom, and spread them out so that the physical measurements of the two sides are the same as the bottom. Assuming you'll be picking up 1 stitch in each stitch across the bottom edge, pick up for the sides at a ratio of about 5 stitches in every 7 rows of the base fabric. If this is difficult to keep track of, try 3 stitches to 4 rows instead.

Cast on stitches for the top of the pocket (the same number as you picked up for each side). You may need to cut the yarn before you cast on, depending on how you pick up the stitches and what cast on you use. Work in rounds, going down the side, across the bottom, up the other side of the picked-up stitches, and back across the cast-on edge. While you could work this pocket using Magic Loop or two circular needles (see appendix, pages 267–70), it is really easiest with a set of five double-pointed needles. The 90-degree angles at the corners are difficult to manage unless you change needles at each corner, and the double points allow you to do this.

Begin working circularly, working two symmetrical decreases at each corner. You could work a double decrease at each corner, but this is impractical because it requires shifting stitches between needles before working each decrease. It's easiest to simply work one decrease at the beginning of each double-pointed needle

**Working a Patch Pocket**

**Picking up stitches for a patch pocket,** folding the fabric, and holding the yarn on the right side. The position of the pocket was outlined in purled stitches to make picking up easier.

**Picking up stitches for a patch pocket** with the yarn on the wrong side

**Patch pocket** in progress

and a second at the end of each needle. To make a flat pocket, you will need to adjust the rate of decrease to match your pattern stitch. In garter stitch, work the decreases every other round. In stockinette, work them on about 5 out of 7 rounds. For other pattern stitches, you'll need to determine the rate of decrease, just as for a square-necked border (see page 225). If you'd like a pocket that pooches out a bit, then decrease more slowly. When 8 or 12 stitches remain, cut the yarn and pull it through these last stitches to secure them. If you work

the pocket in stockinette, the upper edge will have a tendency to curl out. Prevent this by working the top needle in ribbing or in garter stitch on the first few rounds.

A nice variation on the mitered pocket is one with a V opening at the top. To make this, pick up stitches as for the three sides, but do not cast on any stitches for the top of the pocket. Instead of working circularly, work flat, turning at the end of each row. Work a single decrease at the top edges and two decreases at each of the two bottom corners (photo, below right).

## Working a Mitered Pocket

① To start a mitered patch pocket, pick up an equal number of stitches for both sides and the bottom.

**The decreases on this mitered pocket** were worked 1 stitch away from the end of each needle, making the prominent cross that is its most obvious feature.

② Cast on stitches for the top of the pocket, knit across the other three sides, then begin working circularly.

**The decreases on this mitered-V pocket** were worked on the right-side rows with an ssk at the beginning of each needle and a K2tog at the end of each needle. This makes the mitered corners look a little blunt. For crisper corners, reverse the position of the two decreases, using K2tog at the beginning of each needle and ssk at the end.

# Afterthought Invisible Pockets

THESE POCKETS require no prior planning at all, which makes it possible to add them to a finished garment when you hadn't even considered making pockets. It also lets you try on the garment to determine the correct placement for the pockets before you commit yourself. Once you've decided where the pocket opening should be, cut just 1 stitch at the center of the opening. This may seem traumatic, but it's far easier than any other method.

① At the center of what will be the opening at the top of the pocket, snip 1 stitch. Then unravel as many stitches as needed for the top of the pocket, working out in both directions.

② With the right side of the fabric facing you, slip double-pointed needles or two circular needles into the exposed stitches across the top and bottom of the opening. There will be 1 fewer stitch across one edge.

③ If you're working on double-pointed needles, divide the stitches on one side of the opening between two needles.

④ Attach a matching ball of yarn and begin working circularly (shown here in contrasting yarn for clarity). On the first round, purl across the stitches on the front half of the opening to make a neat ridge for the fold at the top of the pocket.

⑤ Knit around until the pocket is the desired depth. Tuck the pocket to the inside of the garment. You may have to shift the needles back and forth to coax them through. This step is much easier if you're using two circular needles. Join the two layers together at the bottom using the three-needle bind off. The final stitch won't have a mate; just bind it off separately.

⑥ There will be gaps at the upper corners whenever you add afterthoughts. Use the tails where you unraveled and joined the working yarn to close up the holes when you weave in the ends.

## Forethought Invisible Pockets

Forethought pockets are made identically to afterthought pockets, with one important difference: you must know where you want the pocket while you're making your sweater. When you get to this point, cut your working yarn, leaving an 8-inch tail. Knit across using a piece of waste yarn, exactly where the opening will be for the pocket. Begin using the working yarn again, leaving another 8-inch tail. When you've completed the piece of the garment with the pocket, pick out the waste yarn, place the live stitches on needles, and proceed exactly as described for the afterthought pocket (page 249).

Forethought invisible pocket. When you use waste yarn to prepare for the opening, be sure to leave long tails (at least 8 inches) so the yarns won't work loose, and to close up any holes later on.

## Adding a Border at the Pocket Top

Pockets can be reinforced and supported by applying an I-cord or a border after the pocket is completed. Flat borders can be worked in any of the following ways:

▷ Horizontally from stitches picked up along the front edge of the pocket. When you pick up the stitches and when you bind off, leave tails long enough to sew down the ends after the border is completed.

▷ From end to end separately and then sewn on.

▷ From end to end and joined to the top of the pocket as you work (see Applied Edging, page 259). Leave long enough tails at the cast on and bind off to sew down the ends of the border. You can also add an I-cord to the edge this way (see appendix, page 274).

A border worked as a ribbing, ready to bind off

Garter stitch border attached as an edging across the top of an invisible pocket

# Knitted Embellishments

Ruffles, cords, and other edgings can be added after the individual garment pieces are completed, or after the pieces have been put together. It's easiest to work with the individual pieces, because they are lighter and smaller than the complete garment, but embellishments that cross seam lines must be attached after the seam has been completed. If you know ahead of time the exact location where the embellishment will be added, a series of stitches worked in reverse stockinette makes a clear anchor for attaching them.

How you pick up for the embellishment will affect how it lies against the fabric. Consistently picking up and knitting will make a ruffle, edging, or cord lie flat against the surface at its base, folding toward the knit side of the pickup row. Alternately knitting and purling as you pick up stitches will make the addition stand straight out from the fabric rather than flopping to one side.

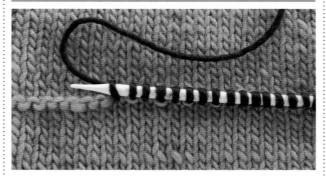

Alternately knitting and purling while picking up stitches along a reverse stockinette ridge

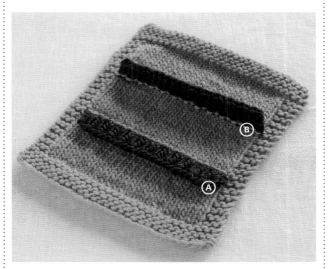

Picking up in knitting makes the addition lie flat against the surface Ⓐ. Alternately picking up in knitting and purling makes the addition stand up instead Ⓑ.

I-cord can be added in all the ways just described for flat edgings (page 252), but it can also be threaded through eyelets and other holes, like those at cable crossings, as well as knitted separately and sewn onto the fabric. (See appendix for I-cord, page 274; I-cord Bind Off, pages 259–60.)

## Choosing from a Variety of Ruffle Options

Add a ruffle by picking up stitches along a line of reverse stockinette stitches, then increasing substantially and working until the ruffle is as deep as you like. Or make a very long strip of knitting (at least two times the width of the area where you want to attach the ruffle), bind it off, and run a piece of yarn through it, in and out between every stitch along one edge. Gather the edge of the strip along this strand of yarn so it ruffles, then sew this edge onto the garment. (For a complete discussion of the various ways to make ruffles, see How to Create a Ruffled Edge, chapter 5, page 165.)

# When You Want to Add Edging

Applied edgings are worked perpendicular to the fabric they are attached to. They can be simple garter stitch, any other noncurling pattern, or lace. You can add edgings to the fabric in several ways.

▷ Pick up stitches and then knit the edging, joining it to the picked-up stitches as you create it.

▷ Knit the edging and pick up 1 stitch in the base fabric at the end of every right-side row to attach it.

▷ Complete the edging as a separate strip, then sew it on.

Edgings are sometimes too long for the edge of the fabric they are applied to. If this happens, try using a needle one or two sizes smaller to prevent the edging from flaring. Or work fewer rows of edging per stitch of the base fabric. To do this, when you reach the end of the row, knit the next 2 stitches of the base fabric together (if you're attaching to live stitches), or skip a row when picking up the next stitch (if you're attaching by picking up stitches). (For more photographs of edgings, see chapter 5, page 165; for more information on working applied edgings, see the appendix, page 259, and Knitting On, chapter 6, page 182.)

## Applied Lace Edgings Three Ways

Lace edging worked as a bind off

The same edging worked across the cast on, picking up 1 stitch at the end of each right-side row and working it together with the last stitch of the edging

A diagonal line of purled stitches was worked in the base fabric, stitches were picked up in the purled stitches, and the same lace edging as above was worked as a bind off.

# Blocking the Finished Garment

If you blocked the garment pieces before assembling them, then completely blocking the garment isn't usually necessary when it's finished. Do block the seams and other points like the corners of collars or front openings that could use a little shaping, and you'll be happier with the way your garment looks and behaves. You can pin these areas to the correct shape and then steam them, or mist them with cool water and leave them to dry.

On the other hand, if you didn't block the pieces or there are larger issues that blocking can address (for example, the two fronts aren't quite the same length), then blocking the complete garment is an excellent idea. My preference is to wash the garment as I would normally launder it. At the very least you should soak it in warm water so that the fibers absorb plenty of moisture. Squeeze it out, roll it in a towel to remove the excess moisture so it's not dripping wet, then lay it out flat to dry, shaping it to exactly the size you want. You may need to pin sections in place or use blocking wires to keep select areas under tension so they look their best. For complete details on blocking, see pages 194–99.

# Caring for Your Finished Handknits

For the most part, the best way to wash any handknit garment is to soak it in warm water with mild detergent, squeeze gently, and soak in clear water to rinse. Remove the excess moisture by rolling in a towel, then lay the garment out flat to dry, shaping as described in Blocking Knitted Pieces (chapter 7, page 194). Sweater-drying racks made of nylon net let air circulate so the garment will dry more quickly while laid out flat to prevent stretching. Many of these are stackable so you can wash several sweaters at a time and dry them in a small space.

▷ Garments made from superwash wool may do better when washed on gentle in the washing machine. Some superwash yarns can be dried (at least partially) in a dryer. Check the washing instructions on the yarn label for guidance.

▷ Washing may ruin garments made from multiple colors if any of the colors run. Test for this by washing the swatch before making the garment or by rubbing the yarn with a damp white paper towel to see whether any dye comes off. You may still be able to wash the garment if you use a product that contains a surfactant (to prevent dye that becomes suspended in the water from settling again on the surface of the fabric), such as laundry detergent, Shout Color Catcher sheets, Synthrapol, or Dharma Professional Textile Detergent.

▷ If the yarn requires dry cleaning, then it's best to follow the guidelines on the label.

# Storing Handknit Garments

Handknit garments should not be hung, unless you want them to stretch. Instead, fold them neatly and store away from sunlight. To avoid moth damage, wash them to ensure that they're clean before storing and make sure they are completely dry. If you have problems with moths, silverfish, or other insects that eat fiber, seal your garments up in plastic bags and check them frequently for problems. If you store your garments in plastic, it's vital that they be completely dry, stored out of sunlight, and in an area that doesn't experience extreme changes in temperature. This is necessary to ensure that condensation doesn't form on the inside of the bag, causing mildew and possibly felting wool or other animal fibers.

# The Elusive Pursuit of Perfection

I wish I could guarantee that, if you take all of the tips and advice in this book to heart and apply them to your project, you'll love the end results. Unfortunately, I can't in all honesty do that. The fact is, you won't see or try on the finished garment until it's, well, finished. Being alert, analyzing your progress, and assessing the fit as you work will help you find or prevent numerous problems, but there's still the possibility that even if everything is exactly what you intended, you won't be happy with the end result.

On the one hand, this will be frustrating. You should justly mourn your failed project (assuming it really is irredeemable).

On the other hand, think of all the things you learned from knitting it so intentionally — from casting on the first swatch to sewing in the last end, your attention to selecting the best structure, texture, color, embellishment, fit, and the best techniques to achieve the end product has elevated the craft of knitting to the level of art.

In the course of the project, you've probably been excited, happy, frustrated, challenged, analytical, and creative. You've entertained yourself (and perhaps others) in the pursuit of the perfect garment and this pastime has come at a very low cost — just the price of the yarn and the pattern, especially when compared to the expense of a dinner out, a movie, or going to the theater, a concert, or a sporting event, which are much more fleeting amusements. If worst comes to worst and you decide to cut your losses, unravel the whole thing, and start over, or to make something else entirely, think of it as getting more entertainment for your yarn dollar. There's no reason why you shouldn't enjoy the whole process once again.

What to do? First, try to figure out what, exactly, is wrong. Put the sweater on yourself or on the person it was intended for and assess the problem with brutal honesty. Is it ugly all over? Does it hang wrong? Is the fit too tight or too loose in places? Are the seams the focus because they're too tight? Are the borders messy? Does one section look noticeably different (messy, tighter, looser, lighter) than the others?

## When Aesthetics Are the Problem

If the sweater fits and all the finishing looks good, but you don't like the way it looks, you do have some practical options for improvement.

**Managing mistakes.** If there are mistakes in the pattern stitch or dropped stitches, see Fixing Mistakes (chapter 6, page 174) for approaches to correcting them. Mistakes of this sort can also be hidden or camouflaged by adding a patch pocket, some embroidery, or an embellishment like a bead or a braid on top of the offending spot. Of course, you'll also need to add similar embellishments in other places to make it look intentional.

**Coping with color.** If the color of the yarn (or the combination of colors in a variegated yarn) gives you visual indigestion, then consider dyeing the garment to tone things down. There was a time when I would have been terrified of the very idea of dyeing my garments, but dyes for both animal and plant fibers are now widely available. Make sure you choose dye that's appropriate for the type of fiber and that you get enough to dye the weight of the yarn. Keep color theory in mind — yellow and blue mix to make green, red and blue to make purple, and yellow and red to make orange — and this applies when you add dye to the color that's already on the yarn.

Test your dye on a little of the leftover yarn in all the colors or on your swatch before you commit to dyeing the whole sweater. Note that you don't have to saturate the color — subtle overdyeing can change its appearance significantly and if you decide you want more color, you can always dye it again. Remember that you can make it darker, but not lighter. Follow the directions that come with the dye carefully and treat your garment carefully so that it doesn't shrink or felt. Acid dyes used on animal fibers can usually be applied while cold and then heat-set, making it less likely that shrinkage or felting will occur.

▷ *Go monochrome.* If you're dealing with a multicolor yarn that came out looking garish, consider choosing one of the colors in that yarn and overdyeing the whole thing with that one color. Depending on how much dye you add, the results will vary. Light overdyeing will result in a garment where there are still noticeable differences in the colors but they are all related, so they look good together. With more dye, the result will be a darker monochromatic garment with varying shades of the same color.

▷ *Tone it down.* Dye the garment with a very dilute solution of the complementary color of your yarn. The complementary colors of the primaries red, yellow, and blue, are green, purple, and orange, respectively. So if your garment is red or pink, use a little green dye; if your garment is yellow, use a little purple; and if your garment is blue, use a little orange. This will tone down the intensity of the original color, making it a slightly deeper shade that is less brash. Overdyeing with a stronger solution of the complement will result in a rich neutral color, ranging from gold to brown depending on what color you started with. If you saturate your yarn with the complementary color, you will probably end up with a dark brownish color. Because it can be difficult to predict the results, always test the dye on some unused yarn or your swatch before dyeing the garment. Remember that you can always add dye to make it darker, but you can't remove the dye if you apply too much.

**Variations in the yarn.** If one section of the garment looks different from the others, try to figure out why. Is the color slightly different (perhaps a ball of yarn from a different dye lot)? Is it a bit looser or tighter (perhaps you used different needles or were more relaxed while knitting)? Did you perhaps work the pattern stitch differently in this section?

▷ If a slight variation in color is noticeable only where the color changes, this might have been caused by a different dye lot, by dirt or a coating on that section of the yarn so that it didn't absorb the dye consistently, or a variation in the temperature when the dye was heat-set. You can sometimes camouflage

Perfection is an abstract and unattainable ideal.
Instead, set your own standard for excellence, pursue it,
and find satisfaction in its achievement.

Borders, Bindings, and Embellishments

this with a sprinkling of duplicate stitches on either side of the transition. See Variations in Dye Lot, Color, and Yarn Quality (chapter 6, page 177).

▷ If there is just a spot of color on an otherwise impeccable garment, or a tiny area where the texture is different, you should be able to hide these using duplicate stitch (appendix, page 272).

▷ If most or all of a garment piece is obviously a different color or the yarn is a different texture, the only way to fix it will be to remove any borders and embellishments from that piece, pick out the seams that attach it to the rest of the garment, and make it over with yarn that really matches. Sometimes, once you reject the problem yarn, you won't have enough left to complete the garment. In that case, use the yarn that's different for borders and embellishments, and cannibalize yarn from the original borders and embellishments to work the replacement.

▷ If you worked the pattern stitch differently in one section of the garment than in another, unfortunately, the only way to fix it is to take it apart and do it over.

## When You Don't Like the Fit

A fact of life with knitting is that you can't really tell about the drape and fit of a garment until it's all put together. This is because the weight of the fabric will cause it to stretch some, while the seams support it, preventing other stretching. A garment knit just a tad more tightly will stretch less, a little more loosely will stretch more. Seams sewn firmly will support the fabric more than stretchy seams. You won't know how the fabric and finishing will interact until it's all completed and you actually get to try it on. Sometimes you won't know the worst until after it's been washed a few times, giving it the chance to either grow or shrink.

### Neck Border Adjustments

If you've very carefully checked before and during knitting to ensure that the garment will fit correctly in the shoulder and neck area, but it's too small or too large there when you put it on, it may be the finishing that's causing the problem.

**Too loose.** The most frequent problem I find in sweaters that fit poorly is that the neck border is too loose. When the neck's too loose, it stretches from side to side under the weight of the sleeves so that the shoulder seams fall too far out, with the result that the

armhole is distorted and the sleeves hang too low, so they appear to be too long. It's easy to verify whether this is the problem. Pinch the neck border in several places and fasten those folds with safety pins until the neck is small enough to bring the shoulder area into proper alignment. If you can do this, then you can fix the problem by removing the neck border and making it smaller. First, count the number of stitches that are consumed in the safety-pinned areas. Deduct this number from the total stitches in the border to find the number of stitches you should have used. Unravel the border, pick up the reduced number of stitches, and work it again.

If the neck border is just a tiny bit too loose, you may be able to fix it by removing the bind off and then binding off again more tightly or by crocheting around the edge.

**Too tight.** If the neck border is too tight (which doesn't happen very often, in my experience), it may be that the bind off or cast on is too tight. Unravel the edge and replace it more loosely. If more extreme measures are required, decide how many stitches the neck border really needs, remove it, and work it again. To enlarge the neck opening further, you can also make the new border narrower with fewer rows than the original one.

### Body and Sleeve Length Adjustments

If you realize you'd really prefer the sleeves or body to be longer or shorter, take the bottom border off and make the adjustment as described in Changing the Length (chapter 6, page 177). If there are seams, you'll need to remove them just far enough to be able to work with the section of the garment under revision, and then replace them.

### Body and Sleeve Width Adjustments

Just like length, you can make changes to the width of garment pieces; see Changing the Width (chapter 6, page 180) for guidance. You'll need to remove any seams in the area where the adjustment will take place, but you don't need to take the whole sweater apart.

Before doing anything drastic in the way of cutting to make a garment smaller, spend some time thinking about whether you're likely to be happy with the results. Baste the sides together with sewing thread along the proposed seam lines and wear the garment to see if you like the fit, remembering that the extra bulk along the seam allowance will be removed. You may find that you're happy with the results. If so, just go on wearing the sweater after you've basted it — no need to cut anything!

## When You're Not Satisfied with the Finishing

If you like everything else about a garment except the finishing, it is always worth doing just that over again. Puckered or messy seams, too-stretchy shoulders, and too-tight bind offs and cast ons can all be fixed. Borders that aren't quite right can be revised, even those that were worked immediately upon casting on.

**Seams** that look messy or are too tight must be picked out and done over to see any improvement. Seams that are too loose can sometimes be saved. You can take several approaches. If the one you choose doesn't work or makes the seam too bulky, take it out, do it over looser or tighter, or try one of the other suggestions:

▷ Crochet firmly along the inside of the seam allowance to reduce the stretching.

▷ Work an applied I-cord along the inside of the seam, or along the outside as a decorative element. (For applied I-cord instructions, see appendix, page 274.)

▷ Pick up and knit stitches along the seam allowance, then immediately bind off firmly.

**Bind offs** that are too tight are easy to fix. Just pull out the tail that secures the final stitch, unravel the bind off and place the stitches back on the needle, then work the bind off more loosely (see Taking Out the Bind Off, page 180). You may want to use the suspended bind off (appendix, page 261), one of the decrease bind offs (appendix, page 259), a larger needle, or consider changing to a bind off with more inherent stretch (see When You Need a Stretchy Bind Off, chapter 5, page 164).

**Cast ons.** Fixing cast ons that are too tight or that look loose and messy is a bit more challenging. Starting with the tail attached to the cast on, pick it out stitch by stitch, placing the resulting loops on a needle. This can be a lengthy process across a long cast on, and the growing tail of unraveled yarn will make it take longer. Cut the tail off whenever it becomes too long to work with easily. If you are a brave soul, instead of picking the cast on out one stitch at a time, snip the bottom strand of yarn every few stitches across the edge and then pluck out the short pieces of yarn. Use a fresh piece of yarn and the sewn bind off (appendix, page 260) to finish the edge with exactly the right amount of stretch, or use new working yarn to work any loose, stretchy bind off.

**Borders** that are too tight, too loose, or look bad should be removed and worked again, but before you take them out, analyze the problem, as described above for Neck Borders and Adjustments, page 256. If a border around a curve flares, it's probably most pronounced in the section that's most curved, such as the underarm of an armhole border or the back neck of a V-necked border. Can you make a pinch or two in the border at this point to make it hug the body? If so, count the number of stitches in the pinches so you know how much to reduce. Rather than taking out the whole border, you may be able to take out just the bind off and the final row or round of the border. Work that last row or round again, decreasing to get rid of those troublesome flared sections, then bind off.

Bottom borders that are too large or too small can be removed and reworked. See Changing the Length (chapter 6, page 177) for instructions on removing a section of the fabric. Remember to plan what you'll change before you begin your revisions, so that you can refer to the original for stitch counts and row counts. When you rework the border, make it the right size.

## When It Can't Be Saved

Some problems can be fixed, but sadly, some cannot. If not, then the yarn can always be unraveled and used over, or you may discover a friend who adores the sweater — and you can generously bestow it upon him or her.

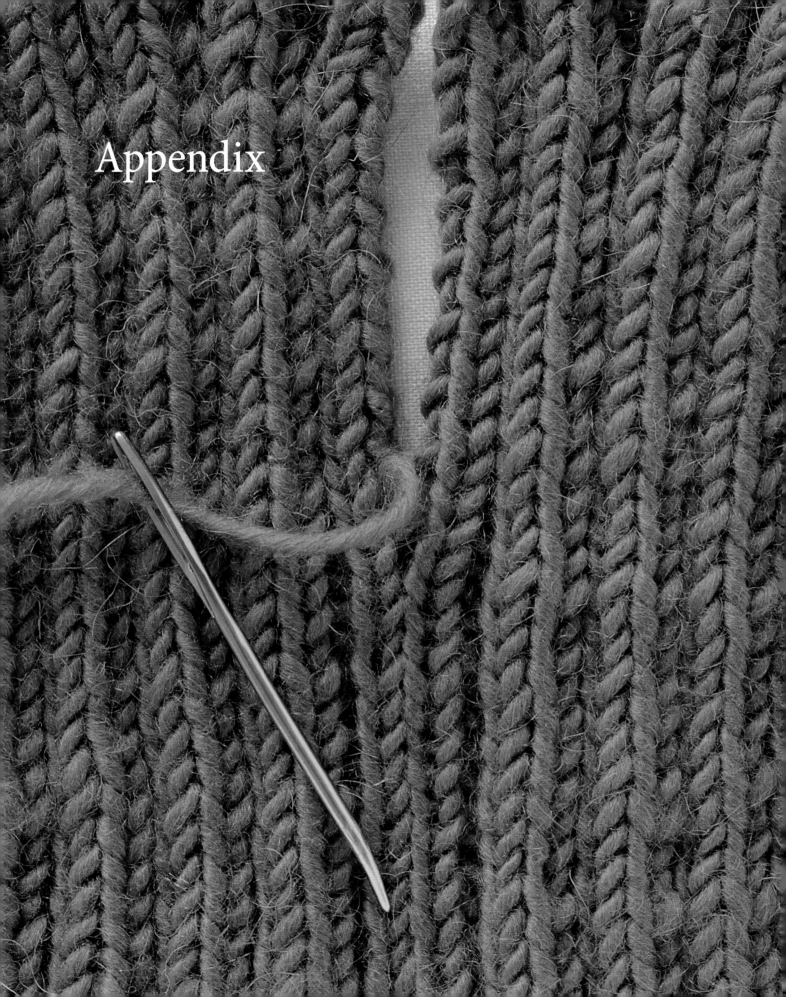

Appendix

# Glossary of Techniques & Terms

## Applied Edging

An applied edging is a separate strip of knitting (decorative or plain) that is added at a right angle to the base fabric. Applied edgings may be attached to live stitches either as a bind off or to stitches picked up for that purpose. Edgings may be applied to live stitches as described below (essentially the same procedure as Knitting On, Method 2 in chapter 6, page 182) or they may be joined to the edge of the fabric using Knitting On, Method 1.

To work an edging by attaching it to live stitches as you go, follow these basic guidelines:

**Step 1.** Cast on the additional stitches required for the edging. If there is a decorative pattern, you may need to cast on 1 additional stitch for joining. If the first row of the edging is a right-side row, cast the stitches onto the beginning of the needle that holds the live stitches to which you'll be joining it. If the first row is a wrong-side row, place the cast-on stitches on an empty needle and work the first wrong-side row.

**Step 2.** Work across the edging stitches on the right side until 1 stitch remains. Decrease to join this stitch to the first stitch of the base fabric. Working an skp decrease will usually look best.

**Step 3.** Turn and work back across the wrong side of the edging stitches in pattern. The join may look neater if you slip the first stitch on wrong-side rows.

Repeat steps 2 and 3 until all the stitches of the base fabric have been decreased away. Bind off the edging.

## Backstitch

A series of small stitches made by inserting the needle at the midpoint of each preceding stitch so that the stitches overlap. The overlapping stitches allow the sewing to be stretched without breaking the thread.

## Biasing

The tendency of flat knitted fabric to skew on the diagonal, or for a tube knit circularly to spiral instead of hanging straight. This is caused by some pattern stitches or yarn that is not "balanced," meaning that the plies have not been twisted the proper amount to equalize the yarn so that it is inert. Yarn that is not balanced also tends to twist back on itself when not under tension.

## Bind Offs

### Basic Bind Off (BO)

K1, *K1, insert the left needle into the first stitch worked, pass it over the other stitch and off the needle; repeat from *. When 1 stitch remains, cut the yarn and pull it through the last stitch to prevent it from unraveling. To prevent the last bound-off stitch from protruding past the edge of the fabric, stop when 2 stitches remain, slip last stitch to the working needle knitwise, cut the yarn, and pull it through the last 2 stitches.

**In pattern.** Continue to work the pattern already in progress while binding off. For example, if working K1, P1 ribbing, knit the knit stitches and purl the purl stitches while binding off.

**In purl.** Instead of knitting while binding off, purl all of the stitches.

### Decrease Bind Offs

A method of binding off that employs decreases rather than passing stitches over, helping to ensure that the bind off is loose and stretchy. For the proper way to pass stitches back to the left needle, see Pass (page 277).

**Ssk version.** K1, *slip 1 knitwise. Insert the left needle into the 2 stitches on the right needle. Knit these 2 stitches together; repeat from * until all the stitches have been bound off. Cut yarn and pull through last stitch. This produces a bind off identical to the basic bind off.

**Purl version.** *P2tog (A), pass the stitch back to the left needle (B); repeat from * until all stitches have been bound off. Cut the yarn and pull it through the last stitch. The result is the same as binding off "in purl."

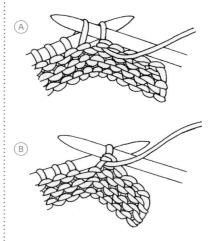

**Russian bind off.** *K2tog-tbl, pass the stitch back to the left needle; repeat from * until all stitches have been bound off. Cut the yarn and pull through the last stitch. The result is the same as the basic bind off, except that if your stitches are on the needle in the standard orientation, the row of stitches immediately below the bind off will be twisted. An excellent choice, however, for those whose stitches are on the needle in the nonstandard orientation, because it will untwist them as they bind off.

### I-cord Bind Off

This bind off can be worked with either the right or the wrong side of the fabric facing you. When working the cord in a contrasting yarn, the tops of the original stitches may peek through the cord. This problem appears on the side facing you while you bind off, so to hide it, work the bind off with the wrong side facing you. If you want both the right and wrong sides to look perfect, work 1 row in the contrasting yarn before beginning the I-cord.

**Setup.** At the beginning of the row, cast on 3 to 6 stitches for the cord.

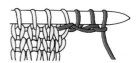

**Step 1.** Knit until 1 stitch remains of the cord, slip 1 knitwise, K1, pass slipped stitch over (this works the last stitch of the cord together with the first stitch to be bound off).

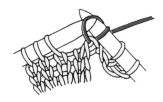

**Step 2.** Pass all the stitches back to the left needle. Do not turn.

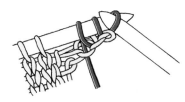

Repeat steps 1 and 2 until all stitches across the row have been decreased and only the cord stitches remain. Cut yarn and pull the end through all stitches.

I-cord bind off is usually most successful with 3 or 4 stitches for the I-cord. If you find working skp cumbersome, you may substitute ssk or K2tog-tbl. I prefer skp because it makes the stitch look slightly taller and maintains the orientation of the stitch parallel to the cord; ssk will result in a slightly shorter stitch, angled away from the cord a bit. The difference may be imperceptible to you, so choose whichever you like best. K2tog-tbl twists the decreased stitches, but that usually will not be noticeable in dark or textured yarns.

## 1-over-2 Bind Off

K3, *pass the first of the stitches just knit over the other 2, K1; repeat from * until only 2 stitches remain. Cut yarn and pull it through the last 2 stitches.

## Picot Bind Off

The picot bind off creates small decorative points along the edge of the fabric. You accomplish this by casting on a few extra stitches, binding them off, and then continuing to bind off a few of the original stitches, making a smooth transition between the added picot stitches and the original stitches at the edge of the fabric. You can easily make larger points by casting on more stitches in step 2, but remember that you'll also need to bind off more stitches to compensate. You can also change the distance between picots by binding off more or fewer stitches in step 3.

**Setup.** Bind off 1 or 2 stitches.

**Step 1.** Pass the stitch on the right needle back to the left needle.

**Step 2.** Cast on 2 stitches using the knitted cast on (page 265).

**Step 3.** Bind off 4 or 5 stitches (beginning with the 2 you just cast on and continuing across the original stitches).

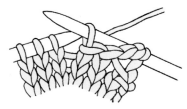

Repeat these three steps until all stitches have been bound off. Cut yarn and pull it through the last stitch. At the end of the row/round, you may need to adjust the number of stitches between picots to make the spacing look even; do this by working K2tog occasionally as you bind off. If you are placing the picots more than 2 or 3 stitches apart, plan the spacing

before beginning your bind off; divide the number of stitches on the needle by the stitches between picots to see how many extra stitches there will be. Split these evenly between the beginning and end of the bind off if working flat, or work K2tog periodically while binding off to reduce the number of stitches if working in the round.

## Sewn Bind Off

**Setup.** Cut the yarn about three times as long as edge to be bound off. Thread it through a yarn needle; you will use it to sew through the stitches. Hold the knitting in your left hand and sew with your right.

**Step 1.** Insert the yarn needle through 2 stitches as if to P2tog and pull the yarn through.

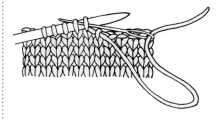

**Step 2.** Insert the yarn needle through the first stitch again knitwise. Pull the yarn through, and slip that stitch off the knitting needle.

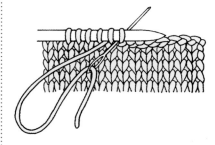

Repeat steps 1 and 2 until you have only 1 stitch left on the needle. Work once more from left to right through this last stitch.

Either side of this bind off could be the "right" side; you'll need to decide which you prefer. If you are left-handed, just reverse the directions in order to sew with your left hand: in step 1, you'll work through 2 stitches from left to right, and in step 2 you'll work through 1 stitch from right to left.

## Suspended Bind Off

This bind off is identical to the basic bind off, but the stitch passed over is suspended on the left needle until the following stitch is worked, preventing it from being tightened by accident.

K1, *K1, insert the left needle into the first stitch worked. Lift this stitch up and pass it over the stitch on the left, but leave it on the tip of the left needle. Keep it there while you work the following stitch. When this stitch slips off the needle, the suspended stitch will also slip off. Repeat from * until all stitches have been bound off.

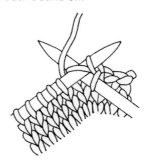

When binding off in pattern, the yarn must be moved to the correct position for the next stitch (in front to purl and in back to knit) *before* lifting the stitch up to pass it over.

## Three-Needle Bind Off

A method of joining the tops of two pieces of knitting while binding off. Hold the two pieces to be joined with either right sides or wrong sides together. The seam formed by binding off will appear on whatever side is facing out while you are binding off. The two needles should be parallel to each other, pointing in the same direction, with the working yarn hanging from one point.

**Step 1.** Using a third needle, knit together 1 stitch from the front needle and 1 from the back needle.

**Step 2.** Repeat for the next stitch on both needles.

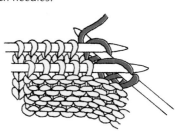

**Step 3.** Pass the first stitch worked over the second to bind it off.

Repeat steps 2 and 3 until all stitches are bound off. Cut the yarn and pull it through the last stitch.

## Tubular Bind Off

**Setup.** Cut the yarn, leaving a tail about three times the length of the edge to be bound off, plus about 6 inches, and thread it through a yarn needle. If this is too long to work with comfortably, start with a shorter length and begin a new piece of yarn when it runs out. If you've been working in K1, P1 ribbing, start with a knit stitch. If the first stitch on your needle is a purl, begin working the tubular bind off with steps 3 and 4.

**Step 1.** Insert the tip of the yarn needle knitwise into the first stitch and slip it off the needle.

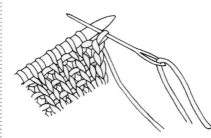

**Step 2.** Insert the yarn needle purlwise into the third stitch and pull the yarn through.

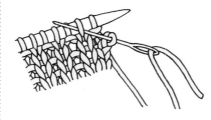

**Step 3.** Insert the yarn needle purlwise into the new first stitch and slip it off the needle.

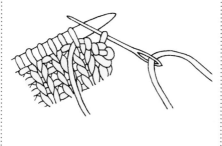

**Step 4.** Bring the yarn needle to the back of the knitting, insert it knitwise into the new second stitch, and pull the yarn through. You've bound off 2 stitches and have worked into the first 2 stitches that remain.

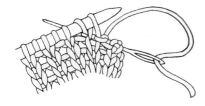

Repeat steps 1 through 4 until all stitches have been bound off. As you become familiar with the process, you'll be able to merge these steps into two smooth movements, working steps 1 and 2 together and steps 3 and 4 together.

You can also achieve the same results by slipping the stitches alternately onto two needles, so stitch #1 is on the front needle, stitch #2 on the back, and so on. If you have been working in K1, P1 ribbing, the knit stitches should be on the front needle and the purl stitches on the back. Work Kitchener stitch (page 276) to join the stitches on the two needles. You may work a few rows of tubular knitting before beginning the bind off. (See Tubular Knitting (page 281) Note that this bind off is *not* a good choice for textured, bumpy, or fragile yarn, any of which will make it difficult or impossible to execute.

## Yarnover Bind Off

Adding yarnovers between stitches as you bind off makes the edge twice as long as it would be otherwise, so there's plenty of room for it to stretch. If the edge is too stretchy, adjust the amount of stretch by working the yarnovers after every second or third stitch.

**Setup.** K1.

**Step 1.** Yo.

**Step 2.** Pass the knit stitch over the yo.

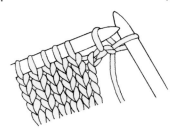

**Step 3.** K1.

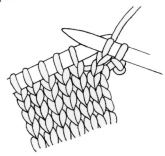

**Step 4.** Pass the yo over the knit stitch.

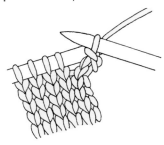

Repeat steps 1 through 4 until all stitches are bound off.

## Buttonhole Stitch

Also called blanket stitch, this is used around buttonholes to firm them up or provide a decorative edge.

Use a yarn needle to sew around the exposed edge of the knitting, catching the loop formed by the working yarn behind the needle with each stitch as shown.

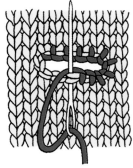

## Buttonholes

For photographs of the finished buttonholes, see chapter 8, page 232.

### Afterthought Buttonhole

This versatile buttonhole allows you to determine where the buttonholes will be placed *after* the knitting is completed, adapt it to any number of stitches, and adjust how stretchy it is by adjusting the tension of the bind off.

**Step 1.** Snip 1 stitch at the center of the spot where you want to add a buttonhole. Unravel just a stitch or 2 to each side. (Usually 3 or 4 stitches make a reasonable width, but how many you unravel will depend on the size of your button.)

**Step 2.** With a new strand of yarn, use the sewn bind off (page 260) to bind off the bottom, going 1 stitch beyond the opening.

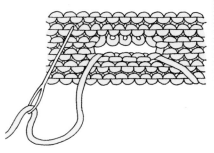

**Step 3.** Turn upside down and bind off the top the same way, joining to the beginning of your bind off.

Weave in all the ends on the back. (For more on "afterthoughts," see Elizabeth Zimmermann's *Knitting Without Tears*.)

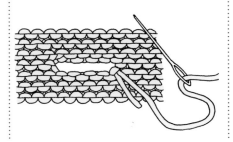

## Buttonhole for K1, P1 Ribbing

This buttonhole is worked over just 1 stitch and is most attractive when placed in a knit stitch when working row 1. The instructions below are for a series of these buttonholes in a K1, P1 ribbing.

**Row 1 (wrong side):** Work across in ribbing, but knit into the front and back of each stitch where you want a buttonhole.

**Row 2 (right side):** Work across in pattern until 1 stitch remains before each increased stitch, ssk Ⓐ, yo twice, K2tog Ⓑ.

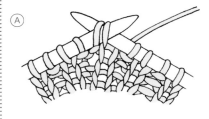

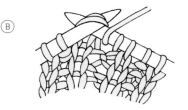

**Row 3 (wrong side):** Work across in pattern. When 1 stitch remains before each double yo, P2tog (working the stitch together with the first yarnover from the previous row) Ⓐ, yo, ssp (working the remaining yarnover together with the following stitch) Ⓑ.

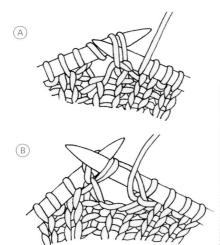

Ⓐ

Ⓑ

**Row 4 (right side):** Work across in pattern, purling into each buttonhole under both strands of yarn.

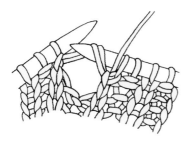

## Buttonhole for K2, P2 Ribbing

This buttonhole is worked over 2 stitches and is most attractive when placed in a 2-stitch purled rib when working row 1. The instructions below are for a series of these buttonholes in a K2, P2 ribbing.

**Row 1 (right side):** Work in pattern until 1 knit stitch remains before the 2 purl stitches where each buttonhole will be placed, ssk, yo twice, K2tog.

**Row 2 (wrong side):** Work in pattern until 1 stitch remains before each double yo, P2tog (working the stitch together with the first yarnover from the previous row), yo twice, ssp (working the remaining yarnover together with the following stitch).

**Row 3 (right side):** Work across in pattern, working K1, P1 into each double yo, working under both strands.

To make a smaller buttonhole, skip row 2 and work row 3 on the wrong side instead.

## Eyelet Buttonhole

Make a yarnover where you want the buttonhole, then knit or purl the next 2 stitches together. You may find it looks better in your pattern stitch to reverse the two, decreasing first and then working the yarnover. When you come to these eyelets on the following row, revert to the original pattern as established.

## One-Row Buttonhole

This makes a tight buttonhole with no stretch. Note that "yarn forward" and "yarn back" mean that you move the yarn between the two needle points, either to the front or to the back. These are not yarnovers; they do not add any stitches. Slip all stitches purlwise. The instruction to "bind off 1" means to pass the second stitch on the right needle over the first one. No additional stitches are knit in order to bind off. This buttonhole looks best when worked on a wrong-side row.

**Setup.** Work across to the point where you want the buttonhole.

**Step 1.** Yarn forward, slip 1, yarn back, slip 1, bind off 1, yarn forward, slip 1, yarn back, bind off 1, slip 1, bind off 1. Pass the last stitch back to the left needle.

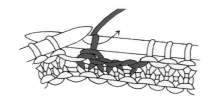

**Step 2.** Cast on 4 stitches using the cable cast on (page 264). Slip the last stitch cast on to the right needle.

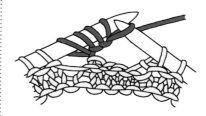

**Step 3.** Bind off 1. Yarn forward, slip 1, yarn back, slip 1, yarn forward, slip 1, yarn back. The buttonhole is complete. Continue across the row.

These instructions are for a 3-stitch buttonhole, but you can bind off any number of stitches to make whatever size buttonhole you work. An odd number will work best. When you cast on in step 2, add 1 more stitch than you bound off in step 1.

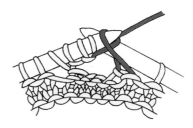

## Three-Row Buttonhole

This makes a looser buttonhole that can be done on any number of stitches. It looks best when row 1 is worked on the wrong side.

**Setup.** Work to the point where you want the buttonhole.

**Row 1.** Bind off the desired number of stitches for the buttonhole. Continue across the row.

**Row 2.** When you come to the gap created by the bound-off stitches on the previous row, cast on the same number using the half-hitch cast on (page 265). Continue to the end of the row.

**Row 3.** Knit into the cast-on stitches so that they twist. Depending on how you twisted the stitches when you cast on, you may need to work into the front or the back to twist them now.

See page 162 for tightening any looseness.

## Cable Cast On

**Setup.** Cast on 2 stitches using the knitted cast on opposite.

*Insert the right needle between the 2 stitches Ⓐ; knit up a stitch, leaving the 2 original stitches on the left needle Ⓑ; insert the left needle up into the new stitch from the front and slip it off the right needle; repeat from *, knitting each new stitch between the last 2 stitches cast on.

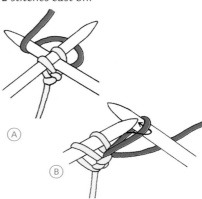

## Alternating-Color Cable Cast On

This is a variation on the cable cast on (see above).

**Setup.** Using two colors of yarn held together, make a slip knot and put it on the needle. These are your first 2 stitches.

*Using the yarn that matches the 2nd stitch from the end of the needle Ⓐ, knit up a stitch in this color between the last 2 stitches Ⓑ and slip it onto the left needle. Twist the two yarns to change colors. Repeat from * until there are enough stitches. Be careful to always twist in the same direction when changing colors.

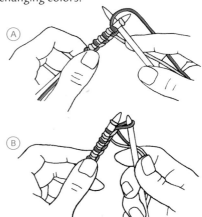

## Channel Islands Cast On

The small picots of this cast on make a very nice edge for K1, P1 ribbing, garter stitch, or stockinette, and the additional strand of yarn used to cast on creates a more substantial, durable edge. You will need two balls of yarn.

**Setup.** Holding both yarn strands together, pull out lengths of yarn measuring about 1 inch for each stitch you are casting on (for example, you need about 10 inches to cast on 10 stitches). The length of the tails recommended is for worsted-weight yarn. If you are using thinner yarn, you'll need less; with bulkier yarn, you'll need more. Make a single slip knot with both yarns at this point and place it on your needle. Cut off one of the strands that is attached to a ball.

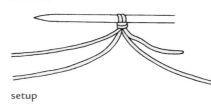

**setup**

**Step 1.** Hold the needle in your right hand with your index finger on the slip knot. Wrap the double strand counterclockwise twice around your left thumb and hold the single strand over your left index finger. Maintain tension on the strands in your left hand by holding them against your palm with the rest of your fingers.

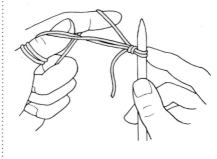

**Step 2.** Put one wrap of the single strand around the needle by taking the needle point over the strand and behind it (making a yarnover). Insert the needle up through all the wraps on your thumb and over the strand on the index finger once again.

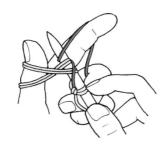

**Step 3.** Pull a new stitch out through the thumb loops using the tip of the knitting needle and let the wraps slip off your thumb. Tighten the thumb strands.

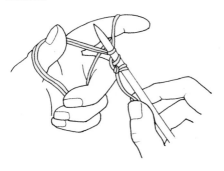

**Step 4.** Replace both the double and single strands on your left hand, wrapping the double strand twice counterclockwise around your left thumb as in step 1.

Repeat steps 2 through 4. Each repeat will cast on 2 stitches. If you need an even number of stitches, adjust for this on the first row by knitting the two strands of the slip knot individually. If you need an odd number of stitches, knit the double strand of the slip knot as if it were 1 stitch.

## Half-Hitch Cast On

This is only one of many ways to work this cast on, which is just a series of half hitches placed on the needle: Hold a needle and the cut end of the yarn against your left palm. *Bring your thumb to the front under the yarn Ⓐ, slip the needle up into the loop on your thumb Ⓑ, slip your thumb out. Repeat from * until the stitches you need have been cast on Ⓒ.

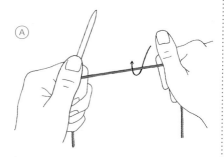

Ⓐ

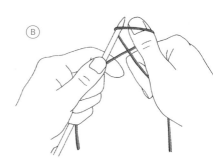

Ⓑ

Ⓒ

## Knitted Cast On

Leaving a short tail, make a slip knot and place it on your left needle. *Knit a stitch, leaving the original stitch on the needle Ⓐ, insert the left needle into the new stitch from the front Ⓑ, tighten up the stitch Ⓒ. Repeat from * until the stitches you need have been cast on.

Ⓐ

Ⓑ

Ⓒ

## Lace Cast On

This is an open and decorative cast on, but also very stretchy.

**Setup.** Place a slip knot on the left needle. Hold it in place with your index finger.

**Step 1.** Bring the yarn forward over the left needle.

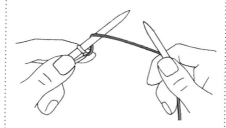

**Step 2.** Insert the right needle between the slip knot and the yarnover.

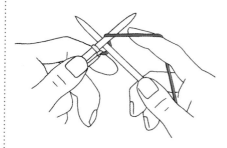

**Step 3.** Wrap the yarn around the right needle and knit a stitch.

**Step 4.** Slip the new stitch onto the left needle knitwise.

Repeat steps 1 through 4 until the desired number of stitches has been cast on. These instructions result in an odd number of stitches. If you need an even number, begin by knitting a stitch in the slip knot, placing it on the left needle, then working the instructions above, or cast on 1 more stitch than you need and unravel the slip knot when you reach the end of the first row.

265

### Long-Tail Cast On

**Setup.** Pull out a length of yarn for the long tail, about three times as long as the desired width of your knitting, plus about 6 inches. Make a slip knot at this point and place it on the needle. Hold the needle in your right hand with the index finger on the slip knot to prevent it from sliding off. Arrange the yarn in your left hand, with the tail over your thumb and the working yarn over your index finger Ⓐ.

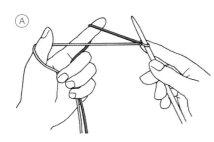

*Insert the needle up through the loop around your thumb Ⓑ, bring it over and behind the front strand on your index finger Ⓒ, then back out through the thumb loop to form a stitch Ⓓ; drop the thumb loop, place your thumb behind the long tail, and use it to tighten the loop; repeat from *.

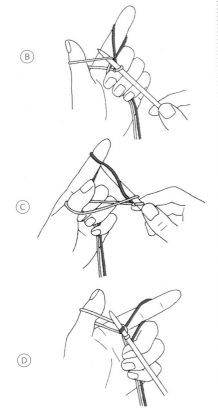

### Alternating-Color Long-Tail Cast On

Using two colors of yarn held together, make a slip knot and put it on the needle. Work as for the long-tail cast on above, with one color on the thumb and the other on the index finger. Between each cast-on stitch, twist the two yarns and swap their positions on your finger and thumb. Be careful to always twist in the same direction. Do not include the slip knot in your stitch count; when the cast on is complete, remove the slip knot from the needle and unravel it later.

### Two-Color Long-Tail Cast On

Hold the ends of both colors together and make a slip knot. Place the slip knot on your needle, put one color on your thumb and the other on your index finger, and work the usual long-tail cast on (above). Unlike the alternating-color long-tail cast on, you do not swap the yarns between each stitch. The color on your thumb will appear at the bottom edge of the knitting, and the color on your index finger will become the first row of the knitting. Do not include the slip knot in your stitch count; when the cast on is complete, remove the slip knot from the needle and unravel it later.

### Provisional Cast Ons

Provisional cast ons are worked using waste yarn so that you can easily remove the cast on and have live stitches at the beginning of your knitting. These are very useful for creating hems or when planning to add another garment section or border seamlessly.

### *Crocheted Provisional Cast On*

**Setup.** You need waste yarn and a crochet hook the same size as your knitting needle. Make a slip knot with the waste yarn and place it on the crochet hook. The yarn, needle, and crochet hook may be held in either hand.

**Step 1.** Cross the crochet hook in front of the knitting needle.

**Step 2.** *Bring the yarn behind the knitting needle Ⓐ and chain a stitch with the crochet hook Ⓑ Ⓒ. Repeat from * until you have the required number of stitches on the needle.

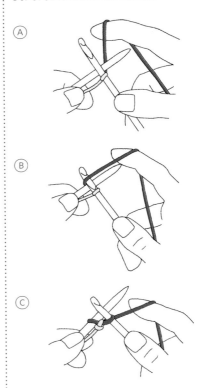

**Step 3.** Cut the waste yarn and pull it through the loop on the crochet hook so it won't unravel.

**Step 4.** Change to the working yarn and knit 1 row, being careful to work into the stitches without twisting them.

To remove the waste yarn later, pick the ending tail back out and unravel the chain, placing the live stitches on a needle.

## Invisible Cast On

**Setup.** Use waste yarn and your working yarn to begin this cast on. Tie the waste yarn around the end of the working yarn. Arrange the waste yarn around your thumb and the working yarn over your index finger. Hold both strands taut against your palm and the point of the knitting needle under the knot; keep the knot from sliding off the needle with your index finger.

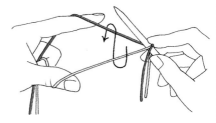

**Step 1.** Point your thumb up and insert the needle under the waste yarn from front to back and over the working yarn to scoop up a strand of the working yarn; 1 stitch is now on the needle.

**Step 2.** Point your thumb down and take the needle behind the working yarn to scoop up a second stitch.

Repeat steps 1 and 2 until there are the required number of stitches.

Cut the waste yarn and tie it to the working yarn to keep it from coming undone. To remove the waste yarn later, untie both ends and pull it horizontally out of the fabric, placing the live stitches on a needle.

## Ribbed Cable Cast On

This is a variation on the cable cast on (page 264), alternating knits and purls.

**Setup.** Cast on 2 stitches using the knitted cast on (page 265).

*Purl up a stitch between the last 2 stitches on the left needle (A) and slip the new stitch knitwise onto the left needle. Knit up a stitch between the last 2 stitches on the left needle (exactly like the cable cast on) and slip the new stitch knitwise onto the left needle (B). Repeat from * until desired number of stitches has been cast on. To work K1, P1 ribbing above this, knit the knit stitches and purl the purl stitches.

(A)

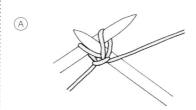

(B)

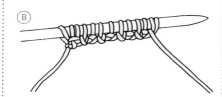

## Ruffle at Cast On

Cast on two or three times as many stitches as you need with a stretchy cast on. Work until the ruffle is as wide as desired, then decrease severely down to the number of stitches you need for your project. For a ruffle that stays flat, work it in garter stitch or some other noncurling pattern. For a ruffle with rolled edges, work it in stockinette. After you decrease, work very firmly for the first few rows, compressing the stitches together to force the extra fabric at the cast on to ruffle.

## Tubular Cast On

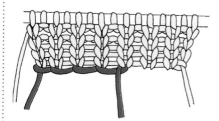

**Setup.** Cast on half the desired number of stitches using a provisional cast on or a half-hitch cast on and waste yarn. If you need an odd number of stitches, round up (for example, for 21 stitches, cast on 11).

**Step 1.** With the working yarn, *K1, yo; repeat from *, ending K1.

**Step 2.** At this point you have two options: You may work tubular knitting for 2 or more rounds to create a tube at the edge of your knitting, or you may skip to step 3. To work tubular knitting, slip 1 purlwise wyif, *K1, slip 1 purlwise wyif; repeat from *. On opposite side, K1, *slip 1 purlwise wyif, K1; repeat from *. Repeat these 2 rows for a full round of tubular knitting. (See Tubular Knitting, page 281.)

**Step 3.** Begin working ribbing. If you want an even number of stitches, make a yo at the beginning of the row, then work *P1, K1; repeat from *, ending P1. If you chose to work tubular knitting in step 2, you may work stockinette or any other pattern stitch at this point. If you did not work tubular knitting, you *must* work at least 1 row alternating knits and purls before continuing.

You may remove the waste yarn now or wait until later. If you used the half-hitch cast on, snip the waste yarn every few stitches and then pull out the short sections.

## Circular Knitting

A method of knitting that makes a tube, also called knitting "in the round." Larger tubes, such as bodies of sweaters, are made on circular needles; smaller tubes, such as socks and mittens, on sets of four or five double-pointed needles, on two circular needles, or on one very long circular needle with a very flexible cable (a method known as Magic Loop).

**Circular needles, working on.** Cast on as usual, then spread the stitches from point to point on the needle. Make sure that the cast-on row doesn't spiral around the needle at any point. Join the beginning and end of the round as described opposite, then work continuously around.

**Double-pointed needles, working on.** Cast all stitches onto one needle, then slip some of the stitches to two or three other needles. Arrange the needles to form a triangle or square (depending on the number of needles). Make sure the right side is facing you, and the cast-on row doesn't spiral around any needle at any point. Join the beginning and end of the round using one of the methods described opposite. Using an empty needle, knit across the first cast-on needle. When you are finished, you have emptied a needle. Use this to knit across the second needle. Continue around, working each needle in succession, using the needle you just emptied as the new working needle.

**Two circular needles, working on.** Cast all the stitches onto one needle and then slip half to the other. Bring the needle points with the first and last cast-on stitches together, being careful not to twist or untwist the cast on where the other ends of the two needles come together, and check to make sure that the knitting doesn't spiral around either needle at any point. Join the beginning and end of the round as described opposite. Holding both ends of the first needle, work all of those stitches onto that same needle Ⓐ. Put down the first needle and pick up both ends of the second needle. Work all of the stitches on the second needle onto itself. Continue around, alternating needles Ⓑ.

Ⓐ

Ⓑ

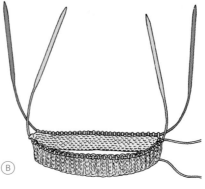

**Magic Loop, working on.**

**Step 1.** Using a very long (32 inches or more) circular needle with a very flexible cable, cast on the required number of stitches. Slide the stitches to the center of the cable. Divide the stitches in half and gently pull the cable through them at the halfway point, making a loop of the cable.

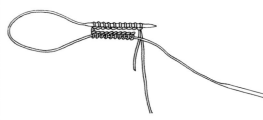

**Step 2.** Slide the stitches up onto the two needle points and make sure the cast on doesn't spiral around the needle. Note where the working yarn is attached to the end of the cast on; this is the end of the round, and the stitches connected to it are the second half of the round. This needle point should be in back.

**Step 3.** Slide the stitches on the back needle down onto the cable, leaving a loop of the cable at the halfway point and the tip of the needle free to work with.

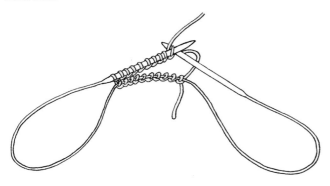

**Step 4.** Knit across the first half of the round using the working yarn.

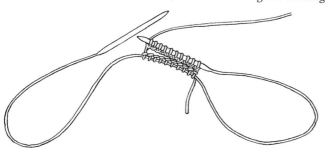

**Step 5.** Push the second half of the stitches up onto the point of the needle, turn the knitting.

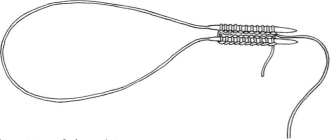

Repeat steps 3 through 5.

## Joining into a Round

There are several ways to join the beginning and end of the cast on when beginning a piece of circular knitting.

**Knit 2 together.** Cast on 1 more stitch than you need. Arrange your knitting so the last cast-on stitch is on the right needle. Slip this stitch to the left needle Ⓐ. Knit the first 2 stitches on the left needle together, using the working yarn and the cast-on tail held together Ⓑ. Drop the cast-on tail and continue with the working yarn only. On the next round, treat the double strand of the first stitch as a single stitch. When working K2, P2 ribbing, knit the second stitch using the doubled strands as well.

Ⓐ

Ⓑ

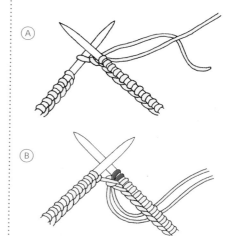

**Swap the first and last stitch.** Cast on the number of stitches needed. Slip 1 stitch from the left needle to the right needle. Insert the left needle into the 2nd stitch on the right needle and pass it over the first stitch. The 2 stitches have traded places.

**Knit with both strands.** Cast on the number of stitches needed. Arrange your knitting so the last cast-on stitch is on the right needle. Knit the first stitch or two using the working yarn and the cast-on tail held together. Drop the cast-on tail and continue with the working yarn only. On the next round treat the double strand of the first few stitches as a single stitch.

## Colorway

A group of colors selected to be used together. Handpainted or variegated yarns have more than one color on a single strand and are sometimes referred to by named colorways to distinguish them from solid-colored yarns. The term *colorway* is also used to refer to a selected group of solid yarns in different colors that will be used together to make a single project.

## Crochet

**Single crochet.** Begin with a slip knot on your crochet hook. *Insert the crochet hook through the fabric and hook up a new loop , then chain another loop through the 2 now on your hook . Repeat from *.

**Slipstitch crochet.** Begin with a slip knot on your crochet hook. *Insert the crochet hook through the fabric and hook up a new loop through the fabric and the loop on the crochet hook. Repeat from *.

## Decreases

**Knit 2 together (K2tog).** Insert the right needle into the first 2 stitches and knit them together. This decrease leans to the right on both the knit and the purl side of the fabric.

**Purl 2 together (P2tog).** Insert the right needle into the first 2 stitches and purl them together. This decrease leans to the right on both the knit and the purl side of the fabric.

**Slip, slip, knit (ssk).** Slip 1 stitch knitwise, slip another stitch knitwise, insert the left needle into these 2 stitches and knit them together. This decrease leans to the left on both the knit and the purl side of the fabric.

**Slip, slip, purl (ssp).** Slip 1 stitch knitwise, slip another stitch knitwise Ⓐ. Pass both of the slipped stitches back to the left needle Ⓑ. Purl the 2 stitches together through the back loops Ⓒ. This decrease leans to the left on both the knit and the purl side of the fabric Ⓓ. See Pass (page 277) for instructions on maintaining the orientation of the stitches.

Ⓐ

Ⓑ

Ⓒ

Ⓓ

## Double Decreases

**Knit 3 together (K3tog).** Insert the right needle into the first 3 stitches knitwise, and knit them together. This decreases 2 stitches and leans to the right.

**Purl 3 together (P3tog).** Insert the right needle into the first 3 stitches purlwise, and purl them together. This decreases 2 stitches and leans to the right.

**Slip 1, knit 2 together, pass slipped stitch over (sk2p).** Slip 1 knitwise; knit 2 together Ⓐ; pass slipped stitch over Ⓑ. This decreases 2 stitches and leans to the left.

**Slip 2, knit 1, pass 2 slipped stitches over (s2kp2).** Insert the right needle knitwise into the first 2 stitches, as if to knit them together, and slip them to the right needle; knit 1 Ⓐ; pass both of the slipped stitches over the knit stitch and off the needle Ⓑ. This decreases 2 stitches and is centered.

**Slip, slip, slip, knit (sssk).** This decrease is worked exactly like the ssk, except that 3 stitches are slipped and worked together. Slip 1 stitch knitwise, slip another stitch knitwise, slip a third stitch knitwise, insert the left needle into these 3 stitches and knit them together. This double decrease leans to the left on both the knit and the purl side of the fabric.

**Slip, slip, slip, purl (sssp).** This decrease is worked exactly like the ssp, except that 3 stitches are slipped and worked together. Slip 1 stitch knitwise, slip another stitch knitwise, slip a third stitch knitwise. Pass all 3 slipped stitches back to the left needle and purl them together through the back loops. See Pass (page 277) for instructions on maintaining the orientation of the stitches. This double decrease leans to the left on both the knit and the purl side of the fabric.

**Slip, slip, pass 2 left, purl 3 together.** This is the wrong-side equivalent of the centered double decrease s2kp2. It is rarely needed because most double decreases are worked on the right side of the fabric. When a centered double decrease is required on a wrong-side row, however, there is no substitute for it, and it's worth the effort. Completed correctly, it looks identical to s2kp2 worked on the right side of the fabric.

Slip 1 knitwise, slip a second stitch knitwise Ⓐ, pass these 2 stitches together back to the left needle knitwise so their orientation changes Ⓑ, purl 3 together Ⓒ. See Pass (page 277) for instructions on changing the orientation of the stitches.

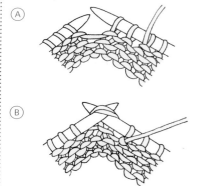

## Dropped Stitch, fixing

**Stockinette stitch.** Turn the fabric so that the knit side is facing you. Insert a crochet hook into the stitch from the front and hook the lowest unraveled strand through to the front; don't remove the crochet hook. Instead, continue to work your way up from the lowest strand to the highest, hooking each one out to the front to reknit another stitch. At the top, put the stitch back on the needle.

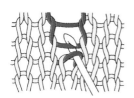

**Ribbing.** Turn your knitting so that the knit side of the stitch to be corrected is facing you and hook the strands back up just as described for stockinette stitch.

**Garter stitch or other pattern stitches.** Where there is a combination of knits and purls facing you, you will need to hook up the knit stitches from the front and the purled stitches from the back. If you find it difficult to insert the crochet hook from the back, simply turn your knitting over and hook up the stitch from the other side, then return to the front to capture the next knit stitch. Take care to work the strands in the correct order from bottom to top.

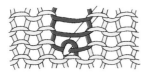

## Duplicate Stitch

A method of embroidering with yarn on the surface of the knitting, following the structure of the knitted stitch.

**In pattern.** To work duplicate stitch in fabric that combines knits, purls, and other stitch manipulations, you will sometimes be duplicating knit stitches (see Knit Side, below) and sometimes duplicating purl stitches (see Purl Side, below). If there are yarnovers, increases, decreases, slipped stitches, twisted stitches cables, or other stitch manipulations, you will simply follow the strand you are duplicating. There are too many possible variations on stitch patterns to give specific guidelines here, but an excellent way of educating yourself in this is to work a pattern stitch and substitute a contrasting yarn for just one row; this will allow you to see exactly the path it follows for that row of the pattern.

**Knit side.** Bring the point of the yarn needle up through the bottom of the stitch. *Insert the yarn needle behind two strands along the top of the stitch (A); insert the yarn needle back through the bottom of the stitch and under two strands to the bottom of the next stitch (B); repeat from *. You may work from either right to left or left to right.

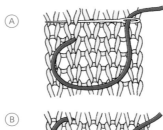

**Purl side.** The yarn should not show on the knit side of the fabric. This technique is used on the wrong side of the fabric for working in ends invisibly or to adjust the tension and alignment of stitches to improve the appearance on the right side. *Insert the yarn needle under 2 purl bumps diagonally from bottom to top (A); insert the yarn needle under the next 2 purl bumps diagonally from top to bottom (B); repeat from *. Work right to left or left to right.

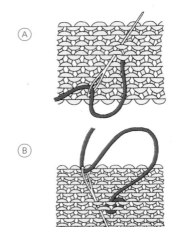

## Eyelet

A small hole in the knitted fabric made with a yarnover. For instructions and illustration, see Eyelet Buttonhole (page 263).

## Felting

The act of making a matted fabric from unspun wool or other animal fibers using moisture, heat, and abrasion. Unspun fibers can also be needle felted by punching barbed needles through them repeatedly. *See also* Fulling

## Frown

Section of a purled stitch that looks like a frown.

## Fulling

The act of making a matted fabric from a loosely knitted or woven fabric by applying moisture, heat, and abrasion. Fulling is an important finishing step in most woven wool fabrics. It is commonly referred to as "felting" in the knitting community. When a knitted fabric is fulled, it results in a thicker, less stretchy fabric, useful for mittens, hats, bags, and jackets. Unintentional fulling can occur if a knitted garment is washed improperly, in the washing machine or by hand with too much agitation. *See also* Felting

## Gauge

Gauge describes the tightness (or looseness) of your knitting. In U.S. knitting instructions, it refers to the number of stitches and rows per inch in your pattern stitch. Patterns from the United Kingdom, as well as from New Zealand, Australia, and Canada, use the term *tension*. Gauge is usually given in stitches per 4 inches but may be per 1 inch, or any other measurement. In the United States, the term *tension* is used more generally when discussing how a knitter holds the working yarn or when referring to uneven tension on the working yarn that has resulted in an uneven fabric.

## Helix Knitting

In this book, helix knitting is suggested as a way of working stripes and garter stitch without a jog at the beginning/end of round and as a way of blending yarns together if there is a variation between dye lots. The instructions here are limited to two-strand helix knitting, but you can introduce more colors by using more balls of yarn.

### Starting helix knitting at the cast on.
Use the two-color long-tail cast on. When the cast on is completed, begin working circularly using the strand that was on your thumb (it's the strand that runs across the bottom of the cast on).

### Starting helix knitting in the middle of your work.
Leave the original yarn attached and begin working with the new yarn at the beginning of the round.

### Changing colors.
When you reach the end of the round, drop the yarn you used on the last round and pick up the yarn that's waiting there from the previous round. Be sure to drop the yarn you just finished to the right of the one you are picking up so they don't get twisted around each other. Be careful *not* to pull firmly on the strand you are now using — it will make the stitch at the beginning of round too tight. Instead, gently draw up any slack so that all the stitches are the same size. When you reach the end of the round, change yarns again exactly the same way. There should be a smooth spiral of the two colors with no jog at the beginning/end of round.

### Binding off.
Change yarns at the beginning of the round as usual and bind off with the one now in use or bind off a section with each yarn.

### Disguising the corner at the bind off and cast on.
Use the tails of yarn at the cast on and bind off to tighten the stitches and smooth out the edge at the cast on and bind off when you weave in the ends.

### Jogless garter stitch.
To work garter stitch in the round without a jog, work helix knitting using two balls of the same color. Knit around with one of them and purl around with the other.

## Hems

Hems can be worked at the cast on or at the bind off. Because of their double thickness, they will sometimes bulge. This can be avoided by working the inner layer on a smaller needle, with thinner yarn, or on fewer stitches than the outer layer.

## Bind-Off Hems

When the garment is the desired length, work one of the Edge Treatments for Hems (page 274) (Folded, Picot, or Rolled). Following this, work in stockinette for the desired depth of the hem. Fold to the wrong side and join the live stitches to the back of the fabric using one of the methods of joining described below.

### Joining Bind-Off Hems

**Bound off.** Knit the live stitches together with a row of stitches on the back of the fabric while working three-needle bind off. *Slip 1 knitwise from the left needle, insert the tip of the right needle under a "smile" in the same column as the stitch you are binding off, then knit the smile and the stitch together. Repeat from * so that there are 2 stitches on the right needle, then pass one over the other to bind it off as usual. You will need to work loosely to avoid creating a noticeably tight row at the top of the hem.

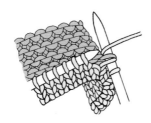

**Sewn.** Use a whipstitch to sew through one of the bumps on the back of the fabric and through the live stitch opposite it on the needle. Be careful to align the columns of stitches so your hem isn't skewed, and to work loosely so it will stretch when the fabric stretches. If your stitches are on a circular needle, you can leave all the stitches on the cable while sewing the hem. On a rigid needle, slip each stitch off as you finish working with it.

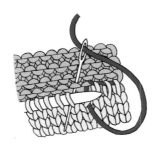

**Woven.** Combine Kitchener stitch and duplicate stitch to sew the live stitches down while creating a new row of stitches. Cut the yarn, leaving a tail about three times the width of your knitting, and thread it on a yarn needle. *Insert the yarn needle knitwise into the first stitch on the knitting needle and slide it off Ⓐ. Insert the yarn needle purlwise into the next stitch Ⓑ, leaving it on the needle, and pull the yarn through Ⓒ. Duplicate stitch the top of the stitch on the back of the fabric where you want to join the hem, inserting the yarn needle up through a smile and then down through the next smile to form the curved top of the stitch Ⓓ. Repeat from * until all live stitches have been attached to the back of the fabric Ⓔ.

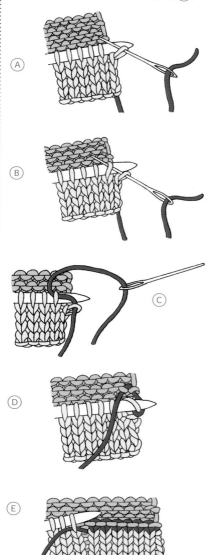

## Edge Treatments for Hems

**Folded.** Work 1 or 2 rows in reverse stockinette (2 rows will make a squarer edge).

**Picot.** Work *yo, K2tog; repeat from *. If a single stitch remains at the end of the row, K1. This makes a picot edge when folded.

**Rolled.** Don't do anything special to delineate the fold at the bottom edge, just continue working in stockinette.

### Cast-On Hems

Use a provisional cast on, then work in stockinette for the depth of the hem. Work a folded, picot, or rolled edge treatment as described above. Work in stockinette until length above the fold equals the length below the fold. Remove the provisional cast on and place stitches on an empty needle. Use a third needle to knit the stitches on the two needles together to join the hem to the body. (See chapter 8, page 236 for an illustration of how to join layers by knitting together.)

## I-Cord

Using two double-pointed needles, cast on 3 or 4 stitches. *Knit across. Slide the stitches to the other end of the needle without turning. Put the needle with the stitches in your left hand. Pull the yarn firmly across the back, and repeat from * until cord is desired length. Cut yarn and pull through all the stitches to secure.

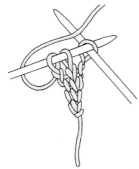

An alternative method of working I-cord, which doesn't require double-pointed needles, is to pass the stitches back to the left needle after completing each row, rather than sliding the stitches to the other end of the needle. Some knitters find this much quicker to work. See Pass (page 277) for instructions on maintaining the orientation of the stitch.

**I-cord, applied.** Using two double-pointed needles, cast on 3 to 6 stitches. With the right side of the fabric facing you and the needle with the stitches on it in your right hand, pick up and knit a stitch through the edge of the fabric. *Do not turn. Slide the stitches to the other end of the needle and shift it to your left hand. Pull the yarn across the back and knit until 2 stitches remain, skp (working the last stitch of the cord together with the picked-up stitch). Pick up and knit a stitch through the edge of the fabric. Repeat from *.

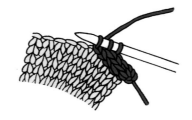

### I-cord Bind Off

*See* Bind Offs, I-cord (page 259)

## Increases

### Knit-Front-and-Back (Kfb)

Knit into the stitch, leaving it on the left needle. Bring the right needle to the back of the work, knit into the back loop of the stitch and slip it off the needle. Pfb is the purled equivalent of Kfb (see Purl-Front-and-Back, opposite).

### Make 1 (M1)

There are many ways to work the M1 increase. Lifted M1s steal yarn from the stitches on either side, so they are tighter than M1s made using the working yarn. The M1 made with a yarnover is a happy medium, looser than a lifted M1 and tighter than an M1 with the working yarn.

**Left slanting, lifted (M1L).** Insert the nonworking needle from the front under the top strand between the two needles (A), then knit into the back of the stitch to twist it (B).

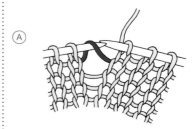

**Left slanting, working yarn (M1L).** Make a small loop of the working yarn close to the needle, twist it clockwise, and place it on the needle.

**Right slanting, lifted (M1R).** Insert the nonworking needle from the back under the top strand between the two needles (A), then knit into the front of the stitch to twist it (B).

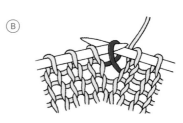

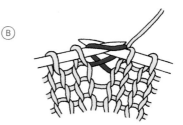

**Right slanting, working yarn (M1R).** Make a small loop of the working yarn close to the needle, twist it counterclockwise, and place it on the needle.

**Yarnover make 1.** Work a yarnover on the increase row, then knit into the back of this stitch on the following row to twist it. This makes a left-slanting M1 and is useful when the other methods are too tight to work easily. To make a right-slanting version of the M1 using a yo, wrap the yo the opposite of the normal way (from back to front over the right needle), then work into the front of it on the following round.

## Purl-Front-and-Back (Pfb)

Purl into the stitch, leaving it on the left needle. Bring the right needle to the back of the work, purl into the back loop of the stitch, and slip it off the needle.

## Lifted (also Raised or Row-Below) Increase

Knit the stitch normally. Then, from the back, insert the left needle into the left half of the stitch 2 rows below. Knit into this stitch Ⓐ. To reverse the slant of this increase, reverse the order: lift up the stitch from 1 row below and knit it, then knit the stitch normally Ⓑ. You may find it easier to lift with the right needle and slip to the left needle before knitting.

This increase can be worked by knitting into the back of the lifted loop to twist it, or into the front to leave it untwisted. Decide for yourself which looks best in your knitted fabric.

## Yarnover (yo)

**Standard.** A stitch worked between two existing stitches that produces an eyelet. Note that the yarn always travels over the top of the right needle. If the next stitch will be a knit, the yarnover must end with the yarn in back. If the following stitch will be a purl, the yarn must continue under the needle from back to front in preparation for purling. With yarn in your left hand, either wrap counterclockwise around the needle with your index finger, or take the right needle around the back and under the yarn Ⓐ. With yarn in the right hand, wrap counterclockwise once around the right needle Ⓑ.

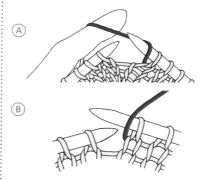

**At the beginning of a row.** An increase worked before the first stitch of the row forming a loop. To work a yarnover at the beginning of a row, place the yarn in front of the right needle if the first stitch will be a knit Ⓐ, which will make a sloppy loop over the needle; work this loop as usual on the following row to prevent it from becoming twisted. Keep the yarn in the back of the right needle if the first stitch will be a purl Ⓑ. This will also make a loop over the needle, but it will be oriented in the nonstandard direction. Work into the back of this loop on the following row to untwist it.

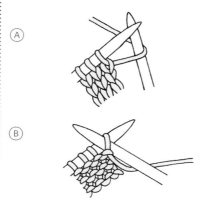

To make a larger yarnover in the standard direction before a purl, you may also wrap the yarn counterclockwise all the way around the right needle before working the purled stitch.

### Double Increases

**Knit-purl-knit (K-P-K).** Knit into the stitch as usual, but leave it on the left needle. Bring the yarn to the front, purl into the stitch, yarn back, knit into the stitch, and slip it off the needle.

**Knit-yarnover-knit (K-yo-K).** Knit into the stitch as usual, but leave it on the left needle, yarnover Ⓐ, knit into the stitch again Ⓑ, and slip it off the needle.

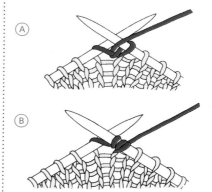

## Intarsia

Intarsia knitting features multiple colors, with a separate yarn supply for each occurrence of each color. The yarn is never carried across the back of the fabric to be used elsewhere in the row. Intarsia is particularly suited to a colored design where there is no repeating pattern, or to large-scale patterns like argyle, where carrying the yarn across the back of the fabric is impractical.

275

## Kitchener Stitch

**Setup.** Hold the two pieces of knitting with wrong sides together. If you are right-handed, point the needles to the right; if you are left-handed, reverse them. Use a yarn needle threaded with matching yarn; if the working yarn is hanging at the edge, cut it to a comfortable length and use it.

**Step 1.** Insert the yarn needle knitwise into the first stitch on the front knitting needle and slip it off.

**Step 2.** Insert the yarn needle into the next stitch on the front knitting needle purlwise, leave it on the knitting needle, and gently pull up the slack in the yarn.

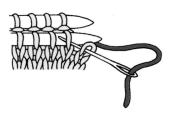

**Step 3.** Insert the yarn needle into the first stitch on the back knitting needle purlwise and slip the stitch off.

**Step 4.** Insert the yarn needle into the next stitch on the back knitting needle knitwise, leave it on the knitting needle, and pull up the slack in the yarn.

Repeat steps 1 through 4. As you work, adjust the tension of the sewn stitches to match the rows above and below.

For those who are mirror knitters (knitting across their stitches from left to right, rather than right to left) and who prefer to work Kitchener stitch in the same direction, simply follow the instructions above.

For those who work in the standard direction, but prefer to sew with their left hand, the terms *knitwise* and *purlwise* can be confusing when working across in the opposite direction. Think of *knitwise* as meaning "insert the needle into the stitch from the right side of the fabric," and *purlwise* as meaning "insert the needle into the stitch from the wrong side of the fabric." Assuming you are working in stockinette stitch, purlwise is inserting from the purl side, and knitwise is inserting from the knit side, which makes it easy to remember.

These instructions are for stockinette stitch. For garter stitch when working from right to left with the yarn in your right hand, work steps 1 and 2 on the front needle, then repeat them on the back needle. If you are working from left to right with the yarn in your left hand, work steps 3 and 4 on both needles.

## Knit To and Fro

This is a method of knitting where right-side rows are worked using the standard method, and wrong-side rows are worked in the opposite direction with the right side of the fabric facing you. This allows you to work flat knitting without turning, with the right side facing you at all times. It is very convenient for working short rows, bobbles, and entrelac, which otherwise require you to turn your knitting very frequently. To knit to and fro, you must learn to knit backward, working in the opposite direction from standard knitting on what would be the wrong-side rows. Directions for knitting backward follow.

**With yarn in your left hand.** With the knit side facing you, the stitches to be worked on the right needle, and the yarn in back, insert the left needle knitwise into the first stitch on the right needle (that is, through the front of the stitch to the back of the right needle) Ⓐ. Bring the yarn over the left (back) needle tip to the front, then under it to the back Ⓑ. You may need to let go of the left needle in order to wrap the yarn. Lift the loop of the old stitch over the tip of the left needle with the right needle, or pull it through with the left needle. Slide the right needle out of the loop.

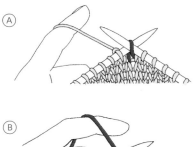

**With yarn in your right hand.** With the knit side facing you and the yarn in back, insert the left needle knitwise (through the front of the stitch to the back of the right needle) Ⓐ. Bring the yarn around the left (back) needle tip from back to front Ⓑ. Lift the loop of the old stitch over the tip of the left needle with the right needle, or pull it through with the left needle. Slide the right needle out of the loop.

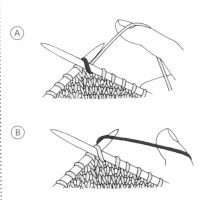

## Knitwise

Designates the way the working right needle is inserted into the stitch on the nonworking needle. Knitwise is from the front of the fabric to the back under the needle, the same way you insert the needle when you knit a stitch. Note that if your stitches are on the needle in the nonstandard orientation, then to slip knitwise you'll need to insert the working needle from back to front instead.

## Lifeline

A thin strand of yarn or cord that is run through all the stitches on a row, as insurance in the event that you have to rip out sections. This is very useful when the yarn is difficult to work with or the pattern stitch is complex. The lifeline is pulled through all the stitches while they are on the needle and then left in place. If a section must be removed, the knitting is unraveled down to the row with the lifeline, and a needle is reinserted through the row. The lifeline prevents any stitches from being dropped during this process. (See photo, page 156.)

## Mirror Knitting

A method of knitting in the opposite direction from standard knitting.

## Nonworking Needle

The needle holding the stitches about to be worked. In standard knitting, this is the left needle. In mirror knitting, this is the right needle. If you are "Knitting To and Fro," then this will be the left needle when working from right to left and the right needle when working from left to right.

## Pass

Move a stitch from the working needle back to the nonworking needle. This can be done two ways. The usual method is to insert the nonworking needle into the stitch from the front of the fabric so that it ends up on the needle in its original orientation. If your stitches are on the needle in the nonstandard position, then you would need to insert the nonworking needle into the back of the stitch to maintain its orientation. Whenever the instruction is given in this book to pass a stitch back to the other needle, without any further instructions about orientation, you should maintain the orientation as explained here.

In just a few instances (when working decreases), you will need to change the orientation of the stitch as you pass it back. If you insert the nonworking needle into the stitch from the back of the fabric, it will be rotated by 180 degrees. If your stitches are on the needle in the nonstandard position, then accomplish the same thing by inserting the needle from the front. In this book if it's necessary to change the orientation while passing back, it will say so explicitly.

"Pass" is also used in the instruction, "Pass slipped stitch over." This action is normally worked on the stitches closest to the end of the working needle, lifting the stitch one or two away from the tip over the other stitch(es) and off the needle. It's used to decrease and in binding off.

## Pick Up/Pick Up and Knit

Throughout this book, the phrases *pick up* and *pick up and knit* are used interchangeably. See also Pick Up and Purl, page 278.

**Along garter stitch edges.** Insert your needle through the tiny bumps at the end of each garter stitch ridge. Wrap the yarn around the needle and knit the stitch out to the front. This works best on straight edges. For curved edges, like armholes and neck openings, pick up 1 stitch in from the edge for a smoother finish, as described for stockinette (below). If the knitting is very firm and it's difficult to work through the bumps, work instead through the loose stitches between the bumps. (See also pages 220–21.)

**Along stockinette stitch edges.** Insert the tip of your needle through the fabric to the back, 1 stitch in from the edge. Wrap the yarn around it and knit the stitch out to the front.

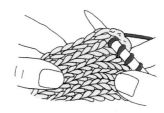

**Along the cast on or bind off.** Insert the needle directly into a stitch (A), wrap the yarn, and knit up a stitch (B). If your knitting is upside down, this is actually the space between 2 stitches, but it looks just like a stitch.

(A)

(B)

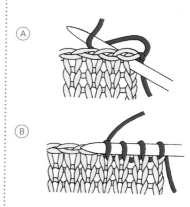

## Pick Up and Purl

With the yarn in front, insert the tip of your needle through the fabric from back to front, a whole stitch in from the edge. Wrap the yarn and purl the stitch out to the back.

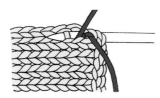

## Purlwise

Designates the way the working needle is inserted into a stitch. Purlwise is from the back of the fabric to the front under the needle, the same way you insert the needle when you purl a stitch. Note that if your stitches are on the needle in the nonstandard orientation, then to slip purlwise you'll need to insert the working needle from front to back instead.

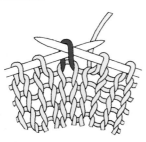

## Right Side

The side of the fabric that's intended to show when the garment is finished, also called the public side.

## Russian Join

The Russian join is used to attach a new ball of yarn or change colors, especially when you want to create a reversible fabric or don't want the ends to show. It does create a thick section in the yarn and the twist will be different, which may be noticeable in some yarns and fabrics.

Use a yarn needle threaded with one of the yarns to pull a short section of the yarn back through its own plies Ⓐ, leaving a small loop at the point where it doubles back Ⓑ. Thread the second piece of yarn through the yarn needle, pull it through the loop in the first yarn Ⓒ, then double it back on itself, pulling a short section of the yarn through its own plies Ⓓ. Smooth out the areas of doubled yarns and trim off any loose ends Ⓔ.

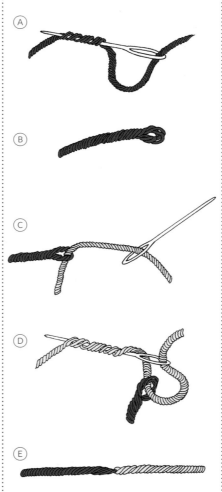

## Seaming

### Mattress Stitch to Join Sides

Mattress stitch is used to join the sides of two pieces of knitting worked in stockinette stitch. With the right side of the fabric facing you, work a full stitch in from the edge. To make a firm, strong seam, sew under just one strand on each side with every stitch Ⓐ. To make a slightly less bulky seam, and one that takes half the time to work, sew under two strands on each side with every stitch Ⓑ.

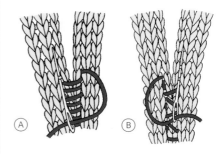

Work alternately on one side of the seam and then the other. As you sew, pull the yarn tight enough so that the yarn you are using disappears into the seam and the two edges draw together, but keep it loose enough that the seam still stretches a little.

For a significantly less bulky seam, assuming the edge is neat and the stitches firm enough, mattress stitch can be worked a half stitch from the edge, instead of a whole stitch. Insert the yarn needle into the center of a stitch and then out again through the center of the stitch 1 or 2 rows higher Ⓒ. You will be sewing under the tops of the stitches rather than under the strands between 2 stitches.

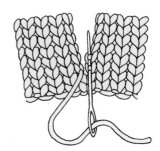

### Weaving to Join Tops and Bottoms

Weaving is used to join the top or bottom edges of knitted pieces to each other by sewing a new row of stitches to join them. While it's obvious that there is a seam, this makes a neat finish with some stretch. The path the yarn follows is the same as for Kitchener stitch, except that Kitchener is worked on two sets of live stitches.

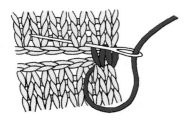

**Setup.** Lay out the pieces as shown, right side up, with the edges to be joined next to each other.

**Step 1.** Find the place in the first row where a stitch comes together to form a V pointing toward the edge of the fabric and insert your needle under those two strands.

**Step 2.** On the opposite side of the seam, find the first stitch where two strands come together to form a V pointing at the edge of the fabric, and insert the needle under those two strands.

**Step 3.** Go back to the first side, and insert the needle under the V of the next stitch. *Hint:* Go back into the same spot you last came out of in step 1. Alternate from side to side until the seam is finished.

You may use weaving when one set of stitches has not been bound off. For instructions on weaving live stitches to dead stitches, see chapter 7, page 208.

### Combination Seams

Use a combination of mattress stitch (see opposite) and weaving (see left) to join the top of one piece to the side of another, such as when joining the top of a sleeve to the body of a sweater. Use mattress stitch to sew under a strand between 2 stitches along the side of the knitting Ⓐ and weaving to sew under the V formed by two strands at the top or bottom of the knitting Ⓑ. Because knit stitches are wider than they are tall, you will sometimes need to sew under two strands/rows along the side edge to make the seam come out even. Adjust the tension of your sewing yarn so that the size of the stitches in the new row you create is the same as those in the top row.

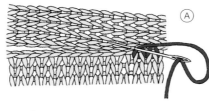

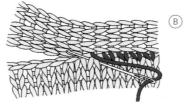

## Three-Needle Bind Off

*See* Bind Offs (page 254).

## Seed Stitch

A knit-purl pattern where single knits and purls are alternated on every row or round to make a checkerboard.

## Short Rows

Short rows are a way of shaping knitting that involves working partway across a row and then turning back before finishing the row. Working a series of short rows makes it possible to shape sloped shoulders or neck edges without binding off, to add darts without cutting the fabric, and to shape sleeve caps while knitting the sleeve onto the armhole.

Each time you turn in the middle of a row, you leave a hole. In lace these holes may integrate well with the lace pattern; in other fabrics, the holes will look like mistakes. The most common way to close the holes is to work a "wrap and turn" at each turning point, which is described here. In garter stitch, the wrap, which appears to be a little horizontal bar, will disappear into the ridged fabric. In other patterns, it will be necessary to take steps to hide the wrap by picking it up and working it together with the stitch it wraps. Instructions for both wrapping and picking up the wraps follow.

Other methods of preventing holes include the "Japanese" and "German," which involve using yarnovers or the running thread between stitches, rather than wrap-and-turn.

### *Wrap and Turn*

Work across until you are ready to turn, slip the next stitch purlwise, change the position of the yarn (from front to back or from back to front), slip the stitch purlwise back to the left needle, and turn. Position the yarn wherever you need it to work the next stitch and continue back across the row.

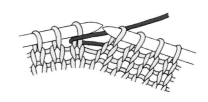

### Pick Up the Wrap

How you pick up the wrap will depend on whether you are knitting or purling and whether the right or the wrong side of the fabric is facing you. What you want to accomplish is to pick up the wrap and to work it together with its stitch in such a way that the wrap falls to the wrong side of the fabric and is hidden. The four possible situations are covered below.

**Knitting on the right side.** When the wrapped stitch is a knit and the right side of the fabric is facing you, insert the right needle tip up into the wrap on the front of the fabric, then through the stitch on the needle, and knit the 2 together. The wrap should fall to the back of the fabric.

**Purling on the right side.** When the wrapped stitch is a purl and the right side of the fabric is facing you, insert the right needle tip into the stitch purlwise, and then underneath the wrap on the front of the fabric. You may need to lift the wrap up with your fingers to accomplish this. Purl the 2 together; the wrap should fall to the back of the fabric.

**Knitting on the wrong side.** When the wrapped stitch is a knit and the wrong side of the fabric is facing you, insert the right needle tip into the back part of the wrap, lift it up and put it on the left needle. Knit it together with the stitch; the wrap should fall to the side of the fabric facing you, which is the wrong side.

**Purling on the wrong side.** When the wrapped stitch is a purl and the wrong side of the fabric is facing you, insert the tip of the right needle into the back part of the wrap, lift it up and put it on the left needle. Purl it together with the stitch; the wrap should fall to the side of the fabric facing you, which is the wrong side.

## Single Yarn

A yarn made of just one strand of twisted fiber, in contrast with a plied yarn, which is constructed from more than one strand, twisted around each other. Also called single-ply yarn.

## Slip Knot

Holding the cut end of the yarn against your palm, wrap it around two fingers, and then a little farther to end in back, forming a loop Ⓐ; pull a loop of the working yarn through the loop around your fingers Ⓑ; slip your fingers out and tighten the knot by pulling the cut end and the loop Ⓒ.

Ⓐ
Ⓑ
Ⓒ

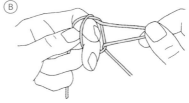

## Slip Stitch

A slipped stitch is one that is simply moved from the nonworking needle to the working needle without working a knit or a purl. If you knit in the standard direction, the stitch will shift from the left to the right needle. If you are a mirror knitter, the stitch will move in the opposite direction.

Stitches can be slipped knitwise (as if you were knitting a stitch) or purlwise (as if you were purling a stitch). They can also be slipped with the yarn in front of the needle (wyif) or in back of the needle (wyib). If you need to change the position of the yarn to the location specified, do this before you slip the stitch. See also Knitwise (page 277) and Purlwise (page 278).

In pattern stitches, where the slipped stitches are not worked again until the following row, they are generally slipped purlwise to prevent the stitches from twisting and tightening the fabric. In decreases and other stitch manipulations where slipping is just one of a series of actions, the stitches are usually slipped knitwise. If no guidance is provided, then decide which way to slip based on what the results look like.

## Smile

Section of a purl stitch that looks like a smile.

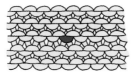

## Splicing Yarn

A method of joining when starting a new ball of yarn. When working with a plied yarn, untwist the plies and pull them apart for 3 to 4 inches, then break off half of them. If you're working with a single-ply yarn, untwist it and pull out about half of the fiber. Do the same with the end you are joining it to. Overlap the two ends of yarn and wrap them around each other in the direction of the original twist. Wet these, give them a bit of a rub, and then carefully knit past the join. If any ends pop out, trim them neatly.

Splicing is most effective in wool yarns or other fuzzy animal fibers. For slippery yarns, such as cotton, rayon, and silk, you can still splice, but it's a good idea to overlap the yarns for 5 to 6 inches. If the yarn has a smooth finish, the splice will still hold together, but the spliced area will probably look noticeably different than the rest of the yarn.

## Steek

Steeks allow you to make the entire garment circularly, so that you can work colored and textured patterns from the right side throughout the construction process. They consist of extra stitches added at armholes, neck openings, and cardigan fronts that serve as seam allowances when the openings are cut open later. For instructions on constructing steeks see chapter 3 (pages 88–97). For cutting and finishing, see chapter 6, pages 186–91.

## Tubular Knitting

Sometimes called "double knitting," this is a method of working a knitted tube on straight needles. Both the front and the back of the tube are on a single needle, with stitches from each alternating across the needle. To work the tube, work across the needle knitting the stitches in the front layer and slipping the stitches in the back layer purlwise with the yarn in front. Working across the needle twice in this manner completes a full round of the tube Ⓐ.

Tubular knitting may also be worked with the purl side out Ⓑ. In this case, purl the stitches in the front layer and slip the stitches in the back layer on each row. This is much quicker than the knitted version because the yarn is held in front throughout.

A few rounds of tubular knitting make an excellent transition between K1, P1 ribbing and the tubular cast on or bind off. It can also be used to form a hem or casing.

## Waste Yarn

Yarn used temporarily to hold stitches or when casting on. Waste yarn should be smooth, nonfuzzy, the same weight as the working yarn, and a different color from the working yarn, so that it knits up at the same gauge as the working yarn and can easily be removed later without leaving any residue.

## Weaving in Ends as You Go

The instructions below assume you are working a knit row in stockinette stitch. In other pattern stitches, it may not be practical to weave in the ends as you go. Note that this same technique of weaving in ends as you knit can be used to secure long floats between motifs when working stranded knitting.

If you don't weave in the yarn ends as you go, you can always sew them in later. For methods of sewing in ends after the knitting is completed, see chapter 7, pages 200–203.

Think ahead and begin weaving in the new yarn about 10 stitches before you first begin using it as the working yarn (see directions for the appropriate hand, below). If you are knitting circularly and forget, you can always sew in the tail of the new yarn later using a yarn needle. If you are knitting back and forth in stockinette, you can weave in the tail of the new yarn on the following row. You'll then be working on the purl side, so hold the tail in front of your work to do this.

After you've knit 2 stitches with the new ball of yarn, begin weaving in the end of the old ball according to the directions below.

**Working yarn in right hand.** Hold the tail in your left hand and behind your knitting. Simply insert your right needle under it while knitting the next stitch, as shown in the illustration. Alternate knitting normally and knitting under the tail until you've worked about 10 stitches.

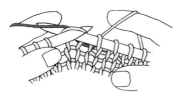

**Working yarn in left hand.** Hold the tail in your right hand and work these two steps.

**Step 1.** Insert the right needle into the next stitch and wrap the tail around the point of it counterclockwise. Wrap the working yarn around the right needle as usual (counterclockwise).

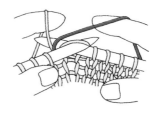

**Step 2.** Unwrap the tail. Knit the new stitch out through the old one.

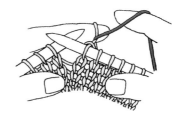

Alternately knit a stitch normally and then knit a stitch catching the tail (following steps 1 and 2) until you've worked about 10 stitches.

## Whipstitch

A method of sewing where stitches pass over an edge, used in joining and finishing.

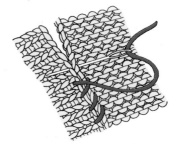

## Working Needle

The needle where newly formed stitches are placed. In standard knitting, this is the right needle; in mirror knitting, this is the left needle.

## Wrong Side

The side of the fabric that will be on the inside of the garment when completed, also called the private side.

# Abbreviations

| | |
|---|---|
| BO | bind off |
| CO | cast on |
| dec | decrease |
| K | knit |
| K1b-tbl | knit 1 through the back loop |
| K2tog | knit 2 together |
| K3tog | knit 3 together |
| Kfb | knit into the front and back of the stitch |
| K-P-K | knit-purl-knit into the stitch |
| K-yo-K | knit-yarnover-knit into the stitch |
| M1 | make 1 |
| M1L | make 1 left |
| M1R | make 1 right |
| P | purl |
| P2tog | purl 2 together |
| P3tog | purl 3 together |
| Pfb | purl into the front and back of the stitch |
| psso | pass slipped stitch over |
| rs | right side |
| s2kp2 | slip 2 together knitwise, knit 1, pass 2 slipped stitches over |
| sk2p | slip 1 knitwise, knit 2 together, pass slipped stitch over |
| skp | slip 1 knitwise, knit 1, pass slipped stitch over |
| sl | slip |
| ssk | slip 1 knitwise, slip 1 knitwise, knit these 2 stitches together |
| ssp | slip 1 knitwise, slip 1 knitwise, pass the 2 stitches back to the left needle, purl 2 together through the back loops |
| sssk | slip 1 knitwise, slip 1 knitwise, slip 1 knitwise, knit these 3 stitches together |
| sssp | slip 1 knitwise, slip 1 knitwise, slip 1 knitwise, pass the 3 stitches back to the left needle, purl these 3 together through the back loops |
| tbl | through the back loops |
| ws | wrong side |
| wyib | with yarn in back |
| wyif | with yarn in front |
| yo | yarnover |
| 2/2 RC | 4-stitch cable: slip 2 to cable needle, hold behind work, K2, K2 from cable needle |

# Symbols

| | |
|---|---|
| ⬚ | Knit on right side, purl on wrong side |
| − | Purl on right side, knit on wrong side |
| O | Yarnover |
| ⋋ ⁄ | Knit 2 together on right side, purl 2 together on wrong side |
| ⋌ | Knit 3 together |
| ⋋ ⋌ | Slip, slip, knit 2 together on right side; slip, slip, purl on wrong side |
| ⋋ | Slip one, knit 2 together, psso |
| ⋀ | Centered double decrease: slip 2 together knitwise, knit 1, pass 2 slipped stitches over |
| Y | Left-slanting increase |
| Y | Right-slanting increase |
| ⍭ | Cast on |
| ⌒ | Bind off |
| Y | Slip with yarn on right side |
| ▪ | No stitch |
| ⌅ | Knit wrap together with stitch |
| ⍭ | Wrap and turn |
| ⍭ | Knit into back loop on right side, purl into back loop on wrong side |
|  | Cable 4 |

# Further Reading

## Books

Abbey, Barbara. *Barbara Abbey's Knitting Lace.* Schoolhouse Press, 2007.

Bernard, Wendy. *Custom Knits.* Stewart, Tabori & Chang, 2008.

Bestor, Leslie Ann. *Cast On, Bind Off: 54 Step-by-Step Methods.* Storey Publishing, 2012.

Eckman, Edie. *Around the Corner Crochet Borders.* Storey Publishing, 2010.
Comprehensive resource for crocheted borders, including how to apply them along shaped edges

Epstein, Nicky. *Knitting on the Edge.* Sixth & Spring, 2004.
Source for a wide range of basic and decorative borders and edgings

Frost, Jean. *Jean Frost Jackets.* XRX Books, 2003.

Hiatt, June Hemmons. *The Principles of Knitting.* Touchstone, 2012.

Huff, Mary Scott. *The New Stranded Colorwork.* Interweave, 2009.
Excellent on steeking, cutting, and finishing cut edges (especially bindings) — and a fun read!

Newton, Deborah. *Designing Knitwear.* Taunton, 1998.
Detailed discussions of garment shaping, garment profiles, fit, fitting larger figures, ease, fabric design, etc.

Paden, Shirley. *Knitwear Design Workshop.* Interweave, 2009.

Parkes, Clara. *The Knitter's Book of Wool.* Potter Craft, 2009.

———. *The Knitter's Book of Yarn.* Potter Craft, 2007.

Radcliffe, Margaret. *Knitting Answer Book.* Storey Publishing, 2005.

———. *The Essential Guide to Color Knitting Techniques.* Storey Publishing, 2008.

———. *Circular Knitting Workshop.* Storey Publishing, 2012.

Robson, Deborah, and Carol Ekarius. *The Fleece & Fiber Sourcebook.* Storey Publishing, 2011.

Stanley, Montse. *Reader's Digest Knitter's Handbook: A Comprehensive Guide to the Principles and Techniques of Handknitting,* 3rd ed. David & Charles, 1993.

Starmore, Alice. *Alice Starmore's Book of Fair Isle Knitting,* rev. ed. Dover, 2009.
Source of color combinations, how to develop designs, center motifs, incorporate steeks

Stuever, Sherry, and Keely Steuver. *Intarsia: A Workshop for Hand & Machine Knitting.* Sealed with a Kiss, Inc., 1998.

Walker, Barbara G. *A Treasury of Knitting Patterns.* Schoolhouse Press, 1998.
Originally published in 1968 and still one of the best references for pattern stitches

———. *A Second Treasury of Knitting Patterns.* Schoolhouse Press, 1998.
First published in 1970. Together with the original treasury, it provides a huge assortment of pattern stitches, with clear instructions and photographs for every stitch.

Wiseman, Nancie M. *The Knitter's Book of Finishing Techniques.* Martingale, 2002.

Zilboorg, Anna. *Knitting for Anarchists.* Unicorn Books, 2002.
Very helpful reference on stitch orientation and on strip knitting

Zimmermann, Elizabeth. *Knitting without Tears.* Fireside, 1973. First published by 1971 by Scribner.

## Magazine and Online Articles

Bernard, Eleanor-Elizabeth. "An Unrecorded Steek," *Knitter's Magazine.* Fall 1996: 83.

Hastings, Marilyn. "Marilyn H's Hidden Zipper," *Knitter's Magazine* 29, no. 3 (Fall 2012): 28–29.

Nicholas, Kristin. "Separating Zipper Tutorial: Handsewing a Zipper into a Handknit Sweater," *Getting Stitched on the Farm with Kristin Nicholas* (blog), October 4, 2006, http://getting-stitched-on-the-farm.blogspot.com/2006/10/separating-zipper-tutorial-handsewing.html.
Includes how to shorten a zipper

*Pickin' and Throwin' Blog.* "Sewing a Zipper into a Cardigan," February 3, 2007, http://picki-nandthrowin.blogspot.com/2007/02/sewing-zipper-into-cardigan.html.
Extensive instructions for attaching a zipper using Wash Away Wonder Tape

Splityarn.com. "Easiest Knitted Sweater Zipper Install Ever." March 27, 2011. http://splityarn.com/2011/03/27/easiest-knitted-zipper-install-ever.
Instructions for attaching a zipper using blocking wires to stabilize the edge

# Online References

**Dharma Trading Company**
800-542-5227
*www.dharmatrading.com*
>Source for dyeing supplies (including Synthrapol and Professional Textile Detergent) and information.

**Knitter's Review**
*www.knittersreview.com.*
>In-depth reviews of yarn, books, tools, and more (updated on an ongoing basis).

**Ravelry**
*www.ravelry.com*
>Online knitting, crochet, and spinning community, with tools for maintaining records of your yarn, needles, patterns, and projects; excellent reference for looking up yarn and patterns, with comments from other knitters.

**Standards and Guidelines for Crochet and Knitting**
Craft Yarn Council
*www.craftyarncouncil.com/standards.html*
>Standard yarn weights, sizing guidelines, knit and crochet abbreviations and symbols.

**YouTube**
*www.youtube.com*
>A search for almost any knitting technique will produce multiple videos you can watch to see how it's done.

# Acknowledgments

As always, there is a long, long list of those whose contributions of time, materials, and support for this project must be recognized.

Thanks first of all to Peggy Jo Wells and Brown Sheep Company, Inc., who very generously provided the vast majority of the yarn for the knitted samples that appear in this book.

Many thanks are also due to the knitters who contributed samples for this book: Nancy Barnes, Peggy Brown, Lyn Day, Sandy Kulik, Joanne Lisa-Strauch, Christine Manhart, Leanne Mitchell, Lawre O'Leary, Jeanne Rippere, Phil Sponenberg, Bonnie Vandenberg, Darcy Whitlock, Cathy Williams, and Linda Wright. Without their help, this book could not possibly have been completed.

Also to Anna Radcliffe, who in addition to the standard duties of an editorial assistant knitted and photographed samples and managed to graduate from college while the book was in production.

Gwen Steege, my editor

Mary Velgos, who always rises to the challenge of designing my very complicated books

John Polak, whose photographs make even the samples I'm not happy with look good

Alison Kolesar, for her clear drawings of techniques

Linda Roghaar, my agent

And, last but not least, to David and Allegra, who put up with a lot in the course of each of my books, and in spite of it all continue to encourage me!

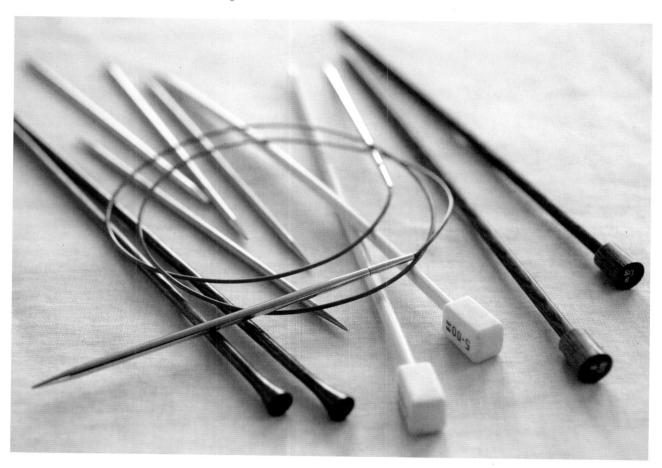

# Index

Page references in **bold** indicate pattern charts.

291

292

## Other Storey Books by Margaret Radcliffe

### Circular Knitting Workshop

Detailed photographic sequences for every classic technique on circular knitting needles, plus 35 demonstration projects.
320 pages. Paper. ISBN 978-1-60342-999-3.

### The Essential Guide to Color Knitting Techniques

Stripes, stranded knitting, intarsia, and more multicolor knitting methods, clearly explained with step-by-step photographs.
320 pages. Hardcover with jacket. ISBN 978-1-60342-040-2.

### The Knitting Answer Book, *2nd edition*

Answers for every knitting quandary — an indispensable addition to every knitter's project bag.
432 pages. Flexibind with cloth spine. ISBN 978-1-61212-404-9.

## More Great Knitting Books

### Cast On, Bind Off *by Leslie Ann Bestor*

A one-of-a-kind reference for more than 50 ways to cast on and bind off, featuring step-by-step photography and detailed instructions.
216 pages. Paper with partially concealed wire-o.
ISBN 978-1-60342-724-1.

### The Knitter's Life List *by Gwen W. Steege*

A road map to a lifetime of knitting challenges and adventures.
320 pages. Paper with flaps. ISBN 978-1-60342-996-2.

### Lace One-Skein Wonders *edited by Judith Durant*

Add delicate lace to your life using these 101 one-skein projects for fingerless gloves, shawls, baby items, scarves, and more!
304 pages. Paper. ISBN 978-1-61212-058-4.

These and other books from Storey Publishing are available wherever quality books are sold or by calling 800-441-5700.
Visit us at www.storey.com or sign up for our newsletter at *www.storey.com/signup.*